REVOLUTION IN
MEXICO'S HEARTLAND

REVOLUTION IN MEXICO'S HEARTLAND

❧

Politics, War, and
State Building in Puebla
1913–1920

DAVID G. LAFRANCE

SR
BOOKS

A Scholarly Resources Inc. Imprint
Wilmington, Delaware

© 2003 by Scholarly Resources Inc.
All rights reserved
First published 2003
Printed and bound in the United States of America

Scholarly Resources Inc.
104 Greenhill Avenue
Wilmington, DE 19805-1897
www.scholarly.com

Library of Congress Cataloging-in-Publication Data

LaFrance, David G. (David Gerald), 1948–
Revolution in Mexico's heartland : politics, war, and state building in
    Puebla, 1913–1920 / David G. LaFrance.
        p. cm. — (Latin American silhouettes)
    Includes bibliographical references and index.
    ISBN 0-8420-5136-8 (cloth : alk. paper)
    1. Puebla (Mexico : State)—History—20th century. 2. Mexico—
History—Revolution, 1910–1920. I. Title. II. Series.
F1326.L32 2003
972'.480816—dc 21

                                                            2003000606

ACKNOWLEDGMENTS

In my research and writing I have accumulated debts to many institutions, programs, and individuals too numerous to mention in their entirety. As for the first, a listing of most of the archives and libraries in which I have worked can be found in the bibliography. I wish to thank them all and particularly the many kind people within each who attended to my requests. Also, I especially want to mention my home institution, the Benemérita Universidad Autónoma de Puebla and its Instituto de Ciencias Sociales y Humanidades, directed by Alfonso Vélez Pliego and Roberto Vélez Pliego, which has over the years gone out of its way, despite my wanderings, to provide me with an abode. For this support I am forever grateful. My appreciation also extends to the Department of American Studies and Mass Media of the University of Łódź, where I spent two invaluable years while writing the manuscript. The Fulbright Hayes Program and the National Endowment for the Humanities also helped finance research for this study.

As for individuals who have in one way or another helped me during my journey to the completion of this study, I first want to express gratitude to Errol Jones, Peter Henderson, and Keith Brewster, who read and critiqued the manuscript. Errol Jones, Marco Reyes, Marco Velázquez, Robert Alexius, Coralia Gutiérrez, Ernesto Godoy, and Loreno Otero put up with me over the years in their always gracious and patient manner. Others who have aided me include Sergio Andrade, Raúl Bringas, Olga Cárdenas, William French, Leticia Gamboa, Gregorio de Gante, Julio Glockner, Agustín Grajales, Lilián Illades, John Mraz, Pilar Pacheco, Columba Salazar, Rogelio Sánchez, Masae Sugawara, and Guy Thomson. My colleagues and friends in Puebla and Łódź also were there to encourage me. At "beaver high," where I witnessed the rewards of obsequiousness and disincentives of professionalism, my cohorts Bess Beatty and William Husband accompanied me, and for that companionship they will be remembered. The staff at Scholarly Resources has, as always, been a pleasure to work with. Finally, I dedicate this book to my parents, Dorothy H. LaFrance and Gerald T. LaFrance, who, although at times are neither fully sure what I do nor why I do it, nevertheless have always supported me.

CONTENTS

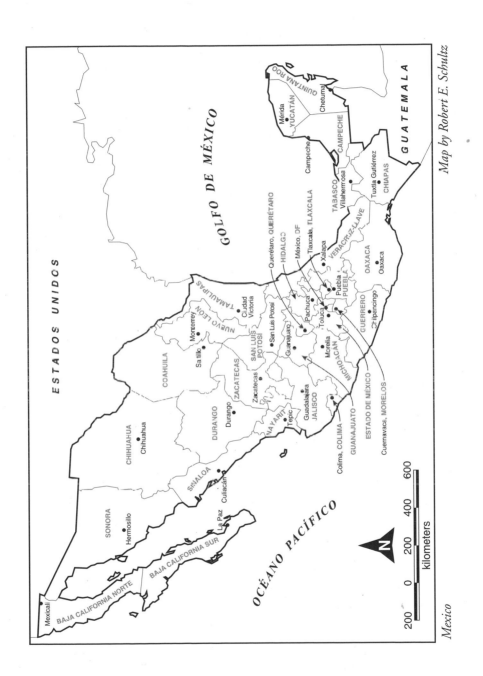

Map by Robert E. Schultz

Mexico

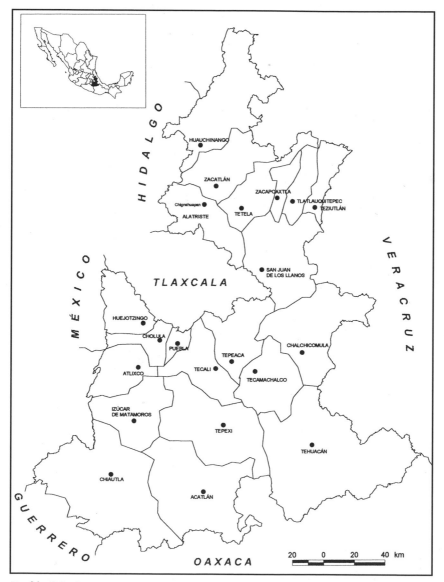

Puebla-Districts

Map by Nereo Zamitiz

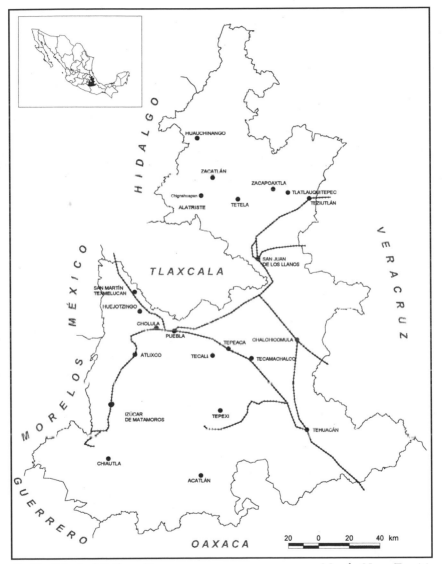

Puebla-Principal Railway Lines   *Map by Nereo Zamitiz*

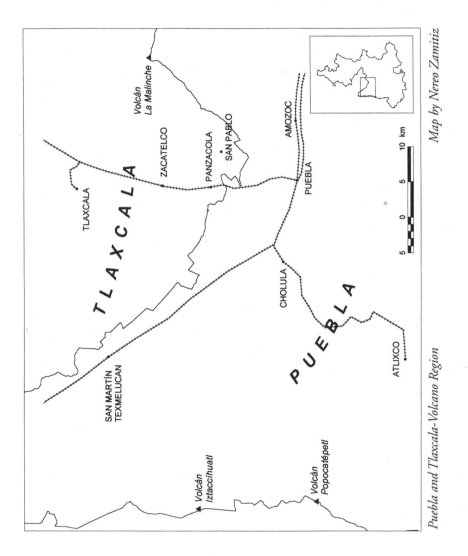

Puebla and Tlaxcala-Volcano Region

Map by Nereo Zamitiz

GLOSSARY

Arenistas	Followers of Domingo and Cirilo Arenas
Cabreristas	Followers of Alfonso Cabrera
Carrancistas	Followers of Venustiano Carranza
Constitucionalistas	Coalition led by Venustiano Carranza, Álvaro Obregón, and Pablo González
Convencionistas	Coalition led by Francisco "Pancho" Villa and Emiliano Zapata
Felicistas	Followers of Félix Díaz
Gonzalistas	Followers of Pablo González
Huertistas	Followers of Victoriano Huerta
Maderistas	Followers of Francisco I. Madero
Magonistas	Followers of Ricardo Flores Magón
Marquistas	Followers of the Márquez brothers, led by Esteban
Obregonistas	Followers of Álvaro Obregón
Porfiristas	Followers of Porfirio Díaz
Villistas	Followers of Francisco "Pancho" Villa
Zapatistas	Followers of Emiliano Zapata

INTRODUCTION

The revolution of 1910, arguably the most studied "event" of Mexican history, still attracts interest and debate because of its complexity, duration, and impact on the country, which is still deeply felt in the twenty-first century. The present work examines the conflict from the perspective of the central state of Puebla between 1913 and 1920 during the so-called Huertista and Carrancista years, when generals Victoriano Huerta and Venustiano Carranza dominated politics. This volume continues my endeavor to explore the longer-term significance of the upheaval in Puebla. This exploration began with an earlier monograph on the Maderista years of 1908–1913, when Francisco I. Madero overthrew the old regime and served as the first revolutionary president.[1]

After twenty-five years of examining the revolution, I believe the most important cause, and driving force behind it, was the deep and persistent desire for local autonomy. This outlook even took precedence over other major issues such as agrarian reform and nationalism, as it was, perhaps, the only overarching phenomenon to involve a cross section of society. Essentially this idea consisted of a wish on the part of people, regardless of category, both to carry on their personal lives as they saw fit and to participate in and thereby have control over political and socioeconomic decision making, free from the interference of outsiders. This idea not only imbued the individual and his local community but also extended to the level of the state.

Yet according to most accounts, by the 1940s, independent, grassroots initiative in the country had largely been curtailed, with local and state structures having been absorbed into a monolithic national political apparatus, which issued orders from above with little input from below. How did this turnabout happen? How did such an important force as local autonomy become assimilated into and consequently muffled by the evolving revolutionary system? This, I believe, is a key question of the revolutionary process. It is central to an understanding of Mexico's recent development, and the principal one that this work attempts to shed light on through an examination of the years 1913–1920, the initial stage of this hegemonic process. This period was one of great violence and destruction, yet also one during which the new state began to emerge, a state that by the beginning of the third decade of the twentieth century had only started to circumscribe local autonomy. Nevertheless, an examination of these crucial years at the regional level helps one to understand how the evolving state became such an overwhelming entity by 1940, with significant consequences thereafter for Mexico.

The literature on the political development of nineteenth-century Mexico indicates that from the beginning of the independence period there had been a desire for and action taken toward asserting local autonomy in many regions of the new nation.[2] The difficulties of the Early Republic of the 1820s–1840s have largely obscured this fact, but it did become apparent during the Reform of the 1850s–1870s. At this time, under the guidance of the dominant Liberal faction, Mexico developed a civic culture, strengthened by the rhetoric of liberalism with its emphasis on individual rights and responsibilities, the development of de jure and de facto local government powers, and the creation of community-based national guards—citizens in arms designed to fight off outsiders, including foreigners. Thus, as the concepts of citizenship and nation solidified, they came to be based on the idea and practice of organization, power, and control from below.

As early as 1825, Puebla's first constitution and laws provided for municipal governments and divided the state into twenty-one districts headed by *jefes políticos* (prefects), reflecting the importance of local and regional affairs. Autonomy then received a boost at mid-century when the Liberals advocated a federalist program, as epitomized in the national constitution of 1857. Throughout the periphery of the state, but especially in the north or Sierra, the Liberals' ideas coincided with particularly strong autonomist tendencies. Indeed, for much of the 1860s and 1870s, Puebla's *jefes políticos* were popularly elected. Even future president and dictator Porfirio Díaz, later vilified for his suppression of subnational rights, gained much support in Puebla when he organized rebellions in 1871 (La Noria) and again in 1876 (Tuxtepec), the latter of which boosted him into power by appealing to Poblanos' (residents of Puebla) concern over local control.

Díaz's dictatorship, the Porfiriato (1876–1911), however, marked a general reversal of this trend. Central authorities circumscribed local and regional organizations and governments in the name of political efficiency and capitalistic development within an increasingly national and even international-based economy. Nevertheless, this process was not smooth as attested to by the many armed uprisings, especially during the late 1870s and the first decade of the twentieth century, as well as by a growing political opposition after 1900.

In Puebla, too, under Díaz local autonomy fell victim to his centralizing project, which cobbled Mexico into a generally coherent nation for the first time since independence in 1821. In the state, governors now appointed *jefes políticos*, and their powers grew relative to the municipalities. In 1885, Díaz broke a long-established practice and named a non-Poblano, Rosendo Márquez, as governor, who, along with Mucio Martínez, another outsider, ruled the state until forced out by the revolutionary movement of Francisco I. Madero in 1911. Furthermore, in 1888, Díaz demobilized the village-based national guard, which in the Sierra had played a key role in the development of local initiative.

The Porfirian assertion of hierarchical and centralized control over what had become a vibrant local political life in many regions of the state did not go unanswered. One of the earliest and most important retorts occurred in 1878 when Alberto Santa Fe and Manuel Serdán (father of Aquiles Serdán, initiator of the revolution in Puebla in 1910) created the Partido Socialista Mexicana (Mexican Socialist Party) and decreed the Ley del Pueblo (Law of the People), calling for municipal liberty as well as agrarian reform. This short but intense rebellion, coming at the beginning of the Díaz period, served as a rallying point for local initiative over the next decades. Subsequently, Poblanos joined other precursor movements, too, most of which made local autonomy a key demand. Especially important was the Partido Liberal Mexicano (Mexican Liberal Party), led by Ricardo Flores Magón. During the decade 1900–1910 the Magonistas (followers of Flores Magón) formed political clubs in Puebla and elsewhere and took up arms against the dictatorship.

In the subsequent Maderista movement (headed by Francisco I. Madero), which began in 1908 and toppled Díaz three years later, one can see the influence of this force from below as hundreds of political clubs and armed groups sprang from the localities. Madero's victory in Puebla and nationwide was made possible by a widespread grassroots mobilization of the citizenry. The Maderistas called for effective suffrage, no reelection, greater municipal power, and an end to the *jefe político*.

Madero had the idea that political change, specifically the choosing of good leaders in free and fair contests, would solve Mexico's woes. Not everyone agreed that this panacea alone would prove effective, but all elements within his coalition, urban and rural, higher and lower, embraced the idea of reform. Hence, free elections took place in which Poblanos were chosen as governors and other mainly state-level personnel, most of whom came from the urban middle classes.

The problem, however, is that the reforms mostly stopped there. Changes in small towns for municipal council, justice of the peace, tax collector, and other posts barely occurred. What positions did turn over took place despite Madero, not because of him. Part of the difficulty consisted of resistance from the conservative opposition, including entrenched officials, whom Madero failed to check and purge. Even more important was the fact that Madero only halfheartedly tried to carry out his program in the countryside.

Rural and lower class people, in particular, had read into Madero's rhetoric and initial actions an intention to redress their socioeconomic problems and now wanted the latitude and means to take the initiative. Madero, however, did not understand this much broader socioeconomic meaning of local autonomy, one that went beyond change in officeholders. Also, he did not trust these rural, mostly lower-class people to wield authority responsibly. Furthermore, to enhance local say over such issues as taxes, education, army service, and commerce, as well as land and water, involved an expansion of democratic, grassroots power, which represented a challenge to the urban-based, mainly middle- and upper-class, status quo. Madero could not accept such an expansion of local power. Therefore, in a misguided effort to gain control over highly unstable rural areas, Madero neither further empowered local government nor ended the *jefe político*. He then denied to his supporters what they wanted most, to participate freely in local politics and select community-based officials in order to run their own affairs.

The expectations Madero engendered soon faded, and opposition to him rose. As the state and nation limped from one crisis to another, even the middle class questioned his leadership. Factionalism and desertions rent the coalition and narrowed his political base. All these problems merely emboldened the conservatives, who had always viewed Madero as a traitor to his upper-class background. In February 1913 the army, led by General Victoriano Huerta, overthrew Madero. Huerta, with urban, middle-class support, acted in the name of stability and the desire to control the radicalized rural elements that demanded local autonomy.

Madero's ouster gained stability for urbanites, but the respite soon ended as mobilized rural groups, fighting nominally under the banners of Venustiano Carranza (Carrancistas) and Emiliano Zapata (Zapatistas), put pressure on the Huertista government in Puebla. A new stage of the revolution had begun, one that would involve the collapse of the old regime and the building of a new state.

For most people in Puebla, outsiders (nonvillagers, non-Poblanos, non-Mexicans) were to be treated with caution, even suspicion. As an extension of this outlook, residents agreed on state rather than federal control over the political system. They did not see eye-to-eye, however, on the degree of autonomy at the municipal level, particularly in the villages and rural areas where more traditional, poorer, less cultured, indigenous people predominated. Urban dwellers, including many workers and other lower socioeconomic elements, embraced modern, progressive, capitalistic, middle-class values. They controlled Puebla City and the larger towns and traditionally held sway over smaller, more isolated entities. Hence, they regarded with distaste, if not fear, the possibility of enhanced influence in the state of these "hordes."

Between 1913 and 1920, then, rural and urban dwellers struggled, although seldom in tandem, against outsiders for the concept of local autonomy held by each. This effort determined the role and fate of the idea in the context of the new revolutionary state in creation. Villagers, who embraced a purer vision of local autonomy, joined leaders, particularly on the periphery of the state, like the Zapatistas in the south, the Marquistas (followers of Esteban Márquez) in the north, and the Arenistas (followers of Domingo Arenas) in the west, all of whom became part of the Convencionista movement. Nevertheless, even these rural elements were not all of one mind. Some pragmatic, moderate, regional caciques sensed opportunities in joining the Constitucionalistas. This turn of events weakened the potential of a united movement in defense of a radical, exclusivist version of the concept.

Puebla's urban elements did not like the outsiders, the Huertistas and later Carrancistas, who came to change the state. Yet they found rural people, with whom they wanted neither to share power nor to coexist as equals, even more repugnant. Consequently, these townspeople played an ambiguous political role, trying to hold on to their limited concept of local autonomy by keeping non-Poblanos and the lower-class villagers at arms length. This exercise required a constant juggling act of compromises, which ultimately produced accommodations with the Carrancistas, the revolutionary group that controlled towns and cities and most closely represented urbanites' values.

In this "negotiating" process, Carrancistas also made compromises, becoming partially absorbed into the Puebla milieu. This fact helped the state's townspeople to fend off total domination by these outsiders, who were persuaded to accept a more Poblano view of the revolution. Consequently, over time a new political culture emerged—one that accepted the reality of a centralized state, yet also one that made some space for and could be accepted by the people of Puebla. By 1920, the idea of a "pure" local autonomy, championed by a dwindling and increasingly isolated rural element, already had become quite circumscribed and muted.[3]

This work is a study of a region (the state of Puebla and its immediate surroundings), which takes a middle or state-level approach to examine politics, warfare, and state building within the context of autonomy. The principal focus is on the state governmental apparatus, what groups controlled it, and what it achieved in the military, political, and socioeconomic realms in the name of revolutionary change. The work also links events at the state level to those of the nation and localities. Puebla's economic and governing elites operated in a context of complex national and local pressures, and their reaction to both shaped the outcome of the conflict and the emerging state.

In order to explain how state building in Mexico occurred, then, this study takes a different approach from other recent works, which tend to emphasize a "bottom-up" perspective.[4] I do not question this focus, as it has offered many and important insights into how so-called subaltern groups helped shape the nascent political system. Indeed, I have attempted in this study to pay attention to such elements. Nevertheless, I also believe that a grassroots perspective alone does not fully explain the important role played by many other groups during these crucial years. Therefore, a view from the middle level allows for inclusion of, for example, state civil and military leaders, the business community, the Church, urban-based workers, and even students, not to mention regional caciques, all of whom merit analysis, along with and in relation to campesinos and related rural people. Thus, out of this other complex mixture perhaps a different and even useful understanding of what happened in Mexico during the revolution will emerge.

This work is divided into three major sections of three chapters each, politics, socioeconomic policy, and warfare. Each principal division follows generally employed periodizations of the revolution at the national level. Puebla in many ways reflected these broader contours of the conflict. Therefore, I believe, the state is most readily understood by employing them, without risk of distorting the reality of what took place there. The first part, encompassing 1913–14, deals with the Huertista period. Its three chapters examine first Puebla's governors and general politics, then socioeconomic matters, and finally the war, which ultimately forced Huerta and his underlings from power. The second part of the book looks at 1914–1917, the years of struggle between the two major revolutionary factions, the

Constitucionalistas (led by Venustiano Carranza, Álvaro Obregón, and Pablo González) and the Convencionistas (Emiliano Zapata and Francisco "Pancho" Villa) and their efforts to control Puebla. In this section, I change the order of the chapters, beginning with the war, which dominated the period, and then looking at the political and socioeconomic situation, which can best be understood in the context of the instability and violence of those years. Growing predictability and legality under the victorious Carrancistas and their newly promulgated national constitution marked the years 1917–1920, which make up the third principal section. Here, I return to the chapter sequence employed in the 1913–14 period as politics, once again, constituted the primary concern of state officials. Finally, a brief tenth chapter relates the fall of the Carrancista government in the state and its replacement by yet another revolutionary group from the north of Mexico, the Sonorans (from the state of Sonora), headed by Álvaro Obregón and Plutarco Elías Calles, erstwhile allies of the Constitucionalistas, who would run the country and Puebla and continue to build the new state until the mid-1930s.

Regarding sources, I have consulted a large number of materials, particularly newspaper and archival holdings, in an attempt to be as thorough and accurate as possible. Although improving thanks to the dedicated efforts of many researchers, most of all my colleagues at the Benemérita Universidad Autónoma de Puebla, the historiography of Puebla for the 1910s remains relatively weak. Hence, in order to write a general political history of the years 1913–1920, it has been necessary to construct events from the bottom up before attempting to interpret the period. Also, given the fact that former governor Maximino Avila Camacho (1937–1941) destroyed the executive-branch holdings of the state archive, any in-depth analysis requires an indirect approach to the ferreting out of information, hence the need to peruse many and varied documents in order to locate ones related to Puebla. Finally, one key component of the picture that I wanted to paint of Puebla during the revolution is largely missing, that of the Catholic Church. Despite the important story that it has to tell, and one, I believe, that would change for the better many of the simplistic stereotypes of its role in the revolution, the Church determinedly maintains its secrecy.

Although this work is a case study, I have compared Puebla to other states for illustrative purposes. Nevertheless, references are possible to only a handful of states, as the regional historiography of the revolution between 1910 and 1920 still exhibits many lacunae. It is my intention that such comparisons shed greater light not only on the inner workings of Puebla but also on Puebla's place in the revolution at the transregional and national levels.

How does Puebla, then, fit into the regional and national picture of the revolution during 1913–1920? Regarding Huertismo (the regime of Victoriano Huerta), Puebla does not reflect fully the traditional view of an all-embracing, repressive, counterrevolutionary regime, one most recently reiterated forcefully by Alan Knight. Neither does it, however, completely fall within the revisionist interpretation by Michael Meyer of Huerta as a moderate reformer who even surpassed Madero in his plans for the country. In Puebla, until at least October 1913 and in some ways until the spring of 1914, the Huertistas were interested in reform and carried out Maderista-era policies. They were even more flexible and democratic (regarding autonomy, the legislature, and to a degree the press, for example) than their Constitucionalista and Convencionista successors. As time passed, however, the regime exhibited increasing intolerance toward its critics and became more repressive as the exigencies of war forced it to step up the *leva* and squeeze more resources out of the citizenry. Nevertheless, the February 1913 overthrow (with foreign collaboration) and murder of Madero should not entirely becloud all of Huertismo. The regime was more tolerant and pragmatic than generally given credit for.[5]

As for Carrancismo (the regime of Venustiano Carranza), suspicion toward, if not always the overt rejection of the northern Mexicans in Puebla, was widespread and in some sectors deep and uncompromising. In this sense, Puebla fits into the larger context of south and southeastern Mexico, to where these newcomers brought and imposed their version of the revolution. The result was years of destructive warfare and alienation of vast numbers of people. Most well known is the case of Morelos where the Zapatistas, described by John Womack and Samuel Brunk, resisted outsiders for the entire decade. As for Chiapas, Thomas Benjamin outlines the so-called *mapache* (raccoon) rebellion between 1914 and 1920, the entire time the Carrancistas were in the state. Led by small- and medium-sized, frontier landholders and composed mainly of cowboy, day workers, and former soldiers, they reacted against abusive intruders and the modernization program of the state government. They "valued their autonomy more than any assistance they might gain from regional or national government." Paul Garner analyzes a popular coalition in Oaxaca representing conservatives and progressives, which developed around regional caciques, particularly in the mountainous region bordering Puebla, all with the basic goal of sovereignty, to challenge the centralizing Constitucionalista machine. This war lasted from 1915 to 1920. Allen Wells and Gilbert Joseph deal with the planter and merchant-led separatist movement in Yucatán, which although shorter-lived attempted to defend the state in the face of the Carrancista takeover in late 1914–15.[6]

This negative attitude toward the Carrancistas was not confined to the south and southeast of the country. Historians also have noted that in northern states, such as Chihuahua, Durango, Querétaro, and San Luis Potosí, where the Constitutionalists' corruption, arbitrariness, and viciousness knew few bounds, they were viewed as barbarians, invaders, conquerors, and occupiers. Indeed, in many places in the north, people preferred the Villistas, as those in the south preferred the Zapatistas.[7]

By 1920, resentment toward the Carrancistas was so widespread that nearly every region of the country rebelled against the regime. Most well known is Sonora, where its state sovereignty movement under Adolfo de la Huerta and Plutarco Elías Calles led the way. Puebla and other states were not far behind.[8]

Given this generalized resistance to and rejection of the Carrancistas and much, if not all, of their program, the question has to be asked: Did there occur in Puebla a popular, grassroots revolution, having as its aim and partial result the overthrow and restructuring of the existing political and socioeconomic order, as posited by Knight, or did only a rebellion of the discontented take place, one within the existing paradigm, as Ramón Eduardo Ruíz claims? Here again, as with Huertismo, Puebla fits somewhere between the extremes. Ruíz portrays well many of the characteristics of the conflict in Puebla that amounted to a "cataclysmic rebellion but not a social revolution," yet it was not totally bereft of a few (and I emphasize few) revolutionary-like traits.[9] The Zapatistas in the southwest of the state did begin to transform local structures as did the Arenistas in the volcano region of the west. Some workers took over factories (with state government backing) while others joined the Red Battalions. Government confiscated properties from the enemy and in other ways intervened in the economy and society in an effort to guide them. Laws were passed to modify the same. Some of the middle class, including students, as well as lower-class rural and urban groups, organized to support the Constitucionalista program and regime, particularly in the early years.

Nevertheless, Knight's idea of revolutionary popularity and spontaneity must be severely circumscribed for four reasons. First, the Constitucionalista program (the degree of its revolutionary character is debatable) was brought from the outside and imposed on a generally reluctant populace. Second, the grassroots mobilization that took place favored a return to previously existing structures, ones perhaps idealized, but ones harking back to the nineteenth century, not new ones. Third, much of the organization and movement that occurred in small towns and rural areas came under the control of federal officers and their local cacique allies, who channeled this discontent and energy largely into self-serving ends. Finally, what grassroots revolutionary action that did take place, occurred, ironically, mostly between 1913 (indeed even earlier in some cases) and 1916, before the Constitucionalistas had begun to consolidate their control and impose their program on the state.

Indeed, one finds few heroes or ideals in this revolution. Most groups and individuals acted on a pragmatic, personal basis. Save for the desire for local autonomy, the only overriding goals were to enhance one's power, materially or politically, seek revenge, or, as in the case of the vast majority of people, hunker down for self-preservation until the whirlwind passed. Discontent abounded, but if any broader aim of political or socioeconomic restructuring were present, it was neither systematically nor widely held. Agrarianism played a key role in certain areas of the state, such as in the Zapatista core area of the southwest and the center, but it was not the universal rallying call to revolution often portrayed for the rural areas of central Mexico. People in the northern sierra and along the mainly mountainous fringes of Puebla exhibited only limited land hunger; they were more concerned with running their own affairs, free from outside control. Here Knight's distinction between *serrano* and agrarian campesinos seems to hold true. Urban elements, including workers, had even less interest in land reform and, indeed, resented it, because it gave power to unpredictable rural people and threatened food and raw material supplies; they did, however, value their autonomy.

Even less did nationalism and foreign relations have an impact on revolutionary mobilization and goals. Hart argues that Mexicans rallied against foreigners and their penetration of the economy, yet it was not an important factor in Puebla. Grievances against the large Spanish community existed, and local acts of violence against them took place. Nevertheless, this sentiment never became effectively channeled, in part because of the inconsistent and confusing message sent by local and state officials, at one time rallying the populace against the Iberians while at another siding with them against popular forces. As for North Americans, their presence in Puebla was minimal and hardly registered in people's consciousness. When the gringos invaded Veracruz in 1914 and far off Chihuahua in 1916, local concerns quickly erased any patriotic reaction. Also, the policies and actions of the great powers toward Mexico, as outlined by Friedrich Katz, had little direct impact on Puebla save for state officials' desire to avoid any incident that would anger foreign governments and the brief William Jenkins "kidnapping" of 1919.[10]

Thus, it seems that Puebla most closely fits into the schema of François-Xavier Guerra and Hans Werner Tobler when taking into account recent, comprehensive works on the conflict. Although Guerra's work ends with 1911, he posits three closely related themes that had been developing since independence and that played key roles in the outbreak of the revolution and would continue to inform events in Puebla in the remaining years of the 1910s: traditionalism versus modernization, the struggle for autonomy in the face of intervening outside forces, and the role of regional caciques as intermediaries between traditional, local society and a modernizing, centralizing state.[11]

Tobler, in his broad survey, claims that for the years 1913–1920 the revolution was not predominantly a peasant-agrarian conflict typified by the Zapatistas but much more varied in terms of motivation, mobilization, leadership, and goals. He adds that Carranza lost control of the country because he failed to root his regime in the popular sectors due to his conservative policies. In the end the First Chief was overthrown because he could not rein in his army. Finally, in evaluating the revolution as a whole, Tobler says it was characterized more by socioeconomic, political, and cultural continuities from the nineteenth century than by any sharp break with the past; the conflict, he says, did "not cause any global reordering of society." All these assertions reflect the situation in Puebla for the Carrancista years.[12]

I

HUERTISMO

1

POLITICS, 1913–1914

The Madero period at the national level quickly ended in February 1913. Early that month army officers Bernardo Reyes and Félix Díaz, nephew of the former dictator Porfirio Díaz, led an attack on the national palace. Although the offensive was repulsed and Reyes killed, the conspirators took refuge in a nearby arsenal. From there the opposing sides shelled each other causing havoc in the center of the nation's capital, an event subsequently termed the Decena Trágica (Tragic Ten Days). Meanwhile, Madero appointed General Victoriano Huerta to head the government's defense. No admirer of Madero, Huerta cut a deal with Díaz behind the president's back; he agreed to remove Madero, take power, and then support Díaz in elections for the constitutional presidency. Huerta carried out the first part of the bargain, even having Madero killed, but he reneged on the second.

Hence, Huerta established a military dictatorship, albeit with the trappings of democratic procedures. He held fraudulent elections, purged the congress, harassed and killed opponents, muzzled the press, and militarized the society, all in an attempt to defeat a growing opposition. To thwart his opponents and gain control over the country, Huerta looked to the state governments and particularly their governors for help. They would serve as crucial elements in the process of consolidation, one that Puebla's independent-minded politicians reluctantly embraced.

The governorship in Puebla, then, played important real and symbolic roles. It wielded much power, and the local political establishment as well as most residents preferred that one of their own occupy it. Under Madero the state had its first native-born governors since the mid-1880s. Nevertheless, this arrangement, in accordance with aspirations of local autonomy, ended under the Huertistas. They replaced Governor Juan B. Carrasco, a civilian and Poblano chosen in a free election, with an outsider and military officer, Joaquín Maass, in June 1913. Although the initial response to Carrasco's removal was muted, the desire for local control of the governorship and other state and lower-level political offices remained strong. When Maass and his successor, Juan A. Hernández, another appointed military man, failed to restore calm and replaced lower-level state and local officials chosen during the Maderista period, discontent mounted. Indeed, even the normally quiescent legislature, into which local autonomous sentiment became channeled, resisted attempts to strip it of all power.

Juan B. Carrasco

Upon assuming the presidency, Huerta inherited Juan B. Carrasco as governor in Puebla, a septuagenarian lawyer and professor who had distanced himself from local politics during the later Díaz and Madero periods. Carrasco, however, was hardly someone upon whom Huerta could stake his policy of consolidation, for the governor lacked a strong political base, either among pro- or anti-Maderistas.[1]

With the Maderista coalition badly fractured in the fall of 1912, particularly over the question of who should become governor for 1913–1917, Carrasco emerged the compromise choice. With the backing of President Madero and the state executive, Nicolás Meléndez, Carrasco won a disputed election, which the federal senate resolved. Thus, upon assuming office on February 1, 1913, Carrasco, in poor health, faced a myriad of problems, not the least of which were charges that Madero had imposed him, thus violating state sovereignty.[2]

Hence, Carrasco faced political enemies from two fronts. On one side were Maderistas who resented his rise to power, the most vociferous of whom had vied for the governorship against him. They included Felipe T. Contreras and Agustín del Pozo, the latter of whom had led an armed revolt against the new state government. These Maderistas also disliked Carrasco's alliance with the opposition Partido Católico (Catholic Party), made in order to help stabilize his administration. On the other side were hard-line conservatives from the Díaz era who opposed any Maderista, even one as moderate as Carrasco, holding office. Once Huerta took power, both groups placed much pressure on the new president to replace Carrasco.[3]

Huerta, however, hesitated to remove Carrasco. Cognizant of Poblanos' deeply held ideal of local autonomy and not wanting to provoke more hostility to his new regime (particularly following the murder of Madero in Mexico City on February 22), the president initially sought reconciliation. He calculated that the Porfiristas (followers of Porfirio Díaz) had little choice but to back his government. Therefore, by staying with Carrasco he could gain the support, or at least the neutrality, of lesser state and local officials. These Maderistas, Huerta hoped, might be willing to accept his administration, provided that a Maderista governor remained in office and peace and stability returned to the state. Indeed, Huerta even went so far as to reach an agreement with Carrasco that Mexico City would not intervene in Puebla as long as the governor controlled the Maderistas and other regime opponents. This early Huerta, then, was not the "slash and burn" assailant of the Maderista revolution as he has traditionally been portrayed, but someone who more carefully considered his moves. Not everywhere did Huerta immediately arrest state chief executives and thoroughly purge Maderista personnel such as in San Luis Potosí. In Querétaro, too, the Maderista governor was kept on, in this case until October 1913.[4]

In the end, Huerta's policy did not work. Carrasco proved incapable of reining in holdover-Maderista officials or suppressing insurgent movements. Maderistas sabotaged the new government from within even as they clandestinely joined the armed rebellion headed by the Carrancistas and Zapatistas in the north and south of the state, respectively. Regime supporters harshly criticized Huerta for allowing Maderistas to remain in office. Some of these complainants coveted Maderista jobs, while others truly were concerned about security. Ultimately it was Carrasco's inability or unwillingness to deal with the rebel threat, aided and abetted by *jefes políticos* and other local authorities, that forced Huerta to demand his resignation.[5]

Huerta ordered Carrasco to cite his poor health as the reason for leaving office and named General Joaquín Maass as provisional state executive. In so doing, the president and state legislature (which approved the change in governors) ignored the five-year residency requirement of the state constitution and ended any chance that elections for a legal successor would soon be carried out. A clear and purposeful break from the Maderista era had taken place.[6]

Joaquín Maass

Joaquín Maass, a 58-year-old career officer from Mexico City, who had fought Indians in Sonora and studied engineering in Europe, assumed the governorship on June 2, 1913. Maass's military background and the fact that he had little to do with Puebla (having arrived in the state only weeks before as military commander) recommended him for the appointment. Furthermore, he was Huerta's brother-in-law. Thus, Maass's takeover ended Puebla's respite from overt, outside political interference during the Madero period and dashed hopes of continued control of the governorship by a local, popularly elected civilian. Indeed, Maass was the antithesis of the ideal local office holder: an outsider and military man imposed by the central government. Furthermore, he had no intention of deferring to Puebla's indecisive and divided political class.[7]

Opposition to Maass's assumption of power, however, was muted. Carrasco quietly retired. A handful of state deputies voiced their objections to a military man heading the state, but when the legislature confirmed Maass, they nevertheless voted for him. Labor activists called for street demonstrations, using the guise of a day of mourning to commemorate Madero, but they never materialized. Indeed, the bulk of the legal political opposition, represented by the decimated and increasingly repressed Maderistas, was hardly in a position to resist. In addition, most of Puebla's power structure initially backed Maass. The elite banking, merchant, and industrial communities even held a lavish banquet in his honor. Conservatives, including the increasingly influential Partido Católico, as well as many moderates, were attracted by promises to fight the Zapatistas and return normalcy and predictability to the state. They had become tired of rebellion and disillusioned with political plurality and elections à la Madero, which seemed only to bring instability. Nevertheless, the desire for local political control in civilian hands, more often an unexpressed belief than a stated goal, remained an important underlying sentiment.[8]

Upon taking office, Maass consolidated power by revamping government at all levels, something Carrasco had not done. He ousted and shuffled personnel, particularly Maderistas, in both the executive and judicial branches. So many and such frequent changes took place, however, especially in the key post of *jefe político*, that confusion and discontinuity resulted. Maass attempted to appoint loyalists, usually outsiders or military men, to the district posts, thus replacing locals who enjoyed some degree of grassroots support and legitimacy. Maass argued that he had to appoint non-Poblanos because, save for the Católico, there existed no truly functioning political party, only loosely organized Maderista-era groups linked to politically ambitious individuals. To name people from these divided factions, he claimed, would only further destabilize the state.[9]

Furthermore, some of the governor's actions took on the taint of revenge. One recently appointed *jefe político* dissolved the town government of San Gabriel Chilac and forced its councilmen into the army. The new secretary of government for the state, Jesús M. Rábago, who hailed from Mexico City, replaced Lino Espinosa Bravo, a member of one of Puebla's most prominent families, known for its support of Carrasco. Attorney General Crispín Ramos, who prosecuted ex-Porfirian governor Mucio P. Martínez a year earlier, was forced to resign. Next, authorities brought charges against Ramos for his role in the Martínez case, but a grand jury made up of state legislators defied the governor and ruled in the defendant's favor.[10]

Even worse from the point of view of independent-minded Poblanos, Maass's administration was perceived as a mere appendage of the federal government, shifting personnel as if they were interchangeable cogs in a vast political machine. Not only was Maass linked to Huerta by marriage, but national authorities took a direct role in appointments at the state level, so much so that even Maass objected that his prerogatives were being undermined. Maass's new secretary of government, Rábago, served in Puebla barely two months before moving on to become subsecretary of government in the national cabinet. Rábago in turn was replaced by Enrique González Martínez, who previously had served as secretary of government in Sinaloa and subsecretary of government in Mexico City. Maass's name surfaced in late 1913 as a possibility to join Huerta's cabinet or even to replace the president himself, as international, particularly United States', pressure mounted on the nation's chief executive to resign.[11]

The effort to consolidate power, however, involved more than the mere selection of personnel. Elective offices also had to be taken into consideration, which forced the new regime to contend with the legal, although weakened, political opposition. The first important step was to fill several vacancies in the 22-member state legislature, thus reshaping the lawmaking body to support Maass. When the congress began its 2-year term the previous January, Carrasquistas (backers of former Governor Carrasco) and Contreristas (backers of Felipe T. Contreras) almost evenly divided power in the lawmaking body while three Partido Católico deputies held the balance of votes needed to form a majority.[12]

By September six seats needed filling, thus providing Maass with the chance to ensure his control of the body. The September vote tally went well for the regime, with the pro-Maass Partido Católico and Carrasquistas gaining spots at the expense of the more liberal Contrerista faction. Then, over the next months, Maass put further pressure on the Contreristas, arresting at least two and forcing others to abandon the legislative body, so that by early 1914 only half its seats were occupied. Likewise, Huerta ordered deputies in the Querétaro state congress to be arrested in order to manipulate its actions.[13]

Despite Maass's efforts to shape the legislature, it still contained members who challenged him on at least two important issues. In one case they pushed for a September 1913 election for constitutional governor (to replace the interim Maass) as the law required, which they wanted to take place simultaneously with the contest for deputies. The conservative majority voted down the initiative. In reaction, deputy Leopoldo García Veyrán organized students, already angered over Maass's educational policy (see Chapter 2), to march on the chamber to protest the decision. For his actions the dissident lawmaker, whose father and uncle had been killed by the Mucio Martínez regime, landed in jail despite his congressional immunity.[14]

In a second challenge to the governor's and by extension the Huerta practice of imposing outside military men on the state, deputies debated whether to further restrict the eligibility requirements for chief executive. This issue reflected the desire to put Puebla under the control of Poblanos. In 1911, following the fall of Mucio Martínez and the advent of the Maderista era, the state constitution had been amended; once changed it provided that governors be limited to one term and that they be state residents for at least five years (as opposed to two years) immediately preceding a vote. Now it was proposed that the chief executive be born in Puebla. For the moment, however, this tactic, too, failed. Nevertheless, it created an important rallying point as well as ideological marker for Poblanos, requiring them to take a stand regarding their relationship to outsiders in general, the central government in particular, and by extension the revolutionary program of the Constitucionalistas once they gained power the following year. In 1917 this idea would be incorporated into a new state constitution.[15]

Federal elections for the presidency and the national congress also had an impact on the state during Maass's governorship. Here, as with the legislature, the governor played mainly a behind-the-scenes role in trying to guide politics along a conservative path. Upon Huerta's assumption of power in February 1913, political clubs in Puebla sprang to life announcing their favorites for presidential elections scheduled for October 1913. Although they faced harassment from holdover Maderista officials, pro-Félix Díaz groups greatly outnumbered those favoring the other most viable ticket, one made up of Francisco Vázquez Gómez and Jesús Flores Magón and supported by the old antireelectionist/liberal faction of the Maderistas. Porfiristas, Reyistas (followers of General Bernardo Reyes, who was killed in the Decena Trágica of February 1913), Catholics, and even some Maderistas backed Díaz. Upon Governor Carrasco's resignation in June 1913, the Felicistas felt especially vindicated and optimistic, even though most would have preferred a civilian replacement or at least the better-known former Porfirian zone commander General Luis Valle rather than Maass.[16]

Optimism, however, turned to apathy once Huerta sent Díaz on a diplomatic mission to Japan in order to undercut the latter's chances at being elected. By October, Huerta's plan to sabotage the election had succeeded, as the legal requirements to make it valid could not be met. Nevertheless, the president carried on with the vote, now aimed at garnering ballots in favor of himself and General Aureliano Blanquet for the vice presidency, a referendum to be interpreted as a mandate to remain in office. In preparation for this ruse, Huerta instructed all governors to increase the vote count. These orders included the arrest of any municipal president, the individual in charge of the electoral process at the local level, who opposed such manipulation.[17]

Meanwhile, earlier in October 1913, Huerta had dissolved the federal congress, arresting some 110 deputies, including a majority of the delegation from Puebla. As such the tainted presidential "election" that took place later the same month also included the selection of a new national legislature and senate. The results for the regime were positive. Consequently, the state's federal congressional delegation took on a whole new look; sixteen of eighteen deputies and both senators, all elected in 1912, were replaced. The winners, duly approved by the now conservative-dominated state legislature, included General Luis G. Valle, Colonel Luis G. Pradillo, the man who rebelled against the state government in February 1913, Porfirista rural officer Colonel Javier Rojas, and Gustavo Maass, the governor's brother.[18]

Maass had little time, however, to take advantage of his increasing control over the state's political system, perhaps to use his accomplishments to catapult himself into higher office. On January 15, 1914, he succumbed in Mexico City to a rapidly deteriorating stomach disorder (cancer?). Even in death, Maass remained the outsider; his local supporters failed in their attempt to have the body returned to Puebla for the funeral. Instead, they had to travel to the nation's capital, Maass's native city, for the burial. State officials thus had to be content with declaring a 3-day mourning period and holding an elaborate mass for the deceased governor, minus the corpse.[19]

Juan A. Hernández

Another military officer, General Juan A. Hernández, succeeded Maass on January 29, 1914, following a unanimous legislative vote. Hernández, born in 1841 in the territory of Tepic (today the state of Nayarit), had joined the army at age eighteen and boasted a long career starting with the campaign against Manuel Lozano (El Tigre de Alica) in his native region and then against the French intervention in the 1860s. In the 1880s he fought Yaqui Indians in Sonora. Most recently, Hernández had served as governor of Colima. Although an unexpected choice to lead Puebla, he was not a complete unknown in the state, as he had briefly served as zone commander there in 1910.[20]

Any significant change in policy between the Maass and Hernández administrations is imperceptible. The new executive's governing council (*consejo de gobierno*), his principal link to the local community, was composed of conservatives, mostly professionals, including Partido Católico head Francisco Pérez Salazar. Furthermore, like his predecessor, Hernández cemented a personal relationship with Huerta, which symbolically underlined his link to the national political structure, not to Puebla; in March 1914, for example, his daughter, Concepción, married Huerta's son, Víctor.[21]

Hernández constantly shifted personnel, not so much to oust Maderistas, as his predecessor had accomplished that, but to find an effective combination of leaders to reverse the deteriorating economic and military situation during the winter and spring of 1914. Again, many of these appointees were outsiders or holdovers from the Porfiriato and generally unacceptable to the local populace. Huerta himself took a direct interest in this process, urging that specific individuals be named to key posts including the *jefes políticos* of both Puebla City and Cholula. Resistance to both changes, however, thwarted the president's wish. In the latter case, protesters claimed that Huerta's man was unfamiliar with the area and too old to take an active part in suppressing increasing numbers of rebels and bandits. As the regime weakened and conditions worsened, officials had difficulty finding individuals to serve in government posts, especially outside Puebla City.[22]

Governor Hernández, like Maass, also had to consult the state legislature. For the most part it followed the governor's lead, for example, it raised taxes for the war effort. Nevertheless, the majority conservatives joined their liberal or independent opponents to thwart the executive's requests to be granted extraordinary powers, which Hernández claimed he needed while the lawmaking body was not in session. Thus, one of the fundamental components of democratic government, the legislative check on the executive, was upheld, in this case on a military, non-Poblano governor, despite the exigencies of economic deterioration and warfare.[23]

Juan Francisco Muñoz Ovando

In July 1914, as the Huerta regime played out its final days in power, the legislature granted Hernández a leave of absence. On the twenty-fourth of the month he officially resigned and fled to Europe with the president. Three days later superior court justice Juan Francisco Muñoz Ovando assumed the governorship, winning the legislative vote over his nearest rival, Catholic lawyer Rafael Cañete, who had served as interim executive in 1911. Once again, visions among Puebla's political class of a return to a locally controlled, legal political order briefly flickered. However, Muñoz Ovando, a native of Tepeaca in the east central part of Puebla and former state treasurer under Porfirian governor Martínez, proved to be little more than a caretaker while the political edifice collapsed around him. The changing of *jefes políticos*, including the naming of his son-in-law to head the post in Puebla City, and efforts to cut deals with the insurgents could no longer stop the revolutionary tide. On August 23, 1914, Jesús Carranza, "First Chief" Venustiano Carranza's brother, occupied the state capital, thus putting a formal end to the Huerta regime in Puebla. By that date, Muñoz Ovando had already gone into hiding, and any hope on the part of the Poblanos that they would soon control their state again quickly dissipated.[24]

During the Huerta period, Poblanos of all stripes demonstrated, although at times mutedly, a desire to wield control over their own political affairs, something they had only briefly enjoyed during the Madero period following the long Díaz dictatorship. Initially, Huerta sought to accommodate them, leaving Governor Carrasco and other holdover Maderista officials in office. Maderista infighting and opposition to his government, however, ultimately forced Huerta to thoroughly purge elements from the previous regime. The two Huertista governors, Maass and Hernández, nonelected outsiders and military men, might have been more tolerated if they had brought stability and predictability to the state following the chaotic months of Maderista rule. Furthermore, they made no pretense that their loyalty lay in Mexico City, not Puebla, and insisted on changing personnel, thus threatening the populace's hard-earned and jealously guarded gains made during the Madero period, particularly that of selecting local people for local office. This last fact, especially, helped to consolidate anti-Huerta resistance among rural elements less inclined to accept a compromised version of autonomy than their urban, more moderate and middle-class counterparts. Nevertheless, despite the authoritarian stance of the Huertistas, some space for political dissent remained in Puebla, a situation that, ironically, would be much less the case under the rule of their successors, the Constitucionalistas.

Poblano discontent in 1913–14, however, rested not only on political grievances. Many people in the state also expected, or at least hoped, that the new regime would carry out a program of economic and social reform. An attempt was made to do this, but given the many constraints upon the government, the changes satisfied almost no one.

2

ECONOMIC AND SOCIAL POLICY
1913–1914

Although the Huertistas came to power at the national level in reaction to what they viewed as the excesses of the Madero years, they realized the impossibility of returning to the status quo ante, to the time of Porfirio Díaz. Mexico's new, authoritarian rulers wanted peace and order and were willing to entertain the idea of change to obtain these goals. What they feared and resisted was radical alteration to Porfirian structures. Indeed, Huerta's government even had a socioeconomic reform program, albeit modest, one that in some aspects even surpassed that of Madero. Hence, the early Huerta (until late 1913), as he is seldom portrayed, was disposed to tolerate socioeconomic experimentation. Nevertheless, like his predecessor, Huerta's short time in office and challenge by armed revolt limited the implementation of such plans.

In Puebla, Madero's fall brought a sigh of relief from many residents as they looked forward to a period of stability under the new regime. This desire for order did not preclude, however, the expectation that the government would carry out at least a modest economic and social reform program. Not only workers, peasants, students, and other so-called popular sectors desired change, but also some of the moderate to conservative elements of society realized such steps were needed. As a result, governors Maass and Hernández attempted to introduce modifications in a number of areas from finances and taxes to labor, land, and education.

In the end, however, these steps, limited as they were in conceptual terms, turned out to be even less significant than intended. The government was inherently cautious. More important, however, as warfare intensified, officials increasingly depended for monies upon the business community and the church, the very groups least tolerant of any meaningful change. By the spring and early summer of 1914, then, the state's elite had lost confidence in the government, openly challenging its economic program and even contemplating its demise. Here, again, one can detect in this rising dissatisfaction an attitude of resentment toward outsiders' running state affairs.

Finances and Taxes

The state faced two fundamental economic problems, financial instability and a lack of funds. Declining income combined with the increasing demand for outlays paralyzed even the most basic government services. Schools closed, employees went unpaid, infrastructural projects came to a halt, hospitals turned away patients, and prison inmates went hungry. Rural areas and small towns especially suffered, although larger communities faced many difficulties, too. Only the military budget increased.[1]

The reasons for this difficult financial situation were many. Nevertheless, what was a loss for the Huertista state and local governments often meant a gain for the regime's opponents. Even as early as midsummer 1913, rebels held large areas of the northern and southern regions of the state (see Chapter 3) where they appropriated tax revenues for their own use.[2]

Furthermore, many people avoided paying taxes. One law, dating from 1897, exempted newly constructed or renovated urban buildings from levies for ten years, depriving the state of some 68,000 pesos in income for 1913. In other cases, individuals had gained reprieves for such situations as an enemy-occupied hacienda, town, or district. Some individuals mistakenly (or conveniently) thought that imposts had been abolished during the Maderista period. Others took advantage of the chaotic times to evade their civic duty. Pulque (traditional fermented drink made from juice of the maguey cactus) merchants, for example, commonly smuggled their lucrative beverage into urban areas. Businessmen and other middle-class interests, frustrated by the ill use of public monies and forced to hand over so-called loans to local officials and military commanders, felt little compunction to comply fully with the law.[3]

What monies were collected were poorly managed. Budgets were speculative and overly optimistic, tax agents enjoyed monopolies and guaranteed cuts of funds collected, and government-run businesses favored politicians and their families and friends. Local governments lacked autonomy to impose taxes without state approval, a cumbersome and politicized process. Lawmakers found it difficult to deny pay raises to public officials, themselves included. Large debts, many of them carryovers from the Porfiriato, weighed on government, eating up revenues in the form of interest payments and impeding efforts to restructure portfolios in order to borrow anew. One property, the Molino de Carmen, originally acquired during the Mucio Martínez governorship, produced less than 2,000 pesos yearly for Puebla City while costing it 15,000 in mortgage payments. Moreover, operating under an outdated 1911 budget and a nearly 12-million-peso debt, double the value of municipal-owned property, the state capital faced bankruptcy, a situation worrisome even to London investors. To make matters worse, Governor Hernández, before leaving office in July 1914, turned over 100,000 pesos of state funds to help finance the desperate administration of President Huerta, who soon fled to Spain.[4]

Officials attempted to deal with the financial crisis in five basic ways. First, they cut public services. This step was already being undertaken on a de facto basis as hospitals, prisons, schools, construction projects, and the like were starved of funds and abandoned while salaries went unpaid. Municipalities, despite professed desires for autonomy, tried (not always with success) to shift the burden of services to the state government, on occasion exaggerating their financial predicament.[5] These steps risked alienating not only the public in general but especially government workers.

The second method was to raise additional revenues by increasing the efficiency of services and tax collection. As such, Governor Maass attacked the abuses of the meat-packing plant (*empacadora*), the flour mill, the sewage authority, and the welfare agency, La Beneficencia, all of which served Puebla City and were controlled by Porfirian-era insiders. The *empacadora* was partially farmed out and its tax exemptions reduced. Butchers cheered the end of the plant's stranglehold on the meat business. Officials also negotiated with Spanish industrialist Benigno Díaz Salcedo, albeit unsuccessfully, to run the corrupt and featherbedded market system for a fixed yearly sum. In another instance authorities tried to get out of a sweetheart deal signed years earlier in which a local entrepreneur paid 280 pesos per year to rent some 406,000 square meters of prime land.[6]

The state also reviewed tax exemption requests in order to keep the tax base from eroding. Denials increased as the state's financial difficulties grew. In April 1914 the longtime reduction in levies on newly constructed and renovated urban real estate was ended. Exemptions rose sharply once again, however, in July and August 1914 as the regime collapsed.[7]

Other measures involved targeting back taxes. Landowners, for example, who paid within a given time period had past levies erased; otherwise they would have to come up with all fees dating from the 1890s. Towns, too, received similar deals.[8] Efforts to collect the personal tax or *chicontepec*, which fell hardest on the lower classes, not only ran into stiff opposition but also revealed the state's desperation for funds. The Maderistas had abolished the impost in July 1911. Nevertheless, the law was erratically enforced. Some localities, dependent on this income, continued to collect it. In other cases, agents saw an opportunity to gather and pocket the defunct impost while falsifying their reports to the state treasury. In November 1913 the *jefe político* of Atlixco faced near rebellion when he attempted to force factory workers to pay up. He claimed Atlixco City desperately needed the additional income, which amounted to between five and six pesos per person, going back to 1910. Moreover, he argued that the mill hands only spent their extra income on alcohol and therefore could afford to pay it. Laborers' protests successfully blocked the tax as higher officials feared that to take a hard line on the issue would only swell the enemies' ranks with defecting workers. Shortly thereafter, however, the financially strapped state reversed itself and reintroduced the law, even attempting to lay its hands on monies from 1910 to 1914, when legally the impost did not exist. The reinstated levy provoked much resistance, including a legal suit. In the end the government partially backed down, ordering all retroactive collections of the *chicontepec* stopped, but an obligation of up to two pesos per month for citizens between eighteen and sixty years old remained in effect. [9]

A third method to raise revenues amounted to volunteerism, oftentimes combined with appeals to patriotism. In the Sierra, where teachers had gone for up to two years without pay, authorities sought donations from private individuals to keep classrooms open. In Tepeaca the municipal president paid instructors out of his own pocket. State deputy Jesús Zafra tried to persuade fellow congressmen to hand over a portion of their expense accounts to the state education budget. At the time of the United States invasion of Veracruz in April 1914, collection boxes were hung on Puebla City streets on behalf of the war effort.[10]

Cutbacks, efficiency measures, and donations never overcame the state's increasing financial straits. Therefore, the fourth step was to raise taxes, but not without provoking a great deal of resistance leading to prolonged legislative debate and intense negotiations with groups affected. Neither Maass nor Hernández could unilaterally impose their will in this matter. Few people escaped paying more in taxes, as imposts were newly applied to or increased on a range of products and services. Augmented levies on, for example, bicycles, charcoal, water, itinerant salesmen, and travel passes in conflicted districts, however, provided only modest amounts of additional income, proved difficult to collect, and contributed to popular resentment.[11]

Therefore, authorities aimed the bulk of their revenue enhancement program at the state's large agricultural, commercial, and industrial interests. Many of these groups had enjoyed special arrangements for decades, paying rates much below that of smaller businesses. In addition, influential urban firms commonly enjoyed reduced prices for public utilities. Small- and medium-sized merchants applauded the effort to raise taxes and equalize electricity and water rates on these competitors.[12]

Pressure from below for more equitable tax treatment, the state's increased need for revenues, and the deteriorating security situation, prompted many of these businesses to renegotiate their financial obligations. Flourmills located on agricultural land had been exempted from taxes on power consumption; henceforth, they would pay a higher rate of three pesos per horsepower per month, one less than the state originally demanded. Sugar and honey producers also agreed to higher levies. The twenty-one hacendados who made up a cattle-raisers group followed suit regarding slaughtered livestock. Pulque, widely drunk by the lower classes, too, was hit by additional levies of up to 100 percent. These steps, however, put upward pressure on basic food and beverage prices.[13]

Finally, the state's largest industry, the cotton textile, also came under similar pressure. Thanks to its size and powerful lobbying group, the Centro Industrial Mexicano (Mexican Industrial Center—CIM), producers traditionally had enjoyed large tax breaks under Porfirian industrialization policy. Its members as a group, like those of other economic sectors, negotiated total tax amounts with the government. The last raise had taken effect in January 1913, which boosted the state's annual receipts from the industry to only 70,000 pesos on a multimillion peso per year business. In September 1913, Maass proposed an increase to 86,000 pesos, which after threats from owners to move their mills to other states, the legislature reduced to 80,000. As conditions worsened a majority of factories closed. Those remaining open, then, faced the burden of still coming up with the full 80,000 pesos and therefore demanded relief. The Hernández administration, needing the income, stalled. Finally, in late July 1914, Governor Muñoz Ovando and the congress exempted levies on mills closed for a minimum of four months, with a corresponding reduction in the total owed by the industry.[14]

These additional sources, however, proved inadequate, and the state began considering others. In February 1914 a tax on properties valued at fewer than 100 pesos was enacted. Although this impost directly hit the poor, its negative impact was partially mitigated by the fact that half the income generated went to the impoverished localities.[15]

Then in April, the legislature added a 50 percent surcharge to all existing state and local imposts. In this instance only after much arm-twisting did Hernández gain the grudging support of Puebla's economic elite. To this point they had increasingly been forced into making ad-hoc payments to local politicians and military officers, allegedly to help sustain the war effort, under threat of jailing and the withdrawal of the federal army to be replaced by less reliable volunteer forces if more monies were not forthcoming. These entrepreneurs, then, opted for the predictability of the state tax collector and the regular military as the lesser of evils. In return the government promised to send another 1,000 federal troops to the state. Not all agreed with this steep increase, however, which came on top of a 30 percent federal surcharge. To enforce the measure, those in favor formed a committee to ensure that everyone paid the new fees, thus guaranteeing that no one gained a competitive advantage. Although indications of discontent had arisen among the state's elites on earlier occasions, this disagreement over taxes marked the first clear division among them about not just general policy but a specific issue that cut to the heart of the regime's ability to survive.[16]

Still short of funds, the state looked to a fifth measure, borrowing. Here, too, however, the results were modest both because the legislature had to approve each transaction, and because the state already carried a large debt, which scared off potential lenders. In an atmosphere of crisis, made worse by the April 1914 United States occupation of Veracruz, then, Hernández called on Puebla's main business groups (*cámaras*) for 2 million pesos. Wanting control over how the money would be spent, they suggested that if the state sold bonds to raise monies dedicated to security and the general debt, they would ensure compliance with the 50 percent surcharge on condition that those taxes collected be used to pay off the bonds. Hernández agreed with the plan. Local banks failed, however, to come up with the sums desired, so the governor sent lawyers Antonio Pérez Marín and Eduardo Mestre to the nation's capital to seek out willing bankers there. Mestre, a son-in-law of former governor Martínez with several important financial institutions as clients, was already selling Puebla City bonds on behalf of the Banco Central Mexicano.[17]

At this point the state legislature balked. It demanded more time to consider the project and asked Hernández to resubmit it, to which he agreed. In early July, however, using the rationale that any further incursion by United States forces had passed, both the governor and legislature dropped the idea.[18]

Then, the business community asked the state to end the hated tax surcharge, now arguing that with Hernández gone, the war was over. The legislature unanimously agreed, citing the need to calm discontent and revive the devastated economy. New governor Muñoz Ovando, however, felt differently, arguing that the state needed the monies to pay soldiers whom he feared otherwise would join the rebels. The governor's viewpoint prevailed, but to little avail. By the time the law was officially repealed, September 1, 1914, Muñoz Ovando had already left office and the Carrancistas controlled the state government.[19]

Communication and Transportation

The state's infrastructure: railways, electrical grids, and telephone and telegraph lines, became regular targets of antiregime rebels. Their impact was mixed. Zapatistas, for example, interrupted the Interoceánico Railroad between Matamoros and Cuautla in the neighboring state of Morelos for months, and trains carried troops to ward off attacks. Yet this firm, as well as others in the region, made more money in 1913 than in 1912 due to traffic diverted from war-plagued northern Mexico. Furthermore, plans persisted into 1914 for the construction of railway lines in the state, an attitude in consistent with fears of widespread violence. Nevertheless, by June and July 1914 the system had greatly deteriorated, even to the point that firewood, which had already been substituted for fuel oil (*petróleo*), was in such short supply that trains became idled.[20]

The electrical, telegraph, and telephone systems also suffered. The Canadian-owned Necaxa hydroelectric works near Huauchinango in the northern Sierra region of the state, inadequately protected by government forces, resorted to private guards and even payoffs to insurgents for protection. The San Rafael paper mill in Mexico State, which received power via lines passing through Zapatista-held areas of the Atlixco district, faced shutdown, threatening a newsprint shortage in central Mexico. Furthermore, not only did these attacks persist, but they sometimes took on unexpected results. Rebels in the Sierra, for example, sold stolen copper wire to finance their movement, sometimes in the form of newly minted coins; they also used it to establish their own communication system. The rebel menace to central government control over outlying areas prompted state authorities to install a more comprehensive phone system enabling districts to be in constant touch with Puebla City.[21]

Business and Industry

Business and industry felt the war, both directly and indirectly. Attacks on infrastructure and plants and equipment were a constant problem. Textile mills and other establishments, especially those located outside population centers, such as the United States–owned Teziutlán Copper Company in the Sierra, became targets. In addition, many small-town banks closed their doors and transferred their capital and personnel to safer locations while Spanish merchants, who had been particularly vulnerable targets since the beginning of the revolution, also took special precautions.[22]

Warfare not only posed direct costs in the form of destruction but also indirect ones that included such things as guards and higher taxes. Furthermore, the climate of insecurity affected business. Puebla City merchants, for example, worried about sales to the northern region of the state. Therefore, they supported the Sierra Pact, an October 1913 truce between rebels and the Huerta government in the area (see Chapter 3). Atlixco officials noticed an upsurge in economic activity in July 1914 when, in the waning days of the regime, forced recruitment into the army was lifted, resulting in more traffic on the streets.[23]

Nevertheless, the business climate, at least in the central, government-dominated region of the state, remained tolerable into the autumn of 1913. Many entrepreneurs held out hope that the new, seemingly probusiness Huerta regime would restore the conditions needed to resume and even increase production following the instability of the Madero period. Several industrialists reopened their mills and a handful even planned expansions or new facilities.[24]

The atmosphere changed, however, after the fraudulent national elections persuaded many people that a political solution to the war was not imminent. Insurgents in the north and south of Puebla were making steady gains (see Chapter 3), and the state's key industry, textiles, faced near paralysis as cotton shipments from northern Mexico faltered. As a result, inflation and currency problems began to hurt the economy. Falling production, distribution problems, and hoarding of basic goods boosted inflation. Meanwhile, capital scarcity, bank closures, and counterfeiting undermined confidence in the financial system, even as the peso devalued forty-nine times on the international market between February 1913 and August 1914. Paper currency, particularly that issued by undercapitalized state banks, lost credibility, provoking a run on coins. Merchants refused to accept bills at face value. Small change needed for daily transactions became scarce, hoarded by speculators and banks, thus disrupting local markets and daily transactions.[25]

Decrees banning the discounting of and refusal to accept paper currency had only limited effect. Rumors of bank closures fueled an end-of-the-year run on financial institutions. To stem the bleeding, the Cámara de Comercio urged citizens to remain calm, and banks took a holiday. Huerta set the reserve requirement at a ratio of three to one to meet the increase in demand. He also named nineteen banks with exclusive right to issue paper money and ordered its obligatory circulation. The banks included Puebla's Banco Oriental, but not before it nearly collapsed, causing great concern and consternation among the business community. To increase the number of small coins and bills in circulation, institutions were urged to make change for larger notes and authorized to emit paper worth one and two pesos. The federal government imported coins, mainly from the United States, and delivered them as well as domestically produced centavo pieces to Puebla's banks; the Cámara in turn oversaw their distribution to businesses, taking care to try to prevent hoarding. Nevertheless, the situation only deteriorated as the regime weakened. Capitalists, such as the heirs of Spanish industrialist and hacendado Ángel Díaz Rubín, transferred money from Puebla to Madrid. Branch banks in smaller cities and towns closed, laying off their employees or sending them to work in Puebla or Mexico City. By July 1914 the Banco Oriental was issuing *cheques* in denominations of between five and fifty centavos on such poor quality paper that, if merchants accepted them, they disintegrated within days.[26]

The juggling of the financial situation and the effort to shore up the banking and currency systems forced the state government and powerful economic groups to deal with one another. Among the latter were the large-scale agriculturalists, businessmen, and industrialists represented by the Cámara Agrícola, the Cámara de Comercio, and the CIM, respectively. These three groups frequently coordinated their actions, referring to themselves as Cámaras Unidas (United Chambers), holding joint meetings and even locating their offices in the same building in Puebla City. Their members' presence in many towns throughout the state made them a powerful lobbying group and, to a degree, an intelligence network equal to that of the government. They did not necessarily approve of the Huerta regime and its methods, seeing it as a poor facsimile of the Porfiriato, but felt that given the alternatives they had little choice but to cooperate with it. Thus, they represented not only a formidable economic presence but to some degree a shadow state government. The administration, much of the time disputed and weak, looked to the Cámaras for help.[27]

Of the three groups, the industrialists wielded the most influence. The CIM represented forty-two textile mills, more than a quarter of the nation's total. Although agriculture represented a larger share of economic production in Puebla, manufacturing, especially textiles, accounted for a significant amount, between 30 and 40 percent. Also, many industrialists had close connections to and investments in the farming and merchant sectors. Furthermore, the largest factory owners tended to be Spaniards; thus their interests axiomatically took on international implications. Finally, more than 8,000 workers plus their families depended directly on the textile industry, and the vast majority of them lived in and near key towns in central Puebla, including the capital as well as Atlixco, Cholula, and Texmelucan. The mill hands' well-being provided the owners with much leverage when dealing with government officials.[28]

As early as July 1913, Carrancista advances in northern Mexico began to affect raw cotton imports from the Laguna region, the principal source of domestic fiber. The major problem was a shortage of railroad locomotives and cars, monopolized by army officers, legitimately and otherwise.[29] The destruction of crops and rail lines as well as the confiscation of Gulf Coast petroleum shipments, needed to power factories, also jeopardized production.[30] Then, to make matters worse, the federal government, short of cash, imposed additional taxes on cotton deliveries and solicited "donations" of cloth for the war effort.[31] Moreover, owners of idle or underutilized mills found themselves locked into fixed electrical power contracts, which they attempted to break, thus creating friction with the also influential Compañía de Luz y Fuerza de Puebla (Light and Power Company of Puebla).[32]

Textile sector complaints produced a steady stream of meetings and missives among industrialists and officials. Pressure on government helped alleviate some problems. Nevertheless, redress, when achieved, generally proved to be fleeting as the economic and military situation deteriorated and central government authority, even over its own officials, weakened.[33]

Although initially divided over relying on United States imports, the CIM eventually accepted the idea; it had became clear that the government could not guarantee shipments from Torreón despite a good harvest, and officials demanded extra monies to defray security costs and repair transportation lines. Furthermore, owners began to fear the creation of a government-monopolized cotton distribution network. In turn, authorities also reluctantly concluded that it was preferable to lose tax revenue and pay out foreign exchange rather than close mills and lay off workers who might then join the enemy. Nevertheless, foreign imports only momentarily relieved the situation. Soon, rising prices and transportation difficulties with the port of Veracruz negated even this option.[34]

By late winter 1914 most factories operated only sporadically, if at all, and at a loss. R. Gavito y Compañía officials wrote in exasperation to the Departamento de Trabajo (Labor Department) saying that the firm had had no major interruptions in production from 1899 to August 1913, but since then its three mills had been operating on a sharply reduced schedule. Moreover, since December 1913, twenty-eight cars of cotton had left Torreón but only two had arrived despite the fact that the company had stationed agents in Mexico City, Saltillo, San Luis Potosí, and Torreón to oversee shipments.[35]

Then in April 1914, Puebla mills faced the loss of one of their last markets, the Yucatán. Customs officials at Progreso taxed Puebla-produced finished cloth as imports because it had been sent through United States–occupied Veracruz. This route was the only viable one as no railroad extended to the far southeast of the country. It took until late July for the regime to remedy the problem.[36]

By August, owners threatened to shut all their mills, throwing their remaining workers on the streets and denying the government needed tax revenue.[37] Indeed, most industrialists, frustrated by having to deal with an increasingly weak and inept government, were ready to take their chances with a new regime. Nevertheless, their willingness to deal with Huerta, if not fully to embrace him, plus their failure to reach out to either the Carrancistas or the Zapatistas before the last desperate moment, left them vulnerable when the revolutionaries did arrive.[38]

Labor

One might expect that in this period of economic and political insecurity, working people would have focused exclusively on protecting their jobs. Employment security was a consideration, but given the organizing experience of the Madero years, aided by government intervention on their behalf, workers no longer demonstrated the docility of the past.[39] Hence, labor activism in 1913–14 took on two additional issues, the six-day workweek and implementation of the 1912 labor accords in the textile industry.

Most employees in the retail and service sectors labored seven days a week, often for ten, twelve, and even more hours at low pay. Some individuals, such as store clerks and especially bakers, were treated as virtual slaves, locked inside the work place in a so-called *encierro* system. Constantly on the job and dispersed among numerous establishments, these people found organizing to be especially difficult. By 1913, however, they had gained two valuable allies, the Partido Católico and larger businesses.[40]

Catholics hoped Sunday off would encourage greater formal religious participation. It might also bolster the Church's effort to steer working people away from class conflict and unionization (*sindicalismo*) into a noncombative, social-Catholic orientation with respect for private property. This trend was closely patterned after traditional mutual societies, but now with a Christian slant. The Church, backed unofficially by government and business, already sponsored labor organizations, schools, and social centers for workers and their families.[41]

Larger businesses also favored the measure. Since sales and profits on Sunday were low in relation to labor and operating costs, this support was a small price to pay to pacify employees and discourage them from organizing into assertive unions. Moreover, other states had similar laws and, the advanced countries of North America and Europe allowed for the practice.[42]

Smaller merchants, however, opposed the idea, because they operated much closer to the margin and could not as easily afford to close on Sundays. Moreover, labor costs for them were low as family members tended to make up most of their workforce. As a result, earlier attempts to implement the measure had always failed as some businessmen refused to close, thus placing others at a competitive disadvantage and therefore undermining the initiative.[43]

Nevertheless, in September 1913 the state legislature passed a law with the support of the Cámara de Comercio and workers represented by the newly formed Unión Cosmopolita de Dependientes (Cosmopolitan Union of Salespersons). Opposition, however, delayed its implementation until February 1914. Nevertheless, by that time, economic conditions had deteriorated to the point that many of its original supporters questioned its wisdom, while at the same time the state tried to convince the business community to back its plan for a 50 percent tax surcharge to bolster security. Consequently, when implemented, Sunday off again failed. Most employers simply ignored it, and Governor Hernández, unwilling to alienate business further, failed to enforce the law. Then the legislature modified and reissued the measure in April, but it was too late. Businessmen's attention was now focused on survival.[44]

The 1912 labor accord between the Madero government and textile industrialists, with workers relegated to observer status, established a set of work rules and a minimum wage in return for a tax break for owners. The imprecisely written agreement, however, left much to interpretation. Huerta's military governors had little experience or inclination to deal with problems within the mills short of outright violence; Governor Maass, for example, had participated in the repression of striking workers at Río Blanco, Veracruz, in 1906–1907. Moreover, the state generally lacked the jurisdiction and means to deal with the issue, thus leaving the federal Departamento de Trabajo to intervene between capital and labor.[45]

The Departamento aimed to control and channel labor along a reformist path. Workers were to nominate representatives to an ideologically moderate Comité Central de Obreros (Central Committee of Workers). In turn the Comité would meet with industrialists to iron out the ambiguities in the 1912 accord. The plan, however, faced opposition from two sides: radical workers who wanted independent unions and conservative owners who objected to any type of worker organization with negotiating power.[46]

The Departamento warned mill hands against their antagonistic attitude toward administrators and failure to adhere to the 1912 agreement, illegal strikes, and taking unauthorized holidays. Otherwise, it could not help the workers to gain credibility with and talk to the owners and might even abandon them to unsympathetic state and local authorities. Furthermore, to entice labor to accept its point of view, Departamento agents established savings and loan programs (*cajas de ahorro y préstamo*) in factories. The Huerta regime also proposed to add the word "Trabajo" (Labor) to the title of the cabinet-level Secretaría de Industria y Comercio (Secretariat of Industry and Commerce), introduce a workers' compensation law, and create state-level Departamento affiliates called Cámaras de Trabajo.[47]

To industrialists the Departamento pointed out the advantages of dealing with a government-controlled, moderate labor organization. Moreover, unlike during the Madero period, worker delegates now would have to be literate, know arithmetic, and have a certificate of good conduct from a local authority or mill administrator. Furthermore, the Departamento agreed to back owners' demands for more energetic action against deemed agitators and troublemakers, including the use of soldiers and spies. According to a policy adopted under Madero, uncooperative mill hands continued to be jailed and inducted into the army.[48]

In an October 1913 labor convention the Departamento outlined its gains and plans. It had set up an office for the unemployed, kept statistics, established a savings and loan program, and published a newsletter. Subsequently, however, little was accomplished. Promises to place Cámaras de Trabajo in each state, create an accident indemnification law, and resolve differences over the 1912 agreement fell victim to owner resistance and the deteriorating economic and military situation. Further consideration of these issues had to wait until after the Huerta period.[49]

Meanwhile many workers moved toward a tacit alliance with their opponents, the owners. In laborers' view, government security, tax, and transportation policy only exacerbated an already poor situation by threatening the closure of mills. Hence, they backed capitalists' demands for more troops, lower imposts, and additional cotton in order to preserve jobs. The entrepreneur Marcelino Presno, who owned an industrial-agricultural complex near Texmelucan, offered his employees positions on his hacienda when cloth production fell. Others allowed half days of work, lowered rent on company housing, and handed out basic foodstuffs to laid-off mill hands and their families.[50]

Property and Land

Agrarian policy in Puebla during the Huerta period can be summed up briefly. Rural tension and conflict prompted official concern and repression. Most violence occurred in a line from the Zapatista stronghold in the south through the volcano region along the western border with the states of Mexico and Tlaxcala to Serrano (person of the Sierra) redoubts in the north. Faced with increasing military threat, hacendado pressure, and the widespread belief in the sanctity of private property, authorities came up with few reform initiatives.[51] At the federal government's behest, state officials named engineers to survey and sell off public lands, but these properties were few and peasants had little money. On occasion the state would buy a rebel-infested property and sell it off to campesinos on condition that they keep it insurgent free. Also, officials encouraged hacendados to make direct arrangements with resident peons or local villagers to buy portions of the hacienda, a practice that would continue into the Carrancista period.[52]

In other words no comprehensive program existed. Most official action consisted of dealing with crises and disputes on an ad hoc basis. Authorities especially became involved in conflicts when they exhibited gross abuse or concerned politically sensitive parties, particularly foreigners. The latter case often included Spaniards, the largest expatriate community in Puebla and owners of significant amounts of property. Here officials tried not only to avoid a diplomatic crisis but also to appear not to favor Spaniards over Mexicans.[53]

Food and Basics

Many, perhaps most, people in the state were not directly affected except on an occasional basis by the war's impact on the infrastructural, business, and political systems. They did feel, however, the negative effects of the violence on basic goods' shortages and prices. Here, again, the problem did not reach critical proportions until late spring 1914.[54]

Violence in the countryside took a toll on production. Nevertheless, the breakdown in rural control systems allowed some campesinos the opportunity to substitute the growing of commercial products such as cane for basic foodstuffs for personal consumption, little of which was noted in statistics. Therefore, the trampling and burning of fields, the pasturing of horses among crops, the occupying and cutting of woodlands, the stealing of livestock, and the destroying of food processing complexes all had, on the whole, a negative effect. Furthermore, the lack of labor became an important issue as men joined fighting forces or went into hiding to avoid the draft. Whole families migrated to safer zones, particularly urban areas, which in turn placed severe pressure on already resource-poor towns to accommodate an influx of new and often destitute people. Finally, the disruptions of the transportation and communication infrastructure also had an impact on production and distribution. Trains were blown up, rails destroyed, and telegraph lines torn down; small farmers simply did not dare carry their small amount of goods to the local market due to fear for their personal safety or of having their wares confiscated.[55]

Slowly and sporadically these conditions began to affect supplies and prices. Some people benefited, such as peasants able to produce and sell in local urban markets or hacendados and businessmen who hoarded for speculative purposes. Nevertheless, most people suffered, especially those who bought most goods that they consumed. Despite an average production year, grain prices, which in normal times would fall at the end of the harvest season, stabilized or even climbed in autumn 1913. They continued upward into the New Year, blamed in part on brokers from Mexico City who bought up wheat and corn at inflated values. In more conflicted areas such as Chignahuapan, Tetela, and Teziutlán in the north, high prices and even shortages of such goods as sugar, salt, and rice were reported. In Huaquechula complaints filtered in about well-organized monopolists who forced peasants to sell cheaply and then marketed the goods in urban areas such as Atlixco at high profits. Rising costs and scarcity were only compounded by the lack of small coins to make purchases. This situation made consumers even more susceptible to dishonest merchants, who charged extra and adulterated such items as lard. One newspaper called these businessmen Jews and promised to publish their names in order to warn the public.[56]

In late April 1914 the state government intervened in the market. Taking its cue from Mexico City, which ordered the state to concentrate grains and livestock in Puebla City because of the United States invasion of Veracruz, Governor Hernández decreed price lids on basic items. He also ordered committees established in each community to oversee distribution. Then the governor forbade the export of products out of certain areas, such as the Matamoros district, because most were being sold across enemy lines to the Zapatistas at higher prices. These steps set a pattern that officials would expand on in subsequent years as conditions deteriorated.[57]

Social Welfare

The war only exacerbated already poor socioeconomic conditions in the state, a situation that dated well before the outbreak of the revolution in 1910. They were especially visible, and most thoroughly recorded, in urban areas. Puebla City, for example, was very unhealthy, despite the modern image public officials tried to project. Open sewers and garbage-laden streets contributed to a high death rate attributed to gastrointestinal ailments, which particularly hit children. Frequent epidemics of smallpox, diphtheria, scarlet fever, tuberculosis, and meningitis also contributed to the toll. Between 1900 and 1910 the city's death rate was 44/1000, compared to 7.6/1000 for United States cities at the time and almost double that of Italy, whose rate was 23.8/1000, the worst in Western Europe. Indeed, for the state as a whole, the average life expectancy had fallen since the late nineteenth century, thirty years in 1895 to twenty-five years in 1910.[58]

After 1910 the well-being of the populace certainly deteriorated, but specific statistics are hard to come by. Little is known about the countryside with its hundreds of small villages where more than 80 percent of the population resided in 1910. If newspaper reports about urban life are any indication of the general socioeconomic situation in 1913–14, it was poor. Crime, unsanitary and unsafe conditions, epidemics, unemployment, public drunkenness and fights, and the lack of monies for social services prevailed. Military authorities had to be warned not to leave corpses hanging after execution and to bury or burn bodies to prevent disease. What health care existed in smaller communities was placed at risk as pharmacies closed for lack of medicines, and their owners fled the violence. In Chignahuapan (population 12,500 in 1912), murders, mainly for personal revenge, rose from eight in 1913 to thirteen in 1914, while other indicators of social instability, such as alcohol and drug abuse, prostitution, and illegitimate births also increased. Warfare and its impact, including the uprooting and migration of rural peoples to less conflicted urban areas, only contributed to already difficult conditions.[59]

Education

Educational policy emphasized financial retrenchment and greater clerical influence in the classroom. One of Maass's first actions was to order that only poor students receive free scholarly materials, thus denying a state-supported subsidy previously enjoyed by all. This action came amidst severe economic difficulty for many municipalities, which could barely afford to keep their school doors open.[60]

Then, in a controversial move that even Maass could not support, the Partido Católico–led bloc in the local legislature attempted to pass a measure automatically granting state validation of private school studies at the high school and university levels. Heretofore, students from nonpublic institutions had to take special exams to determine if they met official standards; public school graduates were exempt. Liberal students, mainly from the Colegio del Estado, decried this threat to the state-monopolized curriculum. They clashed with more conservative colleagues from the Universidad Católica (Catholic University) and Instituto Metodista (Methodist Institute) as well as with police when the liberals tried to storm the congress. In the end the measure was postponed for further consideration, thus diffusing the divisive issue.[61]

Another measure, however, that united students against the regime was obligatory military training in schools, which was part of a general militarization and mobilization effort. Most high school and university-level students soon came to resent the time taken from their lives by marching in slap-dash uniforms with wooden guns under the direction of a low-level officer who was often beneath their social class. In the elementary and junior high schools, parents, too, tired of their sons' and daughters' waste of time and made plans to enroll their offspring in Catholic institutions, where academic instruction took priority over playing soldier.[62]

The Church

Governors Maass and Hernández had a generally close working relationship with the Catholic Church, often in conjunction with the active Partido Católico. Indeed, each side needed the other; for the state, the Church represented a means of social control and a source of funds, while the sacking of ecclesiastical buildings and attacks on priests in the war zones forced religious personnel into authorities' arms for protection.[63]

While Governor Carrasco had attempted to enforce the anti-Church reform laws, Maass and Hernández took a more relaxed stance.[64] Backed by the Partido Católico, both chief executives at least tolerated, if not advocated, expansion of private, mainly church-affiliated schools and Catholic artisan and labor organizations. Nuns were allowed to work in state-run social welfare institutions. Both men cooperated with Archbishop Ramón Ibarra y González. Maass, for example, attended a performance of Catholic school children at which he helped the prelate hand out prizes to students. Hernández and the archbishop exchanged official visits to each other's offices. The governor also suspended the law prohibiting the ringing of church bells in order to welcome Ibarra home from a voyage to Europe, a public event marked by music, fireworks, and the attendance of some ten thousand well wishers. Furthermore, Hernández and Huerta arranged for the archbishop of Antequera (Oaxaca), Eulogio Gregorio Gillow y Zavala, an old friend of both men, to marry their offspring in an elaborate demonstration of political and religious cohabitation. Years earlier Gillow also had confirmed Concepción Hernández in the home of Porfirio Díaz while her father had served as zone commander in Oaxaca. Hernández, along with high military and civilian officials, attended a special mass to pray for the country. Finally, another indication of a tolerant church-state relationship in Puebla in 1913–14 is the fact that the Catholic-oriented newspaper, *El Amigo de la Verdad* (Friend of the Truth), was very well informed about the local political scene.[65]

Despite this outward appearance of close collaboration, however, there is some indication that not all was well between state authorities and the Church. Newspaper accounts claiming that village priests, particularly in Zapatista-influenced areas, were joining the rebels must have strained the relationship and planted doubts about the viability of the regime in ecclesiastics' minds. In early 1914 a report reached Mexico City that the Huertistas in Puebla were in difficulty because clergy and hacendados no longer wanted to finance the government. Furthermore, the two groups were looking for a way to get rid of Huerta. At this point, however, Governor Maass died and

Hernández replaced him. Over the next several months, as the economic and military situation worsened, the new chief executive implemented what appears to be an even more solicitous stance toward the Church.[66]

A look at the Huertista economic and social program in the state clearly reveals it to have been cautious, yet disposed to rectify some of the problems of the past. It showed an understanding of the virtue of adopting some of the Maderista program in order to reduce generalized discontent and stabilize the state, a practical goal that most people supported. The regime tried working with a number of groups, including moderate workers, peasants, and the legislature. Here, Huerta was not, at least early in his time in office, the counterrevolutionary ideologue as he has been portrayed.

Nevertheless, Huerta's governors carried out few of these proposed changes. The exigencies of warfare, especially the constant need for additional funds, pushed Maass and Hernández into the arms of the monied elites. These elements mostly resisted reform, as they disliked taking orders from outsiders and resented having to pay for the war; ultimately they lost confidence in the government and looked for alternatives. Nevertheless, efforts to distance themselves from the regime came too late to avoid being branded Huertista collaborators by the victorious Carrancistas. As a result, businessmen, industrialists, agriculturalists, high-level bureaucrats, clerics, and others would pay a high price for their actions in the near future. Furthermore, Puebla's autonomy would come under even greater assault.

3

WAR, 1913–1914

The political and socioeconomic program of the Victoriano Huerta government can only be understood in the context of warfare. Upon assuming power in February 1913 and thereafter, Huerta faced an array of opponents: unarmed, mainly urban-based political adversaries; rebel movements such as the Zapatistas and Carrancistas or Constitucionalistas (so named with the idea of restoring constitutional order following Huerta's overthrow of Madero); and even the United States, which blocked weapons sales and captured the port of Veracruz.

Thus, while asserting political control and implementing reforms, Puebla's Huertista governors faced the added burden of dealing with urban dissidents and rural insurgents. The most serious threat came from the countryside. In the south of the state, Zapatistas had been battling the government since 1911. In the northern Sierra, locals operated in combination with newly arrived Carrancista officers from the north of Mexico. Much of this anti-Huerta sentiment was couched in long-held, autonomous aspirations. The federal and state governments' response to this challenge took on several aspects. Authorities repressed the unarmed civilian opposition, militarized the society, and built up the security forces in response to the enemy.

The impact of warfare on Puebla's residents in 1913–14 varied greatly. Indeed, for some people it was positive, as weakened central authority opened up opportunities for greater local autonomy and initiative. One, for example, could avoid paying taxes or invade land, made easier by the burning and sacking of official records; one could sell arms and foodstuffs to the army or the enemy; one could seek revenge; or one could get military pay and rank. Nevertheless, for most citizens war meant some degree of inconvenience, depending on such factors as place, time, and socioeconomic status. The northern and southern regions of the state experienced the greatest dislocation while the relatively privileged central area, including Puebla City, fared better. Furthermore, not until the spring of 1914 did most of the state face daily, life-threatening violence.

The Opposition

Urban dissidents

The primarily urban, mostly unarmed, "illegal" opposition to the regime played a minor although not insignificant role in the 18-month-long effort to bring down Huerta and his minions in Puebla. Based mainly in Puebla City and other towns in the center of the state such as Atlixco, Cholula, and Tehuacán, these elements represented a cross section of the populace. Early on they consisted of independents or liberal Maderistas, including bureaucrats and officeholders, students, and radical workers; over time, portions of the business community, professionals, the press, housewives, and others also joined.

The reason for the disillusionment with the regime can be found in the deteriorating political and socioeconomic situation, described in Chapters 1 and 2. Promised stability and prosperity proved short lived. Furthermore, several key events helped shape the public's negative perception of the government, after which in each case antiregime activity (and government repression) rose: Madero's assassination, the imposition of Maass as governor, the fraudulent fall 1913 elections, the April 1914 tax surcharge, and the aftermath of the United States invasion of Veracruz that same month.

Dissident leaders attempted to shape attitudes and organize the populace by offering alternative nationalistic symbols or linking their movement to appropriate old ones. The government and its supporters took up the challenge. Civic holidays became especially contentious as each side saw an opportunity to take advantage of the celebrations. Authorities cancelled the April 2, 1913, commemoration of Porfirio Díaz's defeat of the French at Puebla City in 1867, which came soon after Madero's assassination. On subsequent major holidays the regime strengthened security and made sure its supporters dominated the celebrations. Public employees and students, furnished with uniforms and wooden rifles and trained to march military style, dominated the September 16 independence day festivities; they gathered "voluntarily" to demonstrate their willingness to take up arms to defend the fatherland. Later the same month, officials sanctioned a Partido Católico–sponsored ceremony to mark the 1821 consummation of Mexico's independence by general and emperor Agustín de Iturbide, hero of the nation's conservatives. Similar efforts to control celebrators also took place during the following year's April 2 and May 5 (1862, when Liberals defeated French troops and their Conservative allies at Puebla City) gatherings. According to one high official the government took these actions in order to awaken the military spirit and civic feelings among "*elementos de orden*" (elements of order).[1]

Although dissidents largely failed to win space in official holiday festivities, they did create their own unofficial days to mark special events. In June 1913 labor activists called for demonstrations and strikes ostensibly to honor Madero; the real reason was to protest Maass's becoming governor. Then, as November approached, attention shifted to the 1910 rebellion in Puebla City led by Aquiles Serdán, marking the beginning of the revolution. Once Madero fell from power in February 1913, police kept watch over the martyr Serdán's bullet-hole-pocked house, in which the women of the family still resided, preventing the curious and potential agitators from gathering. Plaques commemorating the battle were removed from the building, and when Serdán backers tried to replace them, authorities arrested the marblesmith who made them. On November 18, the anniversary of the Serdán uprising, flowers appeared on the victims' graves. Workers in one textile mill took the afternoon off to mark the occasion, prompting management to close the factory for a week with no pay as punishment.[2]

The urban-based, heterogeneous, dispersed, protest movement was more a thorn in the side of the regime than any viable threat. Whatever coherence the dissidents managed to exhibit must be credited largely to the second junta Revolucionaria de Puebla (Revolutionary junta of Puebla), largely a hold over from the Maderista era known by the same name. The indefatigable teachers and sisters, Guadalupe, María, and Rosa Narváez Bautista, formed the new junta following Madero's death. They were joined by Carmen Serdán, sibling of the martyred rebel Aquiles Serdán, who herself had been wounded in the November 1910 uprising. The junta was one place where women played a direct and public role during the revolution.[3]

The junta's membership indicates a cross section of Puebla City society. Nevertheless, its leadership remained in the hands of the same type of and, to some degree the same people from the 1910–11 version: middle class, liberal, republican. Many were professionals, like the Narváez sisters and lawyers Rafael Cañete and Jesús Zafra, recruited to serve as president and vice president, respectively, because of their political connections, experience, and moderate, reformist outlook. In addition, the junta gained most of its operating funds from sympathizers in Puebla City and Mexico City, where it had contacts among other anti-Huerta conspirators, including women's groups. In this instance the junta retained much of the myopic outlook of the Madero era, exhibiting from its headquarters in central Puebla City only limited understanding of the socioeconomic needs and wants of mostly rural, peasant, and Indian northern and southern regions of the state.[4]

The junta sent emissaries to the Zapatistas as well as the Carrancistas to sound out their intentions and to undertake alliances. The Puebla City people and southern campesinos, however, could not overcome their mutual distrust. Each blamed the other for Zapata's decision to take up arms against Madero in 1911; beyond this concrete reason, however, there existed a nearly unbridgeable cultural and political gulf between the two groups. The Zapatistas, especially, felt that the junta, weak and isolated and now coming with hat in hand after having backed Madero had little to offer them.[5]

Given its makeup and political proclivities, the junta found the Carrancistas, who by mid-1913 had infiltrated into the northern Sierra, more ideologically compatible. Here, junta agents dealt with Carranza's officers, largely ignoring local leaders. The northern Sierra and Puebla City had a history of mutual antagonism, based partly on cultural differences as well as a long-standing Serrano desire for autonomy. Nevertheless, many people from the region took a more pragmatic stance than the Zapatistas, working, albeit cautiously, with the Carrancistas to oust their common enemy, the Huertistas. Furthermore, the Carrancistas, interested in wielding power at the national level, were much more aware than the Zapatistas of the importance of controlling the state capital and therefore more willing to deal with the junta, despite its isolation and weakness. The strategy worked, for key junta operatives, unlike most of the urban elements they represented, would remain staunch Carrancistas for the remainder of the decade.

As such, the junta Revolucionaria played a modest role in the Carrancista victory over Huerta in the state of Puebla during 1913–14. Its agents joined rebel units to help coordinate action, recruiters added to the insurgents' numbers, spies kept track of enemy movements, smugglers carried messages as well as arms and ammunition, propagandists proselytized the unconvinced, and fundraisers gathered money to help people persecuted by Huerta to reach safety. Many people and organizations took part in this effort, including women, children, storekeepers, state deputies, and even the Instituto Metodista, whose administrators and students employed the school's printing press in the cause.[6]

Zapatistas

The view of events of rural, southern Poblanos differed from that of the urban dissidents in the central part of the state. The opposition in the former area consisted of rebel bands operating loosely under Emiliano Zapata, located in neighboring Morelos state. The Zapatistas had been almost continuously at war since the spring of 1911, first against Díaz, then interim president Francisco León de la Barra, and finally Madero. Madero's demise at the hands of Huerta, however, did little to bring about peace as Huerta had commanded the federal army against the Zapatistas in the fall of 1911 and remained a bitter enemy. Furthermore, the Zapatistas distrusted the urban-based, Maderista-dominated junta Revolucionaria as well as the Constitucionalista interlopers from northern Mexico. Therefore, the Zapatistas continued to fight on their own, hoping to create within the territory they controlled an agrarian-based, autonomous society. Military action aimed more to consolidate gains made during the Madero period and fend off government intrusions than to win national or even state power. This sense of regional identity and self-reliance, not unlike that found in the northern Sierra, would help the Zapatistas successfully to defy central governments and thus keep a large part of the state out of Mexico City's and Puebla City's control for years.

Most Zapatistas greeted Madero's demise with satisfaction, but few saw his successor in a better light. Nevertheless, the abrupt turn in events at the national level did have some impact. Federal agents' blandishments and the announcement of a general amnesty enticed a handful of insurgent leaders to switch sides. The most notable catch was Jesús "Tuerto" (one-eye) Morales, a high-level general. Morales, a saloon keeper from Ayutla, near Chietla, was, as Knight points out, perhaps more inclined to accept a deal, including a reportedly large cash payment, than were his more agrarian rooted colleagues. Indeed, a significant portion of Morales' troops refused to follow him. Madero's overthrow, the Morales defection, and continued government peace feelers momentarily halted the Zapata movement's momentum. Nevertheless, by May 1913, newspapers reported that five districts in southeastern Puebla were virtually overrun by rebels.[7]

If the Huerta regime had any doubts about, however, the resolve and ability of the Zapatistas to take on the federal army, they were dispelled in June 1913 in a fierce battle for the district seat of Chiautla. Located in the heart of sugar cane–producing southern Puebla, Chiautla represented the regime's inability to protect urban centers from the insurgents' advances.

For three days the two sides, involving several hundred men, fought. Led by some of the Zapatistas' principal generals, including Eufemio Zapata (brother of Emiliano), Genovevo de la O, Clotilde Sosa, and Felipe Neri, the insurgents won but suffered many casualties. The defenders, a combination of federal army and irregular troops, fared worse. The dead included Joaquín Ibarro, son of a rich hacendado of the same name, who led a volunteer force, and Chiautla's *jefe político*, Diego Guerrero; it is not clear, however, if Guerrero died at the hands of the Zapatistas or the government, as one version claims he helped the rebels enter the town. The insurgents sacked the community, sending refugees in all directions and forcing the transfer of the district's administrative structure to more easily defend Chietla.[8]

Thereafter, Zapatista actions escalated, especially once the rainy season and harvest ended in October. Even Huertista censorship could not hide the dangerous situation outside the principal population centers, from which soldiers and rural troops only reluctantly ventured. The British embassy, for example, reported some twenty-four instances of so-called banditry in central and southern Puebla for the last week of November 1913: estates attacked, railway hands robbed, kidnappings and ransoms demanded, towns sacked and set ablaze, a hacienda manager tortured to death, and cattle stolen. Rail lines and rolling stock also suffered. By early 1914, Zapatistas operated throughout the south and west of the state, descending from their mountain strongholds into the lowlands to threaten towns as close to the state capital as Cholula, only twelve kilometers distant. Spies, including railroad workers, infiltrated urban areas where they smuggled arms and spread propaganda.[9]

Despite their gains the Zapatista high command, itself peripatetic, only slowly and with difficulty forged the movement into a coherent military, political, and social force. Indeed, the Southerners were fortunate not to be facing a more competent federal army. The Zapatista structure was highly decentralized, allowing for local initiative and homegrown leadership but also presenting many problems. Officers, who gained a given rank depending on the number of people they recruited, often knew little about soldiering and warfare. They squabbled over jurisdictions and perquisites, a situation exacerbated by the arrival in Puebla of personnel sent from headquarters in Morelos. Likewise, volunteers had little experience with firearms, often spoke little or no Spanish, and had only a fuzzy understanding of the movement's program, the Plan de Ayala. Troops were generally poorly trained and organized and lacked discipline. They carried a variety of weapons; horses were at a premium. Soldiers depended on donations from villages or booty from captured towns and haciendas for arms and materiel. Monies were collected from "taxes" on landowners, but troops often went without pay. Over time some of these problems were rectified, or at least ameliorated, as the Zapatista army became somewhat professionalized and institutionalized and its command structure more centralized. This process was not just one of choice but of necessity, as it faced not only the Huertistas but later the more formidable Carrancistas. Nevertheless, these changes tended to distance the army from its original, popular peasant base, a situation worsened by the fact that in Puebla the top leadership came from another jurisdiction.[10]

Historian Ian Jacobs has also noted this tension between the Morelos-based Zapatistas and those of surrounding states. In Guerrero, he says, sporadic armed clashes, raids on villages, and executions took place between the two groups. Indeed, growing distrust of their Morelos cousins by Poblanos and other Zapatistas' would play a key role in the movement's difficulty in projecting and consolidating power in the transstate region. Nevertheless, whatever the gains made in restructuring the Zapatista army, it remained a very different organization than its anti-Huerta counterpart in Sonora. There, Héctor Aguilar Camín points out, soldiers were professional, paid employees of the state, not spontaneous fighters operating in a social context; as a result, units sought to maintain the established order, not overthrow it.[11]

Improving the army was not enough, however, to make the movement effective on an expanded regional basis. Its appeal had to be broadened, and outsiders, not part of the traditional Zapatista peasantry, needed to be incorporated into it. This decision meant accepting Maderista-era officials and others who declared for Zapata following Madero's death. Hacienda administrators, village priests, and townspeople such as merchants also knocked on the Zapatistas' door. Government soldiers switched sides. Finally, they were joined by political refugees from urban areas in central Puebla, in some cases intellectuals such as Manuel Palafox, who became one of Zapata's principal aides. These people gathered under Zapata's tent for any number of reasons, and their loyalty was conditional. Support for the cause in southern and western Puebla, then, became relatively widespread but beyond the Zapatista core constituency rather soft. Furthermore, city people who entered rural Mexico clashed with local culture. Residents greeted them with suspicion and distrust, thereby creating another fault line within the movement's ranks.[12]

Finally, the development of an efficient fighting machine and the expansion of its constituency had to be combined with measures demonstrating the movement's viability as a political entity and socioeconomic provider if it were to succeed. Efforts were made to establish a congress to include representatives from the Zapatista-held transstate region. Land was appropriated and distributed. Hacendados were ordered to honor rental agreements with campesinos. Sales of goods to Huertista-controlled villages were forbidden. Restrictions on alcohol were implemented. Officers' and soldiers' abuse of civilians was investigated. Armies' confiscation of cattle from the poor was prohibited. Schools were ordered established. Finally, in an assertion of defiance and sovereignty as well as promises kept (in contrast to Madero), *jefaturas políticas* (political prefectures) were ended and their archives destroyed.[13]

Not all of these measures succeeded.[14] Nevertheless, the Zapatistas had begun to realize their objective of establishing a separate, self-governing zone, which included southern and western Puebla. This development represented the deepest, most uncompromising strand of autonomous sentiment among the state's rural populace. This outlook rejected not only deals with fellow urban citizens of the state, but also, and especially, the newly arrived Constitucionalistas, outsiders from northern Mexico and ostensible allies in the military struggle against Huerta.

Serranos-Constitucionalistas

The third major anti-Huerta movement during 1913–14 developed in the northern Sierra at the opposite end of the state from the Zapatistas. Here, an unlikely alliance of mestizo ranchers and indigenous villagers joined the Carrancistas, albeit uneasily.[15]

To label this movement Constitucionalista, however, is correct only in the strictest sense. Most Serranos wanted a return to the Constitution of 1857, but their vision of the practical effects of its implementation varied greatly from that of the revolutionaries of Mexico's north who entered their region beginning in spring 1913. The Serranos wanted regional autonomy, a concept so well developed that its more ardent proponents had a name for its logical end, La República de la Sierra, a new state that was to include Puebla's north and part of adjoining Veracruz. Autonomy in practice meant limited federal and state-level intervention in the area: local control over the formation, arming, and disposition of security forces; the end of recruitment in the area for the federal army; tax receipts used for local needs, especially education; and the end of the *jefe político*, giving town governments enhanced power. For the Carrancistas, however, as the Serranos would eventually learn, autonomy meant much less.

Serrano demands largely coincided with those of the Zapatistas; both wanted greater local control over resources and restrictions on outsiders' intervention. The Serranos' concept of autonomy, however, seems to have been somewhat different. They were more disposed to exist within a larger state structure, given their distinct history of arrangements with the national government and their location in an even more isolated, mountainous region of the state.

Nevertheless, the two groups differed on three key issues. First, the Zapatista demand for agrarian reform was not shared so strongly by the Serranos, as most people in the Sierra had access to land. The repercussions of modern, capitalistic agricultural development had not affected the Sierra to the extent that it had in the south of Puebla where modern sugar cane estates and refineries dominated the economy. The Sierra's most important commercial crop, coffee, was grown mainly on family farms. Unlike in the south, no railroad reached into the interior of the Sierra, and commercial operations such as the Necaxa hydroelectric power complex near Huauchinango and the Teziutlán Copper Company mine only had limited impact on a still largely preindustrial society.

Second, many Serranos were Liberals going back to the mid-nineteenth century when they fought Mexican Conservatives and French and Austrian invaders on behalf of Benito Juárez and Porfirio Díaz. As such, they supported or at least tolerated the antiecclesiastical provisions of the 1857 Constitution, a stance that the religiously conservative Zapatistas could not accept.

Third, Serranos were more inclined to deal with the government, whoever was in power. For the Serranos autonomy was relative, while for the Zapatistas adherence to the Plan de Ayala was a near absolute. The Serranos did not oppose all change; they wanted, however, to control its pace on their own terms. Therefore, for the Serranos the main considerations were brokering the best deal possible with the regime in power and determining if and when to shift sides once it weakened. The Zapatistas, however, more fundamentally opposed change, aiming to restore an ideal society based in the past. The Serranos' history of dealing with governments going back to the mid-nineteenth century and their weaker military position compared to the Zapatistas may help explain this difference. Another factor, offered by Knight, is that serrano peasants' cross-class ties made them more flexible in dealing with outside interests. As opposed to traditional, lowland peasants, whose struggle with landlords developed within them greater horizontal or intraclass solidarity, Serranos concentrated more on local political issues, which fostered vertical or geographical alliances among multiple groups. This assertion is confirmed by studies of areas on Puebla's mountainous periphery: Falcón and Soledad García for the Veracruz Huasteca, Garner for the Mixteca of Oaxaca, and Jacobs for northern Guerrero.[16]

For years political life in the north of Puebla had revolved around Juan Francisco Lucas, the recognized power broker of the region whom many called "El Patriarco de la Sierra" (Patriarch of the Sierra). Lucas, a Nahuatl-speaking mestizo, had managed to negotiate the twists and turns of political life since the 1850s by following his keen sense of survival and enjoying support among the majority indigenous population.

Both Díaz and Madero unofficially had recognized Lucas and largely had left the region alone in return for his loyalty. Now most Serranos looked to Lucas to protect their autonomy vis-à-vis the Huerta government; Huerta, too, recognized Lucas's importance and sought his cooperation in keeping the Sierra pacified. The region was an important food and hydroelectric supplier, and it lay near key transportation routes connecting Veracruz and central Mexico. Moreover, peace there freed troops to be sent to other conflicted areas of the country. Lucas was willing to deal with Huerta but could not do so immediately and openly for fear of alienating the many pro-Madero elements in the Sierra; furthermore, he first wanted to assess Huerta's ability to hold on to power.

Once negotiations began, however, others took action, thus putting to the test Lucas's ability to control the region for the new president. Carrancista agents in the Sierra, having arrived from northern Mexico via Gulf Coast ports, successfully began to organize a second front against Huerta. Potential rivals to Lucas questioned his dealings with Madero's killer, especially as Huerta stepped up forced recruitment (*leva*) into the federal army in the region, thus directly challenging one of the most sacred tenets of autonomy. These elements turned to the Carrancistas, hoping that autonomy could be negotiated with the northern revolutionaries, too.

The most important group to ally with the Carrancistas was the five Márquez brothers. Led by Esteban, they were relatively prosperous mestizo ranchers from Otlatlán (Alatriste district) in the western Sierra. Committed and active Maderistas and also natural rivals to Lucas, they gained the backing of diverse socioeconomic elements, especially those who hailed from their sector of the mountainous north.

Soon, Lucas found himself playing both sides and being carried along by events. On the one hand he tacitly participated in the Carrancista rebellion in order to protect his leadership in the region. Indeed, he had little choice as the Carrancistas and their Serrano allies set up headquarters in Tetela de Ocampo, next door to Lucas's hometown. On the other hand he declared loyalty to the Huerta regime and expressed a desire to broker peace. Peace, Lucas realized, was necessary to ensure autonomy; warfare would pull in outsiders and undermine it.

After weeks of acting as intermediary between Huerta and pro-Carranza Serranos, Lucas brokered a formal deal, which called for autonomy, peace, and elimination of the Carrancistas from the region. The October 1913, Pacto de la Sierra (Sierra Pact) provided for the federal army to end recruitment and withdraw. A replacement force, the Brigada Serrana (Sierra Brigade), financed by Mexico City, would be created under the command of Lucas and Márquez. The Brigada would supervise elections for new local officials. Free primary education was to be offered to all, and the American-owned Teziutlán Copper Company's mine, La Aurora, was to remain open, thereby preserving some 2,000 jobs.

Not everyone was happy with the Pacto. Carrancistas saw their gains in the region threatened. They condemned the agreement and continued to organize an army. Mestizo and white townspeople, many of them small businessmen and professionals, feared invasions of their communities by Indian soldiers and the takeover of local political positions by radicals. Consequently, Huerta's forces only slowly withdrew from key population centers, and the selection of new officials produced conflict. Furthermore, monies from Mexico City to finance the Brigada Serrana and education were slow in coming, thus disillusioning even original supporters of the accord.

As a result, by January 1914 the Pacto had largely broken down, and warfare spread throughout the Sierra for the first time. The Márquez brothers, enticed by promises of rank and political office, rejoined the Carrancistas. Lucas had little choice but to go along despite the harm he could increasingly envision for his region.

As the fighting spread and intensified, it took on characteristics of socioeconomic warfare. For the first time since the French intervention of the 1860s, outside troops in large numbers entered the area causing widespread destruction and disruption, forcing the reluctant Serranos to become pawns of larger military and political forces. The conflict also unleashed race, class, and ideological resentment, hostility that Lucas had spent a lifetime trying to control. Mostly poor, rural, and culturally traditional rebels, both Indians and mestizos, targeted urbanized, westernized, economically better off mestizo and white townspeople, including priests and hacendados, and their properties.

Other Insurgent Groups

In addition to the Zapatistas and Serrano-Constitucionalistas, other smaller, poorly organized, and lesser-known insurgent groups also existed in the state, much like elsewhere in Mexico. In San Luis Potosí, for example, thirty-four separate bands existed in September 1913.[17] Indeed, many could more properly be termed bandits. Nevertheless, in Puebla two deserve mention. Because of their geographic location on the western and eastern boundaries of the state plus their loose connections with the Zapatistas and Serranos, they helped form a ring of armed opponents that encircled central Puebla.

The first group, based in the state of Tlaxcala, but with followers in the volcano region along the borders of both states, would later be labeled Arenistas, followers of brothers Domingo and Cirilo Arenas. Before mid-1914, however, the Arenas siblings had yet to assume positions of leadership. Nevertheless, like others in Puebla and beyond, they would form viable fighting units based on family and community ties. The group's agrarian concerns coincided largely with the Zapatistas. Its outlook, however, went beyond the confines of Zapatista agrarianism to include such issues as consumer prices, taxes, and wages and working conditions. These issues were reflective of its membership, which came in part from the varied socioeconomic milieu of the Tlaxcala-Puebla border region, including urban political refugees from Puebla City. Textile-mill hands, railroad and construction workers, and itinerant peddlers as well as campesinos and landless agricultural laborers made up the group. Domingo Arenas, for example, worked as a bread deliverer, herdsman, and factory laborer while the younger Cirilo was a carpenter. As such, the group, commanded by generals Pedro Morales, Felipe Villegas, and Máximo Rojas, not only operated in conjunction with the Zapatistas but also fought at times in the northern parts of the state in cooperation with the Serrano-Constitucionalista forces.[18]

The second group, located in the east along the border with Oaxaca and Veracruz, operated primarily in the districts of Chalchicomula, Tecamachalco, and Tehuacán. Like their Tlaxcalan counterparts, they also used a volcanic region as refuge, in this case the Pico de Orizaba, as well as the Mixteca Alta of Oaxaca. Agrarian issues concerned them, too, but here again other forces influenced the movement, which distinguished it from the Zapatistas and Serranos. One was a radical, mobile, industrial labor element from the Orizaba textile region just across the state boundary in Veracruz. The second was a system of "entrepreneurial" caciquismo, perhaps best exemplified by the Barbosa clan, sustained by the desire to protect its role as power broker between agricultural labor and the large grain-producing haciendas of the region, many owned by Spaniards, and its control of goods passing along the railroad lines connecting Puebla to Oaxaca and Veracruz. In the weeks following Madero's death, Francisco J. Barbosa, Donato Bravo Izquierdo, Juan Lechuga, Prisciliano Martínez, Manuel Oseguera, and Camerino Mendoza raised the flag of rebellion. Mendoza would soon be killed, thus promoting Lechuga to the group's unofficial leadership. During 1913–14, they forged ties with General Gilberto Camacho, whom Carranza had designated to organize the Serranos against Huerta.[19]

United States Occupation

The United States takeover of Mexico's most important port, Veracruz, began on April 21, 1914. Although the invaders did not come close to Puebla, their presence had an important impact on the guerrilla war in the state. In the short run, fighting diminished as rebels and their supporters gauged the Americans' actions and decided how to respond to Huerta's appeals for united action against them. Over the longer run, however, the incident weakened Huerta and accelerated insurgent gains, leading to the president's demise in mid-July.

Huerta immediately took advantage of the situation, playing on the nationalistic reaction and uncertainty about Washington's intentions. Some people envisioned a repeat of General Winfield Scott's 1847 march to Mexico City via Puebla; others were reminded of the French intervention, now patriotically symbolized by the battle at Puebla City in May 1862. As such, the president's offer of an amnesty and calls for a cooperative effort against the foreigners received a positive response.[20]

Most receptive were urban elements, in Puebla City and provincial towns, although intimidation and social pressure may have boosted the level of enthusiasm for the regime's appeals. Men volunteered for special defense units; women joined the Cruz Roja (Red Cross); military training was stepped up in schools and among public employees and workers; anti-American nationalistic demonstrations thrived; priests offered patriotic messages from the pulpit; and the legislature and town councils made official pronouncements in support of the government.[21]

Rebels operating in the state disliked Huerta's plan. After all, by the spring of 1914 they had made substantial gains, even holding the district seats of Chietla in the south and Tetela in the north. Dealing with the president risked undermining these advances, yet to appear to accept the invasion proved equally problematic. As Huerta's agents fanned out across the state, they had some initial success; Juan Lechuga, leader of the eastern insurgents, became their most notable convert.[22]

In the south, the Zapatistas first equivocated, looking for a way around the dilemma. Meanwhile, Huerta's envoys persuaded several lesser officers to defect, but their principal target, Francisco Mendoza, wavered. Then, when Zapatista headquarters in Morelos declared its intention to fight the Americans independently if they continued to march inland, Mendoza fell into line. He subsequently erased any doubts about his loyalty by capturing ex-Zapatista Jesús "Tuerto" Morales, who had traveled to the rebel's camp on Huerta's behalf; Zapata then ordered Morales executed. He was tied to a tree and shot in the back for treason.[23]

In the north, the Serranos rejected Huertista appeals and took a stance similar to the Zapatistas, claiming they would fight on their own; to underline their seriousness they declared a temporary, unilateral cease-fire with the government. They then called, in the names of martyred Chiapas senator Belisario Domínguez, whom Huerta had killed, and Aquiles Serdán, for Mexicans to join them and their Carrancista allies. To gain wider support, they also claimed that the Carrancistas would put into effect the 1878 proagrarian Ley del Pueblo, which Serdán's father had coauthored.[24]

Within a month, then, most of the support that had rubbed off on Huerta thanks to the invasion had largely dissipated. As it became increasingly clear that the foreigners were content to stay on the coast, the oppositions' attention again turned to toppling the regime. Even defectors like Juan Lechuga began to reassess their position. Now Huerta found himself in a weaker position than before the incursion. Everyone took their cue from the realization that the government was too weak to oust the Americans, and the loss of the port of Veracruz only added to its financial and military woes. Furthermore, the president had been forced to withdraw soldiers from key positions in the state in order to defend against a United States march inland. The rebels used the respite in the fighting and the redeployment to regroup, thus seriously crippling any chance for a Huertista victory. The setback was especially devastating in the Sierra, which comprised the lynchpin of Huerta's strategy to control central Mexico. General Joaquín Jiménez Castro had been sent to the region earlier in the year to revive the Pacto de la Sierra; by April he had nearly brought the rebel offensive to a halt and was once again talking peace with Juan Francisco Lucas, but the North American invasion ended the initiative. As a result, Indian rebels entered northern towns, executing wealthy mestizos and dynamiting their homes.[25]

Finally, Huertista supporters lost their enthusiasm once they witnessed his cynical and arbitrary manipulation of the invasion. Army volunteers, many of them urbanites, recruited on the promise of defending the nation against Americans, were instead sent to fight Mexican revolutionaries in the north of the country. Landowners and businessmen resented the confiscation and concentration in Puebla City of livestock, grain, fuel, and other strategic goods as well as restrictions on the sale of war-related material. Merchants were ordered to give employees time off to participate in military instruction or risk being branded traitors. The cash-strapped government drew upon the emotionalism of the moment to urge governors to set up a system by which the public could donate money to the regime. Furthermore, Huerta used the invasion as a smoke screen to intimidate his opposition and to ferret out and repress anyone who dared criticize his government. The manufactured response to the "gringo" invasion and rapid loss of enthusiasm in pursuing the foreigners also has been noted, for example, by García Ugarte, Ankerson, and Wells and Joseph for Querétaro, San Luis Potosí, and Yucatán, respectively.[26]

The Collapse, May–August 1914

Huerta could not turn the United States occupation into his advantage. Within a few weeks following the invasion, full-scale warfare had resumed in Puebla, and the president and Governor Hernández were in an increasingly desperate situation. Everyone detected the scent of a dying government, including heretofore fence-sitters, who now joined the effort to topple it. To encourage the undecided, anonymous handbills circulated in urban areas threatening those who failed to support Carranza.[27]

This bandwagon effect, however, only exacerbated the insurgents' main problem, the lack of coordination and agreement on strategy and policy beyond the mere toppling of Huerta. Indeed, as the end approached, rebels spent nearly as much time and energy manipulating to gain advantage over each other as they did fighting the regime; some even made deals with the enemy in order to trump their insurgent rivals. Save for the Zapatistas, most rebel groups ironically looked to the relatively weak and isolated junta Revolucionaria in the state capital to mitigate this problem. In doing so, they diminished their own dominant position and boosted urban power brokers' influence over the outcome of the war, a situation reminiscent of the Madero period.

These divisions within rebel ranks benefited Huerta's defense and prolonged the conflict. Furthermore, in some places progovernment forces, especially volunteers in the state's population centers, put up a stiff fight. They proved willing to resist to the bitter end against what they saw as outsiders and lower-class rabble in order to protect not just their physical lives and property but their way of life. Furthermore, this resistance set up the possibility of negotiations between attackers and defenders; where consummated it left in place political and socioeconomic structures reflective of local practice and preference, but ones often antithetical to the longer term interests of the revolutionaries.

Following the United States invasion the Zapatistas intensified their efforts, consolidating control of rural areas, thus placing greater pressure on major towns. They targeted key commercial, industrial, and administrative centers, such as Izúcar de Matamoros and Atlixco, located on the Interoceánico Railroad.[28] The southerners alone could not topple the Huertistas, yet they were reluctant to cooperate with other groups except on their own terms. Zapata rebuffed initiatives emanating from the junta Revolucionaria as well as from Carrancista commanders in Puebla's north. He was especially wary of agents claiming to represent various anti-Huerta groups, ordering that they be seized and sent to headquarters, where he determined their fate.[29]

Zapata also demanded that rebels throughout the region recognize the Plan de Ayala, promising to overthrow Huerta and fight until the plan became part of the Constitution. As such, the Tlaxcala-based western insurgents under General Felipe Villegas and Colonel Domingo Arenas, who had been cooperating with the Zapatistas since at least November 1913, now formally pledged their support. They coordinated their operations with the Southerners via Zapatista Colonel Rafael Espinosa. Together they laid siege to towns as close to the capital as Huejotzingo. Nevertheless, the westerners kept their options open by also recognizing the junta Revolucionaria, a fact that Zapata apparently was willing to overlook given the desire to oust Huerta.[30]

The eastern insurgents along the Veracruz-Oaxaca border, headed again by Juan Lechuga, also targeted towns along the Mexicano del Sur (Mexican Southern) railroad line, from Tehuacán to Amozoc, heading toward Puebla City. They, too, kept their options open by playing both sides of the rebel divide, maintaining ties to the Carrancistas in the Sierra via General Gilberto Camacho. Meanwhile they undertook operations with Zapatista commanders such as Francisco Mendoza, attacking Tepexi, for example, which was located in an area where the two groups overlapped. Given the decentralized nature of his movement, however, Zapata could not have sanctioned every action taken with other groups; his local commanders often made arrangements at their own convenience.[31]

Zapatista coordination with the western and eastern rebels contributed to Huerta's downfall by pinning down federal forces and placing pressure on Puebla City, which they virtually surrounded, a situation much like the anti-Díaz, Maderista insurgency of 1911. Yet none of these three groups managed to capture and hold any major town in the state until August, once the regime had disintegrated. As a result, even as these rebel forces made gains in rural Puebla, they constantly had to look over their shoulders to ensure that pockets of Huertista troops and their supporters, located in urban bulwarks, were not counterattacking from behind. Especially for the Zapatistas, larger towns were alien and targets to raid and seek retribution in, not to occupy and curry the support of the local citizenry. In Tepexi, for example, which the Zapatistas briefly overran in late July, their goal seemed merely to sack stores, particularly those owned by militia leaders. In addition, many townspeople, volunteers backed by government forces, fiercely defended their communities. In Atlixco local officials convinced the federal commander, probably without difficulty, to keep his troops in town rather than send them into the countryside after rebels. In some cases, such as in Tehuacán, foreign residents, mainly Spaniards, who provided personnel as well as arms and money, bolstered these grassroots defense forces.[32] Consequently, the Zapatistas and their allies played an important role in the collapse of the Huerta regime in Puebla, arriving at the doorstep of the state capital, but in the end unable to enter it. Instead, the Carrancistas with their Serrano supporters, arriving from the north of the state, would be the first to pass through the threshold and occupy Puebla City.

The Serranos-Constitucionalistas in the north also made steady gains against Huerta beginning in June 1914. Moreover, with a surer supply of arms and ammunition from Gulf Coast ports and a leadership realizing the value of holding larger towns, they successfully took several on their way to the state capital. With the surrender of Teziutlán in late July and the capture of Huauchinango and San Juan de los Llanos in early August, the path was cleared.[33]

This success of the Serrano-Constitucionalista alliance, however, only momentarily obscured a serious division within it. The Carrancista relationship with locals always had been an uneasy one. As outsiders they had little interest in the region's autonomy, paying lip service to it as a means to get Serrano support for their main goal, militarily dominating the region, thereby creating a second front against Huerta and then using this base to capture Puebla City and political power. The Serranos understood Carrancista motives and were concerned, for example, by the replacement of locally named, civilian *jefes políticos* with military officers from the north of Mexico. The Serranos also tried to confine their troops to the Sierra, and once Huerta fell in mid-July, saw little need to contribute more than token numbers of men to the Carrancista-led drive on Puebla City.[34]

Nevertheless, Carranza needed Serrano backing in order to carry out his objectives in the state. What he promised the region's principal leaders, Juan Francisco Lucas and Esteban Márquez, to get their support is not fully clear. It must have included vague promises of regional autonomy and for Márquez, a general's commission in the Constitucionalista army with command in the Sierra plus backing for his political aspirations; Márquez had his eye on the governorship.

Márquez, however, had company. Antonio Medina, an ambitious Carrancista general from Tamaulipas, also aspired to political office. Upon occupying Teziutlán, for example, Medina named it the state capital and promulgated decrees dealing with such issues as taxes and schools. Rather than challenge Márquez directly, a difficult task for an outsider, Medina astutely ingratiated himself with Lucas, taking advantage of the partiarch's desire to gain support against Márquez, whom he increasingly saw as untrustworthy and not meriting leadership of the region.[35]

By summer 1914 friction between Márquez and Medina had become so great that it jeopardized the Carrancista push toward Puebla City. The First Chief authorized Ramón Cabrera, native of the Sierra town of Zacatlán and brother of Carranza's principal aide, Luis Cabrera, to deal with the problem. Márquez and Medina were made military coequals, but Cabrera was to control federal purse strings, establish public services, and create federal offices in the region. In other words, just as Lucas feared, turmoil in the Sierra had allowed Carranza to begin to establish a greater federal presence there.[36]

As the Carrancistas advanced on Puebla City, they entered negotiations with Governor Muñoz Ovando and the Huertista commander General Gonzalo Luque, using the junta Revolucionaria as intermediary. In the capital a majority of the populace and especially the business and professional sectors backed the junta's efforts. The city's denizens, as in other towns in which the junta helped negotiate surrenders, feared the consequences of either a full-fledged battle for the capital or, if federal authority suddenly collapsed, a power vacuum that would allow the feared Zapatistas and their allies to take control. Daniel Guzmán traveled on behalf of the junta to General Medina's headquarters in Teziutlán to arrange a deal. Muñoz Ovando and Luque would hand the city over as long as Medina guaranteed law and order and allowed federal officers to retain their ranks. The politically ambitious Medina agreed despite the fact that such an arrangement with enemy officers contradicted Carranza's orders.[37]

As such, on August 19, General Luque surrendered his nearly nine thousand troops, two thousand of whom were based in Puebla City. The mustering out process was marred two days later, however, when several of Luque's officers rebelled, apparently upon receiving word from Carranza's headquarters that their ranks would not be recognized. They were backed by troops unhappy at being dismissed from the army and paid a mere ten pesos for their service to the nation. Led by General Aureliano Blanquet and his 400-man, Twenty-ninth Battalion, the federals occupied the center of the city as well as the bullring and the Mexicano Railroad station before being subdued. Other scattered incidents took place around Puebla with armed Spaniards joining federal soldiers. Dissidents, joined by mill hands, sacked factories. Others sent an explosives-filled locomotive toward Tlaxcala to kill a group of high-level Carrancista emissaries on their way to Puebla to take formal control of the city. In the wake of the revolt, federal generals Juan Andreu Almazán, Higinio Aguilar, and Benjamín Argumedo fled the state capital to continue their fight against the Carrancistas.[38]

During the revolt, federal soldiers captured Carrancista agent Ramón Cabrera and his younger brother Rafael in Panzacola, Tlaxcala, a short distance from Puebla City. The Cabreras had been on their way to Puebla to relieve General Blanquet of command. Blanquet, apparently aware of their pending arrival, had them executed. Their deaths would have great impact on the future of the state as two other Cabrera siblings would subsequently hold a grudge against the military and especially Huertistas: Luis, Carranza's personal aide and future secretary of the treasury, and Alfonso, who would serve as governor later in the decade (see Chapter 7). In revenge some sixty federal officers and soldiers were shot for their part in the Cabreras' deaths.[39]

Once relative calm was restored, Puebla City was formally delivered to the Carrancistas on August 23, 1914. Muñoz Ovando and Luque handed the state capital first to a delegation of prominent citizens who then turned it over to a second group, consisting of, among others, generals Jesús Carranza, Pablo González, and Francisco Coss.[40]

The Defense

Repression

In dealing with its unarmed, mainly urban opponents, the Huerta regime was tough, and at times even murderous, but it chose its victims on a selective basis; there was no uniform, across-the-board crackdown, at least not until late spring 1914. Indeed, save for the most visible Maderistas, Huertista officials generally were willing to work with members of the former government, overlooking their ties to it, as long as they did not actively oppose the

new regime. High-level Huertista officials even checked the excesses of venge-
ful anti-Maderistas. This level of forbearance would not be found among
the Carrancistas who, after gaining power in 1914, used allegations of even
the most tenuous ties to Huerta as a litmus test of legitimacy; those who
failed were ordered into political obscurity or worse.

The Huerta regime's use of selective and arbitrary repression, including
infiltrators and spies, worked quite well. Although always present to one
degree or another, repression peaked during four periods, reminding people
how bad conditions could be. The first took place in the spring of 1913,
soon after Huerta's takeover of power, when Maderista stalwarts Camerino
Mendoza and Rafael Tapia were hunted down and killed and others, such as
Alfonso Alarcón, jailed.[41]

The second occurred when Maass assumed office in June 1913. He
came to power under pressure to do something about the Maderista threat.
Zapatista-turned-Maderista General Francisco A. Gracia was incarcerated
along with former Puebla City police chief Carlos Ledesma, several *jefes
políticos*, town councilmen, hacienda administrators, and more. Others, such
as the Narváez sisters and Serdán's widow, had their homes searched. In
August the Puebla City jail requested monies to feed twice as many prisoners as it originally budgeted. Maass intimidated the opposition, but he also
received a warning from Mexico City not to incarcerate innocent people,
particularly socially prominent ones, who might have been falsely accused
by personal enemies. If he did so, they cautioned, the regime would lose
prestige.[42]

A third period of more intense repression occurred during and immediately after the October elections. At that time, agents seemed to have singled
out federal and state deputies as well as *jefes políticos* who questioned the
results, accusing them of conspiracy. In one town, voters who cast ballots
for Carranza and Zapata ended up in jail.[43]

Finally, following the United States invasion in April 1914, the government again lashed out, jailing over forty prominent Puebla City residents,
many of them for signing and distributing a circular blaming Huerta for the
incursion. They included lawyer Felipe T. Contreras, journalist and future
governor Luis Sánchez Pontón, Jesús Alfaro, and even former governor
Carrasco. As exemplary punishment, several were inducted into the army
and sent to Veracruz under the command of Gustavo Maass, the former
governor's brother, to face the North Americans.

Instead of bolstering the regime, this move emboldened its opponents.
Many of those arrested had tolerated if not cooperated with the government; Contreras, for example, who had lost his gubernatorial bid to Carrasco,

had backed Maass's takeover of the state government; Sánchez Pontón served as editor of the state's official newspaper; and Alfaro directed the state hospital. Most grievous was the arrest of Carrasco, whose age and infirmities clearly precluded him as a credible threat. His treatment evoked public outrage and prompted the entire city council and the three *cámaras* to protest to the federal government; Mexico City ordered his release but not before much damage was done.[44]

Militarization and Recruitment

To deal with the opposition, Huerta and his governors complemented repression with a program of physical and psychological mobilization of the populace, a policy that amounted to the militarization of society. This effort stressed patriotism and armed preparedness against "anti-Mexican" elements. The government aimed to distinguish itself from and denigrate its enemies in the eyes of the citizenry while creating a last-resort defense force in urban areas. An indoctrinated people would provide an environment in which dissidents would find it difficult to recruit and operate.

Already mentioned above was the attempt on the part of governors Maass and Hernández to link their administrations and the war effort to national civic holidays. These celebrations aimed to raise morale among public employees and students in order to emphasize discipline, motivation, citizenship, and confidence through service to the nation. Such events also offered the opportunity to take counts of military-age men in preparation for future manpower needs.[45]

What started out as an occasional, socially attractive practice session, something to break the monotony of everyday life, soon became more serious. From haphazard marching with a decrepit drum and bugle, equipment progressed to include wooden rifles, uniforms, and shoes. More frequent and obligatory training took place under bona fide military personnel. With the formal militarization of the entire public sector on April 1, 1914, officers took control of the workplace, prison, and classroom. Males became part of the army, and females served as nurses in a Cruz Roja chapter set up by the governor's wife.[46]

Over time, enthusiasm for this project waned, only to return briefly upon the United States intervention. Parents transferred their children to parochial institutions where academics took greater priority; college professors, now captains in the army, complained about the lack of time to undertake training given the need to fight for economic survival; no one liked the modification of the daily schedule, eliminating the mid-day siesta in order to fit in exercises. Students who objected were thrown out of the university. Government workers and especially prisoners had little choice but to accept the program.[47]

Nothing made clearer the growing presence of the military in daily life than the regime's effort to augment manpower. Recruitment took a number of forms. To complement its forces, the government looked to town fathers and business leaders to create volunteer squads. Chambers of commerce and agriculture often took a leading role. Officials calculated that these volunteers, generally made up of the local bourgeoisie, would tenaciously defend their towns against rural "hordes." Many did perform admirably; Atlixco, Tehuacán, and Zacatlán, places with larger business communities and more to protect, proved especially successful.[48]

In rural areas, where isolated haciendas and mills faced a more immediate threat, the regime took a different tack. It required landowners to provide ten armed and mounted fighters who were to join other such units to form contingents totaling at least fifty. The government provided arms and ammunition. Factories, too, were encouraged to raise troops among workers. These irregular forces were to operate as auxiliaries to and under the command of rural forces posted in nearby towns. Huerta also armed haciendas in Querétaro, for example, a practice that dated back at least to Díaz's defense against Madero.[49]

Foreigners, particularly Spaniards, faced a particular dilemma. Most outsiders attempted to remain neutral, a policy generally advocated by home governments and accepted by Huerta, who wished to avoid international complications. Nevertheless, noncommitment played poorly in towns like Tehuacán, where local citizens expected the influential Iberian community to help in its defense, and the Spaniards themselves wanted to protect their substantial interests. As such, some expatriates did play a direct role in the warfare of 1913–14, generally on the side of the regime, a decision for which they would pay once the revolutionaries came to power.[50]

Ideally the regime would have liked only volunteers to fill its manpower needs. This situation, however, was not possible, and as a result it resorted to more coercive and manipulative methods. Soldiers who committed minor crimes were released from jail to resume fighting. Civilian prisoners gained amnesty if they agreed to join the army. Mostly, however, Huerta continued his predecessors' use of the hated *leva* or forced conscription. Along with the constant need for money, this practice became the most important factor in undermining support among the general populace for the regime. *Jefes políticos* and specially designated agents were issued quotas.

They swept towns clear of military-age males, regardless of occupation and civil status. Recruiters accused night-shift workers leaving textile mills of vagrancy and herded them into uniform. Hacienda hands fled to the hills to avoid conscription. Puebla City was forced to issue special exemptions to its freight haulers (*carreteros*) who were deemed essential to the local economy.[51]

Perhaps nowhere did the practice have a more profound impact than in the Sierra, where the *leva* crystallized autonomous sentiment leading to rebellion. In Chignahuapan, for example, as many as one hundred men at a time were shipped out to fight in far-off places such as Querétaro and Zacatecas. The community lived in fear, and the streets were deserted by 6:00 P.M. Locals referred to the *leva* as the *cuerda* or hanging rope and the federal army as the *bandera negra* (black flag), connoting death and destruction.[52]

Security Forces

Despite their many problems, the Huertista security forces in Puebla performed credibly during 1913–14. Their strategy, one imposed in part by default, of defending the principal town and transportation routes also occurred in other parts of the country, as Ankerson has noted for San Luis Potosí. Such displacement of forces in Puebla allowed the army's few heavy guns to be effectively employed and was designed as a holding pattern while the bulk of government forces battled the main threat, the Carrancistas in the north of the country. With a maximum of some seven thousand regular federal and state troops (including rurales), two thousand to three thousand of whom were based in Puebla City, Maass and Hernández had to depend heavily on irregulars and volunteers.[53] Despite its weaknesses, this heterogeneous force held out in most places until after Huerta fled to Europe in mid-July 1914; it was least successful in the Sierra where the Serrano-Carrancista coalition had outside access to arms.

Fielding and maintaining a viable fighting force was complex and difficult. Puebla's defenders were very fragmented: regular federal and state army; federal and state rural forces; irregulars consisting of contingents armed and sometimes financed by the government that were recruited by haciendas, mills, and towns (militias); police; volunteers; and private security units. This structure allowed for much confusion and conflict. Querétaro suffered from the same problem.[54]

Financing an army posed a constant challenge. The federal government, short of funds as it had been in 1911, ordered the state to raise and pay its own contingents. The state in turn pleaded poverty and attempted to shift the burden back to the national treasury. Reluctant to raise taxes, both levels of government looked to the business and agricultural sectors and others who benefited from enhanced security to contribute monies and material. This volunteerism quickly proved inadequate, however, and *jefes políticos* received authority to confiscate strategic items such as horses and rifles. Unpaid and underequipped troops coerced moneyed elements into handing over funds or other material goods, either by using force or threatening to withdraw, leaving the area vulnerable to rebel attack.[55]

In early 1914 the Cámaras reluctantly came to an agreement with Governor Hernández to implement and enforce a volunteer contribution system, which would be equitable and end the arbitrary, strong-arm tactics employed by the military. Many people refused to take part in the plan, however, and those who did insisted that security forces guard only their properties, not those of the nonparticipants. In addition, with state citizens paying directly for the maintenance of federal troops, Hernández now demanded greater authority over their disposition, a stance that conflicted with Mexico City. The resolution of the problem was the implementation of a 50 percent state tax surcharge, which placed the financial burden of security on the entire populace. Nevertheless, given the confusion of spring and summer 1914, this measure was never fully implemented.[56]

Without a clear chain of command, sufficient funds, and adequate preparation time, many troops entered battle poorly trained and equipped. Furthermore, large numbers had been forcibly recruited into the ranks. Some rebelled, such as those headed by longtime Porfirian General Gaudencio González de la Llave. Another troublesome unit, Zapotec Indians from Juchitán, Oaxaca, unpaid and drunk, calmed down only after being assured in their own language that they would receive their salaries. They were soon disarmed and shipped to Mexico City much to the relief of Puebla City's residents. Still other soldiers deserted.[57]

Nevertheless, given these conditions, one must ask why there was not more visible discontent in the ranks and a poorer record of fighting. The answer seems to have two parts. Local irregulars and volunteers, when left to defend their own towns and immediate surroundings did so with tenacity. Regular federal and state troops, too, if allowed to remain in a defensive position in towns, rather than undertake dangerous forays into rebel-controlled rural areas, remained relatively content. In town they imbibed the antirebel outlook of the locals and shared the reality of insurgent besiegement. If they were to desert or even rebel, they had to take their chances with the unpredictable, unfamiliar enemy located in a little-known locale.[58]

The conflict during 1913–14 had great impact on Puebla. For the first time since the revolution began in 1910, the entire populace became caught up in warfare, suffering the consequences of militarization, repression, and violence, harbingers of even worse to come. Nevertheless, these conditions did not manifest themselves fully until spring 1914, not long before the collapse of the regime.

The Huertistas, despite their internal divisions, lack of resources, and limited support in the state, managed to carry on a credible military effort for many months. Two factors changed this situation and subsequently brought the regime to a quick end in summer 1914. The first was the United States incursion into Veracruz, which forced the withdrawal of government troops from key regions of the state, thus giving the rebellion a distinct advantage. The second was the shift in urbanites' attitude toward Huerta. Initially suppressing their autonomous instincts, most townspeople at least passively supported the regime, hoping for a return to stability following Madero and preferring the new government to living under radical, rural, even what was seen as "alien" (culturally speaking) rebels, who also held a much deeper and surer sense of autonomy. City dwellers began to change their view when authorities' increasingly militaristic and repressive policies went beyond tolerable, "middle-class" limits and awakened a long held, although not always visible, distrust of outsiders. This situation underlines the pivotal role of moderate urbanites in a regime's ability to survive a rural insurgency, one that had manifested itself in 1911 for Díaz and would again come to light in 1919–20 in the case of President Venustiano Carranza and Governor Alfonso Cabrera.

Thus, rural-based insurgents, clear only about the objective of overthrowing the government in order to preserve their autonomy and aided by defecting urban elements, defeated an overextended and weakened regime. Consequently, these grassroot revolutionaries let power slip through their fingers by failing to take control of the state capital and its governing apparatus. As a result, divisions among these local rebels, and in the case of the Serranos, a strategic but fateful alliance with the Constitucionalistas, helped place the latter in power in Puebla City. Poblanos would pay a price for this turn of events as these outsiders had only limited appreciation of and concern for the sentiments and welfare of the state's residents.

II

CONSTITUCIONALISTAS VERSUS CONVENCIONISTAS

4

WAR, 1914–1917

A t the national level the surrender of the Huerta regime in August 1914 marked the end of the first act of a long civil war. It now entered a new phase as the victorious anti-Huerta, Carrancista-led coalition disintegrated, and its actors turned on each other—Convencionistas (named after the Convention of Aguascalientes and headed by Francisco "Pancho" Villa and Emiliano Zapata) against Constitucionalistas (led by Venustiano Carranza, Pablo González, and Álvaro Obregón). Following a series of pitched battles in the Bajío region northwest of Mexico City in spring and summer 1915, the balance began to swing toward the latter. Still, it would take another year and a half of conflict before Carranza and his generals plausibly could claim victory.

Contrary to 1913 and the first half of 1914, the following three years in Puebla were dominated by war. Politics, detailed in the following chapter, took a back seat to the violent struggle between the Convencionistas and Constitucionalistas. These groups were composed of various changing factions, creating a fluid and complex situation, but one in which the Convencionistas represented the more exclusivist (least willing to compromise with outsiders) version of local autonomy. Fighting raged throughout the state, and for more than a year (until late 1915) it was not clear who would permanently control the key prize, the central region including the capital. Even when the Carrancistas, thanks to alliances made with regional caciques, achieved this goal, many areas remained contested as the idea of self-rule persisted.

Establishing Control

The Constitucionalista takeover of Puebla City in August 1914 proved to be an important symbolic victory but in the short term a dubiously practical one. Surrounded by hostile forces and internally fractionalized, the Constitucionalistas would spend many months fighting off their enemies while trying to forge a coalition in order to secure the state capital and its immediate environs. They never would manage to dominate the entire state.

The last days of August and September 1914 in central Puebla were chaotic and violent. The fact that the bulk of Huerta's defeated Federal army was located in the region only made the Carrancistas' job of asserting control more dangerous. Carrancista troops occupied strategic spots throughout the capital and surrounding towns to prevent a counterattack. Huertista soldiers were released or offered places in the Constitucionalistas' ranks. Officers were decommissioned, restricted to Puebla City, placed under armed surveillance, and, in some cases, in return for their loyalty, promised regular pay for themselves and their families; others, however, were executed.[1]

As Puebla's war-weary civilian residents cautiously eyed the newcomers from Mexico's north, those suspected of cooperating with the old regime were hunted down with the help of local vigilante organizations called the Junta Depuradora (Purifying Junta) and the Comité para la Salud Pública (Committee for Public Health). Spaniards found where attacks on Carrancista troops took place were disarmed and ordered to remain on their haciendas pending investigation. Factory workers accused of collaborating with the enemy faced summary judicial proceedings. The persecutions even reached individuals found outside the state: hacendado Alberto García Granados, who had served as Huerta's secretary of government (*gobernación*), was shot; former governor Mucio Martínez ended up behind bars. As a result, people fled the country to avoid capture and death. Former Puebla City mayor (*presidente municipal*), Francisco de Velasco, for example, went to Cuba for nearly three years. His family, which remained in Puebla, was interrogated and its properties confiscated. Velasco was declared an "*enemigo del pueblo*" (enemy of the people) and blacklisted; orders were given to shipping lines and immigration officials to prevent his return. Anyone who opposed or openly questioned the Carrancistas was branded a "reactionary," an opprobrium that would harm the lives of people for years. As García Ugarte has noted for Querétaro, where the Carrancistas acted similarly in order to thwart any potential for organized opposition, they "sowed terror among the middle and dominant classes."[2]

Nevertheless, the Carrancistas had difficulty in asserting authority. On August 23, the day they formally took over Puebla City, Federal officers Higinio Aguilar, Juan Andreu Almazán, and Benjamín Argumedo, joined by the Huertista garrison and aided by locals, wrested control of the state's second city, Tehuacán, from the inadequate Carrancista force there. After collecting more than 50,000 pesos, they moved on only to return in October to make a successful repeat performance.[3]

Even more foreboding was the fact that many ex-Federals began to find a new home among the Zapatistas, who aggressively resisted Carrancista incursions into their territory. Clashes between the two sides occurred daily, some of them as close to Puebla City as Huejotzingo, twenty-five kilometers distant. Both Pablo González, overall commander of Constitucionalista armies in the region, and the First Chief's brother, Jesús Carranza, expressed concerns about the security situation, citing the problem of insufficient and poorly organized troops.[4]

Meanwhile, to make matters worse, the Carrancista military leadership vied among itself to determine who would run the state. Carrancista officers from northern Mexico such as Francisco Coss, Cesáreo Castro, Antonio Medina, and Antonio Villaseñor greedily eyed the top positions. Those from Puebla and surrounding states, Domingo Arenas, Gilberto Camacho, Juan Lechuga, Esteban Márquez, Máximo Rojas, and others, already cognizant of their inferior status in the Carrancista movement because of their central Mexican origins, also demanded their due.[5]

Much of the skirmishing between Carrancistas and Zapatistas, as well as the jockeying within the Constitucionalista officer corps, was done with an eye toward an upcoming convention of revolutionary forces first called for by Carranza in July 1914. The objective of the meeting was to iron out the deep fissures within the anti-Huerta coalition. In preparation for the convention, officers in Puebla selected delegates subject to approval by Pablo González and Carranza. The First Chief tried to block the Zapatistas but failed. He also attempted to dilute the military's role at the meeting by allowing for civilian participation. This dispute foreshadowed a serious breach between soldier and citizen that would soon affect Puebla.[6] Finally, the convention got under way on October 10 in the north central city of Aguascalientes. This location marked an approximately midway point between Carranza's forces in the Mexico City-Puebla area and those of the First Chief's other main rival, Francisco "Pancho" Villa, in northern Mexico.

In the end, Carranza lost control of the meeting, and as a compromise he and Villa were forced to renounce their claims to the presidency. In their stead a new government, called the Convención, was created with Eulalio Gutiérrez, the military governor of San Luis Potosí, as its head. Subsequently, Villa and Zapata sought common cause against Carranza. The anti-Huerta coalition had splintered and realigned; Mexico was about to enter another round of bloody internecine conflict, Convencionistas against Constitucionalistas.

Aguascalientes forced revolutionaries of all stripes in Puebla to reassess their positions and choose sides. Calculations of enhancing local autonomy and individual gain, tempered in some cases by personal loyalty, became paramount. Some people tried to postpone making a decision or play both sides. The Constitucionalistas, given their relatively weak military position in the state, their role as outsiders, and their lack of an explicit program aimed specifically at the region's majority rural and working-class population, were the most affected. The Convencionistas (Zapatistas and related groups) avoided most of these problems and generally managed, at least for the time being, to hang on to their original followers.

Following the Convention, Puebla and its surrounding region became especially crucial for Carranza. Villa and Zapata took control of Mexico City, thus forcing Carranza to establish his government in the port of Veracruz, from which he planned to recover the country. Therefore, without dominating at least Puebla's principal towns and the railway lines that passed through it and neighboring Tlaxcala, Carranza would be extremely vulnerable and his counteroffensive plan nearly impossible to carry out.

Even so, Carranza managed to retain the loyalty of General Francisco Coss, Puebla's recently named military commander and governor, generally recognized as the principal Carrancista there. Coss's decision proved crucial in helping to consolidate the Constitucionalista presence in Puebla as a number of other important officers in the state followed his lead.[7] Furthermore, Coss's stance gave him leverage with Carranza, leverage he would attempt to use in coming months as the First Chief's officers competed among themselves for power.

Nevertheless, Coss's example did not prove influential enough to prevent defections to the Convencionistas, particularly by officers from Puebla. In the Sierra, Esteban Márquez, shut out of the governorship and relegated to a command in southern Puebla, far from home and his power base, opted to join the Convencionistas.[8] In the western volcano region, Domingo Arenas likewise felt slighted, having been named a mere colonel in the revolutionary army while Carrancista officers and their Yaqui Indian soldiers from the north asserted control over his area. More specifically, Arenas disliked the naming of rival General Máximo Rojas as governor and military commander in neighboring Tlaxcala, where Arenas's troops also operated. What should have been an army of liberation seemed more and more like one of occupation, he claimed, a sentiment also expressed by autonomous-minded Poblano military and civilian alike. Furthermore, the Convencionista agrarian program more readily fit Arenas's own ideals than did that of the more conservative Constitucionalistas.[9] Gilberto Camacho, one of the first

Poblanos to back the Carrancistas in spring 1913, resented Coss being named governor and military commander. When Coss got wind of Camacho's possible defection, he sent troops against Camacho's brother Roberto, at Texmelucan in November 1914, resulting in some three hundred deaths. Subsequently, Camacho, too, joined the enemy.[10]

The Contenders—Convencionistas

The newly formed Convención government was composed at the national level of a coalition between Emiliano Zapata and Francisco "Pancho" Villa. The mainly northern Mexico–based Villistas played little direct role in Puebla. The Zapatistas, however, continued, as they had since 1911, to be an important faction in the state and now became the principal opponent of the Constitucionalistas. The Zapatistas were not alone but shared action, oftentimes uneasily, with three other significant movements: the Arenistas (followers of Domingo Arenas) in the volcano region of west-central Puebla, the Marquistas (followers of Esteban Márquez) in the northern Sierra, and ex-Federal officers and their troops headed by Higinio Aguilar and Juan Andreu Almazán on the state's eastern border.

These four movements represented only the largest, most clearly identifiable and, save for the ex-Federals, those with clearest ties to the Convencionista government. A myriad of other, generally smaller and more fluid groups also permeated the state. They gathered around leaders who acted both independently and collaboratively with the major movements.

Zapatistas

Nominal allies during the Huerta period, the Zapatistas and Carrancistas had been at odds, if not openly declared enemies since the summer of 1914. The southern campesinos resented the Carrancista capture of the state capital, a prize they wanted for themselves. Yet instead of seeking reconciliation, the Zapatistas held the Carrancistas at arm's length, demanded they recognize the Plan de Ayala, and attempted to recruit their officers. Moreover, Zapatista cooperation with ex-Federals only deepened Constitucionalista distrust. When Carrancista troops fanned outward from the state capital in fall 1914, serious clashes erupted, particularly at Atlixco and Matamoros, cities astride the Interoceánico railway. Only a truce brokered between the two sides by those attending the Convention at Aguascalientes prevented full-scale warfare. Puebla's military commander (and governor), General Coss, reluctantly ordered a suspension of hostilities against the Southerners, save for ex-Federals. Even this limited cease-fire, however, provoked celebratory parties and bell ringing among Puebla City's already less than revolutionary populace.[11]

The protagonists resumed unrestrained action once the Convencionistas declared Carranza in rebellion on November 10. Outmanned, underarmed, and thinly stretched from Aguascalientes to Veracruz, the Constitucionalistas fought desperately but vainly to retain control of Puebla City during November and early December 1914. With the help of ex-Federal generals Aguilar, Almazán, and Argumedo, the Zapatistas defeated the enemy in several hard-fought battles in central Puebla. In the end, by way of a two-pronged advance on the capital city from the north and south, they surrounded and cut it off. Running short of ammunition, facing a larger enemy with artillery, and dealing with a near-starving, sullen, populace, Coss opted to evacuate the plaza. Meanwhile, several hundred people on both sides died in the culminating 4-day battle.[12]

On December 16 the swarthy, white-clad Southerners, led by ex-Federal officers, took control of the state capital. Having just occupied Mexico City along with Villista (followers of Pancho Villa) forces, the Zapatistas now wielded significant real as well as symbolic power throughout central Mexico. The Convencionistas had the Constitucionalistas on the run; indeed, it seemed that rural, traditional, inward looking, lower-class Mexico was about to defeat its urban, modern, outward-looking, upper-class nemesis.

To the surprise of many residents, especially the upper classes, conservatives, and Catholics, the brief Convencionista stay in their city proved to be a break from Carrancista repression, not unlike what happened in Mexico City, Querétaro, and Toluca. Churches reopened; political prisoners, including clerics and former governor Mucio Martínez, were released; merchants readily provided loans to the new arrivals; and local and state government reconvened with the help of Huerta-era officials. However fleetingly a semblance of normalcy reappeared, even to the degree that authorities returned cars stolen by the Constitucionalistas to their rightful owners. Although Zapatista willingness to work with members of the old regime for tactical reasons may have pleased many locals, it gave the Carrancistas a powerful propaganda tool to use against the Southerners.[13]

At this critical juncture the Zapatistas made yet another mistake. They failed to carry out an agreement with Villa to pursue the Constitucionalistas to their redoubt in Veracruz. Several factors help to explain this crucial misstep. As many historians have pointed out, it appears that the Zapatistas did not want to project power such a long distance from their home base of Morelos and southern Puebla. The reason had much to do with the psychological makeup of these so-called provincial country people. After all, what good was a march on far off and little known Veracruz when one's principal objective had already been gained—control over and therefore the ability to work one's own land, the first steps toward the re-creation of an idealized, self-governing, lost agrarian society? The deep-seated sentiment of local autonomy carried much weight.[14]

There were, however, several more concrete reasons that reinforced this inward-looking conservatism and disregard for the relationship between local conditions and broader geo-strategic and political issues. A growing fissure in the Convencionista movement contributed to a lack of arms and especially ammunition, which Zapata had expected to receive from Villa. Also, Zapata and his officer corps soon backed away from their tactical decision to cooperate with ex-Federal officers; the latters' openly conservative, pro-upper-class actions, such as letting Huertista officials out of jail, unsettled the Zapatistas. The Zapatista leadership feared even more the loss of control over their movement to these former adversaries, interlopers whom some people saw as little more than opportunistic mercenaries with no genuine belief in the Plan de Ayala. Finally, the occupation of Puebla City undercut the Zapatistas' ability to carry out operations. Like their recently departed Constitucionalista opponents, the Zapatistas found that control of urban areas, although symbolically important, was often of limited strategic use; indeed, defending and feeding urban centers while dealing with their often hostile populations only impeded armies' abilities to engage the enemy. Much more important were the control of railroad junctions, ports, topographical choke points, and other advantageous positions.[15]

The Zapatista failure to chase and deal a killing blow to the Constitucionalistas allowed the latter to regroup and counterattack along the railroad, from Apizaco, Tlaxcala, to the north and Tehuacán to the east. Following several sharp battles, Coss approached Puebla City early in January 1915 with upwards of thirty thousand troops, double the number he had the previous month, including a contingent of Yaqui Indians from Sonora. To ensure capture of the city by fielding this number of men, the Constitucionalistas took a risk by drawing down manpower in other areas of the region.[16]

Like the Constitucionalistas in mid-December, the Zapatistas also found themselves in a weak position as defenders of Puebla City. Being outmanned, lacking ammunition, and having to provide for the large urban populace exacerbated the factionalism within the Southerners' ranks. Zapata, angry at the lack of support from Villa and distrustful of the ex-Federals who controlled the city in his name, did little to aid the state capital. Furthermore, the ex-Federals came into conflict with old line Zapatistas; Almazán, for example, left the city to its own devices to pursue greater glory, and booty, on the battlefield. As a result, Puebla's fate fell to local Zapatistas and their allies, Fortino Ayaquica, Domingo Arenas, Rafael Espinosa, and Antonio Barona. The Zapatistas put up a nominal resistance before completely withdrawing on January 5, 1915, heading toward the more hospitable mountains to the south and west. They had held the state capital, the only time they would do so during the entire revolution, for a mere twenty days.[17]

Despite their defeat the Zapatistas continued to surround and exert pressure on Puebla City. Indeed, the administrative problems they had faced while occupying the city now became Carrancista concerns. In turn the Zapatistas used the capital as a hostage to obtain arms from the enemy in exchange for allowing food and other goods to enter the metropolis.[18]

Over the longer run the Zapatistas' lack of ammunition, food, and fuel and their difficulty in coordinating their disparate and fractious elements undermined their strength. General Carlos Ledesma, for example, reported that his forces were unorganized and scattered, and that local officers refused to acknowledge higher authority. General Fortino Ayaquica said many of his men had deserted to Convencionista contingents in the state of Morelos because the fighting there was lighter and supplies more plentiful. His requests to President Roque González Garza, who had replaced Eulalio Gutiérrez, for additional material and money were only partially satisfied, further underlining suspicion among Puebla-based Zapatista commanders that Morelos was given priority. Given these problems, by March the Carrancistas had pushed the Zapatistas back from the capital and begun to take the fight to the Southerners in their traditional redoubts in the districts of Acatlán, Chiautla, Matamoros, and Tepexi.[19]

Almost as quickly, however, the tide reversed between April and July. The Carrancistas withdrew forces from Puebla to help protect the railroad lines between Veracruz and the Bajío region of north-central Mexico in order to fight what would turn out to be the defining battles of the revolution against Pancho Villa. Furthermore, Constitucionalista generals in the state bitterly debated among themselves over who should contribute to the fight in the north and therefore forego the economic and political perquisites that each greedily sought to gain by remaining and entrenching himself and his troops in the state. As a result, the Zapatistas recovered much of the ground that they had lost earlier in the year and threatened the capital, nearly forcing its evacuation.[20]

After mid-1915, however, the Constucionalistas once again took the offensive. They were strengthened by Obregón's victory over Villa and then by the United States' recognition of the Carrancista government in October. The first event freed up manpower for deployment to other areas such as Puebla. Both developments persuaded adversaries, such as Acatlán cacique Ricardo Reyes Márquez and General Mariano Cuervo, to switch sides because they believed that the Carrancistas would eventually win.[21]

The Constitucionalistas again pushed the Zapatistas back into the mountainous fringes of the south and west but could not deal a killing blow. The Southerners' advantage of operating in familiar territory among a supportive populace proved insuperable. Furthermore, the Zapatistas developed an effective intelligence network, employing merchants, priests, and local officials who penetrated Puebla City and kept tabs on Constitucionalista activities.[22]

From their redoubts the Zapatistas launched attacks against their adversaries, but materiel and logistical problems, plus internal dissension, continued and precluded any sustained action. Arms and ammunition were so scarce that the Zapatistas used women to buy cartridges from Carrancista soldiers and offered their own troops bonuses for each rifle and one hundred rounds captured from the enemy. Officers even raided each other's storehouses for goods. Increasingly, Puebla-based leaders quarreled among themselves while looking over their shoulders at the vindictive Zapata, based in his Morelos headquarters.[23]

Nevertheless, on occasion the Zapatistas posed a serious threat, such as in May 1916 when they briefly entered the very center of Puebla City. They focused, however, on harassing and raiding soft targets such as small villages, haciendas, mills, electrical generating stations, trains, and telegraph and telephone lines. Material losses and the psychological strain of insecurity, disruptions, and shortages took an especially severe toll on rural Puebla.[24]

Suffering, however, came not only from warfare. The Zapatistas had "taxed" landholders and business people and raided their properties for years. As the war intensified, more innocent and humble people became targets, including campesinos in the Zapatistas' core area of southwestern Puebla. The archival record is full of villagers' complaints, ranging from shakedowns and theft to kidnappings (particularly of young women), murder, and rape. Not unlike their Constitucionalista counterparts, Zapatista commanders from outside the region and ignorant of an area, empathized little with the local populace, even imposing unwanted local officials. Abuse most commonly arose from the need for supplies. The fine lines, however, between asking for goods, then demanding them using force, and finally taking other liberties were easily transgressed. In contested areas, the mere accusation that an individual or family or entire community was "Carrancista" justified such actions, a tactic the Constitucionalistas used in reverse. Furthermore, bandits-cum-soldiers permeated the entire region.[25]

The Zapatista leadership understood the danger in alienating the populace but remained largely helpless to stop abuse, despite warnings and efforts to discipline and professionalize the officer corps. Officers constantly received orders about the problem. In the end, however, the survival of the army, larger and more dispersed and unwieldy than ever before and with little more than a rudimentary commissary structure, depended on "living off the land." Moreover, too many officers and soldiers, including Eufemio Zapata, profited from this brigandage to want to stop it.[26] Thus the reality was one much different than that of the image of a virtuous agrarian rebel enjoying unqualified grassroots support. After mid-1916 the war became mired in virtual stalemate, which lasted another three years. This situation prevented either side from establishing a dominant and secure presence in the state, thus hampering government and the development of the socio-economic infrastructure.

Arenistas

Arenistas, led by Domingo Arenas, played an especially important role in the warfare between 1914 and 1917. Because of its key location in the volcano region on the western fringes of Puebla state and southern Tlaxcala, this group linked anti-Constitucionalista elements in the north and south of Puebla. Furthermore, the short distance from its mountain redoubts to Puebla City and its location on major communication lines also enhanced the group's strategic value.[27]

Consequently, the Arenistas were involved in some of the heaviest fighting of the war. They often spearheaded Zapatista attacks in central Puebla and, as a result, took the brunt of Constitucionalista countermeasures designed to defend this vital region. In one battle, at Texmelucan in March 1915, for example, both Domingo and Cirilo Arenas were wounded and a third sibling, Emeterio, killed.[28]

Never strong enough to operate on their own in any major operation, Arenas and his followers had to rely on their unpredictable Zapatista allies.

Indeed, Zapata distrusted the independent-minded Arenas and commonly withheld support from him. This factor proved exceedingly provocative and dangerous. During the Convencionista occupation of Puebla City in late December 1914 and early January 1915, the Arenistas were left to their own devices in the besieged city, forcing them to withdraw under heavy fire. Again in May 1916, Arenas with some four thousand troops managed to fight his way to the very center of the capital, but ultimately had to retreat when other Zapatista generals failed to back him. In the latter battle Arenas suffered some three hundred casualties. In both cases Arenas was blamed for the defeats.[29]

The Arenistas had other grievances against their Zapatista allies. First, they felt like outsiders in a movement whose top leadership and primary focus of attention were located in neighboring Morelos. Second, the Plan de Ayala, designed primarily for land-poor, village-based campesinos, did not address all the needs of Arenas's followers. His more heterogeneous group also consisted of artisans, laborers, itinerant merchants, and others with a more urban, nonagrarian orientation. Third, because of their location, Arenas's people had had greater contact with a modern, mobile society and its governmental apparatus than had most Zapatistas; this familiarity made them less adverse to dealing with the Carrancistas.[30]

Finally, Arenas did not like playing a secondary role to anyone, even Zapata. He saw himself as an independent operator, protecting the interests of his own people first. As such he had a prickly, even deadly, relationship with many of those around him whom he deemed a threat to his autonomy. Arenas and Zapatista General Fortino Ayaquica, who operated in the Atlixco-Tochimilco area, just south of Arenas's bailiwick of Texmelucan-Huejotzingo, grew to be bitter enemies. Arenas had Rafael Espinosa, the ex-Convencionista governor of the state in late 1914, murdered in an ambush in February 1916, reportedly for talking to the Carrancistas.[31]

Ironically, that same month Arenas himself entered negotiations with the Constitucionalistas. After months of simultaneous fighting and talking, he switched to their side in December 1916. The factor that finally pushed Arenas into the Carrancista camp was Zapata's move to place his fractious generals in Puebla under the overall command of Francisco Mendoza, a longtime loyalist from the south of the state. This step represented a direct attack on Arenas's autonomy. Zapata in turn read Arenas out of the movement, declared him a traitor, and attacked pro-Arenista villages.[32]

Arenas hoped that his new allies would grant him the freedom he wanted but was unable to gain on his own—to run his zone unimpeded. He soon discovered, however, that the Constitucionalistas had little interest in tolerating his dreams of autonomy. In March 1917, only four months after having joined the Constitucionalistas, Arenas wrote Colonel Mariano Plaza inviting Plaza to join the movement, which Arenas claimed was truly revolutionary, dedicated to agrarian reform and opposed to the sanguinary efforts of Villa and Zapata as well as those of Carranza. Meanwhile, as his agents bought arms in Puebla and Mexico City, Arenas resumed contact with both Villa and Zapata as well as with other local Convencionista officers, hoping to recruit or at the least neutralize them. By May his anger over his treatment by Carrancista generals Cesáreo Castro and Fortunato Maycotte had reached the point at which he planned to join in a Zapatista attack on Puebla City.[33]

Marquistas

A third major group operating under the Convencionista banner was that of the Márquez brothers, rancheros from the northern Sierra town of Otlatlán. Allies of cacique Juan Francisco Lucas, they had played a key role in the Constitucionalista defeat of Huerta during spring and summer 1914. Now the brothers expected reward for their help. Head sibling Esteban's appointment as military commander of the south of the state, however, was not enough; instead, he wanted to be in charge of the Sierra where his power base lay. Moreover, he aspired to the governorship. Carrancista generals from northern Mexico, Antonio Medina and Francisco Coss, however, respectively filled both positions.[34]

Therefore, Esteban Márquez spurned his Constitucionalista allies, including Lucas, going on to play a leading role at Aguascalientes and helping to form the new Convencionista government. He parlayed a close relationship with the new president, Eulalio Gutiérrez, into being named the Convencionista governor of Puebla with his capital in the Sierra town of Huauchinango. Within weeks, however, Márquez lost much of his claim to be chief executive when Zapatista officers rejected him and named their own governor, Francisco Salgado. Soon thereafter, in the face of Zapatista pressure, President Gutiérrez himself fled Mexico City, abandoning the presidency and leaving Márquez bereft of a political patron.

Between January and May 1915, then, Márquez operated autonomously in the Sierra. He nominally fought on the side of the Convencionistas against the Constitucionalista coalition of Medina and Lucas, yet remained distanced from the Zapatistas and the Convencionista government, headed now by President Roque González Garza. Márquez's principal ally in the state ended up being Domingo Arenas, and like Arenas he also played an ambiguous role in the larger war between the Constitucionalistas and the Convencionistas-Zapatistas.

Like Arenas, Márquez was motivated more by fervent localism than by any commitment to either of the two major revolutionary factions. He remained willing to work with either so long as the arrangement allowed him to champion Sierra interests as he interpreted them. As such, he also conducted talks with the Carrancistas, but to no avail. They, including Lucas, neither trusted Márquez nor accepted his demand that Medina be removed from the Sierra thus, in effect, giving Márquez a free rein there. Instead, they demanded his unconditional surrender. Finally, after wooing from González Garza, Márquez accepted the inevitable. If he were to have any influence over events beyond his area of the Sierra, he needed a more formal alliance with one of the two national-level groups. Consequently, he renounced his claim to the governorship in May 1915 and agreed to reestablish a closer relationship with the Convencionista government. Like other Convencionista factions, he depended upon the local populace for goods, requisitioning products and taxing people and their properties, oftentimes arbitrarily and forcefully. Confiscated haciendas were run by his troops. Raided state tax offices also provided monies. Furthermore, Márquez used his control of the Necaxa hydroelectric works to shake down its owners as well as businesses dependent upon its power. Copper found at the installation was turned into bullets and coins.

Márquez and his largely ranchero, campesino, and small town mestizo troops plus a sprinkling of Indians, totaled some fifteen hundred to three thousand. They largely controlled the western Sierra (Huauchinango, Zacatlán, and Alatriste districts) and carried the battle into Lucas and Medina's stronghold to the east as well as into the neighboring states of Hidalgo, Tlaxcala, and Veracruz. They focused on controlling the Necaxa complex and interrupting the railroad where it passed along the edge of the Sierra between Mexico City and Veracruz. With electricity from Necaxa cut off and fuel only intermittently able to arrive by train for alternative power plants and pumps, Mexico City faced the constant threat of energy blackouts and water shortages. So effective was brother Emilio in blowing up trains that in July 1915, Carranza declared him "outside the law," thus authorizing anyone, public official and private citizen alike, to capture and immediately execute him.

Like Arenas and several Zapatista leaders in the state, in fall 1915, Márquez renewed efforts to make a deal with the Constitucionalistas. This step came in the wake of Villa's defeat in the Bajío at mid-year, United States recognition of the Carrancista government in October, and the disintegration of the Convencionista coalition. Also, the situation closer to home, including Constitucionalista pressure in the Sierra, the lack of arms and funds, desertions, and internal division persuaded Márquez again to seek peace.

Márquez initially accepted Pablo González's offer of disarmament of his troops in return for their being allowed to return to their homes. However, Carranza intervened to nix the inclusion of Emilio Márquez because of his "outlaw" status and also because of opposition from both Lucas and Medina. As a result, the brothers took a wait-and-see attitude, stockpiling arms and plotting their next move.

After nearly a year of relative inaction, the Márquez once again attempted a comeback, coinciding with the Constitutional Convention at Querétaro in November 1916. They denounced Carranza's failure to restore democracy and called on the people of the Sierra to join their rebellion. Few people paid heed, and the revolt soon sputtered to a near halt. The brothers and the core of their followers fled into the mountains of Veracruz from which they continued to operate, launching occasional raids into the Puebla Sierra.

Ex-Federals

A fourth group of revolutionaries who formed part of the Convencionista coalition were former Federal officers and their followers. Its best known leaders were Higinio Aguilar from the district of Chalchicomula; Juan Andreu Almazán, a native of Guerrero and former medical student in Puebla; and Benjamín Argumedo, an equally ideologically flexible general, originally from northern Mexico. They held sway along Puebla's eastern and southern border with Veracruz and Oaxaca, thus completing, with the Zapatistas in the south, the Arenistas in the west, and the Márquez in the north, a circle around the Constitucionalista-dominated central region of the state.[35]

The ex-Federals, although more conservative and with closer ties to large landholders and urban elites, had most in common with the Márquez movement of the Sierra. Both groups had cooperated with Huerta; both appealed to the conservative, local, autonomous aspirations of rancheros and small-town mestizos; and neither emphasized agrarian reform since land tenure was not the major issue in the mountainous areas of either. Save for their mutual opposition to the Carrancistas, the ex-Federals had little affinity to the Zapatistas; indeed, they had fought each other during the Huerta period. Nevertheless, it was with the Southerners that the ex-Federals had the most contact and cooperation. Having lost the competition with the

Carrancistas to take the state capital in August 1914, Zapata realized the value of potential allies who brought with them not only men, material, and experience but also officers who had a strategic and political vision. Over the long run, however, their lack of agrarian affinity greatly undermined the ex-Federals' ability to gain a lasting foothold inside of Puebla in "natural" Zapatista territory.[36]

The Carrancistas so despised these ex-Federals that the cease-fire arranged with the Zapatistas during the Aguascalientes convention explicitly excluded them. Nevertheless, some three to four thousand ex-Federal forces helped thwart Constitucionalista consolidation of its hold over the state during fall 1914, capturing and sacking Tehuacán twice and controlling much of eastern Puebla. Along with the Arenistas, they also played a key role in the taking of the capital in mid-December. The Carrancista counter-offensive of late December 1914 and January 1915, however, pushed the ex-Federals out of the capital and central Puebla; they retreated to Acatlán, near the Oaxacan border. There they found refuge in the *cacicazgo* (chieftainship) of Zapatista General Ricardo Reyes Márquez.[37]

Before long, internal dissension reduced this already fractious group's viability. Argumedo's heavy-handed actions, including imposing forced loans on Acatlán, prompted Reyes Márquez to intervene. Furthermore, sentiment seems to have turned against Argumedo because of his northern Mexico origins. As a result, officers ousted Argumedo as head of the Zapatista Ejército del Oriente (Army of the East) and replaced him with Aguilar, his principal accuser and a native of the state. In retaliation, Argumedo pointed out Aguilar's own crimes, including selling exemptions from Zapatista taxes to hacendados. Then, in this caldron of personal rivalry and intrigue, a simmering dispute between Aguilar and Reyes Márquez boiled over; Aguilar denounced his southern allies, shot several members of Reyes Márquez's personal staff, briefly took Reyes Márquez prisoner, and fled across the state line to Oaxaca.[38]

Still, the ex-Federals did not disappear. In Oaxaca, Aguilar maintained close relations with the conservative, autonomous movement led there by Guillermo Meixueiro and also increasingly with Felicistas in the Oaxaca-Puebla-Veracruz region. From there he fought Carrancistas first and Zapatistas when necessary but was not beyond talking with either group, always seeking the best deal. Almazán likewise moved his base into the friendlier, neutral confines of Oaxaca's mountainous frontier with Puebla. He maintained ties with both Aguilar and Zapata and also entertained peace feelers from the Carrancistas. Together, Aguilar and Almazán threatened the Constitucionalistas from Chalchicomula south to Acatlán during 1915–16.

There they operated in uneasy conjunction with local leaders, ones more or less tied to the Zapatistas, including Francisco Cruz, Dolores Damián, Juan Ubera, and Reyes Márquez.[39]

Then, sometime in the fall of 1916, their welcome in Oaxaca at an end, Aguilar and Almazán left the Puebla border region for Veracruz, openly to join the Felicista movement, whose leader, Félix Díaz had returned from exile in February that year. Having now broken definitively with Zapata and the lifeless Convencionista government, they made common cause with such prominent, conservative figures with connections to Puebla as Carlos and Mariano Martínez (sons of the ex-Porfirian governor Mucio Martínez), Manuel Márquez (formerly the *jefe político* and police chief of Puebla City), Tecamachalco hacendado Luis Niño de Rivera, and ex-Federal generals Aureliano Blanquet and Gaudencio González de la Llave. From Veracruz they and their Felicista allies attempted to penetrate the more ideologically compatible Puebla Sierra. Save for some spectacular attacks on railroads in the region, however, they met with only modest success. By this date the Carrancistas had the ex-Federals' most logical allies, the Marquistas, on the run. Furthermore, most of their natural constituency, better-off townspeople and landholders, had either fled the region or felt too intimidated to support this latest call to arms.[40]

The Contenders—Constitucionalistas

Ironically, by mid-November 1914, the Constitucionalistas found themselves in a position little different from the Huertistas earlier in the year—weak, divided, isolated, and surrounded by superior hostile forces. Nevertheless, the Carrancistas eventually managed to extricate themselves from their disadvantage vis-à-vis the Convencionistas. Thanks to key alliances with local caciques willing to compromise their autonomy for a price, they gained the upper hand, although large areas of the state remained outside their control. In late 1914, however, victory was yet nowhere in sight. Indeed, the next two and one-half years of fighting would be long, bloody, and frustrating. Once Puebla City was retaken, few decisive battles took place, nothing approaching the magnitude or importance of the encounters between Obregón and Villa in the Bajío. Most action consisted of minor engagements and skirmishes to hold and administer territory while combating an elusive and ever changing enemy, often indistinguishable from the local populace.

This is not to say, however, that Puebla was unimportant to the Carrancistas. Control of the state, especially the center and north, was crucial to the defense of the Constitucionalista capital, the port of Veracruz, and to communications between it and central Mexico. Furthermore, failure to hold Puebla City, the nation's "second" metropolis in 1910, would have been a sharp embarrassment to the Carrancistas. Any thought, however, that just because the Constitucionalistas nominally controlled the state, they also fielded a well-endowed, smoothly running, cohesive army and were embraced by a majority of Poblanos is mistaken. Historian Romana Falcón, for example, has noted the same for San Luis Potosí.[41]

From the moment of their entrance into Puebla City in August 1914, the Carrancistas acted more as conquerors than liberators. Indeed, these young, ambitious, aggressive, even ruthless men from Mexico's far north had little understanding of or regard for Puebla and its people and made no attempt to hide the fact. These "carpetbaggers," as Knight has referred to them, attempted to impose a revolution from above.[42]

Most top Carrancista officers who served in Puebla between 1914 and 1917 hailed from Coahuila, came from modest backgrounds, were under forty years old, and had worked their way up rapidly through the ranks serving as Maderistas and then as Carrancistas. Francisco Coss, a mine laborer, was born in Ramos Arizpe, Coahuila, in 1880. He first tasted action in 1906 with the Magonistas and then in 1910 as a sergeant in the Maderista irregulars. By 1914 he had become a general and governor and head of Constitucionalista forces in Puebla.[43] Cesáreo Castro, although somewhat older, born in 1856 in Cuatro Ciénegas, Coahuila, started out as a Maderista. In 1913 he joined Carranza as a colonel and then quickly rose to a generalship. He served as governor and military commander of Puebla in 1916–17.[44] Antonio Medina, eighteen years old in 1913 (born 1895 in Tamaulipas) when he joined the forces of Lucio Blanco as a captain, also had become a general by late 1914. He spent much time in the Sierra of Puebla as head of the Third Division of the Ejército del Oriente.[45] Pilar R. Sánchez, a farmer with a fourth-grade education, was born on a rancho outside Ramos Arizpe, Coahuila, in 1888. He, too, served first as a Maderista and then Carrancista in the north of Mexico, and obtained a generalship in 1914. Sánchez led the Second Division of the Ejército del Oriente in 1916–17.[46] Pedro Villaseñor, born in San Carlos Candela, Coahuila, in 1878, gained the rank of captain while fighting Orozquistas (followers of Pascual Orozco), and like many of his contemporaries was a general by 1914. He served in several capacities in the state including commander at Tehuacán and Puebla City; chief of operations for the districts of Tepeaca, Tecamachalco, and Tehuacán; and head of the Fifth Division of the Ejército del Oriente.[47]

These men and others like them, preponderantly from northern Mexico, held the top posts (division command and above), made the key decisions, and had the greatest access to the First Chief and his principal generals such as Pablo González and Álvaro Obregón. Meanwhile, revolutionaries from Puebla, also with strong records, were relegated to secondary positions, generally brigade generalships at the highest. This situation caused frustration and resentment and provoked division, even defections, within the officer ranks. Nevertheless, to pursue the war the Carrancistas came to understand the need to work with the Poblanos, especially regional caciques. These individuals had longtime clientalist (i.e., dependent, protectionist) ties into the local society, Garner calls them "cultural intermediaries" in his study of Oaxaca, and therefore held the key to control of and ultimate victory in the state.[48]

This cooperation led to a long-term, productive relationship. Once Constitucionalista officers collaborated militarily with locals, they soon discovered that personal arrangements beneficial to them, economically and otherwise, could be brokered. In turn, regional strongmen wanted security, stability, and autonomy to carry on traditional control of their bailiwicks, which the outsiders could help guarantee. The case of Adalberto Tejeda in the Huasteca region of Veracruz, for example, fits many of these patterns. Tejeda, who would go on to politically dominate his state in the 1920s and early 1930s, did not prove as noxious to the Carrancista cause as many of his counterparts did in Puebla, where this officer-cacique alliance would become so entrenched that it challenged central government control over portions of the state.[49]

Several caciques played a key role in alliances with Carrancista officers. In the south of the state, Francisco A. Gracia operated in the important Atlixco-Huaquechula-Matamoros area. He was a schoolteacher and former Zapatista who had spent a year under Huertista incarceration in Quintana Roo. As a general he held several posts under northern Carrancista officers Francisco Coss and Pilar Sánchez, including command at Atlixco and head of a brigade in the Second Division.[50]

Further south, in Acatlán, Ricardo Reyes Márquez also ended up on the Carrancista side. In the past he had held a series of public posts in his hometown from director of schools and court secretary to *jefe político*, serving the regimes of Díaz, Madero, and Huerta. In 1913–14 he backed Huerta by leading irregular forces against the Zapatistas, briefly joined the Carrancistas once Huerta fell, then allied with the Zapatistas, and finally switched back to the Constitucionalistas in November 1915, once the war began to turn in the latter's favor. A year later he commanded some 650 men with several higher ranking Carrancista officers, all from the North, collaborating with him. He would go on to head the key Acatlán and Atlixco-Atencingo sectors for the First Chief's army, all the while protected by Cesáreo Castro and Pablo González, despite incessant charges of corruption and abuse.[51]

In the west, in addition to Domingo Arenas, who switched to the Constitucionalistas in late 1916, there was Rafael R. Rojas, who dominated Cholula. A bookkeeper and businessman, Rojas came from a clan that had served Porfirio Díaz. At age twenty-four he had dropped out of the Colegio del Estado to help Madero and later collaborated with the Zapatistas. In 1914 he joined the Constitucionalistas, and Francisco Coss appointed him general. He headed the 300-man Cholula or Fourth Brigade of the Second Division of the Ejército del Oriente. In this capacity he played a major role in protecting Puebla City.[52]

In the east, Francisco Barbosa, a ranchero from Ajalpan, near Tehuacán, helped the Carrancistas secure the vast, unstable border region with Veracruz and Oaxaca. Barbosa first fought with the Maderistas in 1911, during which time he lost a brother in the war. He then backed the Constitucionalistas, becoming general in 1915. Under the aegis of Cesáreo Castro he headed the Fifth Brigade of the First Division of the Ejército del Oriente until 1919.[53]

Juan Lechuga, also from the Tehuacán area, fought with Camerino Mendoza during the Maderista rebellion and then became one of the first locally recruited Carrancista leaders in the state in 1913. In 1914 he gained the rank of general and from 1915 to 1917 headed his own brigade in the Ejército del Oriente, serving in Tehuacán as well as in neighboring states.[54]

Just to the north of Tehuacán, Gilberto Camacho headed the federal command at Chalchicomula. One of the original Constitucionalista officers in the state, Camacho had briefly switched to the Convención when his ambitions for governor were thwarted but then reconsidered and joined the Carrancistas in 1915. He was a member of the extended Teziutlán-based Avila Camacho clan, which would dominate Puebla politics from the 1930s to the 1950s and even send one of its members, Manuel Avila Camacho, to the presidency.[55]

In the northern Sierra the Carrancistas gained the backing of octogenarian cacique Juan Francisco Lucas. Widely recognized as the most influential person in the region, he had a stellar military and political record going back to the 1850s and still nominally headed the Brigada Serrana, a post he had held since the Porfiriato. Although too old to take an active role in the fighting, Lucas's influence kept large numbers of Indians and mestizos loyal to the Constitucionalista camp and made it possible for the principal Carrancista commander in the Sierra, Antonio Medina, to thwart the Márquez brothers' bid for dominance. Lucas's successor, Gabriel Barrios, a native of the Sierra and longtime protégé of the patriarch, would finally finish off the Márquez with Constitucionalista backing and then go on to dominate the Sierra until the late 1920s.[56]

In order to put a viable force into the field, the Carrancistas needed men and supplies, two issues that plagued their operations in Puebla. The army arrived in the state with only limited numbers of troops from the North, including Yaqui Indians from Sonora; their strategy was to recruit most forces from central Mexico. The need for men was never ending given battlefield casualties, desertions, and sickness such as malaria, which decimated unacclimated soldiers stationed in the lowlands of southern Puebla.[57] And because much of the heaviest fighting during 1914–1917 took place against the Villistas, many soldiers from the state ended up in north-central Mexico. This fact not only aggravated the shortage of men in uniform in Puebla but also undermined one of the recruiters' principal propaganda weapons, the opportunity to defend one's home turf. In this respect the Convencionistas had an advantage as they kept their forces in the region.

Carrancista alliances with caciques, then, were motivated in large part to gain soldiers. Officers commonly were awarded ranks according to the number of men, arms, and horses they contributed. However, many of these soldiers posed problems: they fought under direct control of local commanders with only limited commitment to the Carrancista cause; like their commanders, they were motivated primarily by local and personal objectives; and they only reluctantly if at all left their home areas to confront the enemy. These issues regarding recruitment were also present in San Luis Potosí.[58]

As a result, Constitucionalista recruiters also attempted to persuade men to join the regular army, focusing their efforts on the industrialized working classes, artisans, shopkeepers, and other urbanized mestizos and small- and medium-sized landholders. Officials reasoned that more urban, moderate elements with jobs and property to protect and free of retrograde cacique control would more readily embrace the broader, modernizing Carrancista vision of the revolution. Agents propagandized in communities, workplaces, and schools. They called on people to defend themselves and the homeland against the threat posed by the lower-class hordes and appealed to local chauvinism by naming fighting units after an area's hero or the town in question.[59]

The result was mixed. Most people, tired of the war, afraid for themselves and their property, and increasingly cynical about the claims of all
factions, did not want to join any fighting unit. Others, motivated by money,
women, or other personal reasons, signed up but never in numbers sufficient to satisfy needs. Only a few inductees, such as students, volunteered
for genuinely idealistic or ideological motives.[60]

Economic and social pressure doubtless played a key role in many individuals' decisions to enter the army, but contrary to the practice of past
regimes, the Constitucionalistas placed some restriction on the use of mi-
nors and apparently did not rely as heavily on forced recruitment or the
leva. In August 1915, Carrancista commanders announced that children
who had not completed primary school would be barred from joining the
military. Although residents from one town in the district of Cholula complained about having to sleep in their fields to avoid being inducted (the
alternative they said was to be shot for being Zapatistas), this seems to have
been more the exception than the rule. Moreover, such coercive actions, as
this case suggests, seem to have taken place mostly in contested, mainly
rural, areas, not where the Carrancistas held secure control. These same
residents added that eighty people from the village who had been forcibly
recruited had later deserted, thus underlining what the Constitucionalistas
fully realized: involuntary inductees were counterproductive as the fluid,
chaotic situation on the battlefield allowed soldiers easily to switch sides;
physical coercion alone was not enough to retain them.[61]

One group, ironically, which voluntarily entered the Constitucionalista
ranks were industrial laborers. Despite their lower-class status, which logically would make them allies of the Convencionistas, they responded favor-
ably to Constitucionalista promises to recognize their longtime demands
for better working conditions. Furthermore, the threat to their livelihoods
because of Convencionista attacks on mills and the railroad along with rising food prices caused by the disruption of the agricultural sector, again
largely as a result of Convencionista action, prompted this decision. In addition, the offer of steady pay helped convince many to trade their tools for
arms.[62]

The Carrancistas enticed textile-factory workers to join their ranks by
vowing to improve pay and hours and increase jobs once peace was reestablished. They also employed the dangerous tactic of reverse psychology, which
accurately reflected the Northerners' attitude toward the Poblanos. At one
meeting, a senior officer challenged laborers by calling them women and
cowards and claiming that the state, which had produced national heroes in

the past, was no longer capable of doing so. Many of the mill hands in attendance took the bait. They formed the Paz y Trabajo (Peace and Work) contingent, which became the Nineteenth Batallón de Línea (Line Battalion) of the so-called Batallones Rojos (Red Battalions), which the Carrancistas created among workers in central Mexico. The Paz y Trabajo unit, as well as other laborers recruited by state military commander General Coss with the collaboration of the Casa del Obrero Mundial (House of the World Worker), saw action in the region as well as in the Bajío in late 1914–15. Nevertheless, Coss openly disparaged Puebla's soldiers, saying they were not as good as those he had brought with him from the North.[63]

Manpower and its disposition became a major source of tension among officers in the field and between them and the secretariat of war. Control over soldiers meant military power and by extension political influence in a context of weak central government. For example, in spring 1915 rival officers jeopardized the Constitucionalistas' ability to protect transportation lines between central Mexico and Obregón's forces fighting Villistas in the Bajío. In Puebla no one wanted to send units to guard the railway network in Tlaxcala and Hidalgo.[64]

Fielding an army also involved supplying troops. Unlike the Convencionistas, who received only limited monies and material from their central government, the Constitucionalistas gained much more help from headquarters, a factor in their ultimate victory. For some people in the state, catering to the army's needs was one of the few ways to make money in difficult economic times. Laid-off workers sought employment in the arms factory established in the Interoceánico railway shops. Cobblers and tailors vied to provide shoes, hats, and uniforms using what political influence they had to gain contracts.[65]

Nevertheless, given the intensity of fighting in 1915–16 and the importance of battling the Villistas, military officers in Puebla reported shortages of every kind.[66] The situation at times became so acute that Carranza even ordered shell casings picked off the battlefield for reuse. The First Chief instructed that infantry units, not cavalry, be formed as the government could not afford to buy and maintain horses. Recruitment faltered and tension rose in the ranks over the dearth of pay and weapons. An estimated 10 to 20 percent of Constitucionalista soldiers in Puebla lacked pistols or rifles; some units reported as many as one-half without proper arms.[67]

Some shortages, however, were artificial. Officers, for example, inflated their needs in order to hoard materiel and keep it from fellow commanders. Furthermore, a thriving black market exacerbated the problem. Unpaid

Carrancista soldiers sold weapons and bullets for cash, either directly to their opponents or more commonly via intermediaries, including a network of Zapatista women. Constitucionalista officers and particularly their cacique allies, many of whom operated in a shadowy world between the two contending camps, made their own lucrative deals.[68]

Carrancista troops commonly abused the civilian population. Crimes were especially egregious in contested areas where the smokescreen of charges of collaboration were used to justify actions against the populace. Simply walking along a railroad line, for example, the easiest way for many rural people to travel to town, could even mean death, as the law considered any unauthorized person near rails to be a saboteur.[69]

Indeed, villagers' accusations of misdeeds against the Constitucionalistas mirrored many of the complaints leveled by rural dwellers at the Convencionistas. Nevertheless, there were three fundamental differences between the two sides' treatment of civilians. First, most Convencionista actions took place in an ambience of social control. Although resented, such actions could at some psychological level be understood if not forgiven because they were most often undertaken by neighbors to sustain homegrown armies in the defense of local interests. Constitucionalista excesses, however, usually took place in an environment of little or no social restraint, against unknowns, and even when committed by regional caciques and their troops, still carried the taint of being outsider motivated.[70]

Second, contrary to the Convencionistas' generally respectful stance toward the church, widespread Carrancista attacks on ecclesiastical property and clerics alienated large sectors of the state's mostly socially conservative populace, rural and urban alike. Third, Convencionista misdeeds seldom directly touched residents of larger towns and cities. Urbanites feared the rural revolutionaries, but they did not have to live with the rebels on a day-to-day basis. They did, however, have to cohabit with the Carrancistas; this arrangement quickly turned sour as the northern interlopers assumed the attitude and comportment of occupiers.

No one felt safe in life or property from attack by the Constitucionalista occupiers. They argued that because they had won the war in a competitive world, this made them the revolutionary elect, ergo capable of and chosen to regenerate a decadent society whatever the cost. In Puebla City the Carrancista leadership confiscated houses of the rich for homes and offices; Pablo González, for example, selected the residence of Spanish hacendado and industrialist Marcelino Presno, just one half block off the city's main plaza. Drunken soldiers went house-to-house robbing and raping, while

others took horses at pistol point in the street. In a parade designed to drum
up support and demonstrate their prowess, soldiers haughtily marched down
the city's principal thoroughfare hauling carts full of loot.[71]

The initial weeks of occupation only turned for the worse in late 1914
and early 1915 when the two sides traded control of the state capital. Before
abandoning the city in December, General and Governor Coss left nothing
of value. He wanted not only to deprive the opposition of materiel, but also
to take retribution on a populace that had never embraced the outsiders.
First he imposed a "loan" on merchants, emptied the pawnshop, and took
some seventy thousand pesos from the city treasury. Then, whatever
Constitucionalista troops could not carry with them was rendered useless,
burned and destroyed. They even razed the Mexicano railroad station and
poisoned the water supply. This scorched-earth strategy resulted in damages
estimated at 2 million pesos. Finally, Coss ordered public employees and
workers to join his army. Those men who refused were shot; others fled for
their lives. As the Carrancistas withdrew from the city, few people, no matter their socioeconomic standing, regretted their departure.[72]

The Carrancista return to the city in January 1915 marked a repeat of
this behavior. To intimidate and punish the city's generally conservative,
pro-Catholic populace, Coss shelled the cathedral, threatening to destroy it
and all of downtown Puebla if the local government and Zapatista garrison
did not surrender. In the end, Coss had his way, yet the pattern of abuse
continued. All who remained in the city during the Convencionista inter-
lude came under suspicion. Coss ordered a number of people, alleged thieves
or Zapatistas, the latter now equated with Huertismo (Huerta's regime), to
be executed in the cathedral's atrium. Others, particularly Spaniards, were
loaded on railroad cars bound for Veracruz to be deported. The more fortunate ones only lost their jobs. For his actions Coss gained the nickname
"Pancho Patadas" (Pancho the [ass] kicker).[73]

Although the excesses of 1914–15 were not to be repeated, Poblanos in
the capital city and in other urban centers found it difficult to ignore their
occupiers. At the least, townspeople had to face arrogant, abusive, armed,
and often drunk soldiers made worse in their eyes by the fact that some were
Yaqui Indians. Prostitution, crime, and a general lack of a sense of order and
predictability, much less security, also upset the populace. Many locals' complaints against the Carrancistas were as mundane as to pay bills for hotel
rooms and foodstuffs delivered to the local garrison or failure to return
"loaned" horses or carriages to their original owners. Nevertheless, even these
minor issues became cumulative and could be crucial to a small
businessperson or farmer in such a precarious economic climate.[74] Then

there were more egregious cases such as that of Major Manuel P. Rodríguez, a friend of General Coss. Among other things, he shot and killed a taxi driver, tortured a soldier, beat up a hotel worker, and raped a 10-year-old girl. He went unpunished as did nearly all other malefactors, thus entrenching official impunity into the bedrock of revolutionary practice, a nightmare that Mexico still lives with today.[75]

While residents contended with the daily, random, alienating abuses of Carrancista occupation, in several areas of the state more organized systems of exploitation developed, based on Constitucionalista officer–regional cacique links. Caciques, bolstered by clientalist or dependent relations and populist actions, had existed for decades in Puebla, deftly switching to support, at least rhetorically, each new regime as it came to power in the federal or state capital. For most central governments a pledge of loyalty and quiescence in the cacique's bailiwick were the only things asked; in return the cacique could do as he wished in his sphere of influence.

The Carrancista presence in Puebla, however, began to erode this long established balance between center and region. Never before had outsiders so deeply and thoroughly penetrated the state. The arrival of the Constitucionalista officers, backed by a formidable and increasingly successful military machine, forced traditional local and regional leaders to change their ways. Some rejected the intruders, attempted to oust them from their zones, and in the process backed the Convencionistas. Others, albeit often reluctantly, tolerated and even collaborated with the Northerners, sensing opportunity to preserve what they could of the old system. Furthermore, officer and cacique alike took advantage of the revolution's undermining of social constraint to exploit for personal gain. Save for Yucatán, where Joseph claims military officers generally "ruled honestly and fairly," this Carrancista "military entrepreneur," as Ankerson calls him, was present throughout the country. Álvaro Obregón is perhaps the best known example, although there were many additional ones on a smaller scale.[76]

In Puebla, the officer-cacique link became an especially formidable combination, one that would evolve not only into economic and social relationships but political ones as well, seriously threatening the regime. In the east of the state, Carrancista General Pedro Villaseñor controlled the strategic and lucrative area around the city of Tehuacán. Taking advantage of the large, well-to-do Spanish presence in the region, he protected haciendas from implementation of the Constitucionalista January 6, 1915, agrarian law and helped owners to sell products to the Zapatista enemy. He peddled arms to the Southerners and their ex-Federal allies, while at the same time persecuting villages that called for land reform, branding them Zapatista sympathizers. He dominated trade routes in the region, including the Mexicano del Sur railroad, and developed commercial links with the anti-Carrancista movement in the neighboring state of Oaxaca. When individuals or towns did not cooperate with Villaseñor, he confiscated what he wanted; livestock gained in such a manner, for example, formed the basis of a lucrative meat trade. To ensure the continuation of the war and his business ventures, Villaseñor made only desultory efforts to engage the enemy. The general also had political ambitions, and Spaniards in the region approached him to start a movement against the First Chief. By 1918, promoted and placed in charge of southern Puebla as well, he spent most of his time in the state capital dealing with his business activities rather than in the field working as an officer.[77]

The two principal caciques of the Tehuacán region, bolstered by Carrancista support, operated in a manner very similar to their fellow officer from the North. Francisco Barbosa, protected by Cesáreo Castro, ran his *cacicazgo* (cacique-dominated area) to benefit himself and his family. He both cooperated with and persecuted hacendados and villagers. He controlled water sources and mines as well as properties in the coffee-producing zone in the Tehuacán Sierra. He pocketed monies destined for his troops and defied orders for their disposition, keeping the bulk of the soldiers in and around his hometown of Ajalpan to protect his economic interests. In the early 1920s, Barbosa would serve as a proagrarian deputy in the federal congress.[78]

Juan Lechuga, too, determined to look after his ill-gotten financial gains and political base, strove to keep his forces in the Tehuacán area, causing a deep fissure between him and General Francisco Coss in spring 1915. Later, when he did agree to move a portion of his troops, he took advantage of the opportunity. In Amecameca, just across the Puebla border in the neighboring state of Mexico, he used them illegally to cut trees on the lands of the San Rafael y Anexas paper factory. He then shipped the timber to Mexico City, where it was turned into finished products at a lumber mill owned by a relative. When a forestry inspector reported the operation, Lechuga had him arrested. Meanwhile the remainder of Lechuga's contingent continued to steal horses, take over pasture, and impose local officials on eastern Puebla. Like many Constitucionalista officers and their cacique allies, Lechuga also controlled portions of the railroad network for personal gain.[79]

The same pattern holds for other parts of the state. In Chalchicomula, Gilberto Camacho embargoed properties, ransacked stores, persecuted and killed political opponents, and jailed uncooperative judges.[80] In the south,

Ricardo Reyes Márquez operated around Acatlán in conjunction with a series of Carrancista officers to maintain and profit from his longtime *cacicazgo*.[81] In the Atlixco-Huaquechula area, Francisco Gracia played a useful role for the Carrancistas by negotiating Zapatistas' surrender.[82] In the west, Constitucionalista leaders in nearby Puebla City tolerated the excesses of Rafael Rojas because he successfully protected Cholula, gateway to the state capital. Rojas, who became rich from his agricultural holdings and milk distribution business, served as a federal deputy and then in 1920, once Carranza fell, became interim governor.[83]

The best example, however, of this officer-cacique relationship and its manifestations took place in the north of the state where Antonio Medina and Juan Francisco Lucas collaborated under the Constitucionalista banner. Medina, the ambitious Carrancista, needed Lucas's influence over the largely indigenous people of the region while the elderly Lucas realized he had little choice but to deal with the outsiders or risk losing his grip over the Sierra. They battled the Convencionista forces of Esteban Márquez, enhanced their economic well being, and in the process exercised political clout in the region, much of which was done without or in defiance of central government authority. Indeed, Medina gained the nickname El Pachón, or Basset Hound, in recognition of his skill in smelling out an opportunity.[84]

Charges abounded that both men put their personal and families' interests above that of the Constitucionalistas. They desultorily pursued the war and blocked peace initiatives, thus prolonging the struggle for economic and political reasons. Neither wanted to share the spoils with Márquez, and trafficking in merchandise and prisoners with the enemy proved lucrative. The war also facilitated speculation in scarce foodstuffs, confiscated properties, and financial paper. They controlled a railroad line and issued their own currency. Profits were invested in land, banks, and mines. Medina reportedly ended up a millionaire.[85]

As long as the fighting continued, Medina and especially Lucas remained indispensable to the Carrancista leadership. Meanwhile, the pair shored up their political base in the region by distributing land to villagers, collaborating with former Huertistas, and arranging for their people to gain local office. Medina also developed ties to the Avila Camacho family of Teziutlán, which would dominate the state in subsequent decades.[86]

Lucas died in early 1917, and his successor, Gabriel Barrios, also backed by the federal army, proved to be even more exploitative.[87] Meanwhile, Medina, blocked from running for the governorship, nevertheless used his power to play an active role in the election for the state's chief executive spot that year. Subsequently, Medina also served as a federal deputy from Puebla between 1918 and 1920.[88]

Warfare took first priority in Puebla between 1914 and 1917. Ambitious and ruthless men struggled to dominate the state. The splintering of the Carrancista coalition in autumn 1914 complicated an already fluid and dangerous situation. The central question facing Poblanos was whether to support the newly arrived Constitucionalistas, made up primarily of outsiders, military men from the North of Mexico, but with a modernizing agenda, or the Convencionistas, people from closer to home, who represented a more traditional, exclusivist Puebla.

Initially, most townspeople backed the Northerners. Some did so out of conviction, as they saw the Constitucionalistas as a progressive force. Others supported the newcomers more reluctantly, either because they had little choice as Carrancista soldiers held their communities, or they feared even more the possibility of rural hordes taking power. Thus, urban elements (save for workers who joined the Red Battalions) primarily played an indirect yet significant role in the outcome of the war, as their generally passive backing of the Carrancistas aided the Northerners in controlling Puebla City and larger towns.

In the state's periphery and in its more traditional small towns and villages, where sentiment for grassroots control over politics and resources was the strongest, there was much resistance to the Carrancistas. In late 1914–15, country folk joined local and regional leaders to fight the outsiders. Many of these groups operated for months and years, as the Zapatistas, Arenistas, and Marquistas attest.

Nevertheless, as the fragile Convencionista coalition weakened and problems within each faction increased, the tide of victory flowed toward the Carrancistas. Given this fact, a number of regional leaders made deals with the Northerners. These caciques, authoritarian power brokers between their followers and the outside world, were disposed to compromise the ideal of autonomy, if it meant their ability to survive and, perhaps, even to prosper as never before.

The Carrancistas, despite their arrogance and disdain for Puebla, realized the need to take advantage of these caciques in order to win the war. Thus, military arrangements were consummated, ones that would play the key role in the Constitucionalista victory and be parlayed into self-serving economic and political relationships. In this process the Northerners, who had arrived in central Mexico determined to show the benighted populace how to carry out a revolution, now themselves received instruction in what it meant to deal with a proud, traditional, largely inward-looking society with deeply held values, which emphasized community, religion, and local autonomy. Their absorption into this milieu, the first step in the creation of a political culture, would soon return to haunt the newly victorious regime. Meanwhile, as armies operated on the battlefield, generals-cum-politicians on both sides sought to destroy what was left of the old governing apparatus and create a new state according to their respective visions.

5

POLITICS, 1914–1917

The Constitucionalistas and Convencionistas were revolutionaries, not aspiring liberal democrats; the niceties of constitutional government adhered to by the Maderistas now seemed quaint and naive. Each faction, where it ruled, brutally wiped away the old institutional order and imposed its authoritarian ways in the name of reshaping Mexico to its liking. For nearly three years, Mexico would be ruled by dictatorships, ones that made even the Huertistas look benign.

The development and initial carrying out of a revolutionary political and socioeconomic program in Puebla took place during the violent years of the conflict. Indeed, the formation of the new state apparatus began even as old structures crumbled, battered by warfare and disruption. In this contest two basic visions for the future collided. On the one hand, the Constitucionalistas, based on formal legal systems (that is, the Constitution of 1857), aimed to transform Puebla into a modern, capitalistic, secular, outward-looking entity, part of a progressive, integrated, twentieth-century nation, à la Porfirio Díaz, albeit minus the severe contradictions. This change was to be carried out via a centralized state, which would regulate the socioeconomic system.

On the other hand, the Convencionistas, based on a combination of formal law and informal custom, determined to preserve a largely agrarian, inward-looking, religious, mostly self-sufficient political and socioeconomic system (capitalism modified with nonmarket practices) with minimal ties even to Puebla City, much less the national capital and beyond. Only a weak central state would exist. Real power would be wielded through an inclusive, decentralized, autonomous structure embedded within and responsible to the regions and villages. In practice both of these visions, Constitucionalista and Convencionista, were conservative, vague, and pragmatic (nonideological), thereby allowing for nearly any action in the name of gaining and wielding power for ends that could always be modified to justify the means.

Many urban dwellers across a range of classes and most medium and large landowners felt uncomfortable in either of these camps. They embraced many of the ideas of modernization and capitalism offered by the Carrancistas but rejected their anticlericalism and the possibility of losing political control. Moreover, their arrogant, paternalistic attitude and authoritarian tactics repulsed this group. Nevertheless, these same people also turned their backs on much of the traditional, backward-looking program of the state's majority rural, mestizo, and Indian population, represented by the Convencionistas. Hence the central political struggle for both the Constitucionalistas and Convencionistas between 1914 and 1917 was to begin the construction of a new, institutionalized, state-governing apparatus, one capable of winning over suspicious and influential Poblanos to support and give it legitimacy. To a large degree the future course of the revolution depended on the outcome of this contest.

Constitucionalistas

The Governors—Francisco Coss

In the chaotic and dangerous days following the Carrancista takeover of Puebla City in August 1914, General Pablo González, head of the Ejército del Oriente, oversaw the creation of a new state government. To avoid having to choose among the factious and bitterly divided higher officer corps, most of whom aspired to the governorship, he first proposed naming a civilian, Luis Cabrera, a Puebla native and one of Carranza's principal aides. This idea, however, was quickly dropped given the anticivilian stance of the army. González then called a meeting of officers in early September, and from it Francisco Coss emerged as governor and military commander, a northern "proconsul," with the two highest posts of the state in his hands. Coss assumed power on September 3, 1914.[1]

Exactly why Coss, a thirty-four-year-old general and native of Coahuila who had worked his way up through the ranks since joining Carranza's forces in 1910, was chosen over other aspirants for the post, all of whom had similar résumés, is not clear. Hard driving, intolerant, radical, and above all conflictive, the mustachioed, intense-looking soldier served the Constitucionalistas' immediate need to strengthen and expand their tentative area of control in the state. In the longer run, however, his lack of political experience, heavy-handed tactics, and inability to get along with the Poblanos and his superiors undermined that goal.[2]

Any illusions that Puebla's economic and political elite had that they might be included in the new state government were quickly shattered. Coss not only banned civilians of the discredited Huertista period but also dissolved the entire previous state apparatus as well as district and local political institutions. He replaced these entities and their personnel with Constitucionalista army structures and officers. The state congress closed, military courts absorbed the judiciary, the *jefaturas políticas* disappeared, and Coss and his staff appointed state and local authorities at all levels. Many of the new personnel were northern Mexicans, including at least two of Coss's relatives. The result was a full-fledged military dictatorship. Indeed, none of the governorships during the Huerta period had equaled the new regime's far-reaching power. Thus, illusions of democratization and greater state and local control, à la Madero, were quickly shattered. Poblanos soon began to chafe under this authoritarian and exclusivist political arrangement.[3]

Coss did not simply exclude people who had served the old regime. He also set up a so-called Comité de Salud Pública (Committee of Public Health), which delved into citizens' political opinions and fingered individuals to be picked up by the security apparatus. Persecutions extended to moderates of the upper political and economic class who had held no or only marginal posts under Huerta. They included 1911 interim governor Rafael Cañete and Miguel Jiménez Labora, a director of the Cámara Agrícola who had worked as former governor Carrasco's private secretary. Puebla City's police chief, Silvino García, a Coss appointee, gained an especially sordid reputation for his harsh treatment of detainees.[4]

A favorite target of Coss was Puebla's influential Spanish community. There was little to lose and much to gain by attacking this disliked group, oftentimes derogatively referred to as *gachupines*. Spain, unlike the other major European powers or the United States, had little leverage over Mexico and therefore could place only limited pressure on Carranza to rein in his subordinates. Appeals to patriotism combined with anti-Spanish measures enjoyed widespread acquiescence if not active support among the lower and middle classes. Anyone who opposed this tactic faced being accused of anti-Mexicanism, a serious charge in the middle of an increasingly xenophobic revolution.[5]

As a result, in an effort to gain peasant and worker support for his nascent regime, Coss decreed the removal from the state's factories and fields of all Spanish citizens, most of whom worked as administrators and managers.

In this instance, however, Coss miscalculated. He gained supporters, tired of abusive Spanish bosses and desirous of their posts, but could not convince Carranza of the wisdom of his action. Given the unstable situation, the outcry among Puebla's political and economic elite, and objections from Madrid and the foreign community in general, the First Chief intervened. When Coss refused to modify the measure, Carranza assigned him to the field to fight rebels and appointed General Cesáreo Castro provisional governor. Castro postponed the decree's implementation. Coss soon thereafter reassumed the governorship, but the law remained in limbo.[6]

Despite the setback, Coss would continue to play the Spanish card throughout his governorship, blaming them, for example, for food shortages, high prices, and attempts to topple his government. On more than one occasion he called upon workers, students, and the urban lumpenproletariat for support while protecting soldiers who attacked and even murdered Peninsulars. Puebla was not alone in formulating an anti-Spanish policy, but compared to Yucatán, for example, Coss's stance was harsh, employing violence against capitalists in general, not just Spaniards.[7]

Ex-Huertistas and Spaniards were not the only groups to feel Coss's wrath. Much of the urban middle and upper class and even sectors of the lower came to resent the governor. Above all they wanted peace, order, and predictability but instead got increased crime, inflation, shortages, arrests and executions, schools turned into barracks, and churches ransacked and converted into stables and whorehouses. Coss had only limited direct control over many of these actions and problems, but he and the Carrancistas tolerated and received blame for them. Indeed, as discontent grew, Coss felt increasingly insecure and thus clamped down even more harshly, much like his Huertista predecessors. Carranza, attuned to the rising backlash to his movement, tried to mediate without jeopardizing military security. These steps only fueled Coss's resentment toward the First Chief and his advisors and divided Constitucionalista ranks in the state. As Garner has noted regarding Carrancista policy in Oaxaca, the rhetoric of populism was already being "slowly but perceptibly transformed into a grim authoritarianism."[8]

Conflict again erupted between Coss and the Carrancista leadership in the wake of the Zapatista occupation of Puebla City in December 1914–January 1915. The underlying issue involved not only his latitude as state commander but also the divisions within the Constitucionalista movement between Coahuilans and Sonorans. Coss complained that in the capture of the city his forces took disproportionate losses because generals Álvaro Obregón and Salvador Alvarado, Sonorans and officers in the Ejército del

Occidente (Army of the West), did not follow plans. Then, upon evacuating the city, the pair ordered Coss to secure the railroad, allowing Obregón's and Alvarado's troops to leave first. As a result, because he was the last to escape, Coss not only again took the heaviest casualties but was also pinned with blame for its loss. Furthermore, when Coss attempted to confiscate horses and saddles from citizens for his forces, Obregón countermanded Coss and insinuated that he was a thief.[9]

In response, Coss threatened to resign the governorship and leave the army. Carranza and Obregón readily accepted the former offer, but because of his value as a commander, allowed him to remain in the field. Moreover, they did not want him to join the enemy. To close the deal, they agreed that Coss choose a temporary successor with the proviso that he could reassume the chief executive spot once security improved.[10]

Within a month, Carranza, over Obregón's objections, had not only acquiesced in Coss's return to the governorship but had also designated him to head the Second Division of the Ejército del Oriente, in charge of Puebla and Tlaxcala. To fend off Obregón and neutralize Carranza, Coss had taken advantage of the delicate security situation and allied with General Pablo González, no friend of Obregón. Moreover, he had mobilized lower-level officers, workers, and radicals in Puebla to come to his defense. Finally, Coss made it known that his loyalty could not be taken for granted; he had been in contact with agents of Eulalio Gutiérrez, the former president of the Convención government and fellow Coahuilan, who now offered himself as an alternative to both Carranza and Villa.[11]

Coss remained convinced that several individuals in Carranza's government were out to destroy his governorship. They included Obregón as well as General Ignacio Pesqueira, secretary of war and a protégé of Obregón, and even worse from a military man's point of view, civilians Luis Cabrera, secretary of the treasury, and Félix Palavicini, secretary of public education. Obregón doubted Coss's loyalty and resented his links to Pablo González, Obregón's principal rival. As for the civilians, Coss's ruthless actions against the populace and the use of his troops for personal gain confirmed their jaundiced view of the military. In turn, Coss reciprocated the civilians' distrust, which reflected most soldiers' contempt for noncombatants in positions of power. After all, the brass asserted that the civilians had had their opportunity with Madero, failed, and deserved no second chance. Furthermore, Coss especially disliked Cabrera because, as a native of Puebla, he paid close attention to and used his influence to intervene in state affairs. Indeed at one point, Coss even had Cabrera's private secretary arrested for criticizing the governor.[12]

Coss jealously defended his power and authority in Puebla, bringing him into conflict with other ambitious officers, particularly Antonio Medina in the Sierra and Juan Lechuga in Tehuacán. Disagreements arose not only over military issues, such as recruiting, troop disposition, and officers' reporting relationships (Coss felt Medina and Lechuga should answer to him), but also over civil matters, such as the creation of military-run courts and the appointment of municipal officials (Coss, as governor, saw this as his prerogative alone), which were key to the control over localities and thus the expansion of one's political base.[13]

These divisions became especially apparent in spring 1915 when Obregón needed additional troops to secure the rail lines between Veracruz and the Bajío as well as to reinforce his army battling Pancho Villa. Neither Coss, Medina, nor Lechuga wanted to send units to help Obregón for fear that gains against the enemy would be sacrificed and that a withdrawal of forces by one officer would give an advantage to others. Moreover, Coss had little incentive to aid his old nemesis, even at one point preventing Obregón's agents from leaving the state with men and materiel.[14]

Pressure on Carranza to do something about Coss mounted. Foreigners and others peppered the government with allegations of his arbitrariness and brutality. Charges of corruption prompted Carranza to order Coss to account for his troops and all payments made to them. In Oaxaca revolutionary elements that had dealt with Coss demanded his removal before agreeing to join the Constitucionalistas. Finally, when Coss got wind that Carranza was planning to replace him, the governor publicly lashed out at his political enemies, including ones in Carranza's cabinet, and threatened to kill Luis Cabrera.[15]

Consequently, the First Chief had little choice but to sack Coss, who left office on May 4, 1915. The step was greeted with general relief. Only a few perfunctory protests from hard-core Constitucionalistas took place. Indeed, one prominent labor leader informed Carranza that he applauded Coss's ouster.[16]

Coss, bereft of public support as governor, agreed to his demotion as long as he could remain in Puebla at the head of his Second Division. When he refused, however, to send a contingent of his troops to Apizaco, Tlaxcala, to protect trains supplying Obregón, the First Chief took further action against him. Carranza stripped three brigades from Coss's division and gave them to General Abraham Cepeda. Coss made noises about rebelling, but Carranza had already neutralized the general's principal subordinate officers. Carranza's problems with rebellious governors-commanders were not isolated to Coss. A month earlier the First Chief also removed General

Máximo Rojas from the governorship of Tlaxcala, thereby leaving him with only his military command.[17]

At this point, Pablo González stepped in to mediate on Coss's behalf. In contrast to his lack of popularity as governor, Coss did enjoy a greater reputation as a soldier. Furthermore, the Constitucionalista core, made up mostly of government employees, students, workers, and others of the urban lower class came out on his behalf; they did not want him removed completely from the scene for fear of a return to power of "reactionaries." Following talks between Carranza and a delegation of officers and civilians from Puebla, González arranged for Coss to reassume his military command as long as he operated wherever the Constitucionalista leadership designated. Furthermore, to help cement his loyalty, Coss was promoted in rank to division general.[18]

Nevertheless, Coss remained unhappy. He attacked the policies of his successor, Governor Luis Cervantes. He persuaded González to shut down the Second Division's influential newspaper, *La Revolución*, and arrest its editors, who had been critical of Coss. Even more, Coss disliked headquarters' now tightened rein over his command and accused González of undermining his authority by dividing up his troops and not allowing him personally to lead them. Finally, in March 1916, once the security situation had improved, González placed the general on leave. Coss went into retirement on his hacienda in the state of Coahuila, but not content, he joined a rebellion against the government in December 1917. The effort fizzled, and Coss headed across the border where he bought a ranch near San Antonio, Texas; there he remained for the duration of the Carranza years.[19]

The Governors—Luis G. Cervantes

Luis G. Cervantes, a young looking, thin-faced, small-statured, forty-year-old lieutenant colonel and medical doctor took the oath of office as governor on May 4, 1915. Although born in Tepic, Cervantes's revolutionary experience began in Coahuila as a Maderista and municipal president of Monclova before becoming state treasurer of Tamaulipas and then Mexico City's first Constitucionalista municipal president. He arrived in Puebla in April 1915 to serve as Coss's chief of staff and private secretary.[20]

Although a newcomer to Puebla and largely ignorant of its particular situation, Cervantes did meet other criteria Carranza wanted. He was young, energetic, and loyal; his modest rank and limited title (governor only) helped temper personal aspirations for greater autonomy (à la Coss) and posed little threat to established generals in the region; he was not tainted by the internecine struggles within the state's Constitucionalista leadership; and, being educated and having administrative experience, he boasted the qualifications to undertake a reform program. Such a step was key to countering enemy measures along the same lines, thus consolidating support among the lower and middle classes and beginning the long process of institutionalizing new political and socioeconomic structures. In other words, unlike Coss, Cervantes was a builder, not a destroyer.[21] Like many Constitucionalistas from northern Mexico, Cervantes was imbued with the liberal, positivistic ideas of modernization, now infiltrated with socialism's emphasis on state intervention and class conflict as the motors of change. Cervantes set out on his mission of reform with a vengeance, eager to apply his outlook to benighted Puebla.[22]

To this point in time, modifications in the state's social and economic systems under the Carrancistas had been focused on tearing down the old. The few new initiatives undertaken had been piecemeal, authorized in part by decrees from the Constitucionalista government in Veracruz, but dictated mainly by the need to appease in order to neutralize opponents and gain recruits. Cervantes took a much more holistic approach. He shaped and implemented central government edicts to what he perceived as Puebla's needs, to the discomfort of many autonomous-minded residents, and codified de facto actions already undertaken by commanders in the field.

In the administrative realm the governor established a Junta Depuradora to purge Huertistas from government and keep track of them; restructured the civil registry; and reopened the judicial system. Economic changes included shifting the unequal tax burden from small businessmen and landholders to the wealthier population; setting up a labor office, recognizing the legal status of unions, and improving wages and conditions for workers; and establishing a local agrarian commission, distributing property to villagers, and controlling the transfer of land titles. Social measures covered several areas: amplification and codification of restrictions on the Catholic Church, including the closure of buildings and legalization of divorce; the passage of laws to eliminate illiteracy; the sponsorship of cultural events; the creation of a Junta Prebostal to enforce availability and prices of basic goods; and the appointment of a Consejo Superior de Salubridad (Superior Council of Health) to oversee public health (see Chapter 4 for detailed treatment of these policies).[23]

Ironically, however, Cervantes's policies in Puebla satisfied almost no one. Although the new governor carried on his predecessor's campaign to ferret out Huertistas in the public sector and persecute them, Constitucionalista hardliners criticized him for not being more aggressive. The lower classes benefited from tax and labor changes yet complained about the regime's moralization and propaganda campaigns and attacks against the Church. For villagers, land reform did not take place quickly enough, while insecurity in rural areas continued. Military officers, who had served under Coss, looked upon Cervantes with suspicion, others coveted his governorship, and pro-Obregón elements saw him as a lackey of rival Pablo González. The Church and conservatives as well as businesspeople and the traditional political class resented the reform program and the persecution of their members. The governor's tolerance for corruption, including that of his brother, Juan, repelled many residents. Everyone blamed Cervantes for the debilitating economic situation, including skyrocketing prices, plummeting currency values, and severe food shortages. Finally, almost no one liked the fact that an outsider held the reins of power and was imposing a non-Poblano-inspired, centralizing program on the state.[24]

As a result, Cervantes's critics circulated reports that the governor was to be removed, rumors reinforced by his known frustration in the job; he resented the lack of power and respect shown him by other high Carrancista authorities and openly expressed his dislike for the state and its people. The most persistent reports of his dismissal occurred in the fall of 1915 once a Carrancista victory seemed largely assured. People from many parts of the state urged that Colonel Eulogio Hernández, a native of Puebla and the current police chief in Mexico City, replace Cervantes.[25]

Hernández's supporters saw him as a viable candidate not only because he was a loyal Constitucionalista officer and Poblano but also because he hailed from Tlatlauqui in the Sierra. There a movement to create a new state (made up of the Sierra area of Puebla and adjoining districts in neighboring Veracruz), based on longstanding autonomous sentiment in the region, was gaining ground. Many Serranos chafed at increasing central government intervention in their traditionally isolated area, including the closing down of local governments and replacing them with military rule. The Constitucionalista commander in the region, Antonio Medina, took advantage of this sentiment by holding local elections in 1915–16 only to have Cervantes order the practice stopped. The politically ambitious Medina may have been involved in these efforts to create a new state. Therefore, Hernández, his backers claimed, was the man to halt this drift toward secession in Puebla's north.[26]

Carranza finally removed his embattled governor in April 1916. Cervantes had done his duty by purging Huertistas, curbing the Church, and establishing a legal basis for reform, but the animosity he had created, especially among Puebla's business and political classes, limited his future usefulness. Now, with security improved, a program for change in place, and the judiciary functioning, Carranza wanted to reconstitute elective government. This step, however, was a delicate one, for in order to work it needed to include the state's largely alienated middle and upper classes. Without their support, political instability would continue, the economic situation would not improve, and the legitimacy of the new state would remain in doubt. Finally, it is clear that the First Chief, himself much more a product of the ideas of nineteenth-century liberal democracy than those of twentieth-century socialist revolution, never embraced the more radical actions of many of his subordinates, including Cervantes.[27]

The Governors—Cesáreo Castro

On April 3, 1916, Carranza's third military governor in Puebla, Cesáreo Castro, assumed office. On this occasion the First Chief passed over the young radicals of his northern entourage and instead tapped a sixty-year-old moderate. Castro, physically a big man who wore a Stetson and carried a paunch, was a lawyer and divisionary general. He boasted administrative and political as well as extensive military experience. He had served as a delegate to the Maderista Antirreeleccionista (Anti-Reelectionist) convention in Mexico City in 1910, fought Huertistas and Zapatistas under Pablo González, led Obregón's cavalry against Villa in the Bajío in 1915, managed the railroad between San Luis Potosí and Tamaulipas, and headed commands at Saltillo, Mexico City, and Querétaro. Moreover, as a native of Carranza's hometown and of the same generation, Castro knew him well, and the two had much in common. The First Chief reportedly trusted Castro implicitly, so much so that he reversed policy and also named Castro military commander of the state.[28]

Governor Castro ameliorated or ended some of his two predecessors' most conflictive measures, ones that especially had aggravated relations with conservatives and the business and political classes. Religious persecution eased and churches reopened. Political prisoners gained their freedom. Exiles returned to the state. The suspended anti-Spanish labor law of October 1914 was annulled. Civilians, many with dubious revolutionary credentials, reassumed high-level state government posts. Bullfights again took place, and obligatory "popular civic concerts," with music and pro-Constitucionalista propaganda aimed at workers, stopped.[29]

In addition, the frenetic pace of reform under Cervantes slowed drastically under Castro. Indeed, a reading of the state's *Periódico Oficial* reveals only one such decree between May and December 1916. Furthermore, what initiatives Castro did take, save for a very modest land reform program, were aimed to offend almost no one: the reopening and repair of schools, the promulgation of an education law, the inauguration of a new state hospital (named after Carranza's brother, Jesús, who died at the hands of rebels in Oaxaca in January 1915), and the holding of local and state elections (see Chapter 6 for detailed treatment of these policies).[30]

Castro's status quo governorship provoked sharp criticism, especially from hard-core Constitucionalistas who wanted more change and saw his actions as a betrayal of the revolution. Direct attacks on the well-connected and powerful Castro were somewhat muted, but his government came under fire. Particularly targeted were General Secretary Marciano González and top legal consultant Felipe T. Contreras, to whom the governor gave day-to-day control. Meanwhile, Castro focused on military issues and, as he was by now well entrenched in the socioeconomic structure of the state, his personal business interests, including meat processing and pulque fermenting. One observer commented, "General Castro is all generosity with foreigners, principally Spaniards . . . [and], along with Marciano González . . . and Felipe T. Contreras, follows a policy of turning his back on the people; only getting rich interests him."[31]

Thus, González and Contreras represented the purists' nightmare, the ingratiation of Carrancista revolutionaries with Poblano pragmatists, a process similar to that already described as happening in rural areas between Constitucionalista officers and regional caciques. González, a general from Nuevo León, arrived in the state in the first wave of northern officers in August 1914 and also served for a time as Coss's general secretary, the second most powerful post in the state government. Contreras, a longtime lawyer with political ambitions (he had run for governor in 1912) and connections, had most recently been practicing his craft in Mexico City, including representing high profile clients before the Convencionista government of Roque González Garza.[32]

Now González and Contreras joined forces. They distributed posts, handed out concessions, and tolerated illegalities, ensuring that they and their families and friends benefited first and foremost. Indeed, this emerging partnership of northern Carrancistas with Poblano power brokers could hardly be represented better than by González's marriage to the daughter of Contreras. In this atmosphere of opportunistic collaboration,

Constitucionalista calls for the wholesale transformation of Puebla rang increasingly hollow.[33]

Creating Legitimacy

The Constitucionalistas' ability to implement their revolutionary program required more than military control and reform decrees. The process had to go further; to be legitimate, the new state apparatus needed the acceptance of most citizens. The effort to bring about this result consisted of three simultaneous initiatives: a propaganda campaign, the replacement of the military dictatorship with a renewed constitutional government, and a reformist socioeconomic program (for treatment of this last point see Chapter 6).

Propaganda

The Constitucionalistas realized the importance of propaganda to convince the wary populace of the virtue of their presence and value of their still partially developed program. Ultimately they hoped to gain the support of enough Poblanos to create a dominant political machine. This proselytizing effort was not just mechanically educational. Carrancista agents also played on the emotions by linking their movement to Madero and local heroes, especially Serdán, in the process creating what Thomas Benjamin calls a "collective memory" of the revolution. Indeed, one of the first actions was to organize a ceremony at the fallen revolutionary's grave. Then in February 1915, to mark the deaths of Madero and his vice president, José María Pino Suárez, a daylong commemoration took place.[34]

Newly arrived Constitucionalistas and their local minions, then, spread the good word, aiming to gain political support as well as recruits for the army. They sent delegations to Mexico City, organized town meetings and public demonstrations, and distributed and translated government decrees into native languages. They manipulated the past by removing plaques from public places that mentioned Porfirio Díaz and former Governor Mucio Martínez and by renaming streets for Madero and Serdán. Ceremonies, holidays, and monuments also honored revolutionary heroes. State and local authorities helped ensure turnouts for these occasions by declaring days free from work and forcing owners to cooperate.[35]

Initially the propaganda campaign was chaotic and haphazard. In April 1915 the movement's leadership moved to solve the problem when it established the Oficina Local de Información y Propaganda Revolucionaria Constitucionalista (Constitutionalist Revolutionary Information and Propaganda Office), an entity similar to that created in other states, such as Oaxaca. Puebla's office was placed under the leadership of longtime revolutionary Guadalupe Narváez Bautista. By selecting Narváez, the Carrancistas hoped to tap into the pro-Madero-Serdán reservoir in the state. In some ways, however, they got more than they had bargained for.[36]

In 1910, Guadalupe Narváez and her two sisters, Rosa and María, ran a school (*instituto*) in their father's middle-class Puebla City home that offered cooking, piano, sewing, and similar classes to young women. After reading Madero's book, *La sucesión presidencial en 1910* (The Presidential Succession in 1910), which criticized the Díaz dictatorship and called for free elections, they became staunch Antirreeleccionistas. Consequently, they joined the more radical Serdán wing of the movement and used the cover of their institute as a base of operations. Along with Carmen Serdán, Aquiles Serdán's sister and fellow participant in the failed November 1910 revolt, the Narváez siblings played a key role in the principal revolutionary junta that coordinated military and political activity in opposition to Díaz and Huerta. When tapped to run the information office in 1915, Guadalupe headed the Cruz Blanca Nacional Constitucionalista (National Constitucionalista White Cross) in Puebla and organized hospitals for the cause.[37]

Guadalupe Narváez energetically worked to expand and intensify the propaganda effort. She established a youth wing made up of Colegio del Estado students; she sent agents into towns and villages to persuade local officials to make speeches and teachers to perform skits on central plazas and in the public schools; she backed civic meetings for soldiers and workers and concerts for bureaucrats; she headed up holiday celebrations; she constructed public bulletin boards; she published and distributed broadsides and a newspaper, *La Hoja Constitucionalista* (The Constitutionalist Sheet); and her office produced a pictoral history of the revolution.[38]

Narváez and her followers, however, went beyond touting Constitucionalista virtues with formulaic platitudes and holding feel-good celebrations. They played the foreigner card, condemning capitalists in general and Arab and Spanish merchants in particular for profiting in scarce basic goods. They helped recruit soldiers and mobilized defense units, yet vociferously condemned military abuses and defended the right of involuntary conscripts to desert and rebel. Moreover, they pushed for worker and campesino activism, labor and land reform, help for the unemployed, the end of state and cacique control over local governments (*municipio libre*—free municipality), and freedom to join the political party of one's choice (as long as it was pro-Carrancista). They collected monies to help pay off the national debt. Narváez also kept tabs on local conditions and people, anti- and pro-Constitucionalistas alike, and reported anomalies to the governors, including Coss (whom she strongly defended), and to the First Chief. As a result, people were jailed, their properties confiscated, and in a few cases individuals even executed.[39]

In the end, Narváez and her agents proved effective in deepening the pro-Constitucionalista beliefs of the already convinced, but they had less success in converting doubters. Her office came under criticism for lavish spending in a time of extreme hardship. In addition, Narváez was a female who led an aggressive, intrusive, even radical campaign for change in a deeply conservative state. As one of her defenders put it, she and her sisters acted like "*hombres valientes*," not "*señoritas*" (like brave men, not young women).[40] Local officials and small-town residents recoiled at teams of young, idealistic, urbanized, anti-Catholic, know-it-alls entering their communities. Workers and bureaucrats, too, resisted having to listen to their patronizing, long-winded discourses on such topics as capital and labor, the financial situation, and the meaning of World War I. The traditional political and economic classes saw Narváez as the spearhead of socialism, more orthodox than the northern Carrancistas and, as a local, perceived to be even more dangerous.[41] Indeed, these attitudes may help explain why, despite all their activity, apparently neither the Narváez adherents nor their Carrancista sponsors ventured to organize feminist groups in Puebla or take other steps to open society to women as, for example, was done in Yucatán under Salvador Alvarado.[42]

Even Carrancista officials came to see Narváez as more of a liability than an asset and distanced themselves from her. Military officers resented her sharp attacks. Others in the leadership came to believe that Narváez exacerbated the fissures between themselves and the general populace (in part because of her anticlerical position) and contributed to a growing left-right split within Constitucionalista ranks. As a result, Carranza ordered radical Casa del Obrero Mundial members removed from Narváez's office. In mid-1916, Governor Castro moved to oust Narváez, but the decision was reversed, apparently upon appeals to the First Chief. Nevertheless, from this point, Narváez and her coreligionists were put on a much shorter leash.[43]

Renewed Government—Creation of a Political Party

Out of the propaganda campaign, the Carrancistas wanted to create a political party that would become a machine to dominate the electoral system. When the Constitucionalistas entered Puebla in 1914, however, the only viable as well ideologically acceptable civilian political group with which to work was the Junta Revolucionaria. Traditional politicians who tried to deal with the newcomers were rebuffed. As such, the Carrancistas looked to the junta to form the nucleus of the new party (naming several of its members to local political posts), hoping to use it to tap into the reservoir of goodwill many people felt toward the local revolutionaries of 1910.[44]

Again, however, Carranza got more than he bargained for. Radical as well as provincial, the now officially named Junta Ex-Revolucionaria Constitucionalista, determined to operate on its own terms. Many local junta members, fearing outside control, objected when in early 1915 the First Chief sent a personal emissary, Dr. Atl (Gerardo Murillo), to Puebla to incorporate the junta into a national organization run from the movement's headquarters in Veracruz. Despite its independent, local orientation, however, the junta's honeymoon with the populace dissipated, as it became identified too closely with the extremist policies of governors Coss and Cervantes.[45]

Governor Cervantes, under pressure to consolidate the Constitucionalista political structure and eliminate the better-organized Partido Católico in the state, ignored the junta's narrow base and named it the Partido Liberal Constitucionalista (Liberal Constitutionalist Party) in July 1915. The new party, however, was confined to the Puebla City area and racked by ideological and personal dissension. Its problems prompted Cervantes to postpone local elections, hoping that in time it could be built into something viable.[46]

Thus, the party lay dormant until mid-1916 when Governor Castro attempted to revive it, again in preparation for elections. He revamped the leadership, replacing radicals with moderates; the Narváez sisters, Serdán, and most of their longtime associates no longer appeared among its prominent members. Castro also organized affiliates throughout the state and sponsored rallies to boost its image. In the end, little worked as the liberals continued their infighting, and the wooing of adherents proved difficult. As a result, the door was left ajar for opponents to organize and challenge the Constitucionalistas' claim to run the state.[47]

Renewed Government—The Judiciary

The first step in the reestablishment of constitutional government was the return of the judicial system to civilian control. Governor Cervantes initiated the process in June 1915, when he opened a Ministerio Público (Public Ministry, that is, prosecutor's office) and state courts. In August he introduced trial by jury (*jurados populares*).[48]

The measures' acceptance and impact were tempered, however, by several factors. Unwilling to cede power, governors retained the right to name judges and other officials. Even when lower level tribunals opened, the chief executives continued to perform the duties of the state's superior court until it began to function in February 1917. Courts' review of a governor's decisions or complaints against the military, including appropriation of private property, was off limits. Implementation also occurred in a slow and piecemeal fashion due to military officers' reluctance to hand over authority, warfare, limited resources, and the lack of qualified personnel with acceptable political credentials. Indeed, the Constitucionalista left criticized Cervantes for naming a committee of experienced but conservative lawyers, jurists, and politicians to oversee the judiciary's recreation. Persons of this ilk, the radicals charged, also gained posts within the revamped system.[49]

Renewed Government—Elections: Local

The desire for genuinely autonomous municipal governments, free from state and particularly *jefe político* interference, harked back to the middle of the nineteenth century. Madero's calls for the end of the *jefatura política* (and implicit liberation of the municipality) came to naught on the shoals of conservative opposition, entrenched officialdom, and the need to assert control over unstable rural areas. Likewise, Huerta found the existing system too convenient to modify. Thus, the institution remained, even in San Luis Potosí, where the local Huertistas reinstated it.[50]

Finally in December 1914, Carranza, desperate to gain support for his regime, issued a decree that amended the Constitution of 1857; the edict (*municipio libre*) permitted direct and popular election of *ayuntamientos* (town governments) with no intermediate authorities between them and the state government, thus ending the *jefes políticos*. For the first time, municipalities enjoyed formal legal autonomy and direct access to the state government. With the old *jefatura política* districts abolished, however, Puebla officials now had to deal with more than 180 freely elected *ayuntamientos* with enhanced prerogatives rather than with twenty-one appointed *jefes políticos*. The structure had changed from a centralized and relatively coherent, albeit undemocratic, one into something much less wieldy and efficient and only potentially representative. At the same time this new configuration challenged state leaders as power had shifted to local authorities.[51]

The initial response to *municipio libre* among Puebla's autonomous-minded populace was generally positive. Local vested interests, many of whom did not embrace the Constitucionalistas and their appointees, pushed for new governments based on direct vote. Indeed, in some areas, in order to accommodate rising demand for local control, Carrancista officers had already begun to oust *jefes políticos* and expand municipal prerogatives. The clearest example was in the Sierra where General Antonio Medina, seeing the advantages, oversaw elections in several major communities. Army commanders exercised similar "vigilance" over local votes in Oaxaca.[52]

Constitucionalista officials at the state and federal levels quickly realized the danger in this ad hoc, grassroots approach. Coss made it known that he would not tolerate municipal presidents who challenged his decisions, and he and Cervantes refused to recognize anti-Carrancista victories. Carranza backed the postponement of elections, and the governors continued to name local officials. In unruly Mexico City, Carranza even planned to eliminate municipal autonomy altogether.[53]

Meanwhile, Carranza worried about selecting delegates to a constitutional convention. He needed loyal town governments to ensure that his candidates won the right to rewrite the nation's magna carta. To this end he annulled the whole previous *municipio libre* effort by ordering universal municipal elections for September 1916, to choose people to serve between October of that year and December 1917. In addition, he barred candidates who had taken part in anti-Constitucionalista armies or governments. Governors were to oversee the legality of the contests.[54]

At this point the division within Constitucionalista ranks openly emerged. On Carranza's behalf, Governor Castro reconstituted the Partido Liberal around a core of moderate pragmatists made up of bureaucrats such as Serdán's uncle, Baraquiel Alatriste, who used his position as head of the post office to serve as Pablo González's personal informant; politicians from the Madero era—including former governor and Partido Católico president Rafael Cañete, Felipe T. Contreras, who broke with Madero over the gubernatorial election of 1912 and then went on to have close ties to Huerta and the Convencionistas, and former revolutionary junta head Daniel Guzmán; textile workers; and army officers like Porfirio del Castillo, who headed the party. For Puebla City municipal president they backed a relative unknown and native of Jalisco, Ramón I. Guzmán, who led the local contingent of Masons and ran the official pawnshop (*monte de piedad*).[55]

The left wing of the movement bolted and formed its own party, the Partido Popular Ley (Popular Law Party). Headed by the Narváez sisters, it consisted of artisans, railroad and textile workers, students, small merchants, and middle-class radicals. They supported the better-known Leopoldo R. Galván, who had served briefly in the post the previous year as a Coss appointee.[56] In the wake of questions about the candidates' eligibility, charges of counting fraud, and the deployment of soldiers in the streets to maintain order, the official candidate, Guzmán, took Puebla City.[57] With the state capital politically secured, Governor Castro annulled elections in other towns where the results did not turn out as planned and ordered new balloting for December.[58]

Renewed Government—Elections: Constitutional Convention

Municipal elections, then, paved the way for the next step in renewing constitutional government, a convention to modify the country's constitution. The vote for delegates was set for October 22, 1916. Despite the short time (five weeks) to establish electoral machinery, including forming districts, selecting candidates, and campaigning, the balloting went off smoothly. The time factor, the lack of interest in the technical issues of rewriting a constitution, and the willingness to concede authority to the Carrancista leadership regarding an issue that seemingly had little immediate and direct state or local relevance resulted in weak opposition and low turnout. Moreover, some people claimed that Carranza and Governor Castro had determined who would win beforehand, thus only increasing the apathy. Whatever the case, Castro's people, appointed or recently elected, now held many municipalities, which facilitated the vote count in favor of Partido Liberal candidates. As a result, Liberals, despite the party's organizational problems outside of Puebla City, took ten of the eighteen delegate posts up for grabs.[59]

Whether Partido Liberal members or not, all the delegates to the Querétaro meeting were Carrancistas and reflected the growing moderate, middle-class, civilian, Poblano orientation of the movement. Professionals accounted for at least thirteen of the eighteen delegates while only two or three were peasants or workers. Although a majority were soldiers, hardly any could be considered "lifers," and two thirds of the total originally hailed from the state. Clearly Carranza and Castro had made strides in softening the policy of "northern imposition" carried out by governors Coss and Cervantes.[60]

Renewed Government—Elections: Federal

The promulgation of the new federal constitution on February 5, 1917, allowed for presidential and national congress elections. The balloting for chief executive on March 11, 1917, elicited little interest in Puebla, as Carranza's victory was a foregone conclusion. He took the state with nearly 58,000 votes compared to 1,200 for his nearest rival, Pablo González; Álvaro Obregón garnered fewer than 200 supporters.[61]

The selection of federal congressmen (eighteen deputies and two senators) on the same day aroused more attention. The contenders, all self-proclaimed liberals, were divided more by personal differences than ideology. Four different parties fielded candidates in Puebla City. The winners tended to be young, Puebla-born or longtime residents of the state, and citizen-soldiers or civilians, many of them professionals, with experience serving the Constitucionalista cause. Only seven had served in the constitutional convention. This new contingent included Carranza's secretary of the treasury, Luis Cabrera; Cholula cacique Rafael Rojas; *agrarista* José María Sánchez; former editor of the state's *Periódico Oficial* during the Maass government, Luis Sánchez Pontón; and convention holdovers Froylán Manjárrez, Porfirio del Castillo, and Daniel Guzmán.[62]

Renewed Government—Elections: State

Unlike national contests, interest in state-level balloting, especially for the governorship, had been building for months. This next step in the reestablishment of constitutional government would allow Poblanos to choose one of their own for the state's highest office for the first time since the vote for Juan Carrasco in 1912.[63] Some half dozen viable candidates participated in the June 10, 1917, contest. They divided along civilian versus military as well as regional lines, however, exposing the profound differences within the Constitucionalista movement.

Among the military several top officers, including provisional governor Cesáreo Castro, Sierra commander Antonio Medina, and even Francisco Coss, from retirement in Coahuila, coveted the office. Each lobbied Carranza for the nod, but none could overcome his preference for a nonsoldier, a stance conveniently reinforced by Puebla's constitution, which limited the permanent governorship to residents having lived in the state a minimum of five years immediately preceding the election.[64]

Not to be deterred, Castro and Medina then championed surrogates, Porfirio del Castillo and Ignacio Hermoso, respectively. Del Castillo, a colonel, was closely identified with the moderate wing of the movement. In 1915 he had served as interim governor of Tlaxcala, where his accommodating policies gained him the wrath of radicals. In 1916 he headed Puebla's Partido Liberal and attended the Querétaro convention; he was elected federal deputy in 1917.[65] Hermoso, an aging hacendado from the district of Chalchicomula, former member of the Junta Revolucionaria, and Puebla City bureaucrat, reportedly had close business ties to Medina.[66]

Then, as if two military-backed candidates representing two distinct regions, central Puebla and the Sierra, were not enough, others also joined the fray. The most important were caciques Francisco A. Gracia from the Atlixco-Huaquechula area and Juan Lechuga from Tehuacán.[67]

Several military-cacique aspirants, then, provided the civilians with a golden opportunity to rally around a single viable candidate. A search began for a native Poblano who had not been dirtied in local politics, which led to Pastor Rouaix. Born in Tehuacán and an engineer, Rouaix had served as Carrancista governor of Durango in 1913–14. There he proved to be a strong progressive, having promulgated the first state agrarian law, and no lackey of the generals. He also had played a key role in the Querétaro convention, backing land and labor reform. At the time of the election he was federal minister of development (*fomento*). With extensive administrative and technical experience, especially in agrarian matters, and a background as a pragmatic moderate who enjoyed widespread support in rural and urban Puebla, he seemed the ideal candidate. Nevertheless, Rouaix did not meet the five-year residency requirement. This impediment probably could have been overlooked, but in addition, the president denied Rouaix's request to quit the cabinet.[68]

Instead, Carranza backed Alfonso Cabrera, a medical doctor from Zacatlán. As a federal deputy, Cabrera had been part of the pro-Maderista renewal bloc (*bloque renovador*) until Huerta closed the congress in October 1913. Most recently he had served as director of medical and health services for the Constitucionalista army and delegate to the Querétaro convention.[69]

Why did Carranza pick Cabrera over the more qualified and known Rouaix? The president may have been unable to spare Rouaix from his cabinet. Moreover, he may have been too radical, given his prolabor and agrarian reform views. Also, the fact that Alfonso Cabrera's brother Luis was Carranza's treasury secretary and perhaps his closest confidant had much to do with the choice. In addition, the Cabreras hailed from the Sierra, and it appears that Carranza calculated that Alfonso Cabrera could more easily gain support in the strategic and volatile area than Rouaix could. If elected, Cabrera would help check not only the rising political aspirations of General Medina but also the movement to carve a separate state, some planned to call it Zempoala, out of the region, an effort that Medina backed and Cabrera opposed. The issue recently had gained renewed urgency by being broached at the Querétaro convention. Carranza hardly wanted the divisive and dangerous specter of regional fragmentation headed by renegade army officers and local caciques to be legitimized. Moreover, he faced the same thorny issue in other regions of the country such as the Huasteca, just to the north of the Sierra, where locals wanted to create a new entity from Hidalgo, San Luis Potosí, and Veracruz.[70]

Whatever Carranza's motives in selecting Cabrera, his action fit a pattern of imposing safe, known people as state chief executive. In Campeche, for example, military governor Joaquín Mucel, who had served since 1914, was "elected" for another two years. In Michoacán, the First Chief blocked radical Francisco J. Múgica in favor of Pascual Ortíz Rubio, who would go on to become president in 1930. In Querétaro, Carranza's brother-in-law, General Emilio Salinas, was appointed governor in early 1917 and then oversaw the "popular" election of Ernesto Perusquía three months later.[71]

Cabrera carried out an effective campaign, making use of federal government political and financial support as well as that of the new Mexico City daily, *El Universal*. He traveled throughout the state, making himself known and voicing general yet appealing promises to a war-weary and economically prostrate populace, calling for agricultural and industrial development, increased educational opportunities, and self-determination for towns. Furthermore, he exploited the weaknesses of his divided, military-backed opponents and emphasized his lack of any connection to the army.[72] In the end, despite the use of troops to intimidate voters and tabulators, Cabrera won every district except Cholula (no vote was held in Chiautla because of the Zapatistas).[73] He received some 52,000 of the 85,000 ballots cast; the two principal military-sponsored candidates, del Castillo and Hermoso, came in second and third respectively, garnering 9,000 to 10,000 votes each.[74]

On the same day, balloting also took place for deputies to the unicameral state legislature. Although the documentation is thin, it appears that most of the twenty-two seats were actively contested. The most controversial race occurred in Puebla City's second district, for which thirteen candidates vied. With the backing of workers, students, and teachers, Gilberto Bosques beat the establishment's candidate, Joaquín Ibáñez, despite Alfonso Cabrera's attempts to manipulate the count. Once elected, Cabrera tried to induce Bosques to drop his radical, pro-labor and peasant stance. When the schoolteacher from Chiautla refused, Cabrera then attempted to have Bosques disqualified by the legislature's credentials committee. Bosques prevailed, thanks to popular support and a connection to Carranza.[75]

Convencionistas

Government in the Convencionista-held areas of Puebla functioned differently than that of the Constitucionalistas. On paper there existed a three-tier, national-state-local governmental hierarchy, like their adversaries had, but for all intents and purposes the state level never worked and the national level disappeared in all but name after less than a year. This situation resulted in a highly decentralized system, which emphasized the power and influence of municipal governments and caciques. Representative of rural and small-town society and popular among campesinos and even many landholders, both of whom distrusted strong, centralized, modernizing government, this arrangement, based on autonomy and localism, exacerbated disunity. Over the longer run this lack of translocal political vision and cohesion undermined the Convencionistas' ability to meet the Constitucionalista challenge.

The one major effort to create a Convencionista government in Puebla proved a disaster, leaving no one running the state. When in December 1914, President Eulalio Gutiérrez named Sierra cacique Esteban Márquez governor, with the capital in Huauchinango, Convencionistas in other parts of the state, largely Zapatistas, objected. Claiming that Márquez had not been selected according to the Plan de Ayala, the Southerners held a meeting in Puebla City, presided over by Eufemio Zapata and other high officials of the movement from Morelos. In it they defied the president and Márquez and chose Francisco Salgado, a relatively obscure officer, as chief executive.[76]

When chosen governor, Salgado was in Convencionista-held Mexico City and showed no signs of wanting to relocate to Puebla. The state capital was under a Constitucionalista counterattack and, anyway, he would have faced a cool reception, given his imposition by the Morelos Zapatistas. Puebla City soon fell to the Carrancistas, and Salgado remained outside the state with his Zapatista patrons. As late as May 1915 he was issuing statements as governor from Cuautla, Morelos, but they meant little. By remaining there, he posed no threat to the high Zapatista officials who controlled him or to Zapatista-allied caciques in Puebla, who wanted free rein from headquarters.[77]

Meanwhile, Márquez, now harboring an anti-Zapatista outlook, remained in the Sierra. There he continued to lay claim to the governorship, even though President Gutiérrez's fall from power in January 1915 negated any real possibility of the Serrano gaining the state's highest office. Finally in May, Márquez gave up his bid to be chief executive when he recognized the Convencionista central government of Roque González Garza in return for a payoff of money and arms.[78]

Even over the longer run, as local Poblano commanders chafed under rule from Morelos, they failed to find enough common ground to establish a state government.[79] As a result, rule in Convencionista-held areas of Puebla became locally based, with the occasional nod given by Márquez to the national Convencionista government and by the southern caciques to Zapata in Morelos. The state remained divided politically on a north-south basis; Márquez had almost nothing to do with Zapatista-allied commanders, save for Domingo Arenas, who had his own difficulties with neighboring caciques and Morelos headquarters.

The structure and nature of local government in Convencionista Puebla varied greatly depending on revolutionary circumstances, officials' leadership, and the reception given to outside initiatives. Most governments were ad hoc affairs, depending on informal networks of village-based kin and friends (note the many siblings who shared leadership posts), especially in the most conflicted areas. In the Sierra, for example, Esteban Márquez, his brothers, and other family and trusted neighbors ran the movement as they saw fit. They appointed local officials, judged people, delivered goods and services, taxed, and in other ways carried out the duties of government without recourse to formal democratic structures. Domingo and Cirilo Arenas operated little differently in their bailiwick in the west. The ex-Federals, Aguilar and Almazán, also utilized a similar, personalized governing mechanism in the areas that they held.[80]

In the core Zapatista region of the southwest, however, a greater semblance of political order and procedure existed. There the direct influence of Zapatista headquarters circumscribed, at least to a degree, traditional practices and resulted in the creation of a more formalized, impersonal (albeit not necessarily more democratic) means of governing. Not to be outdone by Constitucionalista calls for *municipio libre*, Zapata first ordered the election of local governments, which were to be free in terms of internal administration and finances. He underlined this goal by introducing the plebiscite.[81]

Zapata then went further, imposing his own ideas of local government. He called for Juntas de Reformas Revolucionarias (Revolutionary Reform Juntas), composed of the municipal president and six other literate individuals chosen by townspeople. Each junta was to be responsible for a range of issues, including land and labor disputes, law enforcement, statistics, unemployment, and propaganda. Next he outlined a judicial system. He then established regulations detailing the conduct and responsibilities of authorities regarding public services and security, particularly in relation to the army, which depended upon the villages for its survival.[82]

Finally, he set up what amounted to a parallel government, controlled from Morelos headquarters and designed to watch over local officials, the Asociaciones Defensoras de los Principios Revolucionarios (Associations for the Defense of Revolutionary Principles). These groups served as branches of the Zapatista party in each community. Its members were to work with but not to impede the functioning of regular civil and military authorities. The first association was formed in Tochimilco in November 1916.[83]

In other words, Zapata, like his Constitucionalista counterparts, wanted to establish a centralized means to coordinate and control villages, an objective he found difficult to achieve. Ironically, the mere attempt contravened one of the most fundamental bonds between him and the people, local autonomy. As a result, having to support troops from elsewhere, suffering intrusive commissions that judged a community's loyalty, and being forced to relocate into larger and more easily managed towns upset many citizens. As time passed, large numbers of residents saw the Zapatista presence, just as they viewed the Carrancistas, as an imposition from the outside. This growing lack of differentiation between the two sides made it easier to withdraw one's political support or even to switch loyalties to the more powerful Carrancistas.[84]

The Constitucionalista political program started off aggressively and arbitrarily, designed as much to destroy and punish as to build and reward. The drawbacks of this policy soon became apparent, and Carranza replaced Governor Francisco Coss with Luis Cervantes. The latter brought greater predictability and began the systematic implementation of a reform program, yet still proved unable to gain the support of suspicious, if not alienated, Poblanos. They had already seen enough of the Constitucionalistas' modus operandi and wanted little to do with it. Increasingly concerned about the situation in the state and anxious to have his regime's power consolidated there before the writing of a constitution and the holding of elections, Carranza then turned to his old confidant-in-arms, Cesáreo Castro. Castro's more conservative approach as chief executive, although not universally embraced, proved more successful; he created a party apparatus, reopened the judiciary, and oversaw balloting, important steps in creating legitimacy, a political culture, and the building of a new state.

Ironically, however, much of Castro's achievement was based on the fact that he had begun to ingratiate himself with the very elements in Puebla that questioned, if not the revolution itself (although many did), certainly how it was being carried out. Indeed, under Castro, Puebla's traditional political class once again partially revived. They faced disappointment, however, in the demise of Pastor Rouaix as gubernatorial candidate and reluctantly backed Carranza's favorite, Alfonso Cabrera. At this juncture it seems, there was a lost opportunity to create a "progressive consensus," a reformist, moderate, middle-class-led movement that could have expanded the opportunities of the lower classes without the creation of an overbearing state, a situation similar to that described by Peter Henderson in reference to the Francisco León de la Barra interim presidency of 1911. Here, too, a look at Yucatán is instructive. General Salvador Alvarado's rule from 1915 until 1918 was firm, yet moderate, à la Castro. Aided by monies from henequen production, he managed to create a viable, cross-class, reformist coalition until Carranza, wary of Alvarado's rising star, removed him from the state. Alfonso Cabrera lacked the skill, however, to build such an alliance, a fact that would hurt the state. Nevertheless, Puebla did have the opportunity to choose a governor, something not all states enjoyed. Chiapas, for example, remained in the control of military governors until Carranza's overthrow in 1920.[85]

Meanwhile, in the Convencionista camp, battlefield setbacks and internal factionalism meant that any pretensions of establishing a national or even statewide political apparatus faded after 1915. Consequently, politics, as its adherents preferred, became exceedingly local, although generally disorganized and subject to the whim of each group's leadership. Only in the core Zapatista area of the southwest of the state was there any degree of coherency to government.

The Poblanos had generally welcomed the political initiatives of Governor Castro, as they held out the possibility of a return to political control in the hands of locals. Between 1914 and 1917, simultaneously with the creation of new governing institutions, the Constitucionalistas began to implement a revolutionary program to overhaul the state's economy and society. Change in these areas, especially those measures imposed from above by an interventionist, centralizing government, however, came under much closer scrutiny and provoked resistance.

6

ECONOMIC AND SOCIAL POLICY
1914–1917

The successful construction of a revolutionary state also depended on the purging of the old socioeconomic order and its replacement by a new one. Here, as with their political program, the Constitucionalistas had a more comprehensive idea than the Convencionistas had of what they wanted. This vision included equalizing the tax burden, stimulating business and industry, reforming labor and land policies, improving education, and muzzling the Church. The more rural-based, lower-class Convencionistas, at least implicitly, embraced many of these same goals, although industry and labor were less important, while land was more so, and they differed completely over the Church.

Nevertheless, the importance was not so much the difference in programs, but how they were to be carried out and with what goals. Constitucionalistas envisioned a centralizing, outward-looking state undertaking change in order to prod Puebla into the modern world. Convencionistas saw autonomous, locally controlled communities carrying out reform with the goal of reinforcing traditional patterns of life.

In the end, however, neither side's program was effectively implemented. Before structural change could take place, people had to be provided with the basics of life in a time of acute disruption. In addition, Poblanos resented outsiders, mostly the Carrancistas, telling them how to run their affairs.

Constitucionalistas

Finances and Taxes

The Constitucionalistas, in their effort to finance government, faced many of the same issues as their Huertista predecessors had. Now, however, the armies were larger, the warfare more intense, the destruction greater, the economy more inert, and the tax base smaller. Furthermore, the Carrancistas had committed themselves not just to shifting the tax burden from the poor to the rich but also to making improvements in daily life. Beyond the rhetoric, however, it was incumbent upon the regime, at a minimum, to keep paychecks and materiel flowing to soldiers and bureaucrats. These two groups formed the linchpins of the effort to win the war and reestablish viable government, which in turn would enable the carrying out of additional reforms and create legitimacy. Nevertheless, given the extraordinary circumstances between mid-1914 and mid-1915, there hardly existed any official financial structure, particularly outside the largest towns. Besides the impediments of rebel-controlled territory, destruction, and lost production there also existed fluctuating currency values; destroyed records; corrupt, incompetent, and disloyal personnel; and generalized resistance to paying taxes.[1]

Governor Coss raised taxes on alcohol and voided state contracts with the previous regime, but he offered neither any systematic policy nor a way to revive the financial structure. No budget existed, and local commanders and officials arbitrarily collected and dispersed monies for immediate needs. Few public services beyond security were provided. Indeed, the system perhaps can best be described as predatory; witness, for example, the state's confiscation of properties of alleged enemies, properties which were then occupied, rented, and sold for the benefit of those in power. This Carrancista practice also occurred in other states such as Chiapas, Oaxaca, and San Luis Potosí, and resulted in the coining of a new, widely used term, *carrancear*, meaning to sack, pillage, confiscate, rob.[2]

Cervantes became the first governor methodically to deal with finances. To avoid some of the earlier pitfalls of state budgeting, Carranza forbade governors to hand out exemptions from state or municipal taxes or to borrow money without federal government approval. Also, to avoid international repercussions, the First Chief ordered that foreign capitalists such as the Couttolence and Díaz Rubín families be treated civilly.[3]

To get a handle on income and outlays and reduce the estimated 700,000-peso current-year deficit, Cervantes established a budget, the first since 1913, for the last four months of 1915.[4] The new financial plan and other initiatives reflected his strategy to increase revenues by collecting additional monies from large, established economic interests while lowering imposts on marginal groups. As for property taxes, holdings were revalued, cadastral records updated, exemptions ended, and levies increased. Imposts were also raised on business but not before much bargaining. Furthermore, everyone now had to pay in metal or paper at current (depreciated), not nominal, value.

At the same time, Cervantes kept his promise to shift the tax burden by exempting levies on merchants, save for those who sold alcohol, whose working capital was less than fifty pesos. He also forgave back taxes on owners of less than 500 pesos worth of real property if they registered their holdings.[5]

Governor Castro, like Cervantes, continued to make modest gains in the financial sphere. He raised taxes when politically feasible and paid special attention to undervalued properties, including those of the Church. The recalculation of some 680 holdings in Puebla City and the district of Chalchicomula, alone, for example, netted the state a tidy sum given that the real estate was worth some 14 million pesos. Castro also raised state workers' salaries, paid them more regularly, and reorganized and upgraded the treasury.[6]

Furthermore, Castro dealt with the plight of municipal governments whose recently gained political freedom meant little given their bankrupt condition. In response to demands for financial autonomy and to reduce the headache that economically nonfunctioning towns posed to the state, he urged local officials to draw up budgets (subject to state approval). He then turned over to them 50 percent of property taxes collected on rural holdings valued at less than 1,000 pesos, a not altogether generous act, however, since most towns were heavily in debt to the state. The governor also loaned additional monies to localities for paying teachers, which, along with providing for jail inmates, composed most communities' greatest financial burden.[7]

Currency

The destruction and insecurity caused by warfare were only the most obvious causes of falling production and consumption. Next to establishing peace, the government's highest priorities to right the economy were stabilizing the monetary system and gaining control over the communication and transportation network. Problems with currency, well advanced by the fall of the Huerta regime, worsened. The peso devalued between 1913 and 1916 from 2.07 to 23.82 to one United States dollar. In 1916 the government recognized twenty-one different types of paper currency. No one trusted this medium of exchange. Severe penalties for holding enemy-issued money exacerbated the situation. Consequently, the run on coins, especially those of small value, accelerated, both for daily transactions and for speculation.[8]

The resulting scarcity of an acceptable medium of exchange hobbled commerce, led to ad hoc solutions, and forced the acceptance of dubious paper currency. In the Sierra, for example, cacique Juan Francisco Lucas minted his own coins. In Tehuacán, merchants issued chits backed by a deposit in a local bank. Many people resorted to barter. Similar informal measures also took place in other states such as San Luis Potosí.[9]

Abuse and counterfeiting also became commonplace. Shopkeepers and even banks refused to accept paper money. Merchants raised prices based on the gold exchange rate rather then actual inflation. Still others denied customers change thus obligating them to buy unwanted goods. Mills paid in depreciated, large-value bills, sometimes requiring two or three workers to share one note. Speculators, called *coyotes*, aiming to drive down even further the value of Constitucionalista paper, spread rumors of its worthlessness; then with hoarded metal and at low prices they bought the bills that they in turn used to purchase material goods at an artificial discount.[10]

By mid-1915 some observers warned of social upheaval as the lower and middle classes became pauperized. A person who had earned 100 pesos per month in silver during the first half of 1913 received the equivalent of fourteen pesos by mid-1916; at the same time, prices for all basic goods and services had multiplied several fold.[11] Frustrated, officials blamed their enemies for the crisis.[12] In Puebla the Banco Oriental, with its close ties to the Spanish community, came under attack. By defying a September 1915 federal banking law that restricted the counting of reserves, a step taken to boost paper currency's value by limiting money in circulation, the bank provided the government an excuse to revoke its charter of emission.[13]

Then in the spring of 1916 federal authorities issued so-called unfalsefiable notes (*infalsificables*). Despite their being difficult to reproduce, the new bills initially backed by metal reserves and issued at a ratio of ten old pesos for each unfalsefiable, barely slowed down the plummeting currency. By November each new peso's worth had slipped from twenty cents gold to one cent as the money supply continued to expand to pay debts and field the army.[14]

Finally, in September 1916 the government canceled the concessions of all banks of emission. In Puebla, federal agents closed the Banco Oriental, arrested its managers, and began liquidating its assets. They sent its reserves to Mexico City where Carranza planned to establish a single bank of emission.[15]

Communication and Transportation

Along with regulating currency, gaining control over and rebuilding the communication and transportation system proved key to the Carrancistas' objective of stabilizing, no less modernizing the economy. After 1914, all aspects of the system suffered from insecurity and violence. Bandits and revolutionaries alike cut and stole message-carrying copper wire, robbed travelers of their goods, and destroyed vehicles for personal gain while striking a blow against the enemy's infrastructure and economy.

No part of this system, however, was as important and as victimized as the railroad, the lifeline of the country. Several routes passed through Puebla and neighboring Tlaxcala, connecting the national capital to southeastern Mexico, including the port of Veracruz. Not only did much armed conflict occur along these lines but they also became targets of sabotage. Direct attacks on trains became a specialty of both Convencionistas and independents (at times it was difficult to distinguish the two groups), especially after 1915 when many weakened Convencionista fighting units resorted to guerrilla tactics. As a result, major sections of the network remained closed for weeks and months while general maintenance was neglected. Trips that normally may have taken several hours now often took days or even longer or were cancelled.[16]

Dealing with security, although difficult, was straightforward. The railroads sent out scout trains, placed soldiers and armored cars on runs, varied schedules and routes, cancelled night trips, and built a series of guardhouses along the most vulnerable sections. The more problematic issue was what to do about Constitucionalista officers and their cacique allies who controlled the lines and rolling stock (also a problem in San Luis Potosí). They not only used the system for military purposes, thus impeding the transport of nonbelligerent goods, but also operated it as their personal fiefdom, carrying products for private gain and "taxing" anyone else who wished to use it. In fall 1915 businessmen were paying as much as 3,000 pesos in bribes per freight car or locomotive.[17]

In 1915 to deal with the problem, Carranza appointed Alberto J. Pani, an engineer and civilian, director general of the Ferrocarriles Nacionales de México (National Railroads of Mexico). Pani made only modest progress in his challenge to the military. The estimated 325 passenger cars still occupied for living purposes by army officers in October 1916, for example, could have doubled the total of people carried by the entire system.[18] In Puebla, Pilar Sánchez's entourage occupied seven of these carriages, including one for women, while he used others to transport his prized fighting bulls. Additional officers, such as Francisco Barbosa, Juan Lechuga, Antonio Medina, and Pedro Villaseñor, also monopolized wagons and rails, making tidy sums for their efforts.[19] Control of the railroad remained a problem to the end of the Carrrancista period.

Business and Industry

The military and economic situation between 1914 and 1917 provided a poor climate for the development of business and industry. Only the most optimistic, or foolhardy, entrepreneur invested his money in Puebla in those years. Nevertheless, the breakdown of the socioeconomic and political orders provided opportunities for illicit activity, including bribery, black market operations, smuggling, speculation, and theft. For some people these endeavors meant the difference between starvation and survival; still others, less needy, made fortunes.

For the legitimate businessman, arbitrary, changing, and conflicting government policy made conditions worse. This situation not only further destabilized the economy and evoked the business community's wrath but also reflected division within the Constitucionalista movement. Carranza, although no unconditional champion of the capitalist class, understood the need to tolerate monied groups willing to help rebuild the country. Military officers and their cacique allies, however, sought to expand their armed might and political base by appealing to the lower and wage-earning portions of the middle classes. Consequently, they implemented populist, redistributive policies aimed also at punishing business and industry for their support of Huerta. Furthermore, soldiers commonly took advantage of the situation to establish their own economic ventures, thus competing with local entrepreneurs. As a result, the president and his mainly civilian advisors found themselves trying not only to mollify ungrateful capitalists but also to circumscribe the military's oftentimes more radical and in many cases self-serving program.

This tension can be seen in the textile sector. The security situation during fall 1914 and winter 1915 was so desperate that not only could the First Chief do little to aid the industry but he also had to give the military a free rein. As such, the army failed to prevent the sacking and burning of more than half of the state's forty mills in November 1914; the attacks, blamed on anti-Constitucionalista elements, included Carrancista contingents. Owners and managers closed their factories and fled to safety. General Coss allegedly told one industrialist that he (Coss) not only had no troops to protect his mill but also was pleased about its destruction because the owner had not supported Coss for governor. For months the industry remained moribund.[20]

Although still difficult, the industry's relationship with state authorities improved after Coss left office in May 1915. Neither Cervantes nor Castro liked the owners' demanding attitude and threats to close factories, thus potentially ending tax payments and throwing thousands of mill hands on the street. The governors in turn vowed to confiscate plants and run them in conjunction with workers, but this was rarely done. In reality, the state needed the industrialists to restore the economy, ensure social peace, and finance the government because it lacked the wherewithal to run the industry itself.[21]

With Carranza's intervention and an improving security situation, the governors and owners managed to salvage the industry from its nadir of 1914–15. Focused efforts, prompted in part by workers' appeals to save their jobs, gradually helped plants to resume production and avoided any subsequent major shutdown of the industry. Carranza purchased and distributed the La Laguna cotton crop, agents went to Veracruz to oversee shipments to Puebla, the state offered factories short-term loans, and both sides compromised over taxes.[22] By May 1917 forty of the fifty-four mills in the Puebla-Tlaxcala region were operating. Nevertheless, production remained two-thirds below that of 1912, and the cost to produce 100 kilograms of cloth had risen by 60 percent since 1913. Indeed, the CIM claimed, it was now cheaper to import cloth from the United States.[23]

Labor

How to deal with urban labor posed a dilemma for the Constitucionalistas. Tens of thousands of people worked in the 70-kilometer-long industrial corridor from Tlaxcala City through San Martín Texmelucan to Puebla City and on to Atlixco. As military recruits they proved critical to the war effort. Moreover, their support was needed to keep the economy functioning. For their backing, they demanded jobs, security, and currency stability, as well as better salaries and working conditions. For the regime, the first three issues posed less difficulty as capital and labor agreed on them. For example, workers backed owners in pressing the government to provide raw cotton for the mills in order to keep them open. Furthermore, attacks on factories by antiregime elements and bandits prompted mill hands to join their bosses to protect workplaces.[24]

Improvements in pay and conditions, however, divided the two groups. The issue once again illustrates the differences within the Constitucionalistas between the more moderate, civilian-dominated, federal government and the more radical, military-political leadership in the field. Concerned about the economy and the creation of a viable political order as well as the war, Carranza and his advisors attempted to walk a fine line between owners and their workers; his commanders took a narrower perspective, focusing on building support for their military needs and personal gain, often at capital's expense.[25]

Hence, Carrancista military officers favored workers with decrees, the most far-reaching taking place in Veracruz and Yucatán. In Puebla, Pablo González established an eight-hour workday and a minimum daily wage of eighty centavos for all laborers, rural and urban. Incensed, businessmen ignored the threat of arrest and marched on the state government palace in protest. Textile industrialists feared these unilateral steps would undermine the 1912 tripartite pact signed under Madero, lead to chaos in their relations with labor, and put them at a disadvantage with other producers, as the edict applied only to Puebla and Tlaxcala.[26]

Backed by Carranza and the Departamento de Trabajo, industrialists forced González and Governor Coss to compromise. The new minimum remained (most textile factory hands already earned more, as the 1912 accord established a 1.25 peso daily salary for the industry), but the workday would be nine hours (down from the standard ten) at nine-hours' pay, thus disappointing many workers who wanted an eight-hour day at ten-hours' pay. Carranza agreed to call a national meeting to hammer out a new accord for the entire industry, not just for Puebla's. The gathering, however, fell victim to the mounting violence and mill closings of late 1914–15; thus, the issue remained unresolved.[27]

Meanwhile, Carranza sought to ensure worker loyalty to the federal government, rather than to commanders in the field. He sent Dr. Atl to Puebla to establish a branch of the Casa del Obrero Mundial and gain worker support for the army. Governor Coss, who wanted to control the Casa himself, opposed Atl. The First Chief also raised mill hands' wages by 35 percent, cognizant of the fact that such a move would gain workers' favor yet have little immediate repercussion on the industry given currency depreciation, the fact that few plants were operating, and the ability to pass on prices. Nevertheless, when Pablo González soon after upped salaries by another 25 percent, Carranza was angered by his general's unauthorized action.[28]

Once rid of Coss, Carranza further cemented his relations to the state's moderate working majority by sponsoring official unions. In the textile sector the Departamento de Trabajo and Governor Cervantes formed so-called Agrupaciones de Resistencia (Resistance Groups), later named Unión de Resistencia (Resistance Union) at the factory level with a coordinating body (*mesa central*) in Puebla City. This development, taken with the tacit authorization of the CIM, marked the first step in meeting labor's demand to organize and bargain legally. Moreover, it provided Puebla's mostly pragmatic, economically oriented workers an alternative to the more radical Casa del Obrero Mundial. Indeed, to see that the Casa would not prosper, the regime harassed its members.[29]

Similar wage hikes and organizational backing followed for employees of the Compañía de Tranvías, Luz y Fuerza, which controlled the capital city's streetcar and power systems and the hydroelectric generating complex at Necaxa in the Sierra. At Necaxa, General Antonio Medina backed the Casa del Obrero Mundial's attempt to organize workers, a development Carranza wanted to prevent.[30] Another important constituency, shop attendants and service workers also received attention. Cervantes doubled their salaries, imposed the eight-hour day, and, to solve the longstanding "Sunday off" issue, decreed the Sabbath labor free unless owners paid extra.[31]

Then in September 1915, Cervantes and the Departamento de Trabajo established a state-level labor department called the Oficina Técnica de Trabajo (Technical Labor Office). It was followed in December by a tribunal, designed to receive workers' complaints. Cervantes also said that once an implementation study was completed, he would recognize the legal status of unions, something that had already taken place in Yucatán, for example. Owners reluctantly tolerated these steps as their appeals to the federal level over specific decisions generally ended in more favorable rulings for themselves.[32]

Finally, additional pay raises of between 150 and 235 percent (totaling 300 percent over the 1912 base for textile workers) were squeezed out of industry and business in December 1915 and January 1916. Threatened by a general strike among mill hands and transportation workers and pressured by Governor Cervantes, the owners grudgingly conceded, calculating that depreciation and price hikes would minimize the impact on their profits. Furthermore, capital considered higher wages a small price to pay as long as they were not forced legally to recognize the increasingly active government-sponsored union movement, thus preventing it from gaining exclusive bargaining rights and a monopolistic voice in the work place.[33]

After this point, reform slowed even while labor's situation continued to deteriorate. With military recruits from workers' ranks less of a priority and the Casa del Obrero Mundial checkmated, regime officials focused on other issues. The appointment of a more conservative governor, Cesáreo Castro, and the repression of the streetcar workers' movement in Mexico

City in mid-1916 underlined this trend. Reports of inadequate diets, disease, and increasing theft in mills reflected unemployment, scarcity of basic goods, rising prices, and collapse of the currency system.[34]

By October 1916 conditions had reached the point that additional pay raises in *infalsificables*, totaling 500 percent over the 1912 base for mill hands, failed to quell discontent. Workers rejected the nearly valueless currency and demanded to be compensated in gold or its equivalent. Federal authorities authorized such a basis for payment, but Governor Castro failed to work out an agreement between owners and labor. The impasse ended in a series of strikes, which severely hurt the economy, and Carranza ultimately was forced to intercede on the workers' behalf. Like in Puebla, currency issues also fueled much of the discontent among Mexico City workers during 1916.[35]

The promulgation of the new federal constitution in February 1917 with its prolabor Article 123 (which Carranza opposed) again raised the issue of laborers' rights. The article first, however, had to be implemented via legislation. As such, mill hands called for a convention of all workers and owners; they wanted to modify the 1912 accords and use the resulting product as the basis for a law reflecting the new article.

Pastor Rouaix, Carranza's development secretary, an author of Article 123 and aspiring Puebla gubernatorial candidate, took up the demand. He even suggested that industrialists pay their employees to attend a conference. Carranza, under pressure from owners and concerned that such a gathering would be taken over by radicals, intervened. He vetoed plans for a national meeting and instructed his governors to organize labor-management talks at the state level. The president also nixed Rouaix's ambition to head his native Puebla.[36]

Puebla's owners agreed to meet with workers only after Carranza, who wanted the labor issue solved before his May 1917 inauguration, threatened to take over mills. After hard bargaining, they raised the 1912 daily minimum wage of 1.25 pesos by 40 percent (45 percent for piece work) and settled on an eight-hour day. Nevertheless, the hike hardly made up for the increased cost of living, which was three times that of 1912.[37]

When the mill hands broached the subject of giving formal legal status to their organization, the Unión de Resistencia, however, both Governor Castro and the industrialists refused and broke off the talks. In reaction, the workers struck all forty-four mills in the state. By this time, Castro had become so discredited among labor that Carranza resorted to Tlaxcalan governor Daniel Ríos Zertuche and that state's military commander, General Máximo Rojas, to mediate the conflict. The ten-day strike ended only after

Castro and the CIM finally agreed to deal with the Unión and help come up with a state-level accord implementing Article 123.[38]

Property and Land

By controlling real estate, the Carrancistas had two basic goals. The first objective was political and economic, the punishment of enemies through confiscation and the use of appropriated property to finance the movement. The second was political and social, the distribution of land to those without to gain adherents and improve their well-being through the distribution of wealth.

Upon entering the state the Carrancistas plundered and expropriated. Many officers became minimagnates, living in fine houses, driving motorcars and fancy carriages, and ruling expanses of land with numerous workers. Almost no one of means, including the Church, remained immune from their avarice. Indeed, confiscated property formed the basis of wealth for Carrancistas elsewhere, too, as Falcón details for San Luis Potosí general and governor, Juan Barragán.[39]

The movement's leadership quickly realized the perils of this practice. In September 1914, Pablo González ordered that property be taken only upon written consent and that a Junta Interventora de Bienes (Committee for Confiscated Property) be established. It was to investigate owners, take over and run or sell holdings, and deliver the proceeds to the state, thus bolstering government coffers and reducing officers' gain.[40]

Nevertheless, abuses continued. Governor Coss, for example, took over a hacienda without authorization thus jeopardizing its bean crop, which had been contracted for delivery to Carrancista forces in the field.[41] When reports of abuse and corruption within the Junta Interventora became too credible to ignore, Carranza ordered that all intervened properties in the state be turned over to the federal government. This provoked a showdown with Governor Cervantes, who wanted the holdings' income for Puebla. Cervantes soon thereafter was removed from office.[42] Ironically, his replacement, Cesáreo Castro, already held a hacienda near Huejotzingo, which had been taken from Oaxacan archbishop Eulogio Gillow in August 1914.[43]

Meanwhile, owners sought to protect their interests. One method was to transfer titles to a third party. The regime outlawed this practice, because it hid enemies' holdings. It also played into the hands of foreigners, who used both their unofficial immunity to act as third parties and their access to hard currency to buy up real estate from indebted landowners on the cheap. Although not the only expatriate to do this, United States entrepreneur William Jenkins was probably the most successful, becoming a multimillionaire (in dollars).[44] The propertied class also made deals with well-placed Carrancista officers and their cacique allies. Finally, owners placed pressure on Carranza to moderate his land policy, which, given the deteriorating economic situation and the First Chief's preference for private holdings, resulted in their return beginning in September 1915. By mid-1917 nearly all owners not directly connected to the previous regime had regained their properties.[45]

Land reform quickly became a pressing issue, particularly in the central and southern regions of the state where latifundia predominated. Demand for change from below and the need to gain rural support in the face of the enemy's military threat and own agrarian-reform program forced the Constitucionalistas to act. Local commanders took the initiative, handing out so-called provisional military distributions to villagers, thus adding to their ranks and building up their political bases.[46]

To regularize and control the process, Carranza ordered cadastral surveys.[47] Then, he issued his watershed January 6, 1915, law. It authorized the restitution (return of land previously held) or dotation (grant of new land) of parcels to communities, through expropriation of private holdings, if necessary. Governors or military commanders were to establish local-level committees, which would petition state and national agrarian commissions for approval.

Instead of regularizing the process, however, this step accelerated invasions of haciendas and disputes among villages over land and water.[48] For several months, however, little could be done about the situation due to war. Finally, in June 1915, Governor Cervantes established a local (that is, state) agrarian commission, which the following September began to oversee the first nonmilitary distribution of parcels under the Carrancistas.[49]

Nevertheless, a myriad of difficulties plagued the reform program and kept the Carrancista record between 1915 and 1917 extremely modest. Conflicts erupted among peasants over longstanding claims and in the Sierra, Indians and mestizos clashed. Hacendados sought military protection and appealed to politicians. Officers and local and state authorities, including the governors, ignored procedure and made deals with owners and peasants alike. The bureaucratized process took time and money, which few campesinos had, and reflected the regime's preference for private property as well as the desire to minimize economic dislocation. Finally, the lack of resources and warfare both played a role.[50] Meanwhile, officers and their cacique allies further entrenched themselves as arbiters in and beneficiaries of this complex and ever shifting matrix of conflict, playing campesinos against landowners as well as against each other.

Indeed, although complete figures are not available, more land probably was distributed outside the state-administered program than within it. Peasants continued to invade neighboring properties and local commanders issued titles. Domingo Arenas, for example, distributed land both before and after switching to the Carrancista side in December 1916, with barely a nod to Convencionista or Constitucionalista dicta. In some cases, owners, under pressure from peasants and wanting to avoid the uncertainty of dealing with the government or military, made private arrangements, renting or selling land to campesinos, a practice also common in Oaxaca and Querétaro.[51]

Cervantes' government said it handled 277 requests for parcels between May and December 1915 and made distributions in twelve of the state's twenty-one districts. Castro reported 195 petitions between April 1916 and July 1917. Of these, twenty-one (from eight districts) were approved by the state commission and sent on to the national level for final disposition. Later the Secretaría de Agricultura (Agriculture Secretariat) reported much lower figures for the period 1915 to mid-1917: approximately 137 total petitions from villages, and of them twenty-eight approvals (31,500 hectares) at the state level, and seven or eight final concessions (4,400 hectares) granted by the nation. These statistics point out at least two major flaws in the Constitucionalista reform program. The exaggerated proclamations of state and local officials raised expectations among peasants, who were only to be disillusioned by the long, drawn-out approval process, leaving them in most cases with, at best, legally challengeable provisional titles.[52]

Food and Other Basics

Perhaps the most pressing social issue facing the Carrancistas between 1914 and 1917 in urban Puebla and elsewhere, including Chihuahua, Michoacán, Querétaro, and San Luis Potosí, was ensuring that there existed adequate supplies of food and other basics at affordable prices. State and local efforts to deal with the issue established precedents for future direct government intervention in daily economic life.[53]

The causes of scarcity were several. Warfare resulted in damage, theft, and dispersion of planted fields, irrigation systems, seed, equipment, buildings, and livestock. Employees abandoned farms. Owners suspended investments. Additional security measures and the lack of an organized infrastructure, such as access to markets, raised costs, and impeded distribution. The railroad suffered both damage and attack. Urban areas found it difficult to provide for the influx of refugees from the countryside.

People misused what production existed. For example, seed required for the following planting season was consumed. Corn needed for humans was instead used for starch or alcohol or fed to livestock, including soldiers' horses. Thefts of scarce foodstuffs abounded. Moreover, anyone with the wherewithal hoarded grains and speculated on their price.

Government interference in the grain market undercut production and disrupted distribution. Price lids and restrictions on shipments beyond localities or the state, where effective, discouraged investment and encouraged smuggling. Nevertheless, when grain was exported with government authorization, not only out of its locale of origin and out of the state but in some cases even out of the country, shortages arose in given areas. Available food often first went to soldiers and bureaucrats before the general public, and it was also used to induce men to join the army. The railroad was mandated to transport soldiers before basic goods, while officers charged "taxes" to use the system.

Finally, weather, too, became a factor. Drought in 1914 and again in 1915, as well as unusually cold temperatures the latter year, damaged the corn crop; especially affected in 1915 were central and eastern Puebla, the principal grain growing regions of the state.[54]

Falling production and distribution problems already had begun to reach a critical point by mid-1914, prompting Huertista governor Hernández to monitor prices, prosecute greedy merchants, and subsidize sales to the poor. As conditions deteriorated, Governor Coss took harsher and more comprehensive steps, ones that brought conflict with capitalists and the First Chief. He blocked exports from the state, ordered idle holdings into production, banned nonessential uses of grain, and set prices. In addition, he forced delivery to the state of foodstuffs at 10 percent over cost to be distributed to the poor. He also sponsored street demonstrations to condemn hoarders and speculators, particularly the landowning and merchant Spanish community.[55]

Reports abounded that Constitucionalista officers, including Coss, profited from the crisis. The governor, his brother Antonio, and several others controlled goods sold to and confiscated by the state and profited on their resale. Coss was also linked to a larger network, which included Agustín Diez, a Spanish merchant, and Silvestre Aguilar, brother of Veracruz governor and general Cándido Aguilar. They specialized in cattle, grain, and flour gained by forced sale or theft and transported from Puebla to the neighboring state via the Interoceánico Railroad.[56] In Veracruz prices jumped because of the demand generated by the headquartering of the federal government and army there and overseas exporting of grains through the port to obtain hard currency. Indeed, by August 1915, price disparities for corn reached levels of ten to one from one region of the country to another.[57]

Carranza might have overlooked Coss's personal gains, but he could not tolerate his harsh, arbitrary, anti–free market actions; they jeopardized shipments of supplies to troops (which particularly incensed Obregón) and cities and ran counter to the First Chief's policy of gaining merchants' and producers' support, as well as to his belief about how to right the economy. Moreover, Coss's scapegoating of foreigners risked an international confrontation. Consequently, Carranza ordered an end to his governor's practices.[58]

Under Governors Cervantes and Castro the effort to deal with the food crisis became much more systematized. However, strong, state government actions, dictated by the gravity of the situation, continued to bring Puebla officials into conflict with Carranza and the private sector. Cervantes created a Junta Prebostal (Administrative Junta) with far-reaching economic and police powers. It inspected warehouses and companies' books, fixed prices, set profits, redistributed goods among sales outlets, required merchants to save seed for the next year's planting, and controlled shipments. The Junta also obtained grain in other states and set up kitchens to feed the poor.[59]

Cervantes defended the Junta to Carranza, saying the problem was not one of a lack of food but of hoarders and speculators, especially Spaniards, who opposed the government and impeded its operations. He urged the First Chief to reduce prices for basic goods in Veracruz or quintuple salaries in Puebla so that its residents could purchase grains made scarce and expensive by their shipment to more lucrative markets. Carranza responded that the solution to the problem lay not in regulating trade but in free markets and, joined by producers and merchants, put pressure on the governor to end restrictions on commerce.[60]

Meanwhile, a sense of desperation arose as Puebla, normally a grain-surplus state, faced deficits. Scattered reports of severe hunger circulated and the fear of attacks on bakeries and warehouses spread. Labor unions scoured the countryside for foodstuffs, while businessmen with hacendado connections arranged for goods to be sent to their employees. The Instituto Metodista took up collections to buy basics from the United States to distribute to the needy.[61]

Smaller towns as well as rural areas, heretofore less affected by the crisis, began to experience shortages. In some areas, people consumed immature crops. In Tehuacán the export of grains to neighboring Oaxaca, facilitated by General Villaseñor, pitted civil and military elites against each other. In Teziutlán, where the influx of refugees placed a heavy burden on the town, authorities replicated the state's example by setting up a committee to oversee the market. District and municipal officials, in a demonstration of local autonomy, resisted the state's exercise of power to feed Puebla City just as the state authorities opposed the national government's effort to supply Veracruz and Mexico City.[62]

Finally, Carranza ordered the elimination of the Prebostal over Cervantes's objections.[63] Determined not to cede all control of the market to the private sector, however, Cervantes turned around and created another public entity, Almacenes Generales (General Stores), to purchase and sell grains at affordable prices to the needy and government workers. Almacenes not only bought goods directly from producers but also required peasants who had benefited from land distribution, as well as hacendados, to deliver a certain percentage of their crops to local and state governments. Like his predecessor, Cervantes also allegedly took advantage of his position to profit from the crisis.[64]

Hence, Puebla would simply have to wait for the worst of the food crisis to pass. By late 1915 the widespread disruption and destruction due to fighting had eased, and that fall's corn harvest, although estimated to be only one quarter to one half of normal for the region, alleviated some of the immediate pressure. As for the poor, the state-run Almacenes partially succeeded in making basics available at below private-sector prices.[65] Nevertheless, Cervantes and then Castro would have to deal with the problems of seasonal shortages and high costs for at least two more years.

Other Social Welfare Services

Beyond foodstuffs and other basics, the state also faced the challenge of providing several other essential services. In general, this effort was haphazard, limited in resources, and confined to Puebla City and its environs. Also, in this process, the state demonstrated a moralistic tone and interventionist streak, actions not to the liking of all Poblanos.

On the medical front, the Constitucionalistas established a Cruz Blanca, as opposed to cooperating with the traditional Cruz Roja (Red Cross), which was felt to be too closely linked to the Convencionistas. They also created a nursing corps headed by Carmen Serdán and the Narváez sisters. A new state hospital was built and named after the First Chief's brother, Jesús Carranza. Pharmacies came under stricter control, and physicians were required to be licensed. Finally, Governor Cervantes established a Consejo de Salubridad (Health Council); it disbanded, however, in November 1916 due to a lack of funds.[66]

Closely linked to the care of the sick and wounded were public sanitary measures, as gastrointestinal problems from contaminated food and water and contagious disease killed large numbers of people. Nevertheless, the crackdown on adulterated products and control of epidemics made little headway. Merchants ignored government edicts, and military barracks served as breeding grounds for microbes, which were quickly spread by the movement of civilian and soldier alike.[67]

Typhus, always a threat during the dry season, hit Puebla City especially hard in the fall and winter of 1915–16; some 2,000 people died. To combat the scourge, a special police unit was created. It inspected homes and even arrested the unkempt, forcibly cutting their hair and making them strip and wash in special bathhouses. Officials encouraged residents to report on their neighbors' cleanliness. Similar measures in the port of Veracruz during these years, including the demolition of housing, led residents to refer to the "sanitation dictatorship."[68]

The state also did what it could for the needy. The lucky or politically connected, such as Serdán's widow, received pensions, albeit small and erratically paid. A hacienda was divided up among war victims' relatives. Abandoned children, at times numbering in the hundreds, were collected off the street and sent to the orphanage. Money for the jobless was channeled through labor unions, while others found work on public projects. The La Paz textile factory, taken over by the state when its owners refused to keep it operating at a loss, provided a living for several hundred individuals; they produced cloth that the state sold at reduced prices to the poor and used in its social-welfare complex, the Beneficencia. There were never enough resources to fund these efforts, however, and much of the money and material were private-sector donations.[69] Nevertheless, Puebla City can be considered fortunate compared to Querétaro. There, the Carrancista army swelled the floating population by 40,000. Officials turned the entire community into a "hospital," treating thousands of sick and wounded soldiers from the front, and in the process provoked an outbreak of cholera.[70]

Finally, similar to the Maderistas, officials took steps to "clean up" the state in a moral and visual sense. These actions, based primarily on a middle- and upper-class Victorian outlook, a Mexican rendition of North American progressivism, reflected a combination of revolutionary certitude, self-righteousness, and prudishness. Cantinas and *pulquerías* (where pulque was sold) were strictly controlled and closed. Government employees faced dismissal for patronizing bars, brothels, and casinos, or appearing drunk and using foul language or obscene gestures in public. Authorities banned bull and cock fights. Rosa Narváez, to prevent women from becoming prostitutes, proposed to establish a combined factory and school in which they could sew and study to improve themselves. Beggars, deemed eyesores and a nuisance, were fed and dressed or run off the streets.[71]

Not all Poblanos approved of this activist, interventionist state, no matter how well intentioned its actions. The lower classes resented curbs on such activities as drinking and gambling, a fact also noted for Yucatán. Even the middle class disliked being coerced into cleaning in front of their houses or businesses in the name of public sanitation. Nearly everyone accused officials of arbitrarily implementing the law and pocketing monies collected from fines.[72]

Education

Education faced many of the same difficulties as the social welfare system, resulting in limited gains. For lack of resources and security, schools at the elementary and secondary levels, particularly in rural areas, opened only sporadically if at all between 1914 and 1917. Even Puebla City, which received the greatest funding and attention, suspended classes for several months in 1915–16 due to a typhus epidemic.[73]

Carrancista governors attempted to increase state control over and modernize the haphazard system, all with the aim of creating more productive and loyal citizens of the new revolutionary state. At the primary level, municipal and private schools adopted state-mandated curricula, which emphasized a secular outlook and "practical" subjects. A federal initiative required military instruction for male and nursing classes for female students. The state loaned monies to municipalities to open classrooms, raised salaries for personnel, and ordered normal-school professors to teach in rural areas, where soldiers generally earned more than instructors. Adults who completed courses received food as rewards, and subscriptions to *La Mujer Moderna* (The Modern Woman), a magazine edited by the revolutionary feminist Hermila Galindo, were provided to female teachers.[74]

The most ambitious measure was a literacy campaign initiated by Governor Cervantes in January 1916. He decreed that all citizens aged ten years and older would have to know how to read and write by the end of August. Those people who failed were to be jailed and forced to study six hours daily; if the fault could be traced to municipalities or private employers, they were to be fined and forced to pay their citizens or employees to learn. The law accomplished little; 80 percent of the state's population remained illiterate, including 30 percent that did not speak Spanish. Nevertheless, it antagonized those who saw it as another Carrancista-backed intrusion into local affairs and personal lives. In this way and others it appears (direct comparisons are difficult) that Puebla did not have nearly the success of Yucatán. There, for example, Salvador Alvarado created 1,000 new schools, most in rural areas, and hired so many teachers that they rivaled the number of soldiers. Nevertheless, Puebla did not fall into the difficulties of Michoacán. There, the policy of *municipio libre* was interpreted to mean that towns had all responsibility for primary education, which resulted in most schools closing.[75]

Finally, at the high school and university levels, state officials played a more openly political role, realizing the importance of students' support. Nevertheless, Coss's heavy-handed purging of the Colegio del Estado and Escuela Normal (Normal School) of suspect personnel, for which he received much criticism, proved momentarily counterproductive. In time, however, Cervantes ameliorated the situation by finding acceptable replacements for the professorate, building student housing, and backing the Bloc de Estudiantes (Student Bloc). Operating under the aegis of Guadalupe Narváez's propaganda office, it played an important role in carrying the Constitucionalista program to rural areas.[76]

The Church

Anticlericalism ran deeply in the Carrancistas. They saw the Catholic Church as both a rival for the populace's loyalty and an impediment to the creation of a progressive, productive society. This secular, liberal outlook was only reinforced by the Church's support for Huerta and elites in general as well as its ties to the Zapatistas. Indeed, the thought went, without control over the Church, the revolutionary program would be greatly jeopardized. In Puebla, however, they found a people steeped in Catholic culture; people who, even if not active practitioners, recoiled at the drastic actions taken against traditions of respect and practice, a way of life that nearly all considered natural and good, if not sacrosanct.[77]

Again, as he had in other areas, Coss took a harsh stance against the Church. He sacked, burned, and closed houses of worship and other ecclesiastical institutions, using many for barracks, stables, and warehouses. Horses were decorated with sacred vestments. He ordered that confessionals be burned for firewood and held public ceremonies in the cathedral's atrium where "bandits" were executed. He arrested clerics, some of whom were shot. Among those incarcerated were the head of the Universidad Católica, Enrique Sánchez Paredes. Archbishop Ramón Ibarra y González went underground, spending most of the time in Mexico City, before dying while in hiding in early 1917. The archbishop of Oaxaca, Eulogio Gillow, a Puebla native and influential hacendado, fled into exile, living in Los Angeles and New York and only returning in 1921 once Álvaro Obregón became president.[78]

Coss continued by forbidding confession, confiscating all property owned by the Church or its personnel, and secularizing its schools' curricula. He attempted to establish a progovernment, schismatic church, but found no religious official to cooperate. At one point even Obregón, widely known for his anti-Church outlook, felt compelled to stop Coss from expelling all clerics from the state. Coss's detractors labeled him "*comecuras*" or "priest eater."[79]

Human remains, love letters, jewels, and other evidence reportedly found in underground chambers led to wild claims that clerics had been practicing the occult, conducting illicit relationships with women of high Poblano society, and hiding ill-gotten riches. Other officials more credibly charged that priests, at least at the village level, actively backed the Arenistas and Zapatistas. The Southerners' favorable treatment of the Church while holding Puebla City in December 1914 and the carrying of religious symbols into battle supported this view. These allegations contributed to a "clerophobia" among regime officials and its adherents.[80]

Cervantes, albeit less crudely, continued to place pressure on the Church and use it as a political whipping boy. The governor, never happy in Puebla, called the state "*fanático*" (fanatical) and said that despite his dislike for the place he would remain just to oversee the destruction of the Partido Católico. He restricted mass to two hours daily, rented out churches to the highest bidder, encouraged civil marriages, and permitted divorce. When a group of clerics refused to adhere to his regulations, he had them jailed.[81] Such actions were repeated in many states including Oaxaca, Querétaro, San Luis Potosí, and Veracruz.[82]

Large numbers of Poblanos disliked this treatment of the Church. Delegations, many of them largely composed of females, protested to the governors and Carranza. At the Soledad church in Puebla City, neighborhood women attacked soldiers who tried to remove a statue of the virgin. The growing strength of the Catholic Party in 1915–16 also reflected this sentiment. In Querétaro and Yucatán, too, groups, including campesinos and their wives, protested against Carrancista anticlerical policies.[83]

Finally, with the institutional Church on the defensive and no longer willing to sustain parishioners' backlash, Carranza changed policy. Within days of taking power in April 1916, Governor Castro began allowing mass. Church bells rang in the state capital for the first time in a year and a half. Moreover, the governor returned intervened properties to priests.[84]

Nevertheless, Church-state relations continued to be difficult. In Tetela, anti- and pro-clerical factions clashed in the wake of the February 1917 death of cacique Juan Francisco Lucas, a staunch liberal who had kept the local cathedral shuttered. Castro intervened and opened the church. In Tehuacán, parishioners unhappy with the appointment of Spanish priests forced the municipal president to remove the outsiders and replace them with Mexicans. Furthermore, the government continued its program of converting religious buildings into schools, libraries, gymnasiums, and other public institutions. Indeed, the Church "problem" had only begun, bedeviling the state for another two decades.[85]

Convencionistas

Compared to the much more ambitious and complex socioeconomic program of the Constitucionalistas, that of the Convencionistas was modest in aim and scope. Like their basic governmental structure, it was decentralized, loosely coordinated, and locally focused. On occasion the central government issued decrees or provided material or money, but local commanders, caciques, and village officials mostly operated on their own. Only in the core Zapatista area of southwestern Puebla can one detect any systematic policy, one that emanated from headquarters in neighboring Morelos, however, not from the national Convencionista leadership. Policy focused on several fundamental issues: financing the army and town government, overseeing a medium of exchange, distributing land, ensuring the availability of basic goods, and maintaining schools.

Monies to feed and house troops and their animals as well as pay for local government came from imposts on merchants and property owners, fees for licenses and services, and special war levies. As funds were insufficient and many people lacked cash or held worthless currency, they often fulfilled their obligations in the form of goods and labor, such as carrying material for the army or mail for the postal system. Moreover, adult males served in local security forces. Residents of newly captured towns commonly made their initial payment via forced "loans" and the looting of their properties.[86]

Because the army took precedent, basic public services, rudimentary in normal times, virtually came to a halt. Schools closed, prisoners were freed, and corpses remained unburied. Many villages ceased to exist in any formal or functional sense; some were completely or partially abandoned as their residents migrated, voluntarily or otherwise, to more propitious climes.[87]

The major exception to this scenario was in the larger towns of the Zapatista core zone. This remote and well-defended area, which enjoyed a degree of security and stability during 1915–16, reflected Zapata's efforts to systematize government within his domain. In Acatlán and Chiautla, for example, city fathers consulted with Zapatista headquarters about local issues. They managed to preserve a minimum of civic coherence in their communities, albeit with the imposition of extra taxes and the reduction of services. Even so, one is talking about monthly budgetary expenditures in the range of only 300 to 500 pesos per town.[88]

Another economic issue was currency. As it did in Constitucionalista Puebla, the constant fall in the value of paper money and the lack of coins impeded local commerce and tax payments. Furthermore, contrary to popular perception, many rural areas under Convencionista control were neither self-sufficient in foodstuffs nor in manufactured goods. Therefore, they had to go without or deal with merchants in Carrancista-held areas. This factor in turn necessitated dealing in the enemy's currency.[89]

Policy toward this problem was haphazard and contradictory. Both Márquez and Zapata produced their own metal coins, but the amount failed to meet demand. Merchants and town officials resorted to the use of chits to facilitate local commerce, but they were good only within a circumscribed area. Neither form of money, of course, was acceptable in Constitucionalista zones.[90]

For those without access to metal, then, Constitucionalista paper became the de facto currency of Convencionista Puebla. Under pressure from businessmen and soldiers who held the notes, the Convencionista government in 1915 countered Zapata's order and decreed its forced circulation. Although enemy bills were to be revalidated, the process was never fully carried out. Besides, some people, especially merchants and individuals living in disputed areas, preferred unstamped paper, which could be used in Carrancista zones. As a result, confusion reigned. Finally in 1916, Zapata decreed an end to the use of Constitucionalista bills and the production of his own paper money, but the cost, falling value, and lack of popular acceptance proved insurmountable. In the end the Convencionista economy remained dependent on its opponent's currency.[91]

The Convencionistas' overwhelmingly rural, traditional base of support is nowhere so evident as in its labor policy. Despite the large number of industrial workers in the state, they received little attention. Indeed, it seemed as if the Convencionistas wanted purposefully to alienate them. Starting in November 1914, nearly every textile mill in the state came under Convencionista attack. In January 1915, with control of the state capital and surrounding region at stake and the Carrancistas heavily recruiting among Puebla's proletariat, Zapatistas sacked Puebla's largest factory, Metepec, located just outside Atlixco, the state's second-largest industrial center. Two thousand people lost jobs. When the owners complained to Manuel Palafox, the Zapatista minister of agriculture, he threatened to burn the plant. Consequently, several thousand laborers in neighboring factories needed little additional incentive either to remain neutral or join the enemy. Ironically, the Atlixco region as a whole tended to be pro-Zapatista, yet without the support of mill hands, the Southerners never managed to get a firm grip on it.[92] A similar pattern can be seen regarding the railroad. Here again relentless and brutal Convencionista attacks drove its employees and passengers into the Carrancistas' ranks. This failure to recruit industrial labor played a key role in the outcome of the war.

Much more attention, however, was paid to the rural sector, particularly its demand for land. Under pressure from below by villagers and from without by Carrancista initiatives, the Zapatistas expanded and systematized their reform program. A September 1914 decree updated the 1911 Plan de Ayala by allowing for the nationalization of enemies' property. Then the Convencionista government established an agriculture secretariat headed by Zapatista stalwart and Puebla native Manuel Palafox. He sent engineers to Morelos and Puebla to aid communities in recovering lost holdings. Additional decrees followed in 1916 and 1917, including one that established village commissions to deal with agrarian matters.[93]

These initiatives benefited lower classes. Dolores Damián, for example, distributed parcels in the Tehuitzingo-Tepexi area, while Domingo Arenas, Fortino Ayaquica, and Francisco A. Gracia did the same around Texmelucan, Tochimilco, and Coatzingo, respectively.[94] In the Matamoros valley, peasants took advantage of owners' absence to switch production from sugar cane and other commercial crops to basics, thus boosting availability of foodstuffs for self-consumption and sale in local markets. Neighbors of the

Atencingo hacienda tapped into its water supply, thereby gaining victory in a decades-long dispute over the valuable resource. In the Texmelucan valley, Harry Evans and his wife Rosalie managed to hold on to their hacienda but lost everything that could not be nailed down to local villagers who interpreted revolutionary measures as a license to steal.[95]

Nevertheless, the picture of a nascent agrarian paradise in Morelos and areas in adjacent states controlled by the Zapatistas as described by Womack, existed, if at all, in only a small area of Puebla.[96] Furthermore, Adolfo Gilly's portrayal of a revolutionary-cum-socialistic peasantry in the making hardly fits Zapatista Puebla either.[97] Unlike its neighbor, Puebla was a much larger and more complex state and the Convencionistas, including the Zapatistas, within it reflected that fact. In the Sierra, Márquez championed local autonomy; land, better apportioned than in the south, was not the major issue. Ex-Federals such as Aguilar, Almazán, and Argumedo found much of their support among middle- and large-scale landholders who opposed any reform program. They also garnered support from villagers along the eastern periphery of the state where, again, land shortage was not the major problem, and modern, commercial agriculture had not undermined traditional patron-client relationships.[98]

Even within the Zapatista zone of the south and west, the agrarian program faced variation and difficulties. Local commanders and officials often went their own way, ignoring or interpreting orders to fit area needs or personal agendas. Domingo Arenas's radical project of establishing agricultural colonies led to attempts on his life. His example threatened other caciques, many of whom had ambitions to use land reform to convert themselves into budding hacendados and businessmen. Furthermore, the Zapatista leadership opposed Arenas's actions; it wanted a more orderly change designed to preserve tax-paying, commercial crop-producing latifundia upon which the movement depended for cash. In this vein, during all 1915 the only lands to be touched in the Tehuitzingo area by Dolores Damián were those of former governor Mucio Martínez, despite peasants' calls for wider distribution. Acatlán cacique Ricardo Reyes Márquez, by controlling the local judge, made sure that both the well-to-do and campesinos gained property. Furthermore, once Reyes Márquez switched sides to the Carrancistas in fall 1915, he suppressed agrarian commissions in villages. Towns commonly quarreled over boundaries and resources, a situation made worse by colonial-era maps that failed to reflect present-day realities. In some cases, peasants who made their own arrangements with haciendas did not want Zapatista interference; others found officials resistant to carving up latifundia. On occasion, longtime hacienda residents objected to sharing with landless neighbors.[99]

Although the Convencionista agrarian program, by promoting the raising of basic crops, added to the quantity of foodstuffs available for local consumption, this fact could not fully compensate for shortages caused by warfare between 1914 and 1917. Resources, adequate in normal times, could not withstand the destruction of crops, labor deficits, distribution problems, hoarding and speculation, and especially the obligation to field an army. To compound the problem, Reyes Márquez, for example, appropriated foodstuffs from smaller communities such as Tehuitzingo, sending the products to feed prisoners and townspeople in the principal population center of his *cacicazgo*, Acatlán. Other agents bought up crops to be sent to Morelos and even to Zapatista-held Mexico City. Prohibitions on trade with Carrancista-held areas, in the name of depriving the enemy, exacerbated deficits and encouraged smuggling. Renegade soldiers and organized thieves preyed off the populace. Refugees swelled already overburdened towns. Here, again, villages mostly had to face this challenge on their own.[100]

As a result, hunger, disease, and insecurity became a daily fact of life. Villagers resorted to barter and combed the countryside for what they could find to eat. Local authorities imposed price lids, ferreted out hoarders, restricted exports, and warned against the consumption of seed grain or draft animals needed to plant the next year's crop. Armed squads guarded communities from foragers, bandits, and even Convencionista troops. In the Sierra, Márquez ordered the execution of criminals and saboteurs. Commanders on both sides looked the other way as needed goods flowed back and forth across enemy lines.[101]

Finally, with an eye to the future and the idea that previous regimes purposefully had shortchanged rural children, Convencionista officials turned to basic education. They understood that a literate populace was essential for the success of even a traditional, communal, agricultural economy and society. Zapatista headquarters issued its first education decree in fall 1915, but it was not until early 1917 that conditions allowed for any systematic effort to open schools on a regular basis. At this point an office of public instruction was established. It ordered municipal presidents to draw up budgets, hire teachers, prepare classrooms, persuade parents to send their children, and appoint committees to oversee the process and make detailed reports.[102]

Despite this effort, most village schools remained closed between 1914 and 1918, particularly outside of the Zapatista core area. Insecurity, finances, the lack of teachers, epidemics, and general apathy all played a role. Even when classrooms opened, such as in the Tochimilco area where residents' support was considered strong, attendance remained low, highly irregular, and limited to boys. Furthermore, the instruction was of dubious quality.[103]

By mid-1917 the development and implementation of a revolutionary socioeconomic program remained a work in progress. Each faction, Constitucionalista and Convencionista (or perhaps better put, its component groups), sought to gain public support and, therefore, legitimacy through this process. The Carrancista version was the more ambitious, emphasizing, just as for the political system, change via a centralized governing structure to modernize and open Puebla to the outside world. Their initiatives included shifting the tax burden to those most able to pay, creating a central bank, undertaking labor reform, initiating land-tenure improvements with the aim of creating and helping small, entrepreneurial farmers, updating the educational system, and reducing the influence of the Church. The various Convencionista groups, generally isolated in their rural bailiwicks, also understood the need for change, particularly in relation to those issues that impacted them directly, such as education, land, and taxes. Nevertheless, their goal was a conservative one, with reforms to be undertaken by local initiative and designed to strengthen traditional patterns of life.

For both groups, but especially the Constitucionalistas with their more comprehensive and complex goals, these programs proved difficult to accomplish. Warfare and its attendant problems precluded systematic changes until 1916–17, and even then most energy and resources remained focused on providing daily necessities and services, not undertaking grand initiatives. Even so, Governor Cervantes found little support among most moderate and conservative Poblanos, the very people to whom the Carrancistas had to appeal to gain the legitimacy needed to make their revolution work. These people deeply resented the arbitrary and destructive role of Francisco Coss, wanting instead stability and predictability and local control over what change took place, not wholesale innovations imposed from the outside. Thus, the First Chief began to move away from his movement's more radical premises and named as governor Cesáreo Castro, whose mandate was to carry out a more accommodating program. His moderate, inclusive policy brought some results and perhaps had the potential to be even more successful, as was Salvador Alvarado's governorship in Yucatán. Unlike Alvarado, however, Castro followed two unpopular governors, who had poisoned the waters, and he held office for only a little over a year. As with the reconstruction of the political system, then, both the Constitucionalistas and locals found themselves making compromises and creating a political culture in the process of building a new state. The Convencionistas, increasingly marginalized from the central debate of state building, exercised only an indirect influence over these developments.[104]

III

CARRANCISMO

7

POLITICS, 1917–1920

The spring of 1917 marked a watershed in the state-building process, the beginning of the so-called constitutional period. The Carrancistas had won the war, promulgated a new federal magna carta, and established an elected national government, which Venustiano Carranza led, having traded in his military hat for that of president. It looked like the northern Mexican version of the revolution was now truly on the road to success. Now all that had to be done was to ensure that governing institutions were created and political support consolidated at the state level in order to be able to complete the carrying out of the revolutionary program.

In Puebla, too, the reestablishment of formal governmental institutions under the control of the Constitucionalistas had largely been achieved by mid-1917. The judiciary was reorganized, elections held, and local government reconstituted. The remaining tasks were the inauguration of recently chosen governor Alfonso Cabrera and the promulgation of a new state constitution.

The consolidation of public support for the regime, Cabrera's responsibility, proved more elusive. Making his job particularly difficult was the fact that the Constitucionalista coalition had begun to unravel, dividing into factions based on geography (between Poblanos and outsiders as well as among regions within the state), ideology, class, and status (civilian versus military). Apparent by 1917, these differences only deepened, thanks in large part to Cabrera's ineptness. Thus, as the governor's political control weakened, disillusioned pro-Carrancista groups as well as longtime opponents of the revolution began to coalesce into an effective, broad-based opposition leavened by army officers.

The Governorship of Alfonso Cabrera

Alfonso Cabrera had all the requisite attributes to successfully lead the Constitucionalistas in Puebla when he took office on July 20, 1917. The thirty-three-year-old hailed from the state (Zacatlán), came from a modest yet respectable family (father was a baker), was well educated (medical doctor), boasted solid revolutionary credentials (backed Madero, jailed by Huerta, and worked for Carranza), had political experience (organized state Partido Antirreeleccionista and federal congressman), and enjoyed access to the national government (brother Luis served in Carranza's cabinet).[1]

Further consideration of the new governor, however, reveals both a set of circumstances and personal traits that greatly reduced his effectiveness. For many Poblanos, especially the elites who lived in Puebla City, the dapper, mustachioed Cabrera was an inexperienced outsider from the state's north with uncomfortably close ties to Mexico City. Indeed, politicians from central Puebla, jealous of their prerogatives, had been competing with the Mexico City-Sierra axis since the mid-nineteenth century.

To the federal military, the most powerful entity in the state, Cabrera was anathema. He represented the civilian faction of the Carrancista coalition, headed by his despised brother Luis. Soldiers hated Luis Cabrera for his openly antimilitary outlook and financial policies as secretary of the treasury, which negatively impacted their (as well as others') pay. Alfonso Cabrera had also criticized the army and run against its candidates during his victorious 1917 gubernatorial campaign. Furthermore, everyone knew that Carranza ideally wanted his new governor to assert greater control over officers who, with the collaboration of their cacique allies and state and local-level authorities, had begun to entrench themselves into the political and economic fabric of the state, thus reinforcing long-held autonomous tendencies. As a result, torn between his civilian and military advisers, Carranza wavered in his backing of his governor. Thus, Cabrera never felt he received the support and credit he deserved in taking on the army. This situation caused tension between him and the president and weakened Cabrera.[2]

Without the full backing of the state's political class, opposed by the military, and lacking unequivocal support from Mexico City, Cabrera entered office with a fragile and shallow governing base. His absence from the state in recent years, save for his home region of the Sierra, meant that he had not developed ties to other groups or areas. Although labor, students, and to some degree campesinos initially championed him, many soon changed their outlook. Conservatives in general, including the Church and business community, also distanced themselves from the new chief executive.[3]

As a result, Cabrera's administration rested on a narrow combination of hard-core Carrancista "insiders," epitomized by the Narváez sisters (who, after being marginalized by former Governor Castro, regained positions of influence under Cabrera); public employees; a handful of caciques and their backers, such as the Blanca clan in Cholula and Gabriel Barrios in the Sierra; friends and relatives, including brother Ángel and nephews Plinio and Salustio; and police and regional forces. Although Cabrera was considered relatively honest, he used personal ties and monetary and political leverage to gain people's loyalty. Family members filled key posts; the Narváez sisters held the contract to feed prisoners in the Puebla City jail; Barrios received shipments of arms and money; and public workers, required to pledge fealty to the state constitution and scrutinized for political deviation, ultimately owed their jobs to the chief executive.[4]

Furthermore, Cabrera's inexperience and intolerant and dictatorial temperament only exacerbated an already difficult situation. He lacked the ability of knowing when to compromise and deal, a necessary skill in the shark-infested political waters of Puebla. Instead, he saw politics as a zero-sum game in which opponents were to be eliminated, not co-opted. His closest advisors, hard-liners such as the attorney general, Julio Mitchell, and the general secretary, Miguel Moto, reinforced this attitude.[5]

Cabrera misjudged the people of his native state. Many were willing to accommodate the central government if ceded some degree of prerogative and control over state and local affairs, as they had demonstrated with former Governor Cesáreo Castro. Instead, Cabrera pushed them into outright opposition and into the hands of his true enemies, the federal military. Indeed, within months of Cabrera's taking office, it became clear that the objective of widening and deepening the Constitucionalista movement's base and creating a unified revolutionary political machine had come to naught. Over the longer run this development would have repercussions for Puebla as Cabrera boosted the military and fractionalized the political system, a situation that would plague the state in the 1920s.

Propaganda and Control

To enhance his political base and assert control over the state, Cabrera resorted to methods already employed by his predecessors, including propaganda, press manipulation, the promotion of nationalism, and the expansion of security forces under his aegis.

Cabrera first set out to educate the populace, especially the popular classes (*clases populares*) as the newspaper *La Prensa* (The Press) put it, to identify with the state and build its legitimacy. The governor augmented the annual calendar of civic celebrations begun by earlier regimes, thereby linking the past with the present in the effort to create a collective memory essential for establishing social control. They now included November 18–20—Revolution; February 5—Constitution; February 22—Madero and Pino Suárez's deaths; and, in a personal twist, August 21—death of Cabrera's brothers, Rafael and Ramón. Teachers and authorities were ordered to commemorate these days and to instruct their pupils and the citizenry in general about their significance.[6]

Officials made sure that the capital carried out especially elaborate festivities, while other municipalities did the best they could given limited resources. Activities included parades made up of soldiers, civic groups, school children, and bands, as well as speeches, fireworks, theater, poetry, and baseball games, all topped off by the national anthem, with the governor, other dignitaries, and special guests in attendance. Here, sports events played an especially important role, as they represented not only the revolution itself but also its benefits and its future in the form of discipline, health, and physical vigor, all embodied in Mexico's youth.[7]

While Cabrera used civic festivals and nationalism to influence the general populace, his manipulation of the press focused more on shaping opinion among the politically active and literate middle and upper classes. In this vein he employed not only the traditional newspaper of record, the *Periódico Oficial* (Official Newspaper), but other outlets as well to disseminate his views and attack his opponents. *Germinal, La Tribuna* (Tribune), and the local office of the Mexico City daily, *El Universal,* received direct subsidies and other favors from the administration. *La Prensa,* created in October 1917, became Cabrera's principal organ, setting up shop in the state-run poor house.[8]

There also existed, however, an independent press. The most important newspapers, *El Pasquín* (Rag), *El Estudiante* (Student), and *El Monitor,* began in 1918 as Cabrera's initial popularity waned. Although careful to praise Carranza and denounce the Zapatistas and other violent opposition groups, they sharply attacked the governor and his administration, sometimes harshly and in personal terms, charging him with corruption, incompetence, nepotism, abuse of authority, and other acts of malfeasance.[9]

Cabrera initially tolerated these papers, citing the state constitution. Therefore, he confined his efforts to thwart them to suing them, muzzling state employees from talking to opposition reporters, limiting newsprint supplies, and confiscating press runs. By late 1918, however, with his government reeling from a series of setbacks including a general strike, an influenza epidemic, and losses in municipal elections (see below and Chapter 8), a weakened Cabrera forcefully retaliated. Editors, reporters, and newspaper facilities came under illegal harassment and even direct physical attack.[10]

The governor's first opportunity to eliminate a paper occurred in July 1919. *El Estudiante*, produced by Colegio del Estado students, published a letter by rebel Cirilo Arenas, opening the organ to sedition charges. Cabrera expelled and jailed the editors and closed the state college. Nevertheless, the publication survived several more months with direct community support, reflecting the governor's weakening political position.[11]

In the midst of the skirmish over *El Estudiante*, the state introduced a restrictive press law, referred to by its critics as the "ley del candado" (padlock law). It required papers to obtain licenses to publish and prohibited anonymous, antigovernment, and immoral articles, these terms to be defined by regime officials. The outcry against the measure, including pressure from Carranza who wanted to cool the overheated political atmosphere in Puebla, effectively checked Cabrera's ability to implement the law. Thus, the governor's authority was further undermined.[12]

Then, in December, Cabrera attacked *El Monitor*, his most serious critic, which had a large, daily circulation of 15,000. Under financial pressure for back taxes and with its principal personnel jailed, the paper changed hands. Nevertheless, its new editor betrayed Cabrera. He criticized the governor and accepted monies from pro-General Pablo González elements, which opposed Cabrera. In the end, then, Cabrera's attempts to control and silence the press only backfired, contributing to his demise.[13]

Antiforeignism, too, played a role in Cabrera's propaganda arsenal. Unlike some of his predecessors' openly hostile stance toward outsiders, however, he usually took a much more subtle approach. Aware of the need to avoid international imbroglios and desirous of the foreign business community's support, he targeted individuals, usually through the press, but seldom attacked entire groups of expatriates. Furthermore, he avoided taking sides in the Allied-Axis dispute during World War I even as pro-German sentiment, particularly among his opponents in the military, grew.[14]

Nevertheless, in late 1919, with the world war over and in difficult political straits, Cabrera succumbed openly to using the nationalism card. The opportunity arose in October when anti-regime rebels briefly seized United States businessman and consul, William O. Jenkins, from his Puebla City residence. Already ill-disposed toward the rich, influential, and arrogant Jenkins, Cabrera used the flimsiest of circumstantial evidence to throw the American in jail, accusing him of self-kidnapping and collaborating with the enemy. United States protests and pressure from Mexico City gained

Jenkins's conditional release. Nevertheless, determined to pin charges on Jenkins, Cabrera manufactured a case against his prisoner by publishing fanciful stories in *La Prensa*, bribing and intimidating witnesses, and manipulating the judiciary. In the end the governor could prove nothing, yet he used the incident to argue that foreign elements were conspiring with the domestic opposition to undermine his government. In reality, Cabrera had become so weakened that he had little control over events in the state, unable even to protect prominent citizens who resided in the capital city.[15]

Finally, Cabrera built up a security apparatus, beholden to him alone as governor, which he relied on to provide intelligence and coerce opponents. In the capital and its immediate environs he relied principally on police forces of several kinds. They included the regular Puebla City cops (some three hundred fifty foot and mounted personnel), a reserve contingent for emergencies, a state security unit trained for secret operations, and another special group for personal protection. Although not large in number, the latter two categories created much suspicion and provoked constant criticism.[16]

To establish a presence in smaller towns and rural areas, the governor also created regional or social defense forces (*fuerzas regionales* or *defensas sociales*), a practice also undertaken in other states such as Chihuahua and Guerrero. These volunteer units provided their own weapons, while the state appointed unit commanders and furnished ammunition. The maximum number of contingents operating at any one time amounted to some one hundred, totaling about one thousand men (as opposed to Cabrera's original plan for five thousand such troops). Nevertheless, from the beginning the idea caused controversy, forcing Cabrera to get federal government approval. Carranza agreed, but only over the adamant opposition of the federal military, which rightly saw the force as an effort to check its entrenched presence in the state. This situation caused a great deal of conflict in coming months.[17]

Institutionalized Rule

Unlike his immediate predecessors, Cabrera did not have the option of running the state as the lone institutional actor; the new governing structure now included a legislature, a judiciary, and municipal governments. The governor clashed with these entities, which increased opposition to him. Over the long run, however, this opposition formed part of the process of negotiation leading to the creation of a political culture.

The Legislature

When Cabrera took office in July 1917 the new state congress had already convened, thus immediately presenting the governor with the issue of sharing power. Preoccupied with reviewing members' credentials and writing a new constitution, the deputies accepted his argument that conditions demanded a strong hand to ensure continuity and stability. As a result they granted Cabrera extraordinary powers in all areas of government until the new document came into effect in September. At that point, he extended his special prerogatives based on the rationale that they were still needed until specific laws implementing the magna carta could be passed.[18]

By early 1918, however, it became clear that Cabrera had no intention of ceding jurisdiction to the congress, preferring that it remain an advisory body. Therefore, independent congressmen, led by Gilberto Bosques, forced the issue. After much debate and signals from Cabrera that he was willing to compromise, the pro-Cabrera majority voted to remove his powers in all but the key areas of finance and security (*gobernación*). The independents, who wanted Cabrera stripped of all such prerogatives, voted against the halfway measure.[19]

Once presented the bill, however, Cabrera, having taken stock of the increasing influence of the independent bloc and deteriorating conditions of the state, vetoed it. Undercut and intimidated, the Cabreristas fell back into line and refused any further consideration of the issue. Hence, the governor continued to exercise full extraordinary powers in all areas of government.[20]

Opposition deputies, however, challenged the chief executive over a number of other important matters—the budget (particularly unaccounted expenditures), electoral and labor reform, and municipal government creation and prerogatives—many of them issues linked to the question of local autonomy and initiative. Relations between the pro-Cabrera majority and the minority remained tense, with pistols drawn and fisticuffs flying on more than one occasion.[21]

Subsequently the induction of more docile deputies in 1919, made possible by Cabrera's supervising the election, increased his hold over the congress. One of the new legislature's first actions was to reaffirm the governor's extraordinary powers and to approve in advance all measures taken under the prerogative. Indeed, to people who championed the development of viable, local institutions as bulwarks of autonomy, it now seemed little had changed since the Porfiriato.[22]

Ironically, then, the Constitucionalista state legislature wielded less clout vis-à-vis the chief executive than did its Huertista-era counterpart; governors Maass and Hernández, unlike Cabrera, enjoyed no such blanket privilege at the congress's expense. Indeed, it was not until 1921 when Governor José María Sánchez finally ceded the right of extraordinary powers first granted to Cabrera in 1917. In other words, the state had no sovereign legislature from 1914 to 1921. Nevertheless, the situation in Puebla was benign compared to Chihuahua and Oaxaca, where the Carrancistas (and Villistas in the case of the former) tolerated no legislature during the entire time they controlled the two states.[23]

The Judiciary

Puebla's constitution provided for gubernatorial appointment of judges and related personnel, subject to legislative review. Cabrera, however, used his extraordinary powers to avoid congressional oversight, thus making changes he alone deemed proper and mainly selecting people loyal to him. In this way, too, he aimed to project his influence into every corner of the state.[24]

Nevertheless, all did not go as planned. The scarcity of trained and sufficiently loyal personnel forced the governor to look to outsiders, including nonresidents of the state, which the constitution forbade. Moreover, many designees either refused to go to rural areas or faced rejection by locals. Those who did serve often came under the influence of entrenched, anti–central government interests. In some areas, judges found themselves competing with military courts, which federal officers used to check the governor's influence. As a result, Cabrera constantly changed individuals or even shut down tribunals to preserve his control. Huejotzingo, for example, lost its court because of the Arenista threat as did Atlixco when magistrates sided with a rebellious city council.[25]

The greatest opposition to Cabrera from the judiciary came, however, not from the state courts but from the federal district tribunal located in Puebla City. Here judges commonly granted writs of *amparo* or injunctions to complainants who appealed decisions by the state system. Delinquent taxpayers, jailed political dissidents, beleaguered journalists, aggrieved town councils, the shuttered Colegio del Estado, and even William Jenkins gained reprieves issued by these magistrates.[26]

Cabrera complained that these decisions undermined his ability to govern. He attacked the credibility of the judges, charging they were recalcitrant conservatives from the Huerta era and allied with the local opposition.

In part, Cabrera was right. Juan Crisóstomo Bonilla and Juan Dávila y Córdoba, for example, had long careers dating back to the Porfiriato and supported the Zapatistas during the Convención period. Puebla's legal and business community backed the two jurists. The governor also put pressure on Mexico City to rein in or transfer the magistrates; Attorney General Julio Mitchell spent much time in the national capital lobbying officials and defending state appeals of federal district-court decisions to the supreme court.[27]

Local Government

Although Cabrera's relationships with the legislature and judiciary were difficult, they proved tame compared to that with municipalities. Here, a whole range of actors coalesced, particularly around the federal military, to oppose the chief executive in the name of *municipio libre*. Ironically, then, just as the governor aimed to consolidate the Constitucionalistas' hold over Puebla, the movement's program of freeing municipal governments proved to be his greatest headache.

A shift of power from the state to local administrations, facilitated by wartime conditions and the breakdown of central government, had been taking place since before Carranza's *municipio libre* decree of 1914. Puebla's new constitution underlined this trend by granting municipalities the right to hold direct popular elections, to exercise full legal status, and to have the freedom to administer finances. Town fathers began to see their entities as a fourth branch of government and argued that they were no longer subordinate to state jurisdiction. Cabrera understood the ramifications of this outlook, as local councils controlled the electoral process and served as depositories of vested, often anti–central government interests.

In November 1917 then, the governor used his extraordinary powers to decree a new municipal law. It aimed to tighten state control over the 180-plus towns by returning to the pre-1914 centralized system of twenty-one districts, to be called municipalities and run by a council (*ayuntamiento*). Consequently, over 160 other communities lost their municipal status and became subordinated to the newly created twenty-one. In effect, Cabrera reestablished the old *jefatura política* system without the *jefe político*, thus placing himself in direct control over towns. Nevertheless, instead of dealing with one person in charge of each district, the governor now had to work with a council in each municipality, a system not as streamlined as the old one but certainly better, at least from his point of view, than trying to handle nearly two hundred sovereign entities.

The law also aimed to reduce conflict by depersonalizing the election process and decreasing the chances of individuals building up or using local power bases, a longtime problem for state officials tying to centralize power. To achieve these goals, Cabrera ordered that municipal presidents serve only four-month terms and be selected from among sitting council members, not from the public at large. Furthermore, the measure empowered the governor to oversee and intervene in nearly any aspect of municipal life.[28]

Then, to further augment his influence, in October 1918, Cabrera issued a decree that allowed him to decide the validity of votes in areas where enemy forces operated. It also stipulated public, as opposed to secret, balloting and the review of election results behind closed doors. As a sop to local officials who chafed at central government interference and complained about the lack of resources, he authorized towns to establish a new property tax, to be collected and disbursed, however, by the state.[29]

Using these powers, Cabrera readjusted municipal boundaries, changed towns' legal status, supervised elections, named officials, and oversaw public services. At one level it seems clear enough that the governor did desire better functioning local governments; after all, the conflict they engendered and their bankrupt condition constantly burdened the state. At another level, Cabrera clearly did not want autonomous municipalities, especially ones controlled by locally based opponents. His intervention in town politics, therefore, was equally motivated by the desires to ensure traditional state prerogatives vis-à-vis localities and to help loyalists to power.[30]

Instead of solving the municipal problem, however, he turned the issue into a firestorm of protest that crippled his governorship. This backlash was clearly manifested in the December 1918 town elections. Discontent over Cabrera's authoritarian and incompetent rule had grown. Many Poblanos resented his retention of extraordinary powers and arbitrary exercise of authority, such as his closing of the Colegio del Estado, his handling of the economy, and his bungling of a four-month-long textile-industry strike. Still others reacted to the government's inability to deal with the Spanish influenza epidemic (see Chapter 8). As a result, anti-Cabrera forces, largely stymied in the legislature and judiciary, found an outlet in local government, to which they called for the election of pragmatic, nonpolitical leaders; in the vote the opposition took seventeen of the twenty-one municipal councils, including the largest and most influential. Even the governor's hometown of Zacatlán fell to his opponents.[31]

Cabrera quickly counterattacked, taking steps to declare the balloting null and void where he had lost and appointing loyal interim town councils until new elections could be held. Most municipalities ceded to the governor, but a few openly and even violently resisted efforts to reassert control over them, thus straining not only state-local relations but also state-federal ties. In each case, army commanders, joined by antiregime lawyers, backed the independents in defiance of the state. Cabrera administration officials lashed out at their opponents and criticized the national government for its inaction, claiming "obscure forces" operated in Mexico City to the detriment of state authority.[32]

Led by Puebla City, several municipalities appealed to the federal supreme court claiming that the national and Puebla constitutions granted municipal governments (*ayuntamientos*) the status of a power (*poder*) equal to that of the other three branches of the state system, thus insulating them from such intrusions by the governor and legislature. The governor countered by raising the specter of anarchy, bolshevism, and the creation of "little republics." In the end the high court ruled for the state, thus negating a significant expansion of local prerogative. Champions of autonomy were dealt a severe blow.[33]

With the court decision in hand, Cabrera declared the recalcitrant municipalities in rebellion and sent police and state troops to force them to submit. He also ordered tax monies withheld from them. In response several towns openly appealed to the federal army for protection.[34] In Puebla City the business and professional community, students, and workers mobilized to protect the local opposition lawmakers. Faced with such deep and widespread resistance and wary of provoking violence in the capital, Cabrera uncharacteristically backed down. He resumed negotiations with the elected city council, while his own designated body held meetings in another part of the city.[35]

In other towns the situation reached open rebellion. In nearby Cholula the Rojas and Blanca clans had vied for power for years. There, federal units under General Rafael Rojas backed the opposition town government against Leopoldo Blanca who headed the Cabrerista slate. When the state tax collector in Cholula, family member Agustín Blanca, fell to an assassin's bullets, Cabrera sent state police to oust the council and investigate the crime. Rojas's soldiers and residents responded by fighting off the governor's police. State officials' appeals to Rojas's boss, former governor and general Cesáreo Castro, to deal with Rojas fell on deaf ears. Finally, President Carranza intervened and removed the Cholula garrison, allowing the Cabreristas to take power.[36]

In Texmelucan, located northwest of the state capital in the agriculturally rich valley by the same name, a coalition made up of landowners, merchants, and workers and headed by General Macario Hernández backed the

Gabino Lechuga-led opposition. Lechuga, a former officer under Cesáreo Castro, also had served as administrator of a hacienda occupied by the former governor's soldiers. Here, the new Cabrera-appointed council took power relatively smoothly. A few days later, however, Hernández's soldiers assaulted the town hall and ousted the Cabrerista government. They then took up defensive positions preventing state police from arresting Lechuga. Again, General Castro ignored Cabrera's requests to intervene. Finally, Carranza and the war ministry sent a commission to investigate. Federal authorities transferred Castro from the state, thus removing one of Cabrera's most potent enemies. Nevertheless, Hernández remained in Texmelucan another four months, until October 1919, when Castro's replacement, General Jesús Agustín Castro, also forced him out. In turn the Cabrerista municipal council regained office.[37]

In the industrial town of Atlixco a similar pattern emerged. Here the army commander, Margarito Herrera, allied with the community's large population of textile workers. They blamed Cabrera for the loss of a four-month strike in the spring of 1918. So overwhelming was the opposition that state authorities, despite an alliance with cacique Francisco Gracia, initially found it difficult to find people even to serve on a Cabrerista-designated city council. Once formed, the opposition denied the council entry to the town hall, obliging it to operate under the portals on the main plaza. Efforts to oust the elected council by force failed, as armed townspeople and federal troops came to its defense. The governor vainly tried to work out a deal in which one-half of each council fused to create a whole followed by new elections. Eventually the two councils agreed on a plan to share tax revenues. Confusion and conflict erupted again, however, when in a December 1919 municipal vote a third council emerged and began operating in early 1920, also claiming legitimacy.[38]

Not to be outdone a second time by the opposition, Cabrera again changed the state's municipal law in 1919, thus further enhancing his formal control over local affairs. Electoral juntas, heretofore selected by the municipality and charged with overseeing votes, were to be appointed in consultation with the state. Furthermore, town governments could no longer appeal state court decisions. These measures, combined with the removal of Cesáreo Castro from the state and a splintering of the opposition over the upcoming presidential election, finally afforded the governor a degree of relief from municipal conflict by the early months of 1920. Nevertheless, the resentment and acrimony that remained provided ready fuel at the local level for Obregón and González's rebellion of April and May of that year. [39]

Parties and Elections

Upon taking office in mid-1917, Cabrera faced the task of repairing the Carrancistas' political coalition, the Partido Liberal Constitucionalista (PLC). During the Castro governorship the party had divided into two camps, dominated on the one hand by the military allied with centrist to conservative, pragmatic civilians and on the other by liberal to radical, mainly civilian interests. At first a consensus between the groups seemed possible, as the new governor enjoyed support, and many officers who opposed him, as nonresidents, could not officially take part in the political process.

Nevertheless, any hope of reconciliation soon evaporated. Cabrera was disinclined to give any quarter to his critics. In turn, former governor and general Castro, who remained in the state as the military commander, determined to undermine his rival and ward off the threat Cabrera represented to the army's lucrative presence, especially in the regions and localities. As a result the situation became increasingly polarized and volatile.

Cabrera and his supporters branded anyone who questioned his policies a reactionary and dupe of the "military-clerical" faction. The opposition came under attack for Madero's death, the food crisis of 1915, and the flu epidemic of 1918. They were also blamed for the many other, more general, ills that plagued the state such as gambling, prostitution, and alcohol trafficking. In reality, however, groups and individuals existed, such as the independent bloc in the legislature, which found much to criticize about both sides. Nevertheless, over time the governor's authoritarian and inept ways plus effective courting by Castro and his influential allies, including the Cámaras, convinced many neutral people that they had little choice but to cooperate with the anti-Cabrera, military-cacique-conservative-led opposition if such basic goals as an unfettered congress, an autonomous judiciary, and free municipalities were to be achieved.[40]

Thus, the growing coalition of opponents to Cabrera became a formal entity. Made up of a cross section of Poblano society, including army officers, regional strongmen, clergy, the business and professional community, students, small-scale entrepreneurs such as shopkeepers and taxi drivers, and even workers and peasants, it took the name Partido Ignacio Zaragoza (PIZ) (after the nineteenth-century hero of the war against the French) and affiliated with the national Partido Liberal Nacionalista (PLN). Its platform, composed for the most part of boiler-plate liberalism, differed from its rival PLC only in its greater emphasis on protection for and development of agriculture, business, industry, and mining and the lack of a specific anticlerical plank (although it did claim to support fully the new federal constitution, which restricted the Church). Personalities, the civil-military rift, and the desire for power had more to do with this struggle within Constitucionalista ranks than did ideology, save for the seldom voiced yet always present one of autonomy. Nevertheless, there is nothing to indicate that this new party was in any way created and manipulated by the PLC in order to hide the increasing authoritarianism of the Carrancistas as José Alberto Abud Flores says occurred in Campeche.[41]

Consequently, the PLC, despite its rhetoric to the contrary, no longer exclusively represented the revolutionary movement in Puebla. Headed by David Vilchis, a state-government library employee and the husband of Guadalupe Narváez, and a small group of pro-Cabrera stalwarts, its base narrowed. Over time it came to be composed mainly of public employees (bureaucrats, teachers, police, soldiers) and others in some way dependent upon state government for their livelihood.[42]

In July 1918 the two parties vied for the first time in balloting for federal deputies. The PIZ\PLN's slate of candidates included several well-known and generally moderate-to-conservative or military-connected figures such as lawyers Rafael P. Cañete and Luis G. Quintana, doctor Daniel Guzmán, generals Antonio Medina and Rafael Rojas, and colonels Porfirio del Castillo and Eulogio Hernández. A hard-fought and bitter campaign resulted in the PIZ\PLN taking approximately one-third of the nineteen deputy and senate seats at stake, sending to Mexico City a small but influential group of people who supported the military faction at the national level and helped to undermine the Carranza government's working relationship with Cabrera.[43]

Displeased with the opposition's showing in the federal vote, Cabrera set out to ensure that the next contest, that for the state legislature, would go even more his way. In this case he especially wanted to be rid of the independent bloc of deputies whom he blamed as the catalyst for the PIZ\PLN's rise and growing strength. Therefore, he changed the election law (with the upcoming December 1918 local contests also in mind), making it more difficult for opposition parties to participate in arranging for elections and counting votes and giving the governor authority to determine if a contest should take place in areas with large numbers of rebels. In addition, the PLC nominated exclusively friends, relatives, and political appointees of Cabrera, further stamping the party in the eyes of the general populace as a tool of the governor.[44]

PLC-directed bribes and intimidation plus the fact that the vote, which took place in late November 1918, came in the wake of a devastating influenza pandemic, resulted in a low turnout (save for public employees who were forced to cast ballots), which favored Cabrera. All but one of the twenty-one new deputies (Acatlán's contest was voided because anti-Cabrera cacique Ricardo Reyes Márquez controlled the district) backed the governor. As a result, Cabrera faced little opposition in the new legislature, and he continued freely to wield extraordinary powers.[45]

Unable to defeat Cabrera in statewide elections in which the numbers of posts up for grabs were few and could more easily be controlled, the opposition PIZ\PLN completely outflanked the governor a month later in the December 1918 local contests (described earlier in this chapter). By this time, too, Cesáreo Castro no longer hid his desire to undermine the governor. He had criticized Cabrera in the press for months and now sent his troops into the streets to rally the opposition and harass the chief executive's backers. As a result, the PLC suffered significant losses throughout the state.[46]

The bitter conflict throughout 1919 generated by Cabrera's efforts to annul the results of these local contests and impose his own councils, plus the waning of his power in general, highly influenced the country's crucial presidential election scheduled for mid-1920. Cabrera, sharply and openly criticizing the military and facing army-backed municipal rebellions at home, found himself in the uncomfortable position of possibly backing a general for president. Although Carranza had not yet tapped an heir apparent, Álvaro Obregón and Pablo González emerged as the most viable possibilities. Obregón detested the Cabrera brothers, and González was closely linked to Cabrera's principal opponents in the state, General Cesáreo Castro and the PIZ/PLN. Hence, Cabrera hesitated, waiting for the president to indicate what to do.[47]

In the end, Cabrera's procrastination and loyalty to Carranza proved to be a costly mistake for it directly contributed to his fall from power. Both of the unofficial military candidates used the political vacuum created by the governor's inaction to organize against his party in the state. The Obregonistas (followers of Obregón) began campaigning in the middle of 1918. Made up of opponents to Cabrera from within his own party, they wanted to isolate the governor and take control of the PLC from him. The nucleus of the group, based in Mexico City and therefore out of the governor's direct reach, was headed by federal deputy José María Sánchez and lawyer, journalist, and former congressman, Luis Sánchez Pontón. Both men had their own constituencies in Puebla: Sánchez, small farmers and landless peasants in his native Tepeaca and surrounding districts, and Sánchez Pontón, students and workers in the state capital.[48]

Calling themselves independents, the two eventually formed a separate but allied party to the PLC, the Partido Liberal Independiente. They openly attacked the governor and pointedly called for, among other things, "true" *municipio libre*, the guarantee of a free popular vote, a legislature and judiciary unfettered by executive control, regional militias accountable only to municipalities, accelerated agrarian reform, and the immediate implementation of prolabor Article 123 of the federal constitution. All these proposals amounted to a criticism of Cabrera's policies and reflected widespread sentiment in the state.[49]

Before Obregón announced his candidacy in June 1919, the two Sánchez had pro-Obregón organizers in Puebla. The campaign reached the far corners of the state and employed the new technology of cinematography to project images of the candidate to fascinated villagers. Particular effort was made to secure the backing of workers who shied away from the business-oriented outlook of the PIZ\PLN and military officers who resented the heavy-handed pressure of Pablo González, their commander.[50]

Meanwhile, the PIZ/PLN, the most powerful political coalition in the state, also geared up for the election. Its vulnerability, however, became apparent in the form of an internal struggle, which hurt its chances against the rising Obregonistas. The issue was whether to participate in the election and back Pablo González. Originally formed in 1918 to challenge the Cabreristas at the local level and made up of people of many political stripes, the PIZ opted to take no direct part in the contest, arguing that to do so would risk division along ideological lines and divert attention from upcoming municipal votes and the 1920 gubernatorial election (notice the greater concern with local and state issues as opposed to national ones). These people included many who disliked González. Students, who made up an important component of the PIZ, for example, objected to the conservatism of González, while others remembered his brutal actions in conjunction with Governor Coss in 1914–15; among them were Catholics who resented his burning of confessionals and then subsequent hypocrisy of inviting Mexico City archbishop José Mora y del Río to his son's baptism. Nevertheless, the leaders of the other half of the coalition, the PLN, among them businessman Ernesto Espinosa Bravo, former deputy Gilberto Bosques, Colonel Porfirio del Castillo, and deputy and general Rafael Rojas, decided to enter the fray and back González. Thus the anti-Cabrera coalition that had come to include a cross-section of Poblano society lost its momentum.[51]

Politically weakened in general and checkmated both by his distaste for the military and by his loyalty to Carranza, Cabrera proved incapable of extricating himself from his political dilemma. By the time Carranza tapped the civilian Ignacio Bonillas for president, which prompted Governor Cabrera to get actively involved in the race, it was too late. Even the Narváez-Vilchis group of the PLC had already switched to the Obregón camp. Cabrera had been outmaneuvered and lost control of his own party.[52]

Subsequently the electoral campaign turned into a battle between pro-González forces on the wane and pro-Obregón elements on the rise, with the Bonillistas (followers of Ignacio Bonillas) and Governor Cabrera playing a secondary role. Even visits to the state by popular development secretary Pastor Rouaix, who himself was drumming up support for another run for the governorship, failed to boost Bonilla's prospects.[53]

Before the contest could be decided, however, Obregón and then González, citing Carranza's manipulation of the process, revolted. Loyal to the end and accompanied by a small number of public employees and state forces, Cabrera abandoned Puebla city in late April 1920. Upon Carranza's assassination shortly thereafter, the governor, now without a state, became a hunted man.[54]

Puebla's political and economic elites, as well as most other citizens, saw virtue in a homegrown governor. Alfonso Cabrera, a native of the state, was designated to fulfill this desire and consolidate Constitucionalista control over Puebla. Nevertheless, from the very beginning of his time in office he faced stiff opposition, made worse by his incompetence and his reliance upon outsiders, particularly Mexico City. First, conservative, longtime opponents of the revolution as well as federal military officers, whom his civilian administration replaced, rejected Cabrera. Then other groups within the Constitucionalista coalition abandoned him, including even his strongest initial supporters, students, workers, and peasants.

The weaker Cabrera became, the more uncompromising and authoritarian his rule, thus escalating his isolation and further eroding his political base, as traditional enemies and former supporters coalesced into a viable opposition. Ironically, the institutionalization of the revolution, in the form of elections and the reestablishment of the judiciary, legislature, and local governments, provided his critics with mechanisms to more effectively organize against and challenge him. Lacking moral and political support, Cabrera proved unable to control his state movement, which left him vulnerable to the swirling political waters at the national level. Dependent upon Carranza, he fell victim to the rebellions in the spring of 1920 of generals Obregón and González. These insurgencies, partially of Cabrera's own making, enjoyed much local support because they addressed themselves to state and local autonomy.

8

ECONOMIC AND SOCIAL POLICY
1917–1920

With the war won and political institutions in place, the next step, the solidifying of a political base, included the undertaking of socioeconomic reforms. Once accomplished, these measures would mark the triumph of the revolution and signify a key step in the building of a new state. Indeed, they would set Mexico on the path to joining the more advanced countries of the world. This scenario, of course, depended upon local and state governments to carry out such change.

Thus, to this end, Governor Alfonso Cabrera's efforts to consolidate the Constitucionalista political structure in the state of Puebla between 1917 and 1920 went further than the political steps of creating propaganda and control mechanisms and holding elections. Like his immediate predecessors, he attempted to carry out a modernizing, egalitarian socioeconomic program, one designed not only to satisfy the needs and wants of the populace but also to change the fundamentals of the system.

As such, Cabrera tackled many issues, from finances, taxes, and currency to education and the Church, but again, like those who preceded him, with only limited success. Although objective conditions, particularly warfare, had improved by the middle of 1917, Cabrera nevertheless found it difficult to carry out fundamental change given the growing opposition to him. It seemed that everything the inexperienced, authoritarian governor touched only exacerbated his problems. Rather than shoring up his and the Carrancista regime's power, control, and, most important, legitimacy, he undermined them.

Finances and Taxes

Puebla's financial situation had improved little by the time Governor Cabrera took office in mid-1917. Despite his predecessors' efforts (see Chapter 6), the state still faced many of the same problems in obtaining sufficient resources to cover basic necessities, much less carry out the Constitucionalista revolutionary program: corruption, an inadequate collection structure for and resistance to payment of taxes, political in-fighting, and rural violence. As late as January 1920, Cabrera reported that in one-third of the state it remained beyond his government's ability to gather revenues.[1]

Leakage of funds and the system's poor condition drew Cabrera's attention. Outgoing Governor Cesáreo Castro spent thousands of pesos just at the end of his term in office. He left fewer than fifty pesos in the state treasury and two *decenas* (ten-day period) pay owed to state employees. Soon after Cabrera's takeover a state treasury official absconded with 20,000 pesos in pulque taxes.[2]

Institutionalized problems also kept income low. State tax collectors legally pocketed in salaries and bonuses more than 36 percent of the take. Moreover, in the chaos of the revolution, agents had become in essence independent operators, making special (and personally lucrative) arrangements with taxpayers, underreporting revenues, and failing to contact the treasury for months. Some even allegedly used tax proceeds to buy arms for the enemy. Furthermore, property taxes fell short of market-based expectations; cadastral records and valuations were incomplete, outdated, and low, on average by 150 percent, resulting in one to three million uncollected pesos per year in a state with a projected deficit of nearly 700,000 pesos for 1918.[3]

Another issue involved the relationship of the state to federal and local governments regarding how revenues were to be allocated. The state was the primary money gatherer followed by the municipalities, both of which passed to Mexico City 60 percent of monies collected. Towns also handed over an additional allotment to the state, with two-thirds of the total coming from Puebla City alone.[4] This arrangement fueled autonomous sentiment at the local and state levels. In a time of bureaucratic inertia and weakness plus inadequate funds, the arrangement often broke down, leading to infighting. Cabrera exacerbated the conflict by refusing to give timely and complete reports on his disposition of funds, claiming immunity because of his extraordinary powers. Hence, he gave further credence to charges that he used public funds to hire loyalists and finance his political party.[5]

Finally, Cabrera faced the amorphous problem of dealing with a society that had a weak civic culture and therefore saw little reason to pay taxes. Many people (and towns) did not have the cash, and, furthermore, had seen little benefit from the monies they had paid. Others, especially large property owners and businessmen, practiced the art of procrastination and appeal, calculating (generally correctly) that the government, desperate to collect any revenues and too impotent to confiscate assets, would in the end accept less than what the law required. Even recipients of communal land grants (*ejidos*) under the regime's agrarian program balked at handing over imposts. These groups and others sought legal relief, particularly from the more sympathetic federal tribunals. Finally, the regime faced resistance not just from its armed enemies but also from people within its own ranks, such as federal congressman José María Sánchez, who urged his peasant followers in the Tepeaca-Tepexi area not to pay the state. Thus, tax collectors entered towns in Sánchez's bailiwick with an armed escort.[6]

Like his predecessors, Cabrera attempted improvements, including tightening the collection system, denying tax breaks and shifting responsibilities to the municipalities, revaluing properties, raising imposts, borrowing, and reducing expenditures. His most innovative steps were to push for the establishment of state-appointed property valuation committees (*juntas calificadoras de valores prediales*) in the municipalities and to authorize towns to establish and collect for their own use (with 50 percent dedicated to schools) a limited property tax designed to replace the now unconstitutional head tax. On the whole, however, there was little overall planning or restructuring of the existing system; the main concern was to gather enough monies to keep government functioning on a daily basis.[7]

Financial issues embroiled Cabrera in several controversies, particularly with Puebla City, property holders, and the business and industrial community. Contention centered not only on rising taxes but also on the regime's efforts, using its extraordinary powers, to control municipal budgets and do away with owners' input into determining rates, as well as on demands that they open their financial records and inventories to inspection. These conflicts took much time and energy and had negative political ramifications while resulting in only modest revenue gains.[8]

The lines of political and financial demarcation between the state and its capital were open to interpretation, sparking tension leavened by underlying autonomous sentiments. Cabrera wanted Puebla City subordinated to the state. Therefore, upon taking office he forced the handover of the city's hospital, police, and schools. Yet later, when the state ran into financial problems, he foisted responsibility for these same institutions back onto the metropolis in the name of local control. On other occasions the city came under pressure to loan money to the state yet always had difficulty getting repaid. The governor's relations with the capital hit a low point in 1919 when the opposition controlled its council. During this period, Cabrera tried to undermine the municipality by withholding loan and tax payments and interfering with its budget.[9]

Cabrera's property revaluation and tax hike of 1917 ran into stiff cross-class opposition. He held fast over the new rates and reassessment of holdings but prolonged the time for payment of back levies, lowered their amounts, and agreed to accept devalued paper currency as payment. When collections still lagged, the governor placed more pressure on owners, routinely sending soldiers to accompany revenue agents. In early 1919 he again raised imposts. These actions of an activist, tax-gathering, central government did not sit well in a milieu of autonomous sentiment.[10]

Another imbroglio involved the pulque industry. For moral (Cabrera also imbibed the puritanical streak within Constitucionalismo) and economic reasons, the governor chafed at the state's inability to control better the introduction and sale of the alcoholic beverage in Puebla City, the state's largest market. Authorities had ended the notoriously corrupt private pulque monopoly in 1911, yet one-half to two-thirds of the liquid still entered the city untaxed, partly due to corrupt inspectors. The governor stationed police at the city's entrances to collect imposts. Distributors cried foul. They then joined other merchants, who also resented taxes on goods entering the city, to appeal to the federal district court, claiming the governor was trying to impose an *alcabala*, which the federal constitution outlawed. The tribunal decided in favor of the industry, and subsequent appeals to the federal supreme court, which the governor lost, only prolonged the issue. Meanwhile the city, with state backing, raised taxes on bars and cantinas. In protest, owners closed their establishments and also filed lawsuits. This controversy not only deepened cleavages between the state government and both the federal courts and business community but also had an impact on thousands of lower-class consumers whose principal drink rose in price.[11]

A third dispute involved the textile industry, which, along with pulque, provided a principal source of income for the state. Again the CIM vigorously defended its members. Owners claimed imposts per spindle had increased over time, because many factories had closed or were underutilized thus, shrinking the tax base. Cabrera started out with the intention of reducing the burden on cotton mills, but subsequent hikes made to reverse declining total revenues again fueled animosity. This debate drove a wedge between officials and one of the most powerful groups in Puebla and increased the insecurity of thousands of workers and their families, to whom owners portrayed the state as the problem.[12]

A fourth controversy pitted the state and Puebla City against the Canadian-owned Compañía de Tranvias, Luz y Fuerza Motriz (Tramway, Light, and Power Company), which ran the capital's streetcar system and provided it electricity. Puebla City owed the firm between 200,000 and 300,000 pesos, only a small portion of its total accumulated 13,000,000-peso debt going back to the Porfiriato, yet it could not pay. At the same time, Cabrera ended a 1903 agreement with the company, which set a fixed 1500-peso annual contribution to the state orphanage in lieu of taxes. In its stead he imposed an annual impost of 84,000 pesos and claimed the enterprise also owed back taxes totaling 1 million pesos since 1904. Charges and countercharges flew; Cabrera moved to embargo company property, and it threatened to withhold power. Again, nothing concrete was resolved before 1920. Nevertheless, the dispute deepened distrust between government and foreign business.[13]

Save for the power company, however, Puebla unlike Sonora, had no large foreign interests upon which to shift the tax burden. In the northern state, according to Aguilar Camín, this tactic not only resulted in adequate revenues but also minimized government's political problems with native capitalists and served to develop a domestic entrepreneurial class. Furthermore, it contributed to a viable state-arbitrated economy, a Carrancista goal that fell short in Puebla as government and the private sector remained at odds.[14]

When Cabrera's efforts to collect monies from entrenched interests proved inadequate, he looked to the federal government (and to a lesser extent Puebla City) for bailouts. By the end of 1919, his government owed approximately two hundred fifty thousand pesos to Mexico City. No other state received such lenient treatment, helping to confirm critics' allegations that his government was a mere appendage of that of Carranza and particularly the governor's unpopular brother, Luis, whom many people blamed for the entire nation's financial difficulties.[15]

Finally, Cabrera resorted to the risky measures of not paying and laying off public employees. By early 1920 discontent had reached such levels that public servants joined businessmen in street demonstrations against taxes and unemployment. In March the governor used soldiers to disperse them. The very next month he fled the capital never to return as chief executive.[16]

Currency

As in the period from 1914 to 1917, banking and currency problems hurt the state. As part of the federal government's plan to create a single bank of emission, it continued to liquidate the shuttered Banco Oriental (see Chapter 6) and incinerate its currency. This left the Banco Refaccionario Español (Spanish Loan Bank), the second bank, to fill the Oriental's shoes. When the Refaccionario made noises about circulating bills, however, officials accused it, too, of irregularities and moved to close it. These steps jeopardized the financial system and left it without a currency-issuing body, making it dependent on the vagaries of bills circulated by non-Puebla institutions. These actions also directly challenged the influential Spanish community, which controlled the Refaccionario. The bank appealed the state's edict to the courts, thus involving the governor in yet another legal battle. Meanwhile, the proposed national bank of emission was not completed until 1925, long after Carranza's fall.[17]

Thus, unable to gain access to locally issued paper currency, Poblanos increasingly depended on metal. As a result, the extant shortage of small coins for daily transactions worsened, while hoarders and speculators thrived and counterfeiting increased. Merchants abused the public, and so-called *coyotes* profited when making change. Employers, including the government, found it difficult to pay workers. Some businesses closed. Cabrera claimed a conspiracy existed to undermine his government.[18]

Authorities set up a monetary commission to deal with the problem, yet people only reluctantly accepted the coins it issued, because they contained a lower silver content and businesses immediately discounted them. The commission then imported two-peso gold pieces from the United States, yet this measure did little to help the average person, who needed coins of smaller value for daily transactions. Postage stamps and chits became de facto tender, while barter grew.[19]

Finally, during later 1919 as the regime's problems increased, and people sensed impending trouble, coins of all types disappeared. This situation forced the federal government, prompted in part by direct appeals from Cabrera to his brother Luis, the secretary of the treasury, to issue vouchers (*vales*) to keep the economy from collapsing. When forthcoming in January 1920, many people, including state officials, refused to accept this ad hoc tender, which derisively became known as "*vales* Cabrera." Save for people outside the money economy, then, the currency problem had a direct and personal impact on a cross section of the state's populace and significantly contributed to the decline in support for the regime.[20]

Business and Industry

Economic recovery from the nadir of 1914–15 was slow, fitful, and partial. The business and industrial community, frustrated by the poor economy and the necessity of working with Cabrera, compared (not without reason) the present with the allegedly halcyon days of the Porfiriato. In the Díaz era, they claimed, order prevailed, and the entrepreneur had free rein to invest and prosper. Nevertheless, the two sides found themselves having to face a number of other problems inherited from the preconstitutional period: transportation and security and, for the textile industry in particular, tariff rates and the availability of raw cotton.

Rebels, Constitucionalista officers, and lack of resources continued to plague the rail network. Even businessmen who resorted to buying their own cars still faced the problem of ill-maintained lines and undue charges. Furthermore, efforts to raise fees to finance improvements and bring the unwieldy system under the control of the federal agency, the Ferrocarriles Nacionales de México, faced criticism and resistance. No one, it seemed, wanted to make the sacrifice to undertake needed change.[21]

Over time, Puebla had become extremely unsafe, a situation reflected in activity not only by rebels but also by common criminals. Calls for greater military and police protection were met with indifference and almost always, due to bureaucratic infighting and lack of resources, an inability to commit specific units or individuals to given geographic areas or businesses. Indeed, it was difficult to distinguish malefactors from security forces, as the two cooperated in preying off the citizenry. The difficult situation was underlined in 1917, for example, when Spanish industrialist, José Manuel Gutiérrez Quijano, prominent businessman and former president of the CIM, was robbed and murdered as he carried a payroll from the bank to his factory.[22]

In mid-1917, Carranza felt the regime was solid enough to favor Mexico's consumers by reducing tariffs on imported cloth. The lowered rates applied mainly to common varieties, those purchased by the poor and made in Puebla. Angry owners and workers (who feared the loss of jobs) soon forced the president to modify the rates. Meanwhile, the industry continued to face a shortage of cotton, which imports only partially relieved; at the same time, however, Mexico ironically continued to export the raw material to cover hard currency needs. Then the end of World War I prompted a rise in the demand for cotton in the United States, Mexico's principal foreign supplier; as a result, prices soared, making importation even less viable. Both the tariff issue and availability of foreign supplies, then, not only pitted the powerful Puebla industrial community against the federal government but also placed Cabrera in an especially awkward position, as his brother was a principal architect of Mexico City's policies.[23]

Labor

In addition to wages and working conditions, two other major labor disputes marked the Cabrera years. The first had to do with implementation of the new federal constitution. The second involved worker unionization. As for the constitution, Article 123 outlined in general terms labor's rights. Article 57 shifted most responsibilities for workers from the federal government to the states; the Departamento de Trabajo, which had been converted into a mere statistics-gathering center with the establishment of state-level Oficinas Técnicas in 1915, now was to be abolished (although this never took place). The national executive wanted to rid itself of the politically sensitive issue of labor-management relations.[24]

Nevertheless, most states, including Puebla (the exceptions were Coahuila, Jalisco, Veracruz, and Yucatán) lacked laws to put the articles in force. Furthermore, owners, particularly those in larger industries with interstate operations, opposed the shift of authority from the federal to the state level. These industrialists believed they could best wield influence in Mexico City, which they considered more favorable toward capital than the state, where radical, self-serving military officers, other populist leaders, and labor had a more direct impact. Otherwise, they feared that a hodgepodge of state laws would divide them and result in unfair competition from fellow producers in other regions of the country. Workers remained ambivalent about which level of government should promulgate the law; their main concern was that legally binding rules be established, ones that allowed for basic rights and uniformity in their application.[25]

To begin implementation of Article 123, then, Cabrera, over business's opposition, established boards of conciliation and arbitration in October 1917. They functioned moderately well, particularly when dealing with specific, individual grievances. Nevertheless, larger and more complicated issues such as union rights, work rules, minimum wages, and work stoppages were more difficult to resolve as the boards lacked legal authority, given the fact that no labor law yet existed upon which they could base decisions.[26]

The federal constitution's labor provisions animated workers in Puebla and elsewhere, such as Mexico City and the industrial center of Monterrey, Nuevo León, in the northeast of the country. Emboldened as well by Cabrera's backing of the boards of conciliation, the principal labor organization in Puebla, the Unión de Resistencia, unilaterally converted itself into a full-fledged union, called the Federación de Sindicatos (Federation of Unions) (later to be named the Confederación de Sindicatos). It pushed for a pay raise and the implementation of statutes. When the governor failed to close the gap between workers' demands and management's offers, union leaders called for a strike and pleaded their case directly to the state legislature. The lawmakers, led by Gilberto Bosques and the independent bloc, not only set a new minimum wage (80 percent more than the 1.25 pesos per day rate of 1912) but also implemented other provisions of Article 123 by establishing committees at the municipal level to determine minimum pay and introduce profit sharing. By dealing with the Federación, the congress had, in effect, recognized its authority to speak for the workers of the state. Cabrera tried to block the measures but, facing a united legislature and an aroused labor movement, in the end reluctantly approved them, warning, however, of their possibly disruptive consequences. Compared to some of his contemporaries, however, Cabrera proved to be a moderate regarding labor issues in general and the implementation of Article 123 in particular; his contemporary in San Luis Potosí, Juan Barragán, "who faithfully reflected Carranza's approach to the question," for example, made no effort in this respect.[27]

Cabrera's reservations proved to be correct. Owners, led by the textile industrialists, took a forceful stand against the Federación, aiming to break it. All forty textile mills in the state closed their doors in a lockout beginning in early March 1918. Management also appealed the new law to the federal district and supreme courts and, with the employment of bribes, won at both levels. A sustained media campaign, backed by Cabrera, questioned the statutes and attacked legislators and the union leadership, charging them with being Bolsheviks and traitors. A march on May 1, Labor Day, which ended in skirmishes with the police, the destruction of a bakery, and the death of one person, was converted into antiworker propaganda.[28]

Meanwhile, workers and their families struggled to survive. Fifteen percent of Puebla's textile labor force migrated to other states, while others returned to agricultural pursuits, and reports of hunger circulated. Owners exacerbated the situation by ejecting workers from factory housing and placing pressure on landlords and storekeepers to deny them credit. The federal government dismissed appeals to intervene, saying that labor issues were the state's problem. The Federación, never accepted by all workers, increasingly faced internal division.[29]

Finally, growing factionalism within both the union and the CIM over whether to prolong the impasse forced both sides to compromise. With the intervention of Puebla City mayor Leopoldo Galván and federal army officers, including Cabrera nemesis, Cesáreo Castro, an agreement was reached. By mid-June, factories had reopened. Most workers, desperate for an income, returned to their jobs, willing to accept a pay hike close to the owners' original offer and, despite the law, without any new minimum wage or bonus provisions.[30]

Meanwhile, the Federación, which had used the owner-initiated work stoppage as a rallying point to gain supporters, now employed strong-arm tactics, including burning some opponents' homes, to intimidate nonmembers and prevent nonunionized factories from resuming production. Here, again, military officers and their cacique allies, such as Ricardo Reyes Márquez, played a key role in mediating conflicts and providing security for mills and their workers. In this way, they ingratiated themselves with both owners and a significant portion of labor, leaving Cabrera on the outside, further isolating him politically and reinforcing the image of his government as weak and ineffective.[31]

Wounded but not broken, the Federación, backed by the new national labor group, the Confederación Regional Obrera Mexicana (Regional Confederation of Mexican Labor—CROM), continued to try to gain workers' support by challenging owners. A range of issues divided the two sides. Nevertheless, the guerrilla war–like confusion of charges and countercharges and often violent actions and counteractions boiled down to two closely related points: would the union be allowed officially to represent labor and, by extension, would management or the Federación control the workplace?[32]

These questions remained unresolved upon the Constitucionalistas' fall in mid-1920 (the first Puebla state labor law took effect in 1921). Save for inadequate action taken by the federal Departamento de Trabajo and local boards of conciliation and arbitration, no one at the national or state level dealt with these fundamental issues. The state government, preoccupied with other problems, limited itself to declaring the existence of a Bolshevik threat to labor peace, assigning special police agents and its regional force to watch workers, and trying to rein in prolabor town councils such as in Atlixco. Thus, the chaotic situation continued, not only undermining the economy but also alienating both owners and workers from the regime, to which each ironically looked for help in order to iron out differences but both failed to receive it. Nevertheless, the laboring classes in the state, particularly those of the cotton textile industry, had made important strides over the decade of revolution, not the least of which was their development of self-confidence and assertiveness via organization. No longer could they easily be manipulated and controlled by owners or government officials. They were now a force with which to be reckoned. This new, focused aggressiveness was not confined to Puebla; industrialists in Monterrey noted the same situation and reluctantly came to the conclusion that new strategies were needed to come to grips with capital-labor relations. Nevertheless, in Puebla, Nuevo León, and almost everywhere else full and formal recognition of workers' greater influence would not take place until the 1920s and 1930s.[33]

Property and Land

As indicated in Chapter 6, most properties confiscated by the Carrancistas in Puebla during 1914–15 had been returned by mid-1917. Only the state's reluctance to cede several especially lucrative properties to the federal secretariat of hacienda for disposition slowed down resolution of the issue. These cases included the possessions of foreigners as well as those of La Piedad (Mercy), a holding company fronting for the Catholic Church with nearly one hundred fincas and sixty mortgages. Finally, save for a few isolated cases, the issue officially was put to rest by late 1919 as the treasury ministry ordered its oft-corrupt office of Bienes Intervenidos in Puebla closed.[34] Puebla was not unusual in this respect, as the return of expropriated holdings took place in many parts of the country, generally after 1916, once the regime had gained some stability. Nevertheless, it is worth noting that this process took place as early as 1914 in the industrial city of Monterrey, as Carranza had already begun to worry about falling production there.[35]

Meanwhile, the focus shifted to the other side of the issue, agrarian reform. Land and water, arguably the most valuable commodities in a society and economy overwhelmingly rural and agricultural, created a hornets' nest of competing interests; no one it seems, save for the regime itself, wanted the government to control this process and, thus, reap its rewards. Weak institutions and dispersed and contested power, even among the some sixty-eight thousand landowners in the state, only exacerbated the chaotic situation.[36]

Carranza and Cabrera, like their predecessors going back to President Díaz and Governor Martínez, approached the issue of land tenure based on two principles: respect for private property and maximization of production, both of which benefited owners. Only secondarily did distribution concern the regime. As a result, sugar haciendas and woodlands were off limits to subdivision. *Acasillados*, peasants who lived on the hacienda, as well as mill workers were ineligible for parcels. The multistep, bureaucratic process of dealing with petitions took four to five years on average.

Overworked agrarian commissions examined claims from both sides, including resorting to paleographers to decipher old titles, in order to ensure accuracy and check sometimes inflated demands. Decisions provoked long and costly court appeals.[37]

Carranza rejected most petitions for restitutions and instead granted dotations, often of a smaller size. A similar process, for example, also took place in Oaxaca and Querétaro. In some cases, restitutions could not be justified because pueblos lacked proof of ownership. In others, loss of land took place before 1856, the date established in the January 1915 agrarian law and the 1917 Constitution as the base year for recognition of claims. The president sought to minimize restitutions because they generally came from a hacendado's most valuable holdings. In contrast, dotations could be taken from less fertile property, not necessarily contingent to the petitioning village, originating from several different latifundia; in this way, then, the sacrifice was minimized and spread among several owners. In response, rural people complained that dotations denied them productive plots and the right to work the land of their ancestors. Then, adding to the insult, Cabrera ordered villagers who received parcels during 1918 to hand over one-half of their crop to the former proprietors as compensation for their contribution of that season.[38]

Another divisive issue involved provisional distributions made by Constitucionalista officers between 1914 and 1916. Owners, many of whom had abandoned their holdings during the worst of the fighting, now were returning and demanding that peasants, who had meanwhile been working the land, be expelled. In September 1916 former Governor Castro had decreed that campesinos be permitted to continue to till these fields until their definitive status was determined. Cabrera, however, reversed Castro's ruling and ordered peasants off the plots. This step not only increased rural tension and violence but also called into question the integrity and authority of the army and caciques, which had authorized earlier distributions. Cabrera's political opponents in Mexico City, headed by deputy José María Sánchez, investigated the governor's policies. The issue became so volatile that Carranza intervened; in November 1918 the president ruled against the campesinos and quashed the inquiry. As a result, Cabrera lost credibility among many rural Poblanos, a fate shared by his fellow governor in neighboring Tlaxcala, Máximo Rojas, because of the regime's conservative agrarian policy.[39]

Finally, to facilitate dotations, the January 1915 agrarian law called for administrative committees at the village level. This requirement divided communities as factions vied to control these bodies, in the process favoring family and friends. Committees, for example, carved out the best pasturelands and woodlots for themselves and blocked completion of the legal process in order to continue to have reason to take advantage of their neighbors. This behavior led to constant litigation and violence, with which the government had to deal. Even worse, from the standpoint of the state, powerful committee heads began making alliances with anti-Cabrera army officers, regional caciques, and politicians. Cabrera urged federal authorities to bypass the committees and distribute parcels directly to campesinos, but his recommendation was ignored.[40]

Consequently, as indicated in Chapter 6, given the difficulty in gaining parcels via government auspice, most land arrangements were made outside official circles, a situation also noted by Falcón and García for Veracruz. Often campesinos merely squatted, defying both authorities and owners. They also made private arrangements with hacendados. The regime opposed both practices, the second because it undercut government control and implied weakness. Over time, however, as considerations of rural peace and the need to build up a political base, combined with waning revolutionary zeal, took on greater weight, the regime unofficially changed policy. It tolerated extra-official agreements because to do so relieved overburdened agrarian agents, protected hacendado and local elite interests, and maintained production, all the while checking more radical agrarian elements by dividing the peasantry. Then, when the cash-strapped state ordered villages to come up with a compensation scheme before the land petition process could begin, deals made directly with *terratenientes* (large landholders) only accelerated. Thus, peasants and owners (and officials) alike logically asked, Why bother with the official bureaucracy?[41]

Into this situation, then, stepped a myriad of individuals and groups poised to benefit economically and politically in the name of aiding the peasantry. Officials and influence peddlers of all kinds, including army generals, caciques, congressmen, foreigners, regional force commanders, union leaders, municipal presidents, and even local agrarian commission agents cut deals and fought with each other, with landowners and their hired guns, and with campesinos. This complex and constantly changing matrix of relationships twisted and ignored the regulations and procedures of the government's agrarian program.[42]

Here again, the federal military-cacique axis came to the fore, as commanders and traditional regional leaders employed land reform to use the peasantry for personal gain and to build support against the state. Officers such as Cesáreo Castro, Macario Hernández, and Miguel Laveaga, who in the process became landowners themselves, shook down hacendados in the Texmelucan valley and elsewhere. They also manipulated villagers through promises of land while recruiting them to carry arms and work these same officers' fields. General Prisciliano Ruíz created an Indian-based agrarian organization, the Sociedad Unificadora de la Raza Indígena (Unifying Society of the Indigenous Race), which operated in east-central Puebla. Caciques, including Ricardo Reyes Márquez in Acatlán, Francisco J. Barbosa in Tehuacán, and Domingo Arenas in the Texmelucan valley, also used the issue to enhance their *cacicazgos* and enrich themselves.[43]

Another group that seized on the agrarian issue and used it not only to push their anti-Carrancista agenda but eventually to gain high political office in the state in the 1920s were civilians such as Manuel Montes, Luis Sánchez Pontón, and José María Sánchez; all three men became governor. Sensing the demise of the Constitucionalistas, they mobilized peasants, used them for personal ends, and eventually steered them toward the Obregonista opposition. Montes, a bricklayer, gained a following in the volatile Texmelucan valley where he helped form the Confederación Social Campesina (Social Confederation of Campesinos) "Domingo Arenas."[44]

Montes, as well as lawyer and journalist Sánchez Pontón and federal deputy Sánchez, along with Comisión Nacional Agraria (National Agrarian Commission) delegate to Puebla, Pablo Solís, played key roles in the creation of a peasant organization, the Unión de los Pueblos de Agricultores del Estado (Union of Farmers' Villages of the State). It promised expedited land resolutions, protection to small holders, tools, and seed. Originally Cabrera backed the Unión. When it took an independent stance, however, the governor attacked it. He correctly linked it to his personal enemies as well as authoritarian and corrupt village administrative heads and Obregón.[45]

A third group that vied for peasant support was the Federación de Sindicatos. After starting out as an industrial union, it sought backing in the countryside, where prerevolutionary conditions still prevailed. Agricultural laborers earned as little as fifty centavos for a fourteen-hour day. In one village, residents complained about being forced to work twenty-four hours straight for twenty-five centavos. Indeed, little had changed from the 1908 average daily wage of thirty-one centavos for the state. The Federación backed work stoppages in the fields, prompting officials and *terratenientes* to warn about the Bolshevik menace that organized industrial workers posed to the peasantry, to call on the army to intercede, and to jail union organizers. Given the close collaboration between business and agricultural interests in Puebla and the resulting fear of an urban-rural workers' coalition, one can partially account for the lengths to which management went to try to break the union.[46]

Regions of the state became open battlegrounds over the control of land and peasants; Chalchicomula, Cholula-Huejotzingo, and Tepeaca-Tecali-Tecamachalco were especially volatile. In the former two, powerful hacendados such as Marcelino Presno as well as foreigners such as American Diego Kennedy near Texmelucan and Englishman Harry Evans (along with his better known American wife Rosalie) aggressively organized to protect their interests. Furthermore, many peasants in both areas, emboldened by provisional titles received earlier from Prisciliano Ruíz and Domingo Arenas, among others, were not about to cede ground. In Chalchicomula, vigilante groups contracted by landowners murdered village-based agrarian leaders. In one incident, hired guns hauled four men off a train and hanged them; they had been on their way to Puebla City to present their case for land. In the third area, conflict over water plus José María Sánchez's organizing efforts, which faced government opposition, resulted in violence. Sánchez claimed the state killed some thirty people connected to his peasant movement.[47]

Furthermore, Cabrera's largely unfulfilled, proreform rhetoric, disseminated by coverage in the government-controlled press and during ceremonies that included bands and the attendance of high officials, only fed overall peasant frustration. As a result, discontent and violence rose in a context of an awakened sense of campesino self-worth, weakened controls over the lower classes, and a government of disputed legitimacy. Rosalie Evans, for example, made particular note of the insolence and aggressiveness of her workers when she returned to her hacienda in 1918 after several years' absence.[48]

Consequently, official distribution of land in Puebla for the January 1917 to mid-1920 period remained modest. Of 206 original petitions, Cabrera (including the last six months of the Castro administration) approved eighty (75,600 hectares), which he sent to the president. Carranza acted on sixty-six: seven denials, fifty-nine dotations, and no restitutions. The total hectares distributed were 36,400 (out of a national total during Carranza's presidency of 167,000, 21.5 percent) for an average of 550 per dotation. The largest number of actions took place in the districts of Huejotzingo, Tepeaca, and Tehuacán, representing more than 60 percent of the total; none was undertaken for the Sierra, save for the border district of San Juan de los Llanos, as agrarian reform was not a pressing issue there and only one (Acatlán) in the southwest where the Zapatistas carried out their land program. Yet the number of final resolutions granted to the state was larger than to any other.[49]

In other words, despite the generally niggardly land reform program of the Carrancista regime in general, a fact noted in studies of several other regions of the country, Puebla fared relatively well. This fact is probably due to the highly mobilized agrarian elements in the state, a missing element in Chiapas and Yucatán, for example, where little reform occurred. The Zapatistas and Arenistas forced the federal government to combat them with preemptive change in the existing land tenure system. Also, compare Puebla's record to San Luis Potosí, where the Villistas did not make division of hacienda holdings a high priority. There, for the period 1915–May 1920, only four distributions were granted, although they accounted for some 20,000 hectares in a more arid region of the country.[50]

Whatever the efficacy of the official land program, change took place in the state's rural areas. Between 1910 and 1921 the number of haciendas fell from 1275 to 648 while the percentage of the rural population living in hacienda communities dropped from 20.1 to 9.9; at the same time the number of nonagricultural rural communities rose from eighty-three to 275. Meanwhile, agricultural villages remained fairly constant, falling from 1054 to 1013. In other words, haciendas were in decline and people linked to the hacienda economy found new livelihoods in settlements tied to mills, mines, railroads, and other nonagricultural pursuits.[51]

Finally, despite the inadequacy of land reform, Governor Cabrera did correctly foresee one thing: the environmental dangers of poorly considered agrarian policy. He realized that forests had come under severe pressure, particularly by army officers who wantonly cut trees for such things as railroad ties, often sold for personal gain. Now the governor attempted to veto dotations that contained woodlands, which otherwise became especially vulnerable to peasants who saw them as quick and easy sources of cash. Officials also tried to protect the forests in Michoacán, according to Verónica Oikión Solano, only there the main culprits were large landowners and foreign companies. Nevertheless, this protective policy proved exceedingly difficult to enforce, and Mexico and Puebla would not systematically take up the issue until the 1930s.[52]

Food and Other Basic Goods

Cabrera took power in 1917 looking forward to a fall harvest that would end the lingering food crisis, which had devastated the state in 1915–16. Optimistic projections of mid-summer, however, could not foresee a severe freeze of late September and early October. It wiped out 50 percent of the grain and vegetable crop, one that even if fully harvested would have only barely covered the populace's needs, as planting remained below prerevolutionary levels. As a result, an already tense situation in rural areas worsened. In Teziutlán, for example, the poor broke into railroad cars loaded with corn bound for Mexico City. In the national capital merchants could get even more money than the prevailing price in Teziutlán, where it was already at record levels.[53]

Therefore, the state government once again intervened in the market. Cabrera took steps to ensure minimum supplies and lower prices by curtailing exports and undercutting hoarders and speculators. He prohibited corn shipments from municipalities unless officials guaranteed the availability of a 6-months' supply of grain. When producers and merchants refused to cooperate (claiming, and rightly so in some cases, that they did not trust local officials' honesty and competence to handle the corn), the governor mandated that they turn over 20 percent of their holdings to the towns. In Puebla City, Cabrera and the Cámara de Comercio set up special outlets to provide basic goods, including imports from the United States, at below-market prices. He encouraged labor to form purchasing and distribution cooperatives and factory owners to buy and store food for their workers. Farmers also were urged to plant all their land. These measures lasted in one form or another for a year, until the autumn 1918 harvest.[54]

For his policy the governor incurred the condemnation of the federal government and especially merchants. National-level authorities continued to advocate free markets, particularly now that the capital, Mexico City, depended on shipments of grains from surrounding states, including Puebla. Businessmen who dealt in foodstuffs complained that their rights and livelihoods were threatened. Railroad officials and army officers, who controlled lines and rolling stock and saw the curtailment of shipments as a threat to their income, backed them.[55]

Although Cabrera weathered the controversy, including charges that he (among others) personally made money from trafficking in basic goods and the selling of permits to ship them, the policy only marginally helped the consumer while alienating powerful interests within and beyond Puebla. In the end the state lacked the ability fully to curtail smuggling. All in all, food prices in Puebla during the decade 1910–1920 rose considerably for most basic products, despite government intervention: sugar (over 600 percent), rice (67 percent), corn (500 percent), eggs (300 percent), lard (300 percent), and bread (67 percent).[56]

Public Health and Welfare

Other than the basic foodstuffs and a bare-bones *beneficencia* system (hospital, orphanage, poor house, mental asylum), the state's social welfare record amounted to more rhetoric than action. Even efforts to ban bullfights, forbid gambling, and regulate pulque sales became embroiled in a web of conflicting interests, because the government relied on tax revenues from such activities.[57] From all accounts, conditions in Puebla City remained abominable. Outside the state capital they were worse. Garbage, beggars, feral dogs, flies and rats, mud and dust, prostitutes, shoe-shine boys and vendors, armed and drunken soldiers, corrupt police, open sewers, animal and human feces, intermittent power and telephone service, dilapidated public transportation, thieves, speeding motor cars, adulterated foodstuffs, and disease all formed a scourge on life. Despite laws and good intentions, the daily routine virtually went undisturbed, with government-led improvements hardly visible from the perspective of most citizens.[58]

This begrudgingly tolerated policy of official inaction, however, came to an end in fall 1918 when the Spanish influenza pandemic hit a war-ravaged, undernourished, and exhausted Mexico. Puebla authorities took little heed of the approaching disease, even after it had begun killing thousands in cities of northern Mexico, where it had arrived from the United States. Paralyzed by inertia, bureaucracy, ego, and opposition from businesses catering to public entertainment, almost no effort was made to prepare for the menace. Authorities initially downplayed the threat, saying they did not want to panic the populace; later they attributed their inaction to the lack of money. The most pertinent fact, perhaps, in this whole tragic affair is that Governor Cabrera was an experienced medical doctor.[59]

The flu arrived in Puebla City during the first half of October; between then and early December, by which time it had largely passed, approximately 1,500 of the capital's 100,000 residents died as a direct result of the disease while hundreds of others, weakened by the virus, succumbed to other ailments. In early November an estimated one-fifth of the city's populace was ill. Perhaps 5,000 children were orphaned, as the illness especially affected young adults.[60]

At the height of the flu's impact, so many people were dying that unburied and decomposing corpses lay in the hot sun for days in the cemetery. Some individuals, too poor or sick to deal with the dead, tossed loved ones on the street to be picked up and buried in mass graves. The November 2, Day of the Dead holiday, normally a festive occasion, took on a different cast with cemeteries closed to all except diggers laboring in the stench of putrefying bodies. When forced to work in the graveyards, jail inmates rioted in protest. People suffered from hunger because they were too ill to work or even to feed themselves. Hospitals and the civil registry (which issued death certificates) became overburdened, schools closed, and business nearly came to a halt; churches, however, remained open. Morticians, pharmacists, physicians, and vendors raised prices. Quacks peddled homemade potions.[61]

The illness quickly spread to all corners of the state. Limited evidence indicates that it severely hit smaller towns and rural areas; there, sanitary conditions and health measures were even worse than in the state capital. Residents fled their homes seeking safety, only to carry the disease with them. Just across the state line in Tlaxcala, some 600 of Zacatelco's 7,000 residents died, a ratio several times worse than that of Puebla City. Anecdotal reports indicate similar conditions for many other areas.[62]

It is believed that the numbers of deaths attributable to the flu in the state were at least 30,000 and perhaps as high as 45,000 out of a total population of one million. Thirty percent of its residents fell ill to the virus. If this accounting is accurate, it made Puebla one of the hardest hit states in the country, with flu-related fatalities totaling more than combat deaths as of early 1918. In all of Mexico, perhaps five million people caught the virus with between 300,000 and 500,000 (21.4 to 35.7/1000) succumbing to it, half of them between the ages of twenty and forty.[63]

Once the flu's deadliness became apparent, there emerged a serious effort on the part of the private sector in Puebla City to fill the health care vacuum created by official inaction. Called the Comisión Central de Caridad (Central Charity Committee), it was composed of individuals and organizations that in general were from the better off, more conservative elements of Poblano society, few of whom backed the governor. They included the Comisión's president, Francisco Velasco, a former municipal president during the Porfiriato, business organizations, foreign consuls, Catholic groups, the Cruz Roja, and students. It collected 54,000 pesos in donations and paid for medical personnel, sanitation services, medicines, burials, emergency clinics, and shelter, clothing, and basic foodstuffs for the general populace.[64]

Embarrassed by the Comisión and fearful of its political potential, the administration belatedly joined the antiflu effort in order to blunt the group's growing influence. First, Cabrera fired the state's chief health officer, Dr. Luis G. Unda. Then he requested a day's pay from all government employees, an initiative that elicited little enthusiasm among people who already were owed back monies by the state. Nevertheless, the lack of resources and glaring incompetence meant the state government remained a secondary actor in the campaign to restore the populace's health. Implicitly admitting that it had the power to do little else, the state and Puebla City lowered prices for third- and fourth-class burials and ordered coffins to be sold to the public at cost.[65]

However, this did not stop the state from attacking the Comisión, especially when it showed no signs of ceding to government control. Officials accused it of harboring an anti-Cabrera political agenda and purposefully contributing to the crisis. To thwart the body, authorities censored information from the civil registry in an effort to downplay the number of dead and blocked Comisión members from taking part in sanitary operations such as inspecting homes and washing streets. Cabrera's hypocrisy was not lost on the populace. Even the governor's normally supine mouthpiece, *La Prensa*, objectively reported the Comisión's actions and called for it to operate in order to fight disease.[66]

Ultimately the Comisión's initiatives, compared to the government's poor handling of social welfare issues in general and the flu in particular, contributed to the serious setback the Cabreristas suffered in the December 1918 local elections. Indeed, this whole scenario of natural catastrophe, government inaction, private initiative, and subsequent loss of political support reminds one of a more recent event, the 1985 earthquake in Mexico City, followed by the highly contested 1988 presidential elections.[67]

Finally, the difficult conditions of the decade had a negative impact on the population growth of the state. Overall the number of inhabitants fell between 1910 and 1921 by nearly 77,000 from 1,102,000 to 1,025,000, a 7 percent difference. Contrariwise, for the decade 1900–1910 the state's residents had increased by 80,000 and would do the same for the period 1921–1930 by some 125,000. More men disappeared (42,000) from the state than women (35,000) during the decade, as might be expected, given the ravages of warfare. Nevertheless, the difference is not great, indicating that factors other than violent death, such as disease and emigration, also played an important role in the decline.[68]

Education

Governor Cabrera wanted to assert greater control over the state's educational system, for instructional as well as political reasons. His initiatives at the primary level met with little opposition. Indeed, the public school system was in such poor shape that hardly anyone could object to change. In Tehuacán district, for example, whereas 101 schools functioned in 1910, only forty-eight were open in July 1919. Even as of 1921, a year after Cabrera left office, the state's illiteracy rate for people ten years and older stood at 73 percent (67 percent for males, 78 percent for females). Like its predecessors, then, the government attempted to finance local education and recruit teachers. Most important, a 1919 law concentrated many powers heretofore enjoyed by local authorities into the hands of the state. Nevertheless, a lack of monies along with rural violence prevented the measure from being implemented. Puebla was not alone in having only limited success at building up its primary and secondary school system; Oaxaca, too, made little progress in the same realm.[69]

The administration did, however, run into resistance at the Colegio del Estado. Politicized and visible (located in downtown Puebla City and the principal institution of higher learning for the region's elite), the college had battled the Constitucionalistas since 1914. A key issue had been the purging of conservative faculty. Cabrera supported this action, thus initially gaining the support of the institution's prorevolutionary students and professors, yet alienating more cautious elements, which felt quality was being sacrificed for ideology. Even the honeymoon with the left soon faded, however, when Cabrera refused to govern the college in conjunction with them.[70]

By early 1918 then, a growing number of students across the political spectrum had become disillusioned with Cabrera's policies, educational and otherwise. As a result, they created the Agrupación de Estudiantes, recruited colleagues from other institutions in the capital city, including the Escuela Normal, the Instituto Metodista, and the Conservatorio, and began publishing a weekly, *El Estudiante*. The paper took a strident line, making charges (often combined with inflammatory cartoons) against the governor and other known progovernment figures of misdeeds that no other local organ would touch. The group became caught up in the local political scene, as the anti-Cabrera opposition, including the Ignacio Zaragoza party and individuals such as Luis Sánchez Pontón, sought to make common cause with it.[71]

Because of the criticism and the cost of keeping the 1500-student Colegio open, Cabrera threatened to close it. Carranza prevented him from doing so. Then in July 1919, when *El Estudiante* published a letter from rebel Cirilo Arenas, Cabrera shut down the institution and fired the entire faculty, citing a financial exigency.[72]

Meanwhile, students and professors defied the regime by creating a "free school" in the upper level of the Victoria market with the aid of the Federación de Sindicatos and federal army garrison. Officials retaliated by jailing its leaders. Cabrera also decreed a new law regulating the Colegio, giving the state authority over its general as well as day-to-day operations, including the policing of students' actions inside and outside the institution.[73]

After much heated debate, the Agrupación changed its leadership in early November, thus allowing an avowed apolitical faction to assume power as the price for getting Cabrera to reopen the college. Even so, the governor saw to it that the institution's professional schools, location of the greatest degree of activism, remained shut another four months. Puebla was fortunate, however; in neighboring Oaxaca, for example, the Carrancistas closed the main center of higher learning, the state Instituto de Ciencias y Artes (Institute of Sciences and Arts), for four years, between 1916 and 1920.[74]

The governor's heavy-handed measures against this select group of young people gained him few plaudits. Indeed, support for the dissident students came from many quarters, including the local political opposition, labor, the military, and the business community; critics in the federal congress, led by José María Sánchez, moved to condemn Cabrera. Even members of the governor's own party, such as David Vilchis, thought he had gone too far.[75]

The Church

Although not radically antiecclesiastical, Cabrera did continue to carry out a program prejudicial to traditional Church prerogatives. The emphasis was no longer, however, on closing houses of worship, arresting priests, and confiscating and destroying property. Instead, the governor concentrated on taking subtler, yet in the longer term, arguably more effective measures to separate church and state and make the former subordinate to civil authorities. His actions took many forms: restrictions on hours for mass; control over the disposition of ecclesiastical property; secularization of the parochial school curriculum; inventories of Church holdings; the gathering of statistics on baptisms, marriages, and burials; the ouster of foreign priests; and toleration of Protestants.[76]

Resistance to the policy from people of all classes was widespread and grew over time. In some areas, local governments and caciques, such as Ricardo Reyes Márquez in Acatlán, made common cause with clerics against the state. Municipal officials continued to spend scarce resources on religious festivities and to ignore mandates to hold secular civic ones at the same time. Parishioners defied restrictions on mass and orders to remove priests. Evangelical churches came under attack, and several Protestant missionaries lost their lives while plying their beliefs. Clerics refused to supply information about ecclesiastical holdings and their flocks. Church-backed social organizations, such as the Asociación Católica de la Juventud Mexicana (Catholic Association of Mexican Youth) and Unión Popular de Puebla para la Acción Social (Popular Union of Puebla for Social Action) operated openly and actively.[77]

Another indication of the Church's power and defiance toward the state occurred in June 1919, when Enrique Sánchez Paredes replaced Archbishop Ramón Ibarra y González, who had died in early 1917. The investiture took place in a very open way, with public ceremonies, processions, and bell ringing greeting local well-wishers as well as distinguished guests from all over Mexico. Much the same occurred shortly thereafter when Sánchez Paredes returned from an out-of-state trip. Cabrera clearly was powerless even to restrict these ceremonies to behind closed doors. Under heavy pressure from the Catholic community, the governor also returned intact the archbishop's palace and reopened the Universidad Católica.[78]

Cabrera's Church policy was mild compared to the stance of many of his fellow governors. Save for Jalisco, states mainly in the southeast and north of the country, including Campeche, Coahuila, Durango, Sonora, and Tabasco, continued to harshly attack the institution. This geographical division generally reflected the much more conservative orientation of central Mexico. Unlike Puebla, these governments passed laws implementing Article 130 of the federal constitution. Tabasco went furthest, building on an already well-established reputation made when in 1915 the Constitucionalistas changed the name of the state capital from San Juan Bautista (Saint John the Baptist) to Villahermosa (Beautiful Town). In 1919 it limited priests to one for each 30,000 inhabitants and one church for each 6,000 residents.[79]

Like those of his predecessors, Cabrera's record in the socioeconomic sphere was modest. Also, like them, he faced many of the same obstacles, including the lack of resources, some bad luck (especially the flu epidemic), and the need to focus first on daily necessities, which distracted him from undertaking substantive change. Still, he did not have the excuse that generalized warfare (although fighting continued in and the government lacked control over some areas) undermined his efforts.

Cabrera mostly lacked legitimacy, support based on respect that he could call upon when challenging vested interests. Indeed, his authoritarian and uncompromising nature showed more weakness than strength, and his adversaries sensed that. Thus, they felt sufficiently empowered to oppose vigorously his more progressive and much-needed initiatives, which ended up in prolonged political and legal battles. This situation further alienated not only groups that had always cautiously viewed the Carrancistas but also more seemingly natural constituencies that, ironically, came to identify their interests in opposition to his ineffective, hard-line government. Even peasants and workers, who arguably would have been better off under a reformist, centralized state with the power to check large landholders and industrialists in order to redistribute land and improve labor conditions, remained distanced from the regime. The Poblanos may have accepted, probably even wanted, a Cabrera government that simply restored the status quo ante—peace, stability, and predictability—but not one beholden to outside interests and insensitive to local concerns and their desire for autonomy, one that employed arbitrary, dictatorial methods in an attempt to concentrate authority and impose radical change from above. Nevertheless, in the meantime, among the tension and conflict, a political culture was forming.

9

WAR
1917–1920

The Constitucionalistas had won the war for control of Mexico by 1917, but the specter of violence would not go away. Although weakened and no grave threat, Villistas in the north and Zapatistas in the south continued to cause problems. Meanwhile, other groups, many mere bandits, plagued the regime. It seemed that the country would never gain peace. By 1920, then, when the president attempted to impose a weak, civilian successor, officers within the Constitucionalista ranks decided it was time to take over the revolutionary cause from Venustiano Carranza.

In Puebla the curse of warfare continued as well. The violence of 1917–1920, however, was less generalized and lost much of its earlier meaning. Whatever idealism and focus on revolutionary goals that had existed in the earlier battle against Huerta and the subsequent struggle between Constitucionalistas and Convencionistas had largely dissipated. Factionalism rent both groups, the latter having dissolved into its constituent parts. Now the fighting took on a much more personal and vindictive tone, clearly reflecting the desire for aggrandizement and revenge; enrichment via criminal activity also played a role. Nevertheless, the Carrancistas slowly consolidated their military hold over the state yet in the end could never totally defeat the enemy. Meanwhile, as Puebla slowly bled, the majority of its residents, exhausted materially and emotionally by the upheaval, became increasingly disgusted with and alienated from all violent groups. Therefore, despite having checked their opponents, the Carrancistas, fractionalized and lacking popular support, offered little resistance to the rebellion of spring 1920, led by the Obregonistas, northern rivals from Sonora, and joined by the Gonzalistas. In Puebla, a majority backed Pablo González, as the latter seemed to offer the best chance to uphold autonomous principles against another unknown outsider.

The Armed Opposition

While Constitucionalista forces dominated major population areas in Puebla, the armed opposition continued to operate on its more inaccessible, often mountainous borders. Zapatistas in the south, Arenistas in the west, Marquistas in the north, and ex-Federals and others in the east kept constant pressure on Governor Alfonso Cabrera's regime. Although a rebel takeover was no longer a threat despite the fact that insurgents held one-fourth of the state as of mid-1919, warfare drained resources and greatly complicated Puebla City's efforts to carry out its revolutionary program.[1]

Zapatistas

By 1917, after seven years of struggle against de la Barra, Madero, then Huerta, and finally Carranza, warfare in the Zapatista zone of southern and western Puebla had taken on a routine, settling into a pattern of forays into small towns or attacks on trains, mills, and haciendas and then withdrawal into the safety of nearby hills. The frequency, intensity, and location of action depended on the agricultural cycle, on-going negotiations with the Carrancistas, support from Zapatista headquarters in neighboring Morelos, relations among leaders in Puebla, and the personal whim of each general. Given these constraints, then, the objective of Fortino Ayaquica, Marcelo Caraveo, Dolores "El Cojo" (lame) Damián, Juan Ubera, and other Puebla-based Zapatistas was not so much to hold specific territory or population centers as to rob, seek vengeance, and keep Constitucionalista forces off balance. In other words, strategy had evolved into guerrilla warfare with the hope of eventually wearing down the government in Puebla City, resulting in de facto peace and autonomy.[2]

Only occasionally did the Zapatistas muster enough strength to enter larger, better-garrisoned communities such as Atlixco and Matamoros. Nevertheless, although the rebel threat was real, both sides seemed to exaggerate Zapatista potential. The Zapatistas themselves did so in order to impress the enemy and keep their own supporters in line. The Carrancistas employed hyperbole, such as constant warnings of an attack on the state capital (none occurred after mid-1916) or of conspiracies to take over cities or even the state government, in order to demonize the enemy, retain its own backers, and obtain additional resources from the federal government.[3]

The conflict had largely become a stalemate, even to a degree fabricated for the benefit of officers and their troops. Yet the resources expended, the opportunities forgone, and the havoc wrought took a toll. Caught between two (and sometimes more) sides in what now had become a long, drawn-out war of attrition, villagers faced constant insecurity, hunger, and disease. Even in the heart of the Zapatista zone, heretofore more protected from the direct ravages of war, the situation deteriorated as growing banditry and abuses by Zapatista troops increased. Reports of criminal gangs and soldiers' (it became difficult to distinguish between them) going from sackings of churches and factories to assaults on priests and workers, for example, underlines the degree to which personal motivation and the flaunting of traditional institutions and taboos had become driving forces in the war. In turn, such actions exacerbated the general public's feelings of helplessness toward a situation beyond anyone's control. Consequently, more and more people shunned any faction, wanting nothing more than to be left alone to carry on their lives in peace. The Zapatista leadership was aware of this trend but proved incapable of remedying it as the movement's generals in Puebla, increasingly fractionalized, operated independently.[4]

War weariness, declining popular support, internal divisions, a lack of ammunition, and food shortages, then, set the stage for a clear decline in the Zapatistas' fortunes after mid-1918. First, an ongoing offensive in Morelos by Pablo Gonzalez disrupted the movement's general headquarters and pushed large numbers of its soldiers into Puebla. This influx momentarily overwhelmed Constitucionalista garrisons at Chiautla and Matamoros, but at the same time further burdened an already desperately poor people who resented the arrival of even Zapatistas, no less outsiders. Carrancista troops in Puebla under General Cesáreo Castro and cacique Ricardo Reyes Márquez counterattacked, employing airplanes based in Atlixco, slowly squeezing the Zapatista enemy.[5] Then came the flu epidemic of fall 1918. It took a high toll among rural people, civilian and soldier alike, including those in the Zapatista area. Whole villages were decimated, and generals Isabel Guerrero and Epigmenio Martínez succumbed to the disease.[6]

Then, Zapata was killed in April 1919 in a Carrancista-engineered plot in Morelos. His absence further exposed the internal conflict among the movement's commanders in Puebla. Principal among them was the rivalry between Fortino Ayaquica and Cirilo Arenas, who had inherited his brother Domingo's mantle, after Ayaquica killed Domingo in 1917. Also, Zapata's death led to a spate of surrenders to the Carrancistas, culminating in Ayaquica's own relinquishment in December 1919. By early 1920, then, the Carrancistas had the Zapatistas in the state in a difficult position. That spring they would join the Obregonista Agua Prieta (a town in Sonora) rebellion, helping to overthrow Carranza and Cabrera.[7]

Arenistas

As of mid-1917 the Arenistas maintained an uneasy relationship with their ostensible allies, the Carrancistas, while simultaneously talking to the Zapatistas, whom they had rejected as partners in December 1916. The group's leader, one-armed, "El Manco" Domingo Arenas, still held out hopes of creating an autonomous movement in west-central Puebla, one beholden to neither of the two principal antagonists of the greater region.[8] Therefore, neither the Carrancistas nor the Zapatistas were unhappy when in late August 1917, Domingo Arenas fell victim to an apparent assassination plot cooked up by Zapatista officers Gildardo Magaña and Fortino Ayaquica, a longtime rival. Why Arenas met Ayaquica near Tochimilco is not clear; perhaps the two wanted to end their debilitating competition; maybe Arenas thought he could woo Zapatista officers and their men to his side; or as Magaña warned, Arenas may have planned to rejoin the movement and take part in an attack on Atlixco during which he would ambush exposed Zapatista forces.[9]

What is clear is that Arenas stepped into a trap that probably had been organized for weeks. During this period Ayaquica expressed his dismay and frustration at Arenas's gains in the region, including the desertion of soldiers to him. Soon after, Ayaquica executed a general and at least five other officers for attempting to join his rival. Meanwhile, Magaña informed Zapata that the Arenas question would soon be resolved. Arenas's body was decapitated and the corpse sent to Zapata in Morelos, signaling successful revenge for "El Manco's" betrayal of late 1916.[10] After several weeks of hesitation and infighting, the Arenistas eventually settled on twenty-two-year-old Cirilo Arenas, Domingo's younger brother and a former carpenter, to lead the movement. For the time being, at least, the Arenistas remained in the Constitucionalista fold as the Zapatistas immediately initiated a campaign against Arenista villagers.[11]

Also sensing the weakness and disarray within the Arenistas, Carranza and Governor Cabrera moved to assert greater control over their unpredictable partners. From the perspective of both Mexico City and Puebla City, it was time to begin to institutionalize the revolution and curb its heretofore freewheeling actors. Therefore, they moved to place Arenista troops under more trustworthy federal officers. For example, the president, with Cabrera's support, put the subsecretary of war, General Jesús Agustín Castro, in charge of the so-called volcano region where Arenas operated. In the process, former governor and now state military commander, General Cesáreo Castro, Cabrera's principal antagonist, was removed from the Arenista zone.[12]

As a longtime Carrancista officer in the state who had relied on regional caciques to gain both militarily and personally, Cesáreo Castro had understood the Arenas movement's value in maintaining control over the strategic area located at the doorstep of Puebla City. Hence, in 1916, while governor, he negotiated for months with the then-Zapatista Arenas, developing a special and complex relation with the cacique and convincing him to join the Constitucionalistas. This connection not only protected Arenas but also enhanced the value of Castro's presence in Puebla, helping to prolong his stay there, despite Governor Cabrera's hatred toward him and desire to see him transferred.[13] Now Castro was gone. In turn, Arenas and his officers knew that at best they were being targeted for full integration into the Carrancista military structure; at worst they might be eliminated altogether as a fighting force.

When new commander J. A. Castro ordered that Arenas's troops be dispersed and demobilized, the cacique was forced to act. Arenas broke with the Carrancistas in late April 1918, creating a movement independent of either the Constitucionalistas or Zapatistas. Facing two strong enemies and rent by internal factionalism, the Arenistas found the role of principled loner to be difficult. To survive, they lived in caves high on the volcanoes, confiscated villagers' crops, blackmailed hacendados, and practiced banditry. They contacted dissidents outside the immediate region, such as Manuel Peláez and Félix Díaz in Veracruz and peripatetic ex-Federal Higinio Aguilar, but ideological and personal differences as well as logistical difficulties prevented sustained collaboration.[14]

Arenas also approached his two main enemies, coordinating operations with individual Zapatista officers and holding off-and-on peace talks with the Carrancistas, in a complex motif of constantly shifting alliances and intrigue. A peace accord, however, always floundered on Arenista demands for autonomy within its zone. The president and governor refused, insisting on unconditional surrender.[15]

Thus, for over a year, until fall 1919, the Arenistas represented a small threat to Puebla City and its surrounding region. They attacked towns such as Atlixco, Cholula, Huejotzingo, and Texmelucan as well as softer targets like the railroad.[16] Governor Cabrera voiced his concern about the rebel danger and attempted to connect the insurgents to his civilian political opponents. His closing of the state college for several months in 1919–20 for the publishing of a letter from Arenas in a student newspaper may have been an overreaction. Nevertheless, evidence indicates that the movement did enjoy fairly widespread support. Some people, such as hacendados who paid "taxes" or city meatpacking-plant operators who clandestinely slaughtered stolen cattle sent to them by Arenas, backed Arenas for personal gain or protection. Others, however, such as regional forces, students, and, above all, villagers and modest townspeople, were motivated beyond the mere personal, reflecting a widespread sentiment (not confined just to Arenas's supporters) to gain and maintain control over local resources through municipal autonomy. These groups, for example, helped establish a fairly extensive pro-Arenas spy and support network, including in Puebla City.[17]

It probably was no coincidence, then, that three of the most important municipal rebellions against the state government in 1919 took place in the Arenista zone. Although there is no indication that the Arenistas controlled these revolts, the movement's presence contributed to the antigovernment, pro-autonomy atmosphere prevalent in the region. More concretely, in Cholula, for example, cacique Rafael Rojas, who backed the municipal rebellion there, dealt with the Arenistas to gain support against the Cabrera government–backed Blanca clan, which competed with Rojas for domination of the area.[18]

By late 1919, however, military losses, shifting alliances, and infighting left the Arenista movement lacking coherence and momentum. Also, second-in-command Alberto Paniagua died in combat the next January. Then, late the following month, Cirilo Arenas was captured in Puebla City while trying to negotiate his surrender. Despite federal district judge Juan Crisóstomo Bonilla's ruling that Arenas be tried as a civilian (and thereby avoid the death penalty), he was sentenced by a military court and shot in March 1920. For the moment the movement was moribund, but the Arenas name and ideals, particularly agrarian reform, would live on in the Confederación Social Campesina "Domingo Arenas," headed by Manuel Montes in the 1920s.[19]

Marquistas

As of mid-1917 the Márquez brothers of the northern Sierra also found themselves in difficulty. After their last attempt to make a comeback in the region late the previous year, they and their followers had dispersed, many going to Veracruz. Nevertheless, they still posed a threat to the Constitucionalista-imposed peace and security in the region.[20]

Meanwhile, Gabriel Barrios had taken over as commander of the Sierra brigade upon Juan Francisco Lucas's death in February 1917. A longtime aide to Lucas, Barrios (and brothers Bardomiano and Demetrio) more aggressively hunted down rebels and reasserted control over the region than the aging Lucas. Nevertheless, as a result of the Constitucionalista takeover of the Sierra, Barrios, unlike Lucas, owed his position to the Carrancistas; the famous *cacicazgo* would never again exercise the degree of autonomy it enjoyed under the now-deceased patriarch of the Sierra.[21]

President Carranza and Governor Cabrera backed Barrios in his efforts to clear the region of dissidents. With that support he dealt a stunning blow to the Marquistas in mid-August 1917. At some point during the previous months, the brothers had returned to the confines of their own hometown, Otlatlán in the district of Alatriste (Chignahuapan), awaiting developments and sending out peace feelers to the Constitucionalistas. By taking advantage of the Márquez's desire to negotiate, Barrios approached their stronghold. In a surprise, night attack, his forces killed three, Esteban, Emilio, and Gaspar. Several other clan members and close associates also died or were taken prisoner.[22]

Now without centralized leadership, the Marquista movement splintered into competing factions throughout the rugged Sierra. Some effort was made by local groups to ally with Domingo Arenas in the volcano region of Puebla or with Manuel Peláez or Félix Díaz in nearby Veracruz, but local and personal rivalry precluded any systematic cooperation. On at least one occasion, when the Felicistas named one of their own commander of the Sierra, the Marquistas rejected this outside threat to their autonomy and killed the designee. The Sierra rebels did use effectively, however, their knowledge of the terrain and mobility to cross the Puebla Veracruz state border in order to outwit their pursuers. As a result, it would take another two years, until mid-1919, before Barrios, backed by the federal army, repressed the remnants of the Marquistas.[23]

Ex-Federals and Felicistas

No armed opponent better illustrates the complex, constantly shifting myriad of insurgent leaders and their followers that the Constitucionalista government faced between 1917 and 1920 than did the ex-Federals led by octogenarian General Higinio Aguilar and Celso Cepeda. Cepeda was a former army officer from Chalchicomula, who joined the Zapatistas and gained a reputation for blowing up passenger trains. The two headed a loose, ill-defined group, which extended from the northern Sierra along the isolated mountain and prairie of the eastern border with Veracruz and Oaxaca to the south of the state of Puebla. One of them, Juan Andreu Almazán, who had played a key role in 1914–15, now operated out of his native town of Olinalá,

Guerrero, making raids across the border into Puebla state. It was not uncommon for simultaneous reports of attacks on ranchos, trains, factories, or small towns, all attributed to the Aguilaristas (followers of Aguilar), to emanate from the far reaches of this vast, rugged region.[24]

Throughout this area, the ex-Federals made alliances at their convenience, based on immediate tactical goals, irrespective of ideology. In the south, despite their prickly history, Aguilaristas, such as Marcelo Caraveo and "El Cojo" Damián, cooperated with Zapatistas, thus demonstrating not only the former's flexibility but also the weak control that Zapatista headquarters in Morelos held over its officers in Puebla.[25] The ex-Federals made their greatest mark on the northeast and east of the state. There they continued their alliance with the Felicistas, at times placing themselves at the direction of Félix Díaz's loosely organized Ejército Reorganizador Nacional (National Reorganizing Army), which totaled 15,000 to 18,000 men in 1917 and fought from Veracruz through Oaxaca to Chiapas. A combination of Aguilaristas and Felicistas, then, penetrated the eastern Sierra region of Puebla and adjoining districts. In the Sierra they filled the vacuum created by the declining Marquista movement, whose members looked upon these intruders with a great deal of distrust, collaborating with them only out of necessity.[26]

Like other insurgent groups, the ex-Federals also had a network of operatives in the region, such as former governor Mucio Martínez and hacendados. Nevertheless, support for the ex-Federals should not be identified only with reactionaries. Many groups, rural and urban, small and medium landholders, laborers, shopkeepers, and the like saw in the ex-Federals and Felicistas the possibility of moderate reform within a stable context undertaken by and in the control of local people. They preferred this vision to the more radical, agrarian-oriented program of Arenas and particularly Zapata as well as the even more threatening to many, outsider-imposed, centralizing vision of the Constitucionalistas.[27]

Also like its anti-Constitucionalista counterparts, by 1919 the ex-Federal–Felicista movement began to lose momentum. Along the way, members of the last generation of Porfirian-era officials and in some cases their offspring, too, fell. General Aureliano Blanquet, former governor Mucio Martínez and son Carlos Martínez Peregrina, and General Gaudencio González de la Llave and son Porfirio were killed, jailed, or surrendered. Even Higinio Aguilar's heir, Alfonso, offered to cooperate with the government after being captured in Puebla City, where he had sought treatment for malaria. As their situation deteriorated, the insurgents increasingly hit random targets and sowed terror, particularly against trains. Renewed attempts to unite forces with Arenistas and Zapatistas failed, while Aguilaristas and Felicistas fought over control of payoffs from haciendas. Nevertheless, the Carrancistas could not deal the insurgents a deathblow. Finally, in the spring of 1920, most of the rebels took a gamble and made accommodation with Álvaro Obregón and his Agua Prieta rebellion, helping to overthrow Carranza.[28]

Carrancistas

The patterns of military organization and warfare established by the Constitucionalistas during 1914–1917 continued: the officer-cacique alliance and divisions among each group over military, economic, and political issues; corruption; desertions and revolts; abuses of and tension with the general populace; and the slow, erratic, yet cumulative gains made against the illusive and tenacious enemy. Indeed, from the purely military point of view, as of mid-1919 the Carrancistas legitimately could claim to have won the war in Puebla. By that date all the principal insurgent groups had been brought under control, although small, troublesome bands continued to operate in many areas. They posed no direct threat, however, to the regime.[29]

Nevertheless, the state government faced an even more dangerous menace, the federal army. Although muted while Constitucionalista officers held the governorship, the divisions between the military and civilian leadership took on ominous proportions once Alfonso Cabrera became chief executive. Indeed, in the end, it was not insurgents on the battlefield who defeated the regime, but its own armed forces, allied with regional caciques and the generally inward-looking, autonomy-seeking populace. Falcón notes a similar situation in San Luis Potosí, where Governor Juan Barragán, a military man, could not keep his officers under control; Eduardo Nomelí Mijangos Díaz asserts the same for general and governor Pascual Ortíz Rubio in Michoacán.[30]

Since 1913, when the Carrancistas first arrived in Puebla, a subtle and important process had been taking place, one largely overshadowed by warfare. Constitucionalista commanders developed military, political, and socioeconomic ties with the local populace, epitomized by the officer-cacique relationship described in Chapter 4. In some areas these multifaceted links would solidify into bases of support capable of whetting political ambitions. Indeed, nearly every high-level Carrancista soldier at one time or another was reported to covet public office. Nevertheless, the full extent of this phenomenon did not become apparent until 1917, when Carranza moved to establish an institutionalized, constitutional government. Even more crucial, the First Chief made the decision to back civilians for many posts, thus directly threatening military perquisites and ambitions.

The spring 1917 gubernatorial campaign, which divided along civilian-military lines, set the stage for a long and bitter struggle for control of the state between civilian and soldier. The election's winner, civilian Alfonso Cabrera, and outgoing interim governor, General Cesáreo Castro, most starkly represented this struggle. Cabrera, unlike his military predecessors, could not assume the position of army commander as well as governor, yet understood the importance of denying the post to any officer who opposed him. Upon Cabrera's taking office, Castro left the state, yet within two months he returned, reappointed federal commander.[31]

The tenacious, experienced Castro had many supporters in Mexico City and Puebla. An old comrade in arms of Carranza from their native Coahuila, he also enjoyed the backing of General Pablo González's Ejército del Oriente, as well as many other officers in the secretariat of war. Since arriving in the state three years earlier, he had not only served as military commander and governor but had also become one of the state's largest hacendados, expropriating and running abandoned holdings and marketing cattle, pulque, and foodstuffs. As a result of his many and varied activities, Castro also had developed an extensive network of associates and supporters in various walks of life. In numerous ways, they identified their well-being with his presence. Castro's backing would grow as initial acceptance of Cabrera turned into opposition. Many people preferred the relatively laissez-faire administration of Castro (and the federal military-cacique nexus in general), despite the abuses of the army (whose most grievous actions took place in contested, isolated areas), to one that threatened the traditions of local autonomy and action in the name of centralization and efficiency. After all, local initiative was not only a long-standing and highly valued practice but also one that allowed people to exert political control and carry on economic activities free from state-government oversight and taxation. The whole complex, intertwined gamut of local interests developed since independence came into play, and Constitucionalista army officers now, ironically, reinforced it.[32]

Once in power, Cabrera's government continued the antimilitary rhetoric of the gubernatorial campaign, mainly through *La Prensa*. At one level the newspaper focused on the army's many abuses, highlighting tension and conflict between soldier and civilian. In a clear ploy to appeal to the antioutsider and anti-Indian bias of urban inhabitants, the misdeeds of Yaqui Indians, who formed a significant part of the Constitucionalista force in the state, were emphasized. In one article the paper even charged a Yaqui of dancing around and attempting to drink the blood of an innocent victim whom he had just stabbed in an Atlixco cantina (bar). At another level, however, *La Prensa* played even higher stakes by directly condemning the secretariat of war and its officers, calling them a "privileged caste," to which, it claimed, all society was unjustly obligated to pay tribute and vassalage. The newspaper said that the federal army promoted militarism to the detriment of civilian, constitutional rule, a situation similar to the times of Díaz and Huerta. Furthermore, the organ charged that soldiers, particularly Cesáreo Castro, backed the governor's opponents and planned to overthrow his government.[33]

Indeed, in late 1917 it appeared that Cabrera's fears of a coup might come to pass. A rebellion in northern Mexico headed by former governor General Francisco Coss sent shivers through the local political establishment, because many of Coss's colleagues remained in the state. Several of Coss's earlier comrades in arms, such as General Pedro Villaseñor, felt compelled to pledge their loyalty to the government, and soldiers under Cesáreo Castro were concentrated in Puebla City, more to keep an eye on them than to defend the city. Soon thereafter, the war ministry ordered Antonio Medina, who had been reassigned from the Sierra to Puebla City, stripped of command and sent to Mexico City. Medina also had been plotting a revolt, perhaps in conjunction with Zapatistas.[34]

Although an uprising never occurred, Cabrera vigorously expanded the network of regional forces under his command. A handful of these state contingents had first been established in 1915 under Governor Cervantes. As long as military governors controlled them, they drew little concern, but in the hands of the civilian, Cabrera, they were dynamite. Drawn from and based in villages, in theory these troops were to patrol their localities and cooperate with federal units against rebels. In reality, however, they served principally as a means for Cabrera to project power into the far reaches of the state in order to try to check his political enemies in general and the army in particular. Hence, reports filtered out of the countryside connecting these regional forces to attacks on local anti-Cabrera military and political leaders, such as one on General Prisciliano Ruiz's Sociedad Unificadora de la Raza Indígena.[35]

The federal military and its cacique allies read these developments correctly as efforts to discredit them and curb their prerogatives. As a result, the army retaliated. In Atlixco, for example, Francisco Gracia had left the army, accused of collaborating with the enemy, only to head a new state contingent. His former colleagues persecuted him and had him jailed.[36] Francisco Barbosa, ill disposed to tolerate any state interference in his zone of influence, killed a newly appointed regional commander in eastern Puebla.[37]

Elsewhere, open and at times vicious clashes broke out between national-level and state contingents. In one especially egregious case, a regular army unit sacked the southern community of Chila de la Sal (Acatlán district) in December 1917, killing town council members and regional troops. The dispute centered on the disposition of state forces and competition over the lucrative practice of cattle rustling in the region.[38] Dozens of such reports of conflict between federal and Puebla soldiers, each vying for military as well as economic and political domination of the countryside (the *regionales* turned out to be no less abusive of the citizenry than their regular army counterparts), added to insecurity in rural areas and further contributed to alienation from the regime.[39]

Most indicative of the depth to which the federal army, in collaboration with local interests, had penetrated political and socioeconomic life as well as the degree to which this involvement challenged Cabrera's authority, was the struggle over the control of local governments. This process culminated in the December 1918 municipal elections and their aftermath. Federal commanders supported the opposition and backed elected town councils' refusal to relinquish power to Cabrera-designated bodies, not just in Puebla City, Atlixco, Cholula, and Texmelucan (see Chapter 7), but also in Tehuacán, Teziutlán, and Zacatlán. In other words, by 1919, elements of the federal military, backed by a cross-section of the local populace, were in rebellion against state authorities, and neither Cabrera nor Carranza were capable of controlling the situation.[40]

Nevertheless, a reading of reports of the movement of military personnel indicates that Carranza realized the threat these largely autonomous officer-cacique-community relationships posed in the long run to this regime. As early as 1916, once his regime had begun to stabilize, the First Chief attempted to rein in several of these men, including Francisco Barbosa, Francisco Gracia, Antonio Medina, Juan Francisco Lucas, Juan Lechuga, and Pedro Villaseñor, among others. He removed them from active commands; reassigned them, even to Mexico City, where they could be watched; and in some cases cashiered them. Nevertheless, these measures had to be undertaken carefully and individually so as not to provoke desertions and rebellions and undermine the ongoing war effort. Few of these men, however, were effectively tamed.[41]

The case of Cesáreo Castro illustrates well the difficulty of removing a powerful, high-ranking officer with influence. After a brief absence as commander of federal forces in the state following the end of his gubernatorial term in mid-1917, Castro returned to his post despite new governor Cabrera's opposition. Then in May 1918 he was given an indefinite leave and replaced by the subsecretary of war, General Jesús Agustín Castro. The subsecretary launched a vigorous campaign against Puebla's rebels. In addition, he sought to centralize control over the army as well as to professionalize and improve the fighting capability of what had become a lax institution. To this end, he began to overhaul the command structure, renovate the justice system, investigate abuse, transfer and sack errant officers, and demobilize questionable troops. The resulting outcry of protest from many levels of society, both rural and urban, not to mention threats of rebellion by Cesáreo Castro's officers (who logically foresaw their demise, too), forced Mexico City once again to back down; Castro was reappointed to Puebla within three months. It took then, another year of negotiations, the offer of generous inducements, and the 1919 municipal revolt, in which Cesáreo Castro was deeply involved, before he could be forced permanently to leave his military command in the state. Nevertheless, he still occasionally returned to be feted by friends and check on his many interests, both business and political.[42]

Even with Cesáreo Castro's departure, relations between Cabrera and the army did not significantly improve. Castro's replacement, General Pilar R. Sánchez, for example, blamed the governor for a successful rebel assault on Cholula, as a result of the chief executive having substituted a regional unit for a federal contingent that had been guarding the town. Sánchez also accused the state of placing false reports about insurgent attacks in *La Prensa* in order to blacken the army's image.[43]

In the end, then, Carranza's measures to control federal army officers and their cacique allies had limited effect. Given security considerations and widespread local support, regional bosses and northern officers enjoyed significant immunity from the dictates of Mexico City and Puebla City. Indeed, many of these soldiers and their local cohorts, after mid-1919, backed General Pablo González for president. Then in the spring of 1920 most joined the Álvaro Obregón rebellion, which overthrew Carranza. Over the longer run, however, many of these officers would still remain unhappy. Like Carranza, albeit more forcefully, the new Sonoran regime would carry out a policy of centralization and professionalization, which continued to threaten their perquisites. As a result, a number of these men, including Cesáreo Castro, would join the anti-Obregón movement of Adolfo de la Huerta in 1923–24.[44]

By mid-1919, the civilian Carrancista leadership in the state, headed by Governor Alfonso Cabrera, along with the federal military, should have been celebrating their joint success on the battlefield. Although armed opponents, primarily remnants of the Convencionista coalition of 1914–1916, still operated in some areas, the Constitucionalistas now exercised effective control over most of Puebla. Instead, authorities found themselves gravely divided, a situation that pitted the civilian state government against army officers, who since 1914 had ensconced themselves in the political and socioeconomic structure. These military men, epitomized and largely led by Cesáreo Castro (and backed by Pablo González), enjoyed a high level of support from a cross section of Poblanos. They identified the commanders and their troops as bulwarks against the interventionist, centralizing, and, to some, modernizing policies of both Mexico City and Puebla City. Indeed, in several rural areas violent conflict took on the character more of federal army versus state forces than Carrancista versus rebel. Yet, here can be detected interaction leading to the creation of a political culture and the building of a new state.

In the end, Governor Cabrera lost this battle. Even with Mexico City's help, he could never bring the federal officers under control. Already isolated and weakened because of his poor leadership and limited accomplishments, Cabrera could not prevent large numbers of Poblanos, much less soldiers, from backing Generals Pablo González and Álvaro Obregón, first in the presidential political campaign and then in the rebellion of 1919–20. This fact would spell the governor's and the Carrancistas' downfall.

10

REGIME ENDS, STATE CONTINUES

Álvaro Obregón realized that Carranza would never let him win the presidency in a fair and open vote and, indeed, that the regime intended to eliminate him. Therefore, the general rebelled in April 1920, calling for Carranza's overthrow. The summons to revolt, justified by charges of central government violation of Sonora's (Obregón's home state) autonomy, brought widespread support, including that of Obregón's main presidential rival and fellow general, Pablo González. Carranza realized the precariousness of his position and soon fled the capital. This step forced state and local officials to stay and take their chances with the new revolutionaries or follow the president's example.

In early 1920, Puebla governor Alfonso Cabrera was in a difficult position. Support among the general public, both urban and rural, had fallen to a dangerous low. Thus, with his political base greatly reduced and his enemies multiplying, he became increasingly isolated and dependent upon a small number of hard-core followers, especially party functionaries, bureaucrats, and police and state military units. Hence, when Obregón initiated his call to arms, Cabrera had no means to prevent a rebellion within Puebla. The governor fled.

Cabrera's demise opened the door first to a takeover of power by elements closely connected to Pablo González. As a result, the political situation remained cloudy for weeks as local Obregonistas, backed by the new interim president Adolfo de la Huerta, sought to oust the Gonzalistas, headed by cacique and newly named governor, Rafael Rojas. In time the Obregonistas prevailed, taking on the job of building the new state, but their victory failed to answer the old question of who should determine Puebla's fate, locals or outsiders.

Carranza's Fall

The downfall of the Cabrera governorship in Puebla occurred rapidly in spring 1920. As the political situation deteriorated and rumors of rebellion multiplied, Cabrera scurried to shore up his support. The governor found civilian officials to back him, but military men were few. Most soldiers had cool relations with the chief executive; the majority backed Pablo González, although some favored Álvaro Obregón, both Cabrera opponents.

The first public declaration against the regime in Puebla occurred on April 18. Federal deputy José María Sánchez, a staunch Obregonista, and his mainly agrarian followers, seconded by regional forces, took up arms. Then, five days later, came the Sonorans' Agua Prieta plan. Not to be outdone by the Obregonistas, caciques, and González supporters, generals Ricardo Reyes Márquez and Rafael Rojas soon thereafter marched on the capital from the south and west, respectively, while fellow conspirator General Luis Hermosillo cut the Interoceánico Railroad at Texmelucan. As a result, by the time González seconded Agua Prieta on May 4, the Cabrera administration had already lost control of the state.[1]

Meanwhile, the governor had left Puebla City on April 28, using the excuse of having been called to Mexico City for consultations. Over the next several days other state officials, including legislators, joined him in the national capital. In Puebla the reins of power fell to the general secretary, Miguel Moto. When Moto, too, abandoned the city on April 30, leadership devolved to Alfredo Castro Rubio, the *oficial mayor* (chief of staff). Then the federal commander, General Pilar R. Sánchez, fearing being cut off by advancing rebels and facing desertions of his men to the insurgents, also withdrew from the city on May 3. Consequently, Castro Rubio handed the capital over the following day to the Gonzalistas.[2]

While in Mexico City, Cabrera organized a rump state government to be located in his native Sierra. He also planned to use his influence there to protect and aid Carranza if the president decided to flee the capital. The Sierra could be made into a base from which to fight the insurgents or to continue on to Veracruz, where a defense could be established as the Constitucionalistas had done in 1914–15 or, if all else failed, a place from which Carranza could go into exile. As a result, Cabrera and a contingent of followers went directly from Mexico City to Zacatlán, his hometown, arriving on May 9. There, others from Puebla City joined them. In Zacatlán, with the help of the state treasury, which he had conveniently taken with him when leaving for Mexico City (depriving public employees of their pay), Cabrera and a handful of legislators formally reestablished Puebla's government on May 11.[3]

Meanwhile, pursued by his Gonzalista and Obregonista opponents, Carranza fled Mexico City on May 7 but was forced to abandon his Veracruz-bound train on the thirteenth, at Aljibes, Puebla. He headed westward into the Sierra, hoping to find the sanctuary that Cabrera and his brother Luis had promised. On May 17 his entourage reached Tetela, where it had expected support from cacique Gabriel Barrios, whom Carranza and Cabrera had courted since 1917. Barrios, however, did not show up, probably already having committed to the Obregonistas. Consequently, Carranza continued on. After a strenuous trip, the small group arrived in Zacatlán, Cabrera's bailiwick, the next day. Nevertheless, without adequate security, the president decided to move on, still hoping to make it to Veracruz. Carranza's fortune, however, ran out beforehand. Early in the morning of May 21, 1920, while sleeping in a hut at Tlaxcalantongo, outside Huauchinango, troops under the command of Rodolfo Herrero shot him. Herrero, a rebel since 1912, with ties to Manuel Peláez and Félix Díaz, had only shortly before surrendered to the government. He had accompanied Carranza to Tlaxcalantongo earlier that same day, only to return to murder the president. Herrero held a grudge against both Carranza and Cabrera; his family had quarreled with Cabrera as governor and Cabrera and Carranza had ordered Herrero's father to be killed. As if Herrero's animosity were not enough, one of the columns that attacked Carranza's camp that night was headed by Herminio Márquez, brother of Esteban and the other Márquez siblings whom Barrios had eliminated in 1917 on the president's orders.[4]

Upon Carranza's death, Cabrera set out for Central America. He apparently hoped to reach Honduras, where he had friends, and perhaps eventually the United States to join other expatriates. Traveling under a false name and posing as a businessman, he crossed the country to the west coast port of Manzanillo, Colima, where he boarded a steamer bound for Corinto, Nicaragua. In Salina Cruz, Oaxaca, however, he was arrested on July 4, when an army officer who had served in Puebla recognized him. Federal authorities returned him to Mexico City. Perhaps in an effort to calm the political situation, new interim President Adolfo de la Huerta authorized that Cabrera be released on bail, pending his fight against extradition to Puebla where authorities had charged him with embezzlement, murder, and election fraud. Then, as the legal process dragged on, because of bureaucratic and political turmoil, questions about his gubernatorial immunity, and the fear of a high profile, conflictive trial in Puebla, Cabrera fled the

country. He spent several years in Havana, New Orleans, and Panama before returning to Mexico, where he maintained a low profile until President
Lázaro Cárdenas named him director of the Hospital Central Militar (Central Military Hospital) in the late 1930s.[5]

Meanwhile, once it was clear that Cabrera had abandoned the governorship, those few legislators remaining in Puebla City made a last attempt
to salvage what they could of a difficult situation. They named one of their
own, David Vilchis, interim chief executive. Vilchis, however, could find no
support among those deputies who had fled with Cabrera to the Sierra.
Hence, legislative authority ended. Finally, over the next weeks the Sierra-
based representatives and other officials filtered back to the state capital,
hoping to reestablish their lives, some even petitioning to resume their political careers.[6]

Gonzalistas versus Obregonistas

As events played out in the Sierra, in Puebla City the Gonzalistas, led by
Ricardo Reyes Márquez and Rafael Rojas, moved to consolidate power. Acting on dubious constitutional grounds given that the legislature still functioned, albeit now under Cabrera's aegis in Zacatlán, and in the name of
General Pablo González, head of the Ejército del Oriente, Reyes Márquez
named Rojas interim governor on May 8. In turn Reyes Márquez assumed
the position of federal commander. Indeed, by taking advantage of the extraordinary political circumstances and scratching each other's backs, the
two longtime caciques had catapulted themselves into the top two posts in
the state.[7]

Upon occupying the governorship, Rojas began to reestablish government and reach out to the alienated populace. He persuaded the business
community, relieved that he was no Francisco Coss à la 1914, to advance
monies to his administration. Rojas used these funds to pay troops and
public employees and raise teacher's salaries. He also lifted restrictions on
the Colegio del Estado imposed by Cabrera a year earlier. In addition, he
sped up land dotations, returned property to the Church, settled several
strikes and raised worker's pay, partially revamped the judiciary, and began
dismantling the regional forces and the governor's personal police unit that
Cabrera had established. Perhaps most important, Rojas allowed anti-Cabrera
town councils, ones that had been elected in December 1919 and were subsequently blocked from taking power, to assume their posts. The new governor also included among his advisers and official personnel representatives

of the heterogeneous anti-Cabrera Ignacio Zaragoza coalition, from businessman Ernesto Espinosa Bravo and lawyer Juan Crisóstomo Bonilla on the right to more liberal individuals such as army officer Porfirio del Castillo, former deputy Gilberto Bosques, and student activist Gonzalo Bautista.[8] Even United States businessman and consul William Jenkins, no fan of the revolution and one to seldom condone any of its leaders, loaned funds to the new government, hopeful, like many of his class, that under the Gonzalistas conditions would improve. The British vice consul, William Hardacker, reported the city to be quiet and running smoothly.[9]

Nevertheless, Rojas's window of opportunity to shore up his position soon began to shut. First, the governor faced a federal government that at best looked cooly upon his background and pro-González orientation. It preferred his Obregonista opponents in the state, led by José María Sánchez and Luis Sánchez Pontón. Indeed, as early as May 3, reports in the press claimed Sánchez Pontón to be Obregón's choice for governor. Second, Rojas had an image problem, which was used effectively against him in Mexico City. As a typical cacique with a checkered past, one who had been appointed by another of the same ilk, Rojas represented the inward-looking, traditional, conservative Puebla, one that outsiders and opponents of his government could and did easily stereotype and use to their advantage. Third, as Puebla's Cabreristas realized that they were not going to regain power on their own, they began to make deals with the Obregón camp. They preferred to ally with the Sonorans rather than come to terms with their long-time Gonzalista opponents.[10]

Pressure mounted on the new pro-Obregón Adolfo de la Huerta government in Mexico City to do something about Rojas. Especially strident were local Obregonistas, livid that they had failed to take Puebla City in early May. Moreover, a series of upcoming elections, scheduled to take place in early August for the federal congress and in September for the presidency, made it critical that pro-Obregón town councils be in place to oversee the balloting.[11]

Reluctant to confront Rojas directly, for fear of provoking violence, President de la Huerta instead squeezed the governor. First, in early June, Rojas's military support was greatly undermined when pro-Obregón general Fortunato Maycotte replaced Reyes Márquez as head of federal troops. The Obregonistas also cemented alliances with other officers in the region, such as Higinio Aguilar, reduced the forces of others, like Francisco Barbosa, and reorganized the commands of yet others, including the Arenistas.[12]

Pushed by Sánchez Pontón and the local Obregonistas, de la Huerta questioned Rojas's legitimacy. Backed by a vote in the senate, the president ruled that the governor had not been legally appointed and that, since all constitutional powers in the state had disappeared during the rebellion, Mexico City now had authority to regularize the situation. Therefore, Rojas was ordered to adhere to a process in which the president would submit three names, including Rojas's, to the senate. In turn, that federal body would chose one as the legitimate interim governor. Rojas knew that Obregonista favorite Sánchez Pontón would be on the list, and therefore, that he had little chance of surviving such a procedure.[13]

In response, Rojas argued that the state's superior court, unlike the executive and legislative branches, had continued to function during the upheaval and, as a result, represented legal continuity. Hence, that panel, he declared, had power to name the governor. Otherwise, he emphasized, to hand over this prerogative to the federal government would be to subvert state sovereignty, condone federal intervention, and contradict a basic ideal of the revolution.[14]

At this point, however, Rojas's coalition fractured. In late June several key state government officials resigned and publicly condemned him. They included Gilberto Bosques (head of *gobernación*), Aurelio Aja (director of social welfare), and Porfirio del Castillo (police chief). They disagreed with Rojas's interpretation of who should choose the governor and, as liberals, were unhappy about the increasing role of conservatives and business interests in his administration. This shift toward the right reflected Rojas's search for greater support among elements that had made accommodations with the Gonzalistas over the years and who had no desire to see another set of northern revolutionaries assume power in the state. These three individuals, however, also had another motive for abandoning Rojas. They had political ambitions, which were jeopardized by remaining with the besieged state government. Consequently, in the upcoming August vote they would be elected to the federal congress.[15]

Then word circulated that the governor would be ousted come what may. Desperate, Rojas tried to short-circuit de la Huerta by handing over executive power to Roberto Labastida, the head of the state superior court, on July 16. Outraged, local Obregonistas, led by José María Sánchez, stormed and occupied state government buildings, threatening the lives of officials and shutting down the government. Federal troops under General Maycotte took control of the city. In the end, Judge Labastida, no hero, turned the government over on July 21 to Sánchez Pontón, who meanwhile had been approved by the senate.[16]

Reform-minded Sánchez Pontón, who came to power intending to ameliorate the divisive political atmosphere, soon found himself at its mercy.

Initial efforts to revamp town councils by appointing bipartisan, representative members quickly fell victim to Obregonista pressure and threats against the governor. As a result, Sánchez Pontón, employing Cabrerista-era extraordinary powers (which were still in effect) and tactics, ended up overturning pro-Gonzalista local governments and appointing in their stead pro-Obregón ones. Otherwise, his administration faced the real possibility of an "embargo" to be led by José María Sánchez. In some cases the governor's actions even meant putting back into power Cabreristas who had recently switched to the Obregón camp.[17]

Consequently, among widespread reports of intimidation and sporadic violence, the August elections were held with the results, as expected, favoring those who backed the Sonorans. The following month, Obregón won the presidential vote, taking nearly 94 percent of the ballots cast in the state.[18]

By September 1920, then, with the federal congress, the presidency, and the governorship in Obregonista hands, the Carrancista period, the second major era of the revolution, in Puebla had ended. Political life in the state, however, would remain exceedingly atomized, divisive, and violent for another decade or more. The search for stability was to be found neither in the state's formal political structures nor in an authoritarian figure or group that could manage to gain informal control of the entity. The past years of wrenching military upheaval would now settle into a pattern characterized more by relentless, personalized, political infighting, exacerbated by interventions from Mexico City. Despite this chaos, however, the fundamental question of what relationship Puebla, given its autonomous sentiments, was to have to the larger, national political context was slowly being worked out. Beneath the surface, the broad contours of a political culture, already beginning to emerge, contributed to the creation of a new state, albeit one which would not become fully developed and institutionalized until the 1940s.

CONCLUSION

The revolution in Puebla was based on hope for change by people acting on the historically embedded idea of local autonomy. Nevertheless, the effort to carry out this ideal within the revolutionary context revealed division among Poblanos about what this concept meant in practice. As a result, two partially overlapping yet also opposing views came into conflict. Although linked in theory, they clashed over the degree to which autonomy, when actually implemented, should allow individuals and communities to determine their destinies.

One group, radical in outlook, mostly lower and lower-middle class, and principally rural and small-town based, rejected accommodation with the forces of outside change. It emphasized an uncompromising local autonomy to allow the preservation of traditional ways of life, including the power to make and carry out policy related to such concrete issues as commerce, education, labor, land, military service, religion, and taxes. A second group, more moderate and pragmatic in outlook, mostly urban dwellers and including workers, rejected this pure or exclusivist version. Adherents to this second position cautiously accepted some of the forces of change of the era brought from the outside. These included limited centralization or circumscribed state control over their political and socioeconomic lives, modernization, individualism, and a market economy. These changes, however, could not be imposed from the outside.

This disagreement, which arose early in the revolution, divided and weakened the first revolutionary coalition under Madero. In the end, with the backing of many in the second group, the Huertista military took power to check the rising tide of those who pushed for a broader and more radical implementation of the ideal of local autonomy, championed by radicals. Thus, the more moderate, modernized, urban elements momentarily gained some of their goals through the coup that brought the Huertistas to power. Relative stability returned to the state and, although Governors Maass and

Hernández were central government-appointed military men and outsiders, they did allow a limited degree of political space at the state and local levels by keeping the legislature open and permitting municipalities to function. Authorities even demonstrated enough flexibility, in their effort to bring peace to the state, to negotiate the Pacto de la Sierra of October 1913, an indication of their realization of the importance of local autonomy in Puebla.

For the time being, these compromising elements found the Huerta government tolerable, if not ideal (Puebla's political and economic elite still wanted control of the governorship, for example). Nevertheless, intensifying warfare, carried out by the more traditional, rural elements, which rejected interference by the Huertista outsiders (yet, ironically, accepted help from extra-state groups, the Carrancistas and Zapatistas, who entered the Sierra and the south of Puebla, respectively), forced the weakening regime to become increasingly repressive and squeeze its city-based supporters for larger sums of money to finance the conflict. Disillusioned by the breakdown of law and order, growing authoritarianism, and the rising financial burden, these groups abandoned Huerta and his governor by the late spring and summer of 1914.

These urban elements then saw their rescue in the Carrancistas, who, the thinking went, although outsiders, also could be tolerated if they, like the early Huertistas, brought stability and allowed for political space. This illusion quickly dissipated, however. Conflict worsened as rural elements defended their version of uncompromising autonomy. Pragmatic urbanites, too, soon resented these people from northern Mexico who closed all avenues of political activity. They even persecuted people who had had the remotest association with the Díaz and Huerta governments, making this the basic litmus test of revolutionary worthiness. Furthermore, the arrogant, aggressive newcomers, soldiers all, under governors Coss and Cervantes, carried out a harsh, arbitrary, interventionist policy, which aimed to centralize power and force the allegedly priest-ridden, benighted Poblanos into the twentieth century. As a result, Puebla's moderate, civilian city dwellers became virtual pariahs in their own communities.

At this point, one group of the countryside, less isolated and dogmatic, more pragmatic caciques at least paid lip service to supporting the revolution brought from the North. For generally strategic reasons they made military and economic alliances with Constitucionalista officers. By 1916, thanks to these arrangements, the Carrancista military situation had improved, with the Constitucionalistas managing to contain the armed, rural opposition, with its purer form of autonomy. Nevertheless, the political outlook remained somber as Poblanos of all stripes came to reject the

Carrancista program, particularly its interventionist, socioeconomic aspects, thus blocking attempts to forge a coherent and viable revolutionary movement in the state.

With the Carrancista program at a dangerous stalemate, the First Chief turned to an old colleague in arms, Cesáreo Castro. Castro introduced a policy of reconciliation, aimed at shoring up the deteriorating Constitucionalista base by reaching out to the moderate and conservative, mainly urban, elements, including ones who had had connections to the old establishment. Among the new governor's actions were the reestablishment of political institutions, including local government, in which Poblanos could participate, the holding of elections, and the tempering of some of the more interventionist and radical revolutionary programs such as property confiscation and restrictions on the Church.

Castro's moderate program made gains, and by 1917 it looked as if the Constitucionalista revolutionaries and the Poblanos had finally begun to arrive at a workable arrangement. Relative calm had returned as the war was now limited to the peripheries of the state, and the formal political apparatus had been largely reconstituted. Furthermore, newly elected Alfonso Cabrera, a civilian and Puebla native, took over as governor in the middle of that year through election.

This scenario, however, quickly altered. Governor Cabrera was not seen as legitimate by the power brokers of central Puebla. Federal army officers resented the civilian Cabrera's rise to power. Rejected by the state political establishment and the army, the governor allied with the hard-core, pro-Carrancista element. Cabrera proved to be a poor administrator, of authoritarian bent. The state government, because of its own doing and bad luck, failed adequately to deal with a series of crises.

By the middle of 1919, then, Cabrera had lost effective control of Puebla. Moderate urban dwellers and workers, disillusioned by his unwillingness to compromise, joined the growing opposition, leavened by conservative and military elements. Local and regional groups also gathered around federal officers, now a key symbol and enforcer of local autonomy against central government authority. Increasingly weakened and marginalized, Cabrera's administration remained a virtual spectator as Poblanos rallied to the cause of generals Pablo González and Álvaro Obregón, first during the presidential campaign and then when the two revolted and overthrew Carranza in April–May 1920. Cabrera soon fled, bringing an end to the Carrancista revolution in Puebla.

The Constitucionalistas could not fully tame Puebla. They won the war but not the revolution. They subdued the enemy on the battlefield but never gained the Poblanos' acceptance of the Carrancistas. Nevertheless, by the time of the fall of the Carrancista regime in May 1920, many refurbished, if not totally new, state structures were in place. In this process it is possible to detect the beginnings of the creation of a political culture, one that would still take many more years fully to develop. The two sides, Poblanos and outsiders, had begun to make compromises and adjustments to each other regarding their respective expectations of how and by whom the state should be run.

The northern revolutionaries, who arrived in the state in 1914 convinced of the justness of their cause and determined to carry it out, ended up becoming partially absorbed into the complex webs of Poblano socioeconomic and political life. Save for the defeated Marquistas and Arenistas and marginalized Zapatistas, urban and pragmatic rural Poblanos demonstrated willingness to compromise on their idea of local autonomy. Ultimately they tolerated aspects of the northern Mexicans' revolutionary program. The most overt examples of this tolerance, perhaps, are the acceptance by urban moderates of the policies of Governor Cesáreo Castro in 1916–17 and the arrangements made among federal officers and regional caciques during the entire period, 1914–1920. In this process, of course, the long-held ideal of local autonomy in its purest form became muted. Yet despite its dilution, it served an important purpose: helping to shape the revolution to the needs and expectations of the people of the state, not to some abstract set of ideas imposed by outsiders.

Hence, it seems accurate to say that revolutionary actions and aims took place in Puebla between 1913 and 1920, but no revolution in a holistic sense transpired. Some groups and individuals rebelled with goals for overall change, but they were few, and in the end the structures they modified were numbered. Some peasants invaded land, and a few received dotations under the government reform program, but most made deals with hacendados, all within a traditional capitalistic–private property framework. Workers gained marginally better conditions and the unofficial right to unionize, yet real wages declined, and laborers did not control the means of production. Urbanites found themselves generally worse off, with economic opportunity and services diminished while personal freedoms were more circumscribed. The middle class, with hardly any political access between 1914 and 1917, even thereafter found a system structured much like and only somewhat more transparent than during the Porfiriato. Students watched the government cut budgets and close institutions for economic and political reasons. Landowners initially fled, yet were able to return after 1917 to resume control of their properties, many of them handed back by a government more interested in production than redistribution of wealth. Hacendados did now face a more assertive peasantry, yet one disposed to compromise. The business and industrial community suffered economically and would not resume near-normal activity until the 1920s. They, too, would now have to deal with employees and workers less inclined to accept the patterns of management-labor behavior of old, yet whose principal demands were materialistic, not ideological. The Church lost control of many of its properties, yet parish-level priests stayed throughout the conflict and high officials returned after 1918. Moreover, the Church as an institution, and not just its spiritual message, remained an integral part of most people's lives. The press, although marginally freer, was still subject to intimidation, harassment, and co-optation.

Only in the loosest sense, then, did the victorious Constitucionalistas carry out a revolution in Puebla. It was imposed and only grudgingly tolerated. Nevertheless, this interaction initiated the building of a centralizing and powerful state, one that the Porfiristas could only have imagined. The emerging governing apparatus, however, not fully consolidated until the 1940s, would continue for at least another twenty years to accommodate, through much promise and limited action, grassroots demands for change, thereby continuing the process of creating a hegemonic political culture at the cost of local autonomy.

NOTES

Introduction

1. LaFrance, *Mexican*.

2. Buve, "La historia"; Carmagnani, "El federalismo"; Guardino, *Peasants*; Hernández Chávez, "Federalismo"; Hernández Chávez, *La tradición*; Mallon, *Peasant*; Mallon, "Reflections"; Perry, *Juárez*; Rendón Garcini, "Díaz"; Salinas Sandoval, *Política*; Thomson, "Federalismo"; Thomson, "*Montaña*"; Thomson with LaFrance, *Patriotism*; Zoraida Vázquez, "El federalismo."

3. For fuller treatment of the concept of political culture and its connection to the Mexican revolution, see: Joseph and Nugent, *Everyday*.

4. See, for example, Guardino, *Peasants*; Joseph and Nugent, *Everyday*; Mallon, *Peasant*; Tutino, *From*; and Wells and Joseph, *Summer*.

5. Knight, *Mexican* 2:94–103; Meyer, *Huerta*, 156–78.

6. Benjamin, *Rich*, 123–43; Brunk, *Emiliano*, 81–231; Garner, *La revolución*, 105–7; Wells and Joseph, *Summer*, 270–85; Womack, *Zapata*, 159 370.

7. Katz, *Life*, 618–19; Martínez Guzmán and Chávez Ramírez, *Durango*, 214–16, 234, 242–48; García Ugarte, *Génesis*, 61, 71–4, 78; Ankerson, *Agrarian*, 77–9, 84; Falcón, *Revolución*, 104, 111–12, 116–22.

8. Aguilar Camín, *La frontera*, 445–6.

9. Knight, *Mexican*, 2:x–xi; Ruíz, *Great*, ix–x.

10. Hart, *Revolutionary*, 348; Katz, *Secret*, 119-549; Vanderwood, "Resurveying," 146–47.

11. Guerra, *México*, 329–42; Vanderwood, "Resurveying," 146–7, 155–61.

12. Tobler, *La revolución*, 285–94, 373, 400, 670–71.

1. Politics, 1913–1914

1. This section is based mostly on LaFrance, *Mexican*, 206–9, 225–34.

2. Tecuanhuey, *Los conflictos*, 175–98.

3. Ibid., 201–2.

4. Ankerson, *Agrarian*, 61–2; Falcón, *Revolución*, 70–1; García Ugarte, *Génesis*, 44.

5. MWG, Márquez Huerta to Díaz, March 12, 1913, 2:105; MWG, Luna Bonilla to Díaz, April 21, 1913, 3:220; MWG, Zamatiz to Díaz, May 11, 1913, 5:511; PG, Muñoz to Díaz, March 7, 1913, 40; PG, Luna Bonilla to Díaz, May 18, 1913, 41B; SDN/AH, Márquez H. to Mondragón, April 22, 1913, XI/481.5/ 219:117:146; *País*, April 25, May 31, 1913; LaFrance, *Mexican*, 232–3.

6. LaFrance, *Mexican*, 238.

7. *País*, January 16, 1914; Peral, *Gobernantes*, 172–3.

8. FM, Urrutia to Conde et al., June 21, 1913, 59; *Diario*, May 15, 1913; *Imparcial*, June 4, 1913; *País*, June 2–4, 23, 1913; Tecuanhuey, *Los conflictos*, 210–2.

9. *País*, June 15, 1913.

10. SDN\AC, Flores et al. to Barbosa, September 9, 1914, D\III\3-172:47; *Imparcial*, September 5, 1913; *Mexican Herald*, May 31, June 7, 1913; *País*, June 6, 7, 9, 23, 1913.

11. FM, Urrutia to Maass, August 9, 1913, 87; FM, Rábago to Maass, August 11, 1913, 87; INEHRM, Rábago to Maass, September 5, 1913, 1:8/20:201; *Amigo*, January 2, 1914; Garciadiego Dantán, "Alemania," 437.

12. ACE\A, 22:January 7, March 27, June 7, 1913; ACE\E, Legislature—report, March 17, 1913, CCI:9592; ACE\E, Espinosa Bravo to Legislature, May 28, 1913, CCII:9633; *Amigo*, January 23, 1913; *Imparcial*, June 6,1913; Tecuanhuey, *Los conflictos*, 205–10.

13. ACE\A, 22:July 22, August 5, 9, 1913; FM, [Urrutia] to Maass, June 24, 1913, 59; *Amigo*, August 6, 23, 1913; *Imparcial*, June 6, 17, July 14, 21, 23, August 7, September 22, 23, 1913; *País*, July 24, August 7, 1913; *Periódico Oficial*, July 25, August 12, 1913; García Ugarte, *Génesis*, 45; Tecuanhuey, *Los conflictos*, 227.

14. ACE/A, 22:September 27, 1913; VC, Sánchez Pontón to Carranza, February 1, 1915, 26:2620; VC, García Veyrán to Carranza, February 4, 1915, 26:2686; *Amigo*, September 30, 1913; *Imparcial*, September 27, 29, 1913; *País*, August 7, 1913.

15. ACE\E, Mora to Legislature, August 29, 1913, CCIII:9664; *Amigo*, September 7, 1913.

16. PG, Fralde to Díaz, March 22, 1913, 37; PG, Castaños to Díaz, March 26, 1913, 41A; PG, Zamatiz to Díaz, March 27, 1913, 37; PG, Gómez Haro to Díaz, April 2, 1913, 38; PG, Rayón to Díaz, April 2, 1913, 38; PG, Díaz to Martínez et al., April 3, 1913, 37; PG, Ruíz to Díaz, May 22, 1913, 44; PG, del Corral to Díaz, June 2, 1913, 42; PG, Contreras to Díaz, June 12, 1913, 43; PG, Quirós Martínez to Díaz, June 12, 19, 1913, 44; PG, Vital to Díaz, June 22, 1913, 44; *Amigo*, March 8, 11, 1913; *Diario*, April 6, 1913; *Imparcial*, March 7, 1913; *Mexican Herald*, March 8, April 7, 1913.

17. FD, Instrucciones, October 22, 1913, 1:80; *Mexican Herald*, October 23, 27, 1913; *País*, August 3, 1913; Meyer, *Huerta*, 149–54.

18. ACE\A, 22:November 10, 1913; ARM, Diputados Federales to Congress, August 25, 1913, 56:93:22; *Imparcial*, November 13, 16, 1913; *País*, November 6,

10, 13, 18, 19, 1913, January 16, 1914; *Revista Moderna*, October 23, 1913, n.p.; Meyer, *Huerta*, 145–9; Tecuanhuey, *Los conflictos*, 221, 224–6.

19. FM, Alcocer to Maass, Jr., January 15, 1914, 89; *Amigo*, December 4, 1913; *Imparcial*, November 28, December 10, 1913; *Mexican Herald*, January 16, 1914; *País*, November 2, 11, 28, January 2, 16, 29, 30, 1914; *Periódico Oficial*, January 16, 1914.

20. ACE/A, 22:January 21, 1921; FM, Alcocer to Hernández, January 29, 1914, 89; *Amigo*, January 19, 20, 22, 30, 1914; *País*, January 19, 20, 1914; *Periódico Oficial*, January 23, 1914; LaFrance, *Mexican*, 53; Peral, *Gobernantes*, 174.

21. *Amigo*, February 13, March 10, 1914; Gillow y Zavala, *Reminiscencias*, 391; LaFrance, *Mexican*, 71, 131, 205.

22. ARM, Hernández to Alcocer, January 31, 1914, 58:95:262; FM, Alcocer to Hernández, March 19, 1914, 89; MGR, Alcocer to de la Torre, January 26, 1914, 95:156; MGR, Alcocer to Hernández, January 29, 1914, 95:261; *Amigo*, January 31, 1913, February 2, 19, 22, March 4, 9, 1914; *Imparcial*, June 5, July 29, 31, 1914; *País*, August 15, 1913, February 14, March 12, 15, 23, 1914.

23. ACE\A, 22:August 5, 1914; ACE\E, Hernández to Legislature, March 26, 1914, CCVII:9913; ACE\E, Posadas et al. to Governor, CCVII:9913; *Amigo*, April 30, August 9, 1914; *País*, March 3, 5, 1914.

24. ACE/A, 22:July 14, 24, 27, 1914; ARD, Serratos [Serdán] to Medina, August 4, 1914, 9:C:23; VC, López to Carranza, August 24, 1914, 13:1332; *Amigo*, July 30, August 2, 6, 10, 1914; *Imparcial*, July 27, 29, 31, 1914; Tecuanhuey, *Los conflictos*, 232.

2. Economic and Social Policy, 1913–1914

1. ACE/A, 22:July 9, 1913; ACE\E, Carrasco to Legislature, May 28, 1913, CCIII:9687; MGR, Joaquín [illegible] to Sec. Gobernación, November 27, 1913, 94:358–9; *Amigo*, February 26, June 18, 1914; *Imparcial*, July 21, 22, October 1, 1913, July 5, 1914; *País*, July 14, November 19, 1913, January 8, February 13, 14, March 3, 1914.

2. ACE\E, Hernández—*informe*, June 30, 1914, CC:9905; *País*, December 24, 1913.

3. ACE\A, 22:March 16, 1914; ACE\E, Maass to Legislature, August 12, 1913, CCIII:9694; ACE\E, Hernández to Legislature, March 28, 1914, CCVI:9855; MGR, Joaquín [illegible] to Sec. Gobernación, November 27, 1913, 94:358–9; *Imparcial*, July 25, 1914; *Mexican Herald*, April 4, 1914; *País*, January 16, March 13, 1914; *Periódico Oficial*, August 1, 19, 1913.

4. ACE\A, 22:August 9, 1913; *Amigo*, September 18, December 18, 1913, July 17, 1914; *Imparcial*, July 14, September 10, 26, October 4, 1913; *Mexican Herald*, January 12, 1914; *País*, July 5, 26, August 4, 1913, January 2, March 3, 29, 1914; *Periódico Oficial*, October 24, 1913.

5. ACE\E, Carrasco to Legislature, May 28, 1913, CCIII:9687.

6. *Imparcial*, September 26, October 4, November 27, December 6, 1913; *País*, July 18, 23, 24, 30, 1913, March 3, 1914.

7. ACE\A, 22:February 23, March 16, August 1–31, 1914; ACE\E, Hernández to Legislature, March 28, 1914, CCVI:9855; *Imparcial*, July 25, 1914; *País*, January 13, 1914.

8. *Imparcial*, September 6, 1913; *País*, January 9, 1914.

9. ACE\A, 22:March 23, 1914; ACE\E, Sánchez et al. to Governor, March 19, 1914, CCVI:9844; DT, Pérez Jiménez and López to Esteva, November 1, 1913, 37:24:1; DT, Subsec. Gobernación to Sec. Fomento, November 24, 1913, 37:24:6, December 5, 1913, 37:24:8–9; MGR, Esteva to Sec. Gobernación, November 6, 1913, 94:256; MGR, Joaquín [illegible] to Sec. Gobernación, November 27, 1913, 94:358–9; *Amigo*, March 24, 1914; *Imparcial*, November 29, 1913; *Periódico Oficial*, March 31, 1914; LaFrance, *Mexican*, 103, 154.

10. *Imparcial*, July 22, 1913, May 24, 27, 1914; *País*, November 19, 1913, March 13, 1914.

11. *Mexican Herald*, January 28, 1914; *País*, August 8, 1913, February 13, 1914; *Periódico Oficial*, March 31, 1914.

12. Gutiérrez Álvarez, "Conflicto," 43–4; *Imparcial*, July 13, 1913; *País*, August 13, 1913.

13. ACE\E, Álvear to Legislature, August 31, 1913, CCIII:9719; *Amigo*, July 13, August 21, 23, September 2, 1913, March 5, 1914; *Imparcial*, June 1, August, 29, 30, September 12, 22, October 9, November 7, 1913; *Mexican Herald*, March 6, 1914; *País*, July 27, November 30, 1913, March 5, 1914; *Periódico Oficial*, September 19, 1913, March 17, 1914; LaFrance, *Mexican*, 68–9, 156.

14. ACE\E, Maass to Legislature, September 11, 1913, CCIII:9734; ACE\E, Hernández to Legislature, March 28, 1914, CCVII:9907; ACE\E, Muñoz Ovando to Legislature, July 3, 1914, CCVII:9907; ACE\E, CIM to Legislature, July 9, 1914, CCVII:9907; ACE\E, Martínez Yáñez et al. to Governor, July 27, 1914, CCVII:9907; *Amigo*, September 16, 30, 1913, March 13, 28, 1914; *Imparcial*, September 22, 24, October 1, 1913; LaFrance, *Mexican*, 155.

15. ACE\A, 22:March 6, 1914; *Amigo*, December 14, 1913; *Periódico Oficial*, February 10, 1914.

16. ACE\A, 22:February 28, 1914; *Amigo*, February 5, March 1, 7, 20, 25, April 7, 1914; *Imparcial*, March 21, 1914; *Mexican Herald*, February 13, March 22, 1914; *País*, January 16, 18, 22, February, 6, 7, 17, 24, March 21, 1914; *Periódico Oficial*, February 20, April 17, 1914.

17. ACE\E, Hernández to Legislature, May 27, 1914, CCVII:9887; ACE\E, Hernández—informe, June 30, 1914, CC:9905; INEHRM, Rábago to Maass, September 5, 1913, 1:8/20:201; *Amigo*, December 10, 1913, May 9, 13, 23, 1914; *Imparcial*, December 13, 1913, May 8, 9, 15, 18, 25, 1914; *Periódico Oficial*, May 5, 27, June 5, 1914.

18. ACE\A, 22:July 6, 1914; ACE\E, Martínez Yáñez et al. to Hernández, June 6, July 6,1914, CCVII:9887; ACE\E, Hernández—informe, June 30, 1914, CC:9905; *Amigo*, July 9, 1914.

19. ACE\A, 22:July 17, 1914; ACE\E, Alcázar et al. to Muñoz Ovando, July 17, 1914, CCVI:9904; ACE\E, Muñoz Ovando to Legislature, July 23, 1914, CCVI:9904; *Amigo*, July 25, August 11, 14, 1914; *Imparcial*, July 19, 22, 1914; *Periódico Oficial*, August 18, 1914.

20. GBFO, Pearson and Sons—report, March 7, 1914, 2026:371; GBFO, Carden to Grey, June 25, 1914, 2029:470; GBFO, Méndez Riva to Carden, July 23, 1914, 2030:259, July 24, 1914, 2030:270, July 28, 1914, 2030:317; GBFO, Pearson to Undersec., July 28, 1914, 2030:328; JB, Camacho to Carranza, October 26, 1913, I:8; RDS, Canada to Bryan, August 6, 1913, 28:56–7; *Amigo*, February 12, June 3, 7, July 15, 1914; *Imparcial*, August 3, 19, October 9, 13, 1913, March 1, 6, 1914; *Mexican Herald*, August 10, October 1, 1913, February 13, 14, April 18, 1914; *País*, August 8, 1913, January 6, February 12, 13, March 9, April 30, 1914; Knight, *Mexican*, 2:131.

21. RG/G, Álvarez to Sec. Gobernación, August 12, 1913, 1a913(5)1; *Amigo*, August 8, November 23, 1913; *Mexican Herald*, September 7, October 10, 1913; *País*, July 12, August 3, November 25, 1913, February 3, March 11, 1914.

22. RDS, Canada to Bryan, February 23, 1914, 34:865; *Amigo*, December 4, 5, 1913, January 7, July 22, 1914; *Mexican Herald*, October 30, 1913, March 20, 1914.

23. *Amigo*, July 22, 1914; *País*, November 5, 1913.

24. DT, Gavito y Cía. to Esteva, December 16, 1913, 39:24:1; TLP, Evernden to Stockholders, October 29, 1913, 1197; *Imparcial*, July 14, September 21, October 10, 1913; *Boletín Departamento Trabajo*, 1.1(July 1913). 102.

25. *Amigo*, December 23, 25, 1913, January 17, 20, May 26, July 11, 1914; *Imparcial*, December 17, 1913, June 14, 1914; *País*, July 14, August 3, November 2, 10, 12, 14, 23, 30, 1913, January 5, 16, 19, February 4, 1914; Gamboa Ojeda, *Los empresarios*, 92.

26. AJE\I, Velasco to Banco Hispano Americano, June 2, 5, 1914, 1919:5; CDHM, Rivero Collada to Sec. Hacienda, January 20, 1914, 50:335:8:—; *Amigo*, November 12, December 25, 1913, January 5–8, 17, May 26, July 28, August 10, 1914; *Imparcial*, June 8, 1914; *País*, November 10, 12, 14, December 6, 12, 1913, January 7, 15, 19, February 4, March 2, 1914; González Loscertales, "Bases," 272–3, 284–5.

27. *Imparcial*, June 28, July 25, December 11, 1913; *País*, January 7, 1914; Gutiérrez Álvarez, "Conflicto," 176; Gutiérrez Álvarez, *Experiencias*, 318.

28. Gamboa Ojeda, *Los empresarios*, 32, 83; Palacios, *Puebla*, 196, 239; Ramírez Rancaño, *Burguesía*, 101–2, 119.

29. DT, Ortega Elorza to Esteva, July 31, 1913, 41:6:5; DT, Esteva to Sec. Fomento, August 18, 1913, 46:3:1–5; *País*, July 11, 30, 1913; Gamboa Ojeda, *La urdimbre*, 277–9.

30. DT, Cía. Mexicana de Petróleo "El Aguila" to Cía. Industrial Atlixco, January 6, 1914, 84:21:2; DT, Díaz et al. to Esteva, February 10, 1914, 81:1:1; GBFO, Sanderson et al. to Undersec. State, December 2, 1913, 1678:454.

31. *Imparcial*, May 11, 1914; *País*, November 20, December 25, 1913; Gutiérrez Álvarez, "Conflicto," 379.

32. DT, DT—report, [March n.d., 1914], 75:5:1; DT, Riva Cervantes to Ortega Elorza, April 21, 1914, 75:5:16.

33. DT, Jenkins to Esteva, February 10, 1914, 85:5:1; DT, Velasco to Director, April 6, 1914, 81:6:14; *País*, February 7, 1914.

34. DT, Gavito y Cía. to Esteva, February 9, 1914, 80:15:—; *Imparcial*, September 10, December 13, 1913; *País*, November 4, 1913, February 9, 1914; Ramírez Rancaño, *Burguesía*, 102–5, 109–10.

35. DT, Gavito y Cía. to Esteva, February 27, 1914, 80:15:25–6; *País*, March 5, 1914.

36. DT, Cardoso to Molina Enríquez, June 20, 1914, 85:7:1–2; Ramírez Rancaño, *Burguesía*, 122–6.

37. DT, Subsec. Industria to Sec. Guerra, August 4, 1914, 85:8:4; *Amigo*, August 4, 1914.

38. Ramírez Rancaño, *Burguesía*, 126–30.

39. Gutiérrez Álvarez, *Experiencias*, 306.

40. DT, Galicia et al. to DT, December 9, 1913, 35:25:1; *Amigo*, May 1, 1914; *País*, August 25, 29, 1913.

41. DT, Círculo Mutualista Obreros Católicos to DT, January 13, 1913, 44:12:26; *Amigo*, March 8, August 9, 1913, February 1, May 17, 1914; *Imparcial*, October 13, 1913; Ceballos Ramírez, *El catolicismo*, 311–416.

42. *Imparcial*, August 20, 1913.

43. *Amigo*, August 20, 1913; *País*, August 29, 1913, January 14, 1914.

44. DT, Rojas and Peña to Director, February 13, 1914, 35:25:3–4; MGR, Serafín de la Torre—decree, January 28, 1914, 95:185–96; *Amigo*, February 14, March 21, 1914; *Imparcial*, August 20, September 8, 29, December 22, 1913, March 21, April 9, June 2, 1914; *País*, August 21, 1913, January 8, 27, February 4, 17, 1914; *Periódico Oficial*, January 30, February 17, April 3, 1914.

45. DT, DT—report, [n.d. 1913], 51:14:33; DT, Sierra y Domínguez to Esteva, March 14, 1913, 51:24:5; DT, Sierra to Esteva, March 30, 1913, 35:9:3–4; DT, Díaz and Guerrero to Esteva, March 26, 1913, 35:5:8; DT, Director to Meza, April 23, 1913, 49:22:12; DT, DT to Hernández et al., May 2, 1913, 49:18:6; DT, Ortega Elorza to Esteva, June 16, 1913, 51:15:3–4, August 1, 1913, 50:5:16; DT, Ortega Elorza to Esteva, June 28, 1913, 35:36:7–8; DT, Chávez et al. to Esteva, July 4, 1913, 35:10:1; DT, Cadena et al. to Esteva, August [n.d.], 1913, 35:12:1; DT, DT to Sec. Hacienda, September 19, 1913, 47:28:1–3; DT, Coughlin to Director, October 8, 1913, 35:23:7–8; *Amigo*, February 28, November 27, 1913; *Imparcial*, August 9, 1913; LaFrance, "Labour," 59–74; Gutiérrez Álvarez, *Experiencias*, 309.

46. DT, DT—report, [n.d. 1913], 51:14:38; DT, Carbajal to Esteva, May 13, 1913, 50:5:49; DT, DT to Governors, May 30, 1913, 50:13:1–3; DT, González Cosío Hnos. to Director, June 24, 1913, 35:27:1.

47. DT, Esteva to Obreros, [n.d. 1913], 47:7:10; DT, Proyecto Exposición, [n.d.] 1913, 50:13:10–35; DT, Sierra to Esteva, March 30, 1913, 35:9:3–4; DT, DT to Obreros La Hilandera, April 7, 1913, 35:20:3; DT, DT to Governors, May 30, 1913, 50:13:1–3; DT, Mora to Sec. Fomento, June 16, 1913, 50:12:16; DT, Ortega Elorza to Esteva, June 27, 1913, 51:15:20, June 28, 1913, 35:36:7–8; DT, DT to Ortega Elorza, July 4, 1913, 51:15:23; DT, Director to Obreros El Pilar, September 22, 1913, 35:31:2; *Imparcial*, June 14, 1913; *Independiente*, July 4, 5, 1913.

48. DT, Comité Ejecutivo Industriales—meeting, April 15, 1913, 47:16:15–8; DT, Olivares et al. to Obreros, April 30, 1913, 47:19:2; DT, Esteva to Obreros, April 30, 1913, 47:7:5; DT, Cardoso to Director, June 6, 1913, 73:6:1–2; DT, DT to Governor, June 11, 1913, 73:6:3–4; DT, González Cosío Hnos. to Esteva, July 20, 1913, 35:28:1; *Boletín Departamento Trabajo*, 1:1(July 1913): 33–4; Gutiérrez Álvarez, "Conflicto," 372–7.

49. DT, Director to Jefe Estación et al., October 16, 1913, 50:3:23–4; *Amigo*, April 2, 1914; *Imparcial*, October 22, 1913; Gómez Álvarez, *Puebla*, 34–6.

50. DT, Echeverría and Marrón to Esteva, September 12, 1913, 36:24:14; DT, Quiroz et al. to Esteva, January 4, 1914, 36:24:47; DT, Director to Gutiérrez, February 18, 1914, 76:9:2; DT, Gutiérrez to Esteva, March 11, 1914, 36.24.49, *Imparcial*, November 28, 1913; *País*, December 13, 1913, March 2, 1914; Gamboa Ojeda, *La urdimbre*, 280–2; Gómez Álvarez, *Puebla*, 36; Knight, *Mexican*, 2.135.

51. ARM, García Granados and [illegible] Patzer to Sec. Gobernación, July 11, 1913, 55:92:100; *Imparcial*, August 15, December 22, 1913; *Mexican Herald*, April 29, 1913; *País*, January 30, 1914.

52. *Imparcial*, July 12, 1913; *Mexican Herald*, July 14, 17, 1913; *País*, March 26, 1914; *Periódico Oficial*, July 8, 1913.

53. CDHM, Cologán to Ministro Estado, September 2, 1913, 47:292:1:37; *Imparcial*, July 5, August 2, September 3, October 21, 1913, March 24, 1914; *País*, August 3, 1913, February 19, March 9, 1914.

54. *Imparcial*, August 19, 1913; *Mexican Herald*, March 4, 1914.

55. ACE/A, 22:January 5, 1914; ACE/E, Hernández to Legislature, February 20, 1914, CCVI:9834; GBFO, Stronge to Bart, July 19, 1913, 1674:409; *Amigo*, June 20, 1913, March 1, June 23, 26, July 16–8, 1914; *Imparcial*, June 18, July 12, 24, 1913; *País*, November 28, December 25, 1913; Hoyos Hernández, "Vida," 33.

56. *Amigo*, February 6, 15, 19, 20, March 25, July 7, 18, 1914; *Imparcial*, October 9, 1913; *Opinión*, April 25, 1914; *País*, November 28, 1913, February 7, March 20, 1914.

57. ACE/E, Yáñez et al. to Legislature, April 24, 1914, CCVI:9869; SDN/AH, Sec. Gobernación to Governor, April 22, 1914, XI/481.5/220:119:572; *Amigo*,

April 28, May 1, June 27, 1914; *Imparcial*, April 29, May 2, 3, 16, June 1, 29, 1914; *Periódico Oficial*, April 28, May 1, 1914.

58. Henderson, *Worm*, 30.

59. ACE/E, *Boletín de Estadística del Estado*, April 15, 1912, p. 300, CCI:9575; *Amigo*, February 4, March 8, 16, July 22, 1914; *Imparcial*, December 3, 1913, March 9–11, 28, June 20, August 31, 1914; *Mexican Herald*, April 9, 1914; *País*, January 18, February 9, March 9–11, 1914; Kuri Camacho, *La realidad*, 2:75; México, Dirección General Estadística, *Compendio*, 8.

60. *Imparcial*, July 24, 1913; *Periódico Oficial*, July 18, 1913.

61. *Imparcial*, September 7, 14, 17, 18, 25–7, 29, October 18, 1913.

62. *Amigo*, November 25, 1913; *Imparcial*, September 15, 22, 1913.

63. JFL, Pineda—broadside, December 6, 1913, 1913; *Amigo*, August 6, 1913, May 9, June 25, July 18, 1914.

64. TO, Espinosa to Ramírez, March 11, 1913, 410(1913).

65. *Amigo*, March 8, August 5, 9, 1913, March 7, 10, 15, 18, May 17, June 2, 1914; *Imparcial*, October 21, 1913; *País*, March 12, 18, 1913; Esparza, *Gillow*, xxviii; Gillow y Zavala, *Reminiscencias*, 391.

66. VC, Cabrera to Zubarán Capmany, January 30, 1914, 6:786; *Imparcial*, December 7, 8, 1913; *Mexican Herald*, May 19, 1913.

3. War, 1913–1914

1. FM, Urrutia to Governor, August 26, 1913, 88; FM, Urrutia to Governors, September 9, 1913, 88; FM, Alcocer to Governors, March 18, 1914, 89, [May 4, 1914], 90; RDS, Shanklin to Bryan, September 9, 1913, 28:1092–4, September 15, 1913, 29:25–6; *Imparcial*, September 15, 1913, April 3, May 2, 1914; *Amigo*, August 23, 1913, March 20, 1914; *País*, April 1, 1913; *Periódico Oficial*, May 5, 1914.

2. CIM, Cardoso to Depto. Trabajo, June 5, 1913, 1:120–1; DT, Casas to Esteva, November 27, 1913, 51:10:23; *Amigo*, November 19, 1913; *Imparcial*, September 21, November 25, 1913; *País*, April 28, June 7, December 1, 1913.

3. INEHRM, Galindo et al.—certificate, [n.d.], 1:6/1:16; INEHRM, Serdán—report, [n.d.], 1:6/12:44; Jaime Espinosa, "Rosa," 83–4.

4. INEHRM, Galindo et al.—certificate, [n.d.], 1:6/1:16; INERHM, Bonafide to Carranza, July 15, 1914, 1:6/2:14; INEHRM, Vega Reza-certificate, January 30, 1941, 1:6/2:5; *Amigo*, January 5, 1914; Álvarez Aguilar et al., *Carmen*, 35; Jaime Espinosa, "Rosa," 83–4, 87–9.

5. INEHRM, Vega Reza-certificate, January 30, 1941, 1:6/2:5.

6. INEHRM, Narváez—report, January 28, 1914, 1:6/2:10; INEHRM, Instituto Metodista—report, [n.d.], 1:6/2:59; INEHRM, Serratos [Serdán] to González Galindo, May 29, 1913, 1:6/2:6; INEHRM, Narváez and Serdán to Galván, July

18, 1913, 1:6/1:12; INEHRM, Serdán et al.—memorandum, [May n.d.], 1914, 1:6/2:11; INERHM, Bonafide to Carranza, July 15, 1914, 1:6/2:14; INERHM, Medina to Sec. Junta, July 16, 1914, 1:6/2:15; INEHRM, Ángulo to Narváez de Vilchis, June 1, 1939, 1:6/6:69; INEHRM, Vilchis—certificate, November 25, 1953, 1:6/11:16; SDN\AH, Bouchez to Sec. Guerra, May 11, 1914, XI/481.5/220:119:577; VC, Castro—report, [n.d.], 151:17234; Jaime Espinosa, "Rosa," 87–9.

7. C/ADN, Mondragón to Jefe División Oriente, April 1, 1913, MP/7115/4; GO, Franco Pliego to Ministerio Público, March 20, 1913, 13:2:31; GO, Zapata to Ministerio Público, March 20, 1913, 13:2:29; JA, Ramos Martínez to Mendoza, March 11, 1913, 2:86; JA, Mendoza to Ministerio Público, March 20, 1913, 2:91; SRE, Cologán y Cologán to León de la Barra, February 24, 1913, 12–11–55; *Amigo*, March 8, 1913; *Diario*, May 11, 1913; *Imparcial*, March 3, 7, 10–2, 14, April 10, 11, 1913; *Mexican Herald*, May 12, 1913; *Periódico Oficial*, March 25, 1913; Knight, *Mexican*, 2:3–4, 6; Vela González, *Diario*, 91; Womack, *Zapata*, 81.

8. C/ADN, Estado Mayor—report, June 6–7, 1913, MP/7115/4; *Amigo*, June 20, 1913, *Imparcial*, June 11, 12, 14, 15, 1913; *País*, June 11, 13, 16, 1913.

9. GBFO, Carden to GBFO, December 8, 1913, 1679:380; GO, Mendoza to Zapata, October 17, 1913, 13:9:25; GO, Acacia to Zapata, February 17, 1914, 14:3:14; PHO, Sosa Pavón—interview, March 27, 1973, 1/48:1:129–30; *Amigo*, September 2, 1913, January 5, 1914; *Imparcial*, August 14, October 8, 1913; *País*, August 27, November 1, 19, 1913, February 4, April 15, 1914.

10. GBFO, Espinosa to Sosa, November 25, 1913, 1679:371; GO, Zapata to Mendoza, January 3, 1914, 17:3:2; PHO, Cuéllar Montalvo-interview, March 8, 1973, 1/45:/:9–14; *Imparcial*, October 14, 1913.

11. Aguilar Camín, "Relevant," 108, 115; Jacobs, *Ranchero*, 99–101.

12. SDN/AH, Sec. Gobernación to Sec. Guerra, November 5, 1913, XI/481.5/219:117:655; *Imparcial*, November 24, December 1, 7, 8, 1913; *País*, June 26, 29, August 15, November 19, December 7, 20, 21, 1913, January 29, 1914; Brunk, *Emiliano*, 81–110.

13. AJE/I, Peña to Sec. Tribunal Supremo, May 14, 1913, 1913; CGS, Zapata to Amezcua, February 3, 1914, 1:3:27; GO, Zapata to Zapata, September 22, 1913, 13:8:20; GO, Bautista to Zapata, December 28, 1913, 13:11:48; GO, Ayaquica to Zapata, February 12, 1914, 14:3:12; GO, Anzures to Zapata, August 7, 1914, 16:1:106; JA, Zapata—decree, October 28, 1913, 2:117, February 10, 1914, 2:130; JA, Mendoza —circular, February 12, 1914, 2:132; *Imparcial*, April 28, 1913.

14. GO, Ayaquica to Zapata, February 12, 1914, 14:3:12, February 18, 1914, 14:3:15; GO, Anzures to Zapata, August 7, 1914, 16:1:106.

15. This section is based on Thomson with LaFrance, *Patriotism*, 284–93.

16. Falcón and García, *La semilla*; Garner, *La revolución*; Jacobs, *Ranchero*; Knight, "Peasant," 31, 34.

17. Ankerson, *Agrarian*, 64–5.

18. GO, Cozatl et al. to Zapata, October 1, 1913, 13:9:29; Buve, *El movimiento*, 139–43, 336, 359–60; del Castillo, *Puebla*, 125–43; Henderson, *Worm*, 51–2; Ramírez Rancaño, *La revolución*, 15–6, 20–1, 33–42.

19. C/ADN, Vallejo to Sec. Guerra, April 24, 1914, MP/7115/4; FM, Luján to Governor, July 20, 1914, 90; SDN/AC, Sec. Guerra to Barbosa, May 20, 1911, D/III/3-172:25; SDN/AH, Luján to Sec. Guerra, March 30, 1914, XI/481.5/ 220:119:785; *Imparcial*, June 10, 1913; *País*, June 25, 1913; Bravo Izquierdo, *Un soldado*, 32–75; Sánchez Lamego, *Historia*, 5:354–6.

20. ACE/E, Hernández—informe, June 30, 1914, CC:9905; JFL, Rojas—broadside, April 22, 1914, 1914; JFL, Jiménez Castro to Medina, April 22, 1914, 1914; JFL, de la Torre to Jefe Político Chignahuapan, April 22, 1914, 1914; JFL, Luna Bonilla to Lucas, May 5, 1914, 1914; Meyer, *Huerta*, 201–2; *Puebla a través*, 172.

21. C/ADN, Rojas to Sec. Guerra, April 23, 1914, MP/7115/5; *Imparcial*, April 24, 25, 27, 29, May 1, 2, 10, 1914; *Opinión*, April 25, 1914; *País*, April 24, 27, 30, 1914; *Periódico Oficial*, April 28, 1914; Contreras Cruz et al., *Puebla*, 5:253–4.

22. C/ADN, Vallejo to Sec. Guerra, April 24, 1914, MP/7115/4; SDN/AC, Peredes Colín to Barbosa, April 23, 1914, D/III/3-172:35; *Imparcial*, April 30, 1914.

23. C/ADN, Hernández to Sec. Guerra, April 27, 1914, MP/7115/4; Brunk, *Emiliano*, 103–4; Womack, *Zapata*, 186.

24. FIC, Abreu Sala—report, May 7, 1914, 29:7:3–10; JFL, Márquez—broadside, April 18, 1914, 1914, April 25, 1914, Planes y Decretos; JFL, Pineda—broadside, April 20, 1914, 1914; JFL, Soto to Pres. Municipal Tlapacoya, April 27, 1914, 1914; *Imparcial*, May 18, 1914; Benjamin, *Rich*, 116; Rivera Moreno, *Xochiapulco*, 185.

25. SDN/AC, Lechuga to Barbosa, May 15, 1914, D/III/3-172:39; *Amigo*, April 6, 30, May 2, 1914; Sánchez Lamego, *Historia*, 5:356–9.

26. FM, Alcocer to Governor, April 22, 23, 27, 28, 1914, 89, May 3, 1914, 90; *Imparcial*, May 3, 7, 1914; *País*, April 30, 1914; *Periódico Oficial*, May 1, 19, 1914; Ankerson, *Agrarian*, 69; García Ugarte, *Génesis*, 49; *Puebla a través*, 172; Wells and Joseph, *Summer*, 264.

27. *Amigo*, May 2, 1914.

28. CIM, Cardoso to Depto. Trabajo, July 27, 1914, 1:257; CIM, Cardoso to Carvajal, August 3, 1914, 1:258; C/T, Campero to Carranza, July 15, 1914, MVIII; GO, Ayaquica to Zapata, July 19, 1914, 14:8:34, July 23, 1914, 15:3:82, July 26, 1914, 15:3:137; *Amigo*, July 12, 23, 1914.

29. GO, Medina to Zapata, July 25, 1914, 14:8:49; GO, Ayaquica to Zapata, July 28, 1914, 15:3:57; GO, Espinosa to Zapata, August 13, 1914, 16:1:48; GO, Galván to Zapata, August 17, 1914, 16:2:62; GO, Zapata to Galván, August 23, 1914, 17:3:69.

30. GO, Villegas et al.—decree, June 23, 1914, 14:7:28; GO, Villegas et al. to Zapata, June 24, 1914, 14:7:31; GO, Espinosa—certificate, July 7, 1914, 15:2:122; GO, Acta Plan de Ayala, July 19, 1914, 19:1:12; *Amigo*, July 28, 29, 1914.

31. GO, Zapata to Ortega, July 6,1914, 17:3:56; GO, Zapata to Gracia, July 23,1914, 17:3:50; *Amigo*, July 11, August 6, 9, 12, 13, 1914; *Imparcial*, June 23, 26, 30, July 31, 1914; *Mexican Herald*, June 18, 21, 1914; Sánchez Lamego, *Historia*, 5:355–6.

32. GO, Gracia to Zapata, July 29, 1914, 14:8:106; SDN/AC, Barbosa—circular to Spaniards, July 4, 1914, D/III/3-172:42; *Amigo*, June 23, 26, July 19, 1914; *Mexican Herald*, May 22, June 14, 1914.

33. C/T, Estrada to Carranza, August 21, 1914, XXI-4; FM, Alcocer to Jefe Político Zacatlán, May 28, 1914, 90; INEHRM, Pérez to Mariguita, June 29, 1914, 1:6/6:30; JFL, Medina to Lucas, July 20, 1914, 1914; MWG, González to Camacho, May 29, 1914, 16:2390; RDS, Canada to Bryan, July 27, 1914, 39:1295; *Amigo*, July 19, 22, August 1–3, 5, 1914; *Imparcial*, May 14, 15, 17, 23, 29, July 21, 25, 1914; *Renovador*, June 25, 1914.

34. JFL, Lucas to Medina, July 18,1914, 1914; RDS, Burke to Canada, August 4, 1914, 41:118.

35. *Amigo*, August 3, 4, 1914.

36. C/T, Carranza to Medina, June 28, 1914, XXI; JFL, Márquez—manifesto, June 23, 1914, Scrapbook; *Renovador*, June 25, July 16, 1914.

37. ARD, Serratos [Serdán] to Oficiales Ejército Constitucionalista, July 12, 1914, 9:C:15; ARD, Serratos [Serdán] to Medina, August 4, 1914, 9:C:23; ARD, Grajales Murphy to Robles Domínguez, August 12, 1914, 14:58:3; C/T, Acevedo to Carranza, July 26, 1914, MVIII; INERHM, Medina et al.—certificate, August 11, 1914, 1:4:2–3; INEHRM, Sec. Junta Revolucionaria to Medina, May 12, 1914, 1:6/2:12; INEHRM, Mestre to Gómez, June 8, 1914, 1:6/6:26; INEHRM, "El Antiguo" to Jefes Revolucionarios, June 18, 1914, 1:6/5:17; INEHRM, Téllez to Fernández de Lara, July 29, 1914, 1:6/12:15; INEHRM, Bañuelos to Fernández de Lara, July 31, 1914, 1:6/12:16; INEHRM, Fernández de Lara to Bonilla and Arenas, August 4, 1914, 1:6/12:18–9; INEHRM, Hidalgo and del Castillo to Junta Revolucionaria, August 11, 1914, 1:6/2:35; *Mexican Herald*, July 20, 1914; Gutiérrez Álvarez, *Experiencias*, 325.

38. ARD, Serratos [Serdán] to Medina, August 4, 1914, 9:C:23; CDHM, Luque to Consul España, August 19, 1914, 48:307:17:5; C/T, González to Carranza, August 20, 21, 1914, XXI-4; C/T, Rosales to Hay, August 21, 1914, XXI-4; C/T, Cañete to Carranza, August 21, 1914, XXI-4; C/T, Jefe 2a División Centro to González, August 21, 1914, XXI-4; MWG, Report, August [n.d.], 1914, 20:2804; MWG, Luque to Obregón, August 17, 1914, 18:2711; PG, Ruíz Ceus-report, October 17, 1918, 48; VC, Carranza to Carranza, August 22, 1914, 13:1308. The Junta Revolucionaria estimated that 5000 rebels of all stripes were operating in the states of Puebla and Tlaxcala as of mid-July; see INEHRM, Bonafide to Carranza, July 15, 1914, 1:6/2:14.

39. C/T, Jefe 2a División Centro to González, August 21, 1914, XXI-4; C/T, Carranza to González, August 23, 1914, XXI-4; C/T, Cabrera to Carranza, August 23,

1914, XXI-4; RDS, Silliman to Bryan, August 28, 1914, 40:753; Porras y López, *Luis*, 17–8.

40. CDHM, Luque to Consul España, August 19, 1914, 48:307:17:5; *Liberal*, August 23, 1914. The delegation consisted of Rafael Isunza (former governor), Miguel Jiménez Labora, Roberto L. Turnbull, Egidio Sánchez Gavito (industrialist), Eduardo Chaix, Guillermo Hardacker (British consul), Manuel Rivero Collada (Spanish capitalist and consul), and Francisco Barrientos (superior court justice).

41. Gamboa Ojeda, *Camerino*, 44–9; LaFrance, *Mexican*, 230.

42. FM, Urrutia to Maass, June 24, 1913, 59, July 16, 1913, 87; *Imparcial*, June 4, 11–3, 15, 20, 23, 24, July 13, 18, August 23, 30, 1913; *Mexican Herald*, June 2, July 27, 1913; *País*, June 12, 14, 15, July 12, August 15, 1913.

43. *Imparcial*, November 3, 4, 1913; *Mexican Herald*, October 2, November 2, 1913; *País*, November 1, 5, 1913.

44. FM, Alcocer to Jiménez Labora et al., May 14, 1914, 90; FM, Alcocer to Quintana, May 14, 1914, 90; *Amigo*, May 13, 14, 18, 19, 21, June 4, 1914; *Imparcial*, May 14–6, 23, 31, 1914; *Mexican Herald*, May 10, 1914; LaFrance, *Mexican*, 233.

45. FM, Urrutia to Governor, August 26, 1913, 88; *Periódico Oficial*, September 23, 1913.

46. FM, Alcocer to Governors, March 18, 1914, 89; RDS, Shanklin to Bryan, September 15, 1913, 29:25–6; *Amigo*, November 25, 1913, March 20, 25, 30, May 9, August 1, 1914; *Imparcial*, September 6, October 28, November 25, 1913, March 17, 25, 26, 30, April 3, 16, 20, July 14, 1914; *Mexican Herald*, March 18, 28, 1914; *País*, August 9, 1913, March 23, 26, 27, April 14–6, 22, 1914; *Periódico Oficial*, April 24, May 19, 1914.

47. *Amigo*, November 25, 1913, March 27, 30, August 1, 1914; *Imparcial*, September 3, 10, 11, 14, 15, 1913.

48. *Amigo*, August 29, September 27, 1913, June 10, 1914; *Imparcial*, July 7, 12, August 8, September 5, 1913; *País*, July 9, 25, 30, August 29, 1913, January 13, 1914.

49. ARM, Urrutia to Governors, August 27, 1913, 56:93:55; FM, Urrutia to Governors, August 30, 1913, 88; FM, Rábago to Governors, September 2, 1913, 88; GBFO, Stronge to Bart, June 24, 1913, 1674:45; *Imparcial*, June 29, July 6, 1913; García Ugarte, *Génesis*, 43; Knight, *Mexican*, 2:85; Vanderwood, "Response," 551–79.

50. CDHM, Ministro to Ministro Estado, May 10, 1914, 47:298:1:10; SRE, Maass to Huerta, August 10, 1913, 16-10-37; *Imparcial*, May 11, 1914; Fabela and Fabela, *Documentos*, 15:14–5, 75–6.

51. ACE/E, Hernández to Legislature, April 21, 1914, CCVI:9867; ACE/E, Calderón and Alcázar to Hernández, April 21, 1914, CCVI:9867; *Amigo*, November 16, 19, 25, December 5, 13, 1913; *Mexican Herald*, November 27, 1913; *Periódico Oficial*, August 29, 1913; Ankerson, *Agrarian*, 64; Falcón, *Revolución*, 81; García Ugarte, *Génesis*, 49; Knight, *Mexican*, 2:78; Wells and Joseph, *Summer*, 261.

52. JFL, Lucas to Mondragón, [May 10], 1913; *Mexican Herald*, March 1, 1914; Kuri Camacho, *La realidad*, 2:68–9.

53. C/ADN, Blanquet to Maass, October 23, 1913, MP/7115/4; GBFO, Gage to Rice, March 20, 1914, 2036:28–31; RDS, Shanklin to Bryan, September 4, 1913, 28:837–8; *Mexican Herald*, May 10, 1913, January 3, 1914; *País*, January 22, 1914; Ankerson, *Agrarian*, 68.

54. FM, Cauz to Maass, May 10, 1913, 87; FM, Alcocer to Governors, November 13, 1913, 88; FM, Alcocer to Hernández, February 2, 6, 1914, 89; *Imparcial*, July 24, 1913; García Ugarte, *Génesis*, 43.

55. ACE/E, Maass—informe, January 3, 1914, CC:9775; FM, Urrutia to Maass, July 15, 1913, 87; FM, Alcocer to Hernández, January 20, 29, 1914, 89; FM, Lujan to Hernández, May 8, 1914, 90; *Amigo*, December 25, 1913, January 14, 17, 19, 20, 1914; *Imparcial*, June 13, 1914; *País*, April 30, 1914.

56. ACE/E, Hernández—decree, March 20, 1914, CC:9905; ARM, [illegible] to Subsec. Gobernación, January 21, 1914, 58:95:140; CIM, Cardoso to Comisión Proveedora, April 29, 1914, 1:225, May 9, 1914, 1:227; FM, Alcocer to Hernández, January 31, February 2, 3, 6, 7, 1914, 89; *Imparcial*, June 15, 1914; *País*, February 4, 1914.

57. ACE/E, Maass—informe, January 3, 1914, CC:9775; RDS, Canada to Bryan, January 22, 1914, 34:142–3; *Amigo*, July 30, 31, 1914; *Imparcial*, July 16, 19, 1913; *País*, January 7, 1914.

58. *País*, January 30, February 17, 1914.

4. War, 1914–1917

1. C/T, Cabrera to Carranza, August 31, 1914, XXI-4; MWG, Ejército Constitucionalista—report, August 24, 28, 29, 1914, 19:2753, August [n.d.], 1914, 20:2804; PG, Campaña Constitucionalista—report, August 23, 1914, 48; RDS, Jenkins to Shanklin, November 18, 1914, 43:96–7; WFB, Memorandum, [September n.d.], 1914, 145[1]; *Periódico Oficial*, September 15, 1914.

2. C/T, Cañete to Carranza, August 21, 1914, XXI-4; C/T, Jefe 2a División to González, August 21, 1914, XXI-4; *Demócrata*, September 28, October 6, 8, 1914; *Mexican Herald*, September 23, October 22, 1914; *Pueblo*, October 3, 20, 22, 23, 26, November 7, 8, 1914; García Ugarte, *Génesis*, 61; Knight, *Mexican*, 2:180, 183, 444–5; Velasco, *Autobiografía*, 61–3, 74.

3. C/T, Reyes Márquez to Ministro Guerra, August 27, 1914, XXI-4; C/T, Gavira to Carranza, October 23, 1914, XXI-4; PHO, Cuéllar Montalvo-interview, March 8, 1973, 1/45:/:17; Paredes Colín, *El distrito*, 111–2.

4. C/T, Cañete to Carranza, August 21, 1914, XXI-4; C/T, Domínguez to Hay, August 21, 1914, XXI-4; SDN/AH, González to Carranza, October 1, 1914, XI/481.5/220:119:632; VC, Carranza to Carranza, September 12, 1914, 15:1496; *Mexican Herald*, September 13, 28, 1914.

5. MWG, Ejército Constitucionalista–report, August [n.d.], 1914, 20:2804; PG, Campaña Constitucionalista-report, August 29, 1914, 48.

6. CR, Castro to Mesa Directiva, October 8, 1914, 1:6:32; CR, Camacho to Neyra, October 9, 1914, 1:6:48; CR, Maycotte to Hernández García, October 9, 1914, 1:6:53; CR, Coss to de la Torre, October 9, 1914, 1:6:71; SDN/AH, González to Carranza, October [n.d.], 1914, XI/481.5/220:119:629; Cumberland, *Constitutionalist*, 166; Womack, *Zapata*, 113–4.

7. C/ADN, Lechuga to Carranza, November 6, 1914, MP/7115/2; C/T, Coss to Carranza, November 2, 1914, XXI-4; CR, Coss et al. to Villarreal, November 3, 1914, 5:2:47–66; CR, Durán et al.—decree, November 11, 1914, 2:7:58; JFL, [Lucas]—report, November 13, 1914, Scrapbook; RDS, Coss to Convención, November 2, 1914, 42:536.

8. JFL, Medina to Lucas, September 2, 1914, 1914; Kuri Camacho, *La realidad*, 2:75–6.

9. Buve, *El movimiento*, 338; Henderson, *Worm*, 53; Ramírez Rancaño, *La revolu-ción*, 47, 54–5.

10. INEHRM, *El Gráfico*—article, [June n.d.,] 1945, 1:6/11:22; JB, Alvarado to Carranza, December 9, 1914, 1:2; RDS, Jenkins to Shanklin, November 18, 1914, 43:95–6; SDN/AC, Gracia to Castro, August 13, 1917, XI/III/3-2791:76; VC, Ortiz to Carranza, January 20, 1915, 25:2490; VC, Camacho to Carranza, March 22, 1915, 32:3407; Fabela and Fabela, *Documentos*, 1:395.

11. C/T, Carranza to González, August 31, September 5, 1914, XXI-4; EZ, Cilia to Zapata, November 1, 1914, 2:1:4; GM, Argumedo et al. to Zapata, September 10, 1914, 27:12:203; GM, Zapata to Argumedo et al., September 21, 1914, 27:12:204; GM, *El Liberal*—typed copy, October 19, 1914, 26:1:14; INEHRM, Apreza to Serrato [Serdán], August 16, 1914, 1:6/6:33; GO, Zapata to Aguilar, August 25, 1914, 17:3:72; GO, Zapata to Medina, August 25, 1914, 17:3:73; GO, Zapata to Rojas, August 25, 1914, 17:3:75; *Demócrata*, October 26, November 7, 1914; Fabela and Fabela, *Documentos*, 15:213–4.

12. C/ADN, Coss to Carranza, November 24, 1914, MP/7115/2, December 13, 1914, MP/7115/2; C/ADN, López to Carranza, December 16, 1914, MP/7115/2; C/T, Coss to Carranza, November 10, 1914, MVIII; RDS, Silliman to Bryan, November 14, 1914, 42:658; EZ, Ayaquica to Zapata, November 18, 1914, 2:2:46, December 4, 1914, 2:4:48; EZ, Damián to Zapata, November 28, 1914, 2:3:39; JB, Coss to Carranza, December 3, 1914, 1:18; JB, Alvarado to Carranza, December 12, 15, 1914, 1:2; JB, Obregón to Carranza, December 16, 1914, 2:27; RDS, Jenkins to Shanklin, January 7, 1915, 43:796; SDN/AH, Coss to Carranza, December 8, 1914, XI/481.5/220:119:700, December 12, 1914, XI/481.5/220:119:709; *Mexican Herald*, November 14, 17, 18, December 3, 8–10, 16, 1914; *Monitor* (Mexico City), December 9, 10, 12, 16, 1914; Almazán, "Memorias," April 7, 1958; Quirk, *Mexican*, 141; Womack, *Zapata*, 222.

13. ACE/E, Fuentes and Vital to Pres. Legislature, December 16, 1914, CCVIII:9936; *Mexican Herald*, December 19, 21, 29, 1914; *Monitor* (Mexico City), December 19, 20, 22, 23, 31, 1914; Ávila Palafox, *¿Revolución*, 233–4; Cordero y

Torres, *Diccionario*, 4:9509–10; Cordero y Torres, *Historia compendiada*, 2:431; García Ugarte, *Génesis*, 71–2; *Puebla a través*, 172; U.S. Senate, *Investigation*, 2:2082.

14. Knight, *Mexican*, 2:233; Tutino, "Revolutionary," 47–8. For a recent study that argues against the idea of Zapatista inability and unwillingness to project power, see Pineda Gómez, "La revolución," 2:405–7.

15. EZ, Serratos [Serdán] to Zapata, December 31, 1914, 3:1:69; EZ, Mendoza to Zapata, January 1, 1915, 3:2:39; *Monitor* (Mexico City), May 25, 1915; Brunk, *Emiliano*, 140–4; Knight, *Mexican*, 2:309–10; Womack, *Zapata*, 222–3.

16. C/ADN, Obregón to Carranza, December 31, 1914, MP/7115/2; EZ, Robles to Palafox, December 26, 1914, 2:7:5; JB, Obregón to Carranza, December 29, 1914, 2:27, January 5, 1915, 2:28; VC, Carranza to Diéquez, January 7, 1915, 24:2372; *Mexican Herald*, January 6, 7, 1915; *Monitor* (Mexico City), January 2, 1915; Almazán, "Memorias," April 8, 1958; Fabela and Fabela, *Documentos*, 15:146–7; Obregón, *Ocho*, 245, 249–53.

17. EZ, Rodríquez to Ejército Libertador, January 6, 1915, 3:3:49; EZ, Reyes Márquez to Zapata, January 7, 1915, 3:3:64; EZ, Torres to Zapata, January 8, 1915, 3:3:122; JB, Obregón to Carranza, January 6, 1915, 2:28; RDS, Silliman to Bryan, January 8, 1915, 43:387; RDS, Vecino de México to Canada, January 12, 1915, 43:1229, January 14, 1915, 43:1230 1; *Mexican Herald*, January 7, 1915; Almazán, "Memorias," April 7, 8, 1958; Cordero y Torres, *Crónicas* (1966), 192–4; Quirk, *Mexican*, 154.

18. C/T, Obregón to Carranza, January 13, 1915, XXI-4; C/T, Fuentes Dávila to Carranza, January 23, 26, 28, 31, 1915, XXI-4; C/T, Coss to Carranza, January 23, 28, February 5, 12, 13, 1915, XXI-4; EZ, Serratos [Serdán] to Zapata, December 31, 1914, 3:1:69; EZ, Ayaquica to Zapata, January 30, 1915, 4:2:202; GM, *La Convención*—typed copy, January 15, 1915, 25:2:32; SDN/AH, Galindo to Sec. Guerra, [January n.d., 1915], XI/481.5/220:118:10; *Mexican Herald*, January 10, 12, 15, 20–6, February 1, 5, 1915; *Monitor* (Mexico City), January 21–3, 1915; Almazán, "Memorias," April 10, 1958; Fabela and Fabela, *Documentos*, 15:253.

19. C/T, Carranza to Coss, February 20, 1915, XXI-4; C/T, Coss to Carranza, March 29, 1915, XXI-4; EZ, Zenteno to Palafox, January 7, 1915, 3:3:111; EZ, [Zapata or Palafox] to Cotero, January 12, 1915, 4:1:50; EZ, Trinidad Ruíz to Zapata, January 13, 1915, 4:1:52; EZ, Mendoza to Zapata, January 15, 1915, 4:1:88; EZ, Molanco to Zapata, January 31, 1915, 4:2:232; EZ, Sánchez to Zapata, February 25, 1915, 6:1:133; EZ, Damián to Zapata, March 14, 15, 1915, 7:1:93; EZ, Bravo to Zapata, March 17, 1915, 7:2:32; EZ, Gracia to Zapata, March 18, 1915, 7:2:51; RGG, Ledesma to González Garza, January 31, 1915, 5:208; RGG, Ayaquica to González Garza, February 20, 1915, 6:12, March 1, 1915, 6:4–5; RGG, González Garza to Ayaquica, March 11, 1915, 6:2; RR, Palafox to Zapata, January 11, 1915, 3:46:795; RR, [Zapata] to Villa, February 20, 1915, 3:46:805.

20. ARM, González to Carranza, July 18, 1915, 60:98:267; C/T, Cervantes to Carranza, May 4, 1915, XXI-4; C/T, González to Dávila, July 21, 1915, LXVIII-4;

C/T, González to Carranza, July 24, 1915, XXI-4; JB, Carranza to Obregón, April 29, 1915, 3:12, May 18, 1915, 3:15; JB, Cervantes to Acuña, July 15, 1915, 1:17; RDS, Jenkins to Silliman, July 20, 1915, 47:119; *Mexican Herald*, May 17, 22, 1915; Brunk, *Emiliano*, 177.

21. C/T, González to Carranza, July 14, 1915, XXI-4; PG, Cervantes et al.—manifesto, September 14, 1915, 8; *Mexican Herald*, September 3, 1915; Womack, *Zapata*, 245–9.

22. EZ, Zapata to Ayaquica, January 23, 1917, 13:3:7; EZ, Magaña to Zapata, April 26, 1917, 13:12:15; PG, Flores to González, February 22, 1916, 11; PG, Jiménez—project, October 25, 1916, 14; PHO, Hidalgo Salazar—interview, [n.d.] 1973, 1/50:1:99–100; *Demócrata*, March 29, 1917.

23. CGS, Zapata to Amezcua, April 15, 1916, 1:3:58; EZ, Marín to Zapata, October 30, 1915, 16:2:31; EZ, Ramírez to Zapata, December 7, 1915, 10:10:54; EZ, Díaz to Zapata, December 14, 1915, 10:10:14, March 21, 1916, 11:9:2; GM, [Anonymous] to Córdova, April 5, 1917, 28:21:491; JA, Zapata to Espinosa, November 2, 1915, 3:203; PG, Jefe Depto. Estadística to González, May 20, 1916, 31; RGG, Ayaquica to González Garza, May 1, 1915, 16:86; RGG, González Garza to Ayaquica, May 17, 1915, 16:87; Brunk, *Emiliano*, 192.

24. C/ADN, Ferrocarriles Nacionales to Sec. Guerra, June–November 1916, MP/7115/2; C/T, González to Carranza, May 25–6, September 12, 1916, XXI-4; EZ, Cruz to Zapata, March 12, 1916, 11:8:8; EZ, Ayaquica to Zapata, April 16, 1916, 12:2:83; GM, Zapata to Juárez, November 6, 1915, 31:2:98; JA, Paz to Zapata, August 16, 1916, 3:265; PG, Rodríquez to Zapata, April 9, 1916, 50; PG, Jefe Depto. Estadística to González, May 20, 1916, 31; RDS, Canada to Lansing, May 26, 1916, 53:585; *Demócrata*, November 11, 15, 17–9, December 30, 1915, January 4, 7, March 14, 1916; Chaffee, "Adoption," 18–9.

25. EZ, Ánimas et al. to Zapata, September 16, 1914, 1:20:2; EZ, Reyes Márquez to Zapata, May 6, 1915, 19:1:16; EZ, Marciano Vetiz et al. to Zapata, June 1, 1915, 8:4:24; EZ, Lozano Sánchez to Zapata, September 18, 1915, 10:2:40; EZ, Palma et al. to Zapata, October 1, 1915, 10:4:5; EZ, Ponce to Zapata, April 23, 1916, 12:3:43; EZ, Vibar to Mejía, June 19, 1916, 12:7:2; EZ, Franco to Zapata, December 30, 1916, 20:6:8; EZ, "Sus Amigos" to Zapata, February 27, 1917, 13:6:13; EZ, Rodríquez to Moyano, April 21, 1917, 13:12:3; EZ, Díaz to Zapata, May 6, 1917, 13:13:30; GM, Cruz to Mendoza, January 20, 1916, 30:11:223; PG, Hill to González, January 8, 1916, 16; RGG, Damián to González Garza, May 7, 1915, 17:149; RR, Ayaquica to Zapata, November 18, 1914, 3:43:760; Hoyos Hernández, "Vida," 132–4.

26. CGS, Amezcua et al.—decree, November 3, 1915, 1:2:8–10; GM, Escuela Militar—project, December 3, 1915, 29:10:555; GM, Zapata to Huerta y Saavedra, October 15, 1915, 31:2:38; GM, Zapata to Mejía, January 31, 1916, 31:3:96; GM, Zapata—circular, March 18, 1917, 28:1:18; GM, Paniagua to Espinosa Barreda, March 28, 1917, 28:1:27; JA, Díaz Soto y Gama to Mendoza, February 26, 1917, 4:292.

27. *Demócrata*, September 17, 1915; Knight, *Mexican*, 2:223; Kuri Camacho, *La realidad*, 2:76–8.

28. C/T, González to Carranza, June 13, 1915, XXI-4; EZ, Arenas to Palafox, January 29, 1915, 6:2:103; FM, Pres. Provisional—memorandum, December 26, 1914, 75:13; SDN/AH, [document incomplete] to Sec. Guerra, April 12, 1915, XI/481.5/221:120:111; *Monitor* (Mexico City), March 22, April 3, 1915; *Pueblo*, May 26, 29, 1916; *Puebla a través*, 165.

29. SDN/AH, Castro to Obregón, May 25, 1916, XI/481.5/222:120:26; Almazán, "Memorias," April 8, 1958; Henderson, *Worm*, 53; Ramírez Rancaño, *La revolución*, 91–4.

30. Buve, *El movimiento*, 145–8.

31. Henderson, *Worm*, 58; Peral, *Gobernantes*, 179–80; Ramírez Rancaño, *La revolución*, 86–7.

32. GM, Zapata—announcement, December 15, 1916, 28:2:88; JB, Obregón to Carranza, December 3, 1916, IV:6; PG, Castro to Rojano, August 3, 1916, 3; PG, González to Rojano, August 5, 1916, 3; PG, Arenas to Rojano, [August n.d., 1916], 3; PG, Arenas to Medina, October 19, 1916, 34; VC, Cepeda to Carranza, 99:11265; Henderson, *Worm*, 58–60; Ramírez Rancaño, *La revolución*, 87–90, 125–31.

33. C/ADN, Jara to Carranza, April 25, 1917, MP/7115/2; C/T, Carranza to González, January 1, 1917, XXI-4; EZ, Zapata to Arenas, April 10, 1917, 13:14:9; EZ, Ayaquica to Arenas, May 6, 1917, 13:14:9; EZ, Magaña to Zapata, May 19, 1917, 12:14:30, May 30, 1917, 13:15:64; GM, Arenas to Plaza, March 31, 1917, 28:1:35; Henderson, *Worm*, 60; Ramírez Rancaño, *La revolución*, 132–5, 148–50.

34. This section is based on Thomson with LaFrance, *Patriotism*, 294–300.

35 Garciadiego Dantán, "Higinio," 437–58; Garciadiego Dantán, "Revolución," 337–40; Peral, *Los que*, 33–5; Ruíz, *Great*, 251.

36. VC, [Anonymous] to Acuña, October 7, 1915, 55:6028; Almazán, "Memorias," February 10, 11, 1958; Garciadiego Dantán, "Revolución," 291–2; Knight, *Mexican*, 2:212–4; Womack, *Zapata*, 212–3.

37. C/ADN, González to Carranza, October 3, 1914, MP/7115/1; C/ADN, Canseco to Carranza, October 22–9, 1914, MP/7115/1; C/T, Carranza to González, August 28, 1914, XXI-4; RDS, Funston to Adjutant General, November 1, 1914, 42:308; RDS, Canada to Bryan, November 6, 1914, 42:357; RR, Damián to Zapata, September 28, 1914, 3:43:756(2); RR, Rojas to Vicente, October 24, 1914, 3:41:486; SDN/AC, Almazán to Sec. Guerra, May 31, 1922, X/III/2-1153:300; Almazán, "Memorias," February 13, April 7, 1958; Paredes Colín, *El distrito*, 111–2.

38. CR, Aguilar to Reyes Márquez, January 25, 1915, 3:2:13; EZ, Aguilar to [Zapata], January 26, 1915, 4:2:116; EZ, Damián to Zapata, February 11, 1915, 5:2:12, February 12, 1915, 5:2:58, February 26, 1915, 6:2:33; Garciadiego Dantán, "Higinio," 456; Salmorán Marín, *Diario*, 206–9.

39. C/T, Tejeda to Carranza, February 23, 1915, XXI-4; C/T, Carranza to Aguilar, March 9, 1915, XXI-4; C/T, González to Carranza, June 8,1915, XXI-4;

C/T, Aguilar to Carranza, September 27, 1915, XXI-4; C/T, Villaseñor to Carranza, [n.d.] 1915, XXI-4; EZ, Reyes Márquez to Zapata, February 26, 1915, 6:2:35; EZ, Fernández de Lara to Aguilar, February 28, 1915, 7:1:3; EZ, Damián to Zapata, April 7, 1915, 7:4:54; EZ, Aguilar to Pres. Municipal Ixcaquixtla, July 22, 1915, 19:3:63; PG, González to Segura, May 30, 1916, 23; PG, Zapata to Aguilar, June 6, 1916, 50; RDS, Canada to Lansing, May 4, 1916, 53:271–2; RR, Aguilar to Zapata, April 14, 1916, 3:46:829; SDN/AC, Jara to Subsec. Guerra, May 3, 1916, XI/III-2:76; VC, Report, May 22, 1915, 40:4356; VC, Murguía Santayo to Carranza, July 9, 1915, 44:4855; VC, Galicia to Carranza, October 26, 1916, 100:11411; Almazán, *En legítima*, 3; *Demócrata*, November 21, 1915, September 11, 1916; *Mexican Herald*, September 21, 1915; Almazán, "Memorias," April 20, 1958; Salmorán Marín, *Diario*, 210, 215–6.

40. EZ, Magaña to Zapata, May 19, 1917, 13:14:30; JA, Cuartel General Zapatista—circular, [n.d. 1916], 3:259; PG, Zapata to Salas, June 7, 1916, 50; RDS, Traut to Sec. Navy, October 20, 1916, 57:372; RDS, Canada to Lansing, November 19, 1916, 58:21–6; SDN/AH, Aguilar—circular, May 27, 1917, XI/481.5/223:120:68; *Excélsior*, September 10, 1917; Almazán, "Memorias," February 11, 1958; Garciadiego Dantán, "Higinio," 458–63; Garciadiego Dantán, "Revolución," 345; Henderson, *Félix*, 121, 125–40.

41. Falcón, *Revolución,* 103–4. Garciadiego Dantán also makes this point for the country as a whole; see, "Revolución," 297–8.

42. Knight, *Mexican*, 2:235–6.

43. SDN/AC, de la Fuente to Sec., March 19, 1943, X/III-2:839; SDN/AC, González Garza to Sec. Defensa, March 19, 1943, X/III-2:843; Gutiérrez Álvarez, *Experiencias*, 332; Knight, *Mexican*, 2:266; Peral, *Gobernantes*, 176–7.

44. SDN/AC, Empleos, etc., [n.d.], XI/III-2:43–4; Peral, *Gobernantes*, 183–4.

45. Cordero y Torres, *Diccionario*, 2:432–3; Peral, *Diccionario*, 348–9.

46. SDN/AC, Hoja servicios, [n.d.], XI/III/405:142, 1080; Peral, *Diccionario*, 485–6.

47. SDN/AC, Hoja servicios, [n.d.], XI/III/1-372:188; Peral, *Diccionario*, 540.

48. Garner, *La revolución*, 118.

49. Falcón and García, *La semilla*, 71–82.

50. SDN/AC, Hoja servicios, [n.d.], XI/III/3-2791:1; Peral, *Los que*, 244. For descriptions of additional caciques in the state, see Juárez Lucas, "Conflictos," 28–66.

51. PG, Reyes Márquez to González, November 3, 1916, 31; SDN/AC, Reyes Márquez to Sec. Guerra, February 6, 1920, X/III/2–1153:52, [n.d. 1922], X/III/2-1153:315; SDN/AC, Urquizo to Reyes Márquez, February 16, 1920, X/III/2-1153:53; *Demócrata*, November 10, 1915; *Excélsior*, January 10, 1919; *Monitor* (Mexico City), January 8, February 25, May 17, 1919; *Monitor Republicano*, November 1, 1919.

52. PG, Narváez to González, July 31, 1915, 26A; SDN/AC, Hoja servicios, [n.d.], X/III/2-651:48, 197; SDN/AC, Rojas to Sec. Guerra, September 14, 1916, X/III/2-651:628, April 16, 1917, X/III/2-651:76; SDN/AC, Rojas to Barrios Gómez,

December 31, 1919, X/III/2-651:111; SDN/AC, Miguatecal et al. to Sec. Guerra, April 2, 1921, X/III/2-651:545; SDN/AC, Hoja servicios, February 2, 1922, X/III/2-651:215; SDN/AC, Rojas to Obregón, May 29, 1923, X/III//2-651:663; Hernández Enríquez, *Historia*, 2:29–30; Peral, *Gobernantes*, 187–8.

53. SDN/AC, Castro to Barbosa, March 5, 1919, C/III/3-172:185; SDN/AC, Hoja servicios, January 17, 1934, D/III/3-172:850; Barbosa—interview; Peral, *Los que*, 79.

54. SDN/AC, Hoja servicios, May 31, 1918, XI/III/2-403:285; Peral, *Los que*, 281–2.

55. *Excélsior*, November 9, 1919, March 2, 1920; *Monitor* (Mexico City), November 8, 1919; see also footnote 12.

56. Thomson with LaFrance, *Patriotism*, 293–307.

57. SDN/AC, Villaseñor to Sec. Guerra, November 30, 1915, XI/III/1-372:252; SDN/AC, Villaseñor to Obregón, August 3, 4, 1916, XI/III/1-372:262, 268; SDN/AC, Galindo—report, November 22, 1916, XI/III/1-405:265.

58. Barbosa—interview; Falcón, *Revolución*, 105.

59. *Pueblo*, March 9, 1915.

60. JB, Obregón to Carranza, [March] 10, [1915], III:2; SDN/AH, Jiménez to Carranza, January 5, 1915, XI/481.5/221:120:46; VC, Martínez de la Vega to Carranza, March 23, 1915, 32:3419; Ruíz, *Great*, 243.

61. PG, Vecinos to González, June 3, 1915, 3; VC, Oficina Información Propaganda—announcement, August 4, 1915, 47:5183; *Pueblo*, August 5, 1915.

62. Contreras Cruz et al., *Puebla*, 5:279; Gamboa Ojeda, *La urdimbre*, 290–1.

63. C/T, Flores to Carranza, March 10, 1915, XXI-4; C/T, Carranza to Flores, March 11, 1915, XXI-4; RDS, [Anonymous] to Canada, May 7, 1915, 45.191, SDN/AH, Bautista López to Carranza, November 14, 1914, XI/481.5/220:119:678; Ramírez Granados, *El 19o*, 6–10, 18–95, 104; Cumberland, *Constitutionalist*, 257; Meyer, "Los obreros," 1–37.

64. C/T, Coss to Espinosa Mireles, [n.d.] 1915, XXI-4; C/T, Carranza to Medina, March 13, April 11, 23, 1915, February 2, 1916, XXI-4; C/T, Carranza to Lechuga, March 24, 1915, XXI-4; C/T, del Castillo to Carranza, March 25, 1915, XXI-4; C/T, Tejada to Carranza, March 24, 29, 1915, XXI-4; C/T, Carranza to Coss, April 11, 17, 28, 1915, XXI-4; C/T, Norzagaray to Carranza, April 4, 11, 28, 1915, XXI-4; C/T, Carranza to Dávila, May 13, 1915, XXI-4; JB, Lechuga to Carranza, March 23, 1915, II:13; JB, Carranza to Coss, April 7, 15, 22, 1915, I:18; VC, Rojas to Carranza, March 12, 1915, 31:3266.

65. C/T, Carranza to Blanco, February 13, 1915, XXI-4; C/T, Blanco to Carranza, February 17, 1915, XXI-4; PG, Ledermann to González, July 5, 1915, 18, July 23, 1915, 14, May 23, 1916, 14; PG, Larraza and Alatriste to González, August 16, 1915, 5; VC, Díaz to Carranza, May 9, 1916, 76:8427; *Demócrata*, September 9, 1915, March 8, 1916.

66. C/T, Dávila to Carranza, January 16, 1915, XXI-4; C/T, Carranza to Dávila, February 2, 1916, XXI-4; C/T, González to Carranza, March 23, 1917, XXI-4;

CTB, Castro to Obregón, [May n.d., 1916], 11:12:79:96; JB, Dávila to Barragán, September 1, 1915, V:24.

67. C/T, Dávila to Carranza, [n.d.] 1915, XXI-4; C/T, Carranza to Coss et al., March 12, 1915, XXI-4; C/T, Carranza to Tejeda, April 20, 1915, XXI-4; C/T, González to Carranza, June 8, 1915, XXI-4; C/T, Carranza to Dávila, January 21, 1916, XXI-4; JB, Lechuga to Carranza, March 24, 1915, II:13; JB, Villaseñor to Barragán, September 7, 1915, VII:27; JB, Dávila to Barragán, September 10, 1915, V:24; PG, Cervantes to González, January 11, 1916, 17; SDN/AC, Vecinos Tepeaca—broadside, November 6, 1914, 876-7.XI/III/3-2623:21; VC, Medina to Carranza, May 3, 1915, 38:4111.

68. C/T, Aguilar to Carranza, March 14, 1915, XXI-4; C/T, Coss to Carranza, [n.d.] 1915, XXI-4; C/T, Medina to Carranza, January 12, 1916, XXI-4; C/T, Dávila to Carranza, January 18, 1916, XXI-4; PHO, Cuéllar Montalvo—interview, March 8, 1973, 1/45:/:26; PG, Pineda to González, December 30, 1915, 25; RDS, Parker to Lansing, October 2, 1916, 56:567–8; *Mexican Herald*, September 21, 1915.

69. DT, Juárez to Valero, October 10, 1914, 85:2:1; PG, Vecinos Coronanco to González, June 3, 1915, 3; PG, Parra to González, October 29, 1915, 24; PG, Hernández et al. to González, December 21, 1915, 16; SDN/AC, Ruíz—announcement, May 22, 1916, 867.7.XI/III/3-2623:29; VC, Guerrero et al. to Carranza, February 11, 1916, 67:7402; VC, Méndez and Méndez to Carranza, May 25, 1916, 80:8800; *Monitor* (Mexico City), May 25, 1915.

70. Kuri Camacho, for example, says that Carrancista troops were less disciplined than the Convencionistas in the Sierra campaign; see *La realidad*, 2:76–8.

71. C/T, Carranza to González, September 29, 1914, XXI-4; VC, Rodríquez to Carranza, August 22, 1914, 13:1310; VC, Juárez to Carranza, August 24, 1914, 13:1328; VC, [Anonymous] to Carranza, September 14, 1914, 15:1515; VC, Colombres to Carranza, March 25, 1915, 33:3477; *Periódico Oficial*, September 15, December 8, 1914; Cordero y Torres, *Crónicas* (1966), 83–4; Cordero y Torres, *Diccionario*, 3:7659; Knight, *Mexican*, 2:235–6.

72. GM, "El general Zapata comunica…"—typed ms., December 18, 1914, 25:2:37; RDS, Silliman to Bryan, December 18, 1914, 42:1535; *Mexican Herald*, December 16, 18, 19, 1914; *Monitor* (Mexico City), December 18, 19, 21, 22, 1914; Cordero y Torres, *Crónicas* (1966), 192; Cordero y Torres, *Diccionario*, 4:9485, 9509; Knight, *Mexican*, 2:235–6.

73. C/T, Saviñon to Carranza, January 25, 1914 [sic 1915], XXI-4; VC, Rivadeneyra to Carranza, February 10, 1915, 27:2798; *Monitor* (Mexico City), January 12, 1915; Cordero y Torres, *Crónicas* (1955), 18, (1966), 192–4.

74. PG, Fernández to González, May 1, 1915, 11; PG, Pons to González, August 1, 1915, 5; PG, Brachetti to González, October 4, 1915, 6; PG, Cervantes to González, December 2, 1915, 26A; VC, Jara to Carranza, January 19, 1915, 25:2470; VC, Domínguez to Carranza, June 26, 1916, 86:9614.

75. PG, Negrete to González, May 29, 1915, 26A.

76. Ankerson, *Agrarian*, 85–6; Hernández Chávez, "Militares," 181–212; Joseph, *Revolution*, 113; Tobler, "La burguesía," 213–37.

77. SDN/AC, Biography, June [n.d.], 1915, XI/III/1-372:1094; SDN/AC, Villaseñor to Obregón, July 5, 1915, XI/III/1-372:1084, December 26, 1915, XI/III/1-372:1087; SDN/AC, Jefe Estado Mayor to López Araiza, March 31, 1916, XI/III/1-372:1090; SDN/AC, Valderrama to Sec. Guerra, August 9, 1916, XI/III/1-372:1499; SDN/AC, Castro to Villaseñor, July 30, 1917, XI/III/1-372:353; SDN/AC, Jefe Operaciones to Sec. Guerra, May 27, 1918, XI/III/1-372:274; VC, Agente to Ugarte, September 27, 1915, 53:5857; VC, Ramos et al. to Carranza, January 11, 1916, 65:7203; VC, Pacheco et al. to Carranza, January 12, 1916, 65:7210; VC, Soldados to Carranza, February 10, [1916], 148:16979.

78. SDN/AC, Sec. Guerra to Barbosa, February 20, 1917, D/III/3-172:80; SDN/AC, Revolucionario Digno to Obregón, April [n.d., 1917], D/III/3-172:87; SDN/AC, Jefe Operaciones to Sec. Guerra, August 24, 1917, D/III/3-172:93; SDN/AC, Sec. Guerra—memorandum, September 5, 1917, D/III/3-172:838; SDN/AC, Castro to Jara, December 5, 1917, D/III/3-172:121; SDN/AC, Jara to Castro, December 5, 1917, D/III/3-172:119; SDN/AC, Jefe Estado Mayor to Ríos, January 17, 1919, D/III/3-172:171; SDN/AC, Castro to Sec. Guerra, March 31, 1919, D/III/3-172:173; SDN/AC, Sec. Guerra—memorandum, February 27, 1919, D/III/3-172:183; SDN/AC, Sec. Guerra to Castro, February 27, 1919, XI/III-2:249; SDN/AC, Barbosa to Bouchez, March 5, 1919, D/III/3-172:185; Barbosa—interview; *Prensa*, June 5, 1918; Peral, *Los que*, 79.

79. C/T, Coss to Espinosa Mireles, [n.d.] 1915, XXI-4; C/T, Carranza to Lechuga, March 24, 1915, XXI-4; PG, Olivera to Martínez, December 26, 1914, 51; SDN/AC, Ejército Oriente to Sec. Guerra, May 16, 1916, XI/III/2-403:126; SDN/AC, Sec. Fomento—memorandum, June [n.d.], 1917, XI/III/2-403:237; SDN/AC, Sec. Guerra—memorandum, July 28, 1917, XI/III/2-403:240; VC, Barbosa to Carranza, January 12, 1915, 24:2408. Lechuga was not the only Carrancista officer to exploit forests in the region and commandeer the railroad to transport logs; see MI, Military Attaché–report, September 29, 1919, 1:70.

80. *Excélsior*, September 1, 1918, March 1, November 9, December 3, 1919; *Monitor* (Puebla), November 8, December 6, 1919; *Universal*, March 2, 1919.

81. SDN/AC, Covarrubias to González, June [n.d.], 1916, X/III/2-1153:832; SDN/AC, Pérez Aranda to Governor, June 8, 1917, X/III/2-1153:846; SDN/AC, Sec. Guerra—memorandum, July 4, 1917, X/III/2-1153:852, October 9, 1917, X/III/2-1153:385, February 4, 1921, X/III/2-1153:232; SDN/AC, Comisión Revisora to Sec. Guerra, February 16, 1922, X/III/2-1153:259; VC, Reyes Márquez to Carranza, July 8, 1917, 114:13035; *Monitor* (Puebla), January 1, 1919; *Monitor Republicano*, November 1, 1919; *Prensa*, January 8, 1919.

82. SDN/AC, Atlizqueño et al. to [Sec. Guerra], November 25, 1916, XI/III/3-2791:12; SDN/AC, Sec. Guerra to Gracia, February 26, 1917, XI/III/3-2791:37; SDN/AC, Sec. Guerra to Comandante Militar, March 5, 1917, XI/III/3-2791:

39; SDN/AC, Gracia and Sánchez to Sec. Guerra, March 12, 1917, XI/III/3-2791:41.

83. JB, Cervantes to Acuña, July 15, 1915, I:17; PG, Narváez to González, July 5, 1915, 18, July 31, 1915, 26A; PG, Flores to Comandante Militar, July 31, 1915, 11; SDN/AC, Hoja servicios, [n.d.], X/III/2-651:48, 197; SDN/AC, Cuanech et al. to Sec. Guerra, July 24, 1916, X/III/2-651:31; SDN/AC, Miguatecal et al. to Sec. Guerra, April 2, 1921, X/III/2-651:545; Hernández Enríquez, *Historia*, 2:30.

84. Peral, *Diccionario*, 348–9; Thomson with LaFrance, *Patriotism*, 294–301.

85. Thomson with LaFrance, *Patriotism*, 294–301.

86. Ibid.

87. Ibid., 306.

88. Camp, *Mexican*, 374; Thomson with LaFrance, *Patriotism*, 301.

5. Politics, 1914–1917

1. C/T, González to Carranza, August 25, 1914, MVIII, August 28, 1914, XXI-4; C/T, Carranza to González, August 26, 1914, MVIII; Fabela and Fabela, *Documentos*, 15:155–6; Joseph, *Revolution*, 94.

2. RDS, Mitchell to Sec. State, March 30, 1929, 89:916; SDN/AC, Cepeda de la Fuente to Sec. Guerra, March 19, 1943, X/III.2:839; SDN/AC, González to Sec. Defensa, March 19, 1943, X/III.2:843; del Castillo, *Puebla*, 254; Gutiérrez Álvarez, *Experiencias*, 332; Peral, *Gobernantes*, 176–7.

3. ACE/E, Salgado to González, September 10, 1914, CCVIII:9935; PG, Martínez to González, September 8, 1915, 15; TO, Coss and González—decree, September 9, 1914, 422(1914); *Mexican Herald*, September 7, 12, 1914; *Periódico Oficial*, September 11, 15, 1914; *Pueblo*, October 17, 1914; Contreras Cruz et al., *Puebla*, 5:254–6.

4. C/T, Carranza to Comandante Militar, October 12, 1914, XXI-4; SDN/AH, Coss to Carranza, October 24, 1914, XI/481.5/220:119:647; *Demócrata*, November 6, 1914; *Pueblo*, October 2, November 7, 8, 1914.

5. CDHM, Romero Sánchez and Muñoz—broadside, September 14, 1914, 48:308:24:1. There were 1,335 Spaniards in the state in 1910, a small percent of the total population (0.12) but nearly half (47.8%) of the foreigners resident; see Gamboa Ojeda, "Los españoles," 193.

6. CDHM, Quijano Rueda to Ministro, September 27, October 8, 1914, 48:308:24:1; CDHM, Ministro to Ministro Estado, October 7, 1914, 47:298:2:4; *Periódico Oficial*, September 29, October 9, 1914; Gutiérrez Álvarez, *Experiencias*, 341–2.

7. C/T, [n.d.] 1915, Coss to Carranza, XXI-4; INEHRM, "La Comisión"—handbill, March 31, 1915, 11:2:10; RDS, Jenkins to Shanklin, January 7, 1915,

43:803; RGG, Consulado General México, New York—*Boletín*, January 15, 1915, 62:623; SDN/AH, Coss to Carranza, April 4, 1915, XI/481.5/221:120:113; *Revolución*, April 5, 1915; Joseph, *Revolution*, 136–7.

8. RDS, Jenkins to Shanklin, November 18, 1914, 43:97, January 7, 1915, 43:802–3; RGG, "Varios Poblanos" to González Garza, October 16, 1914, 62:357–8; Garner, "Constitutionalist," 90.

9. SDN/AH, Salinas to Carranza, January 9, 1915, XI/481.5/221:120:60; VC, Coss to Carranza, [n.d.], 151:17241.

10. C/ADN, Obregón to Carranza, January 16, 1915, MP/7115/2; C/ADN, Millán to Carranza, January 19, 1915, MP/7115/2; C/T, Carranza to Obregón, January 12, 1915, XXI-4; JB, Obregón to Carranza, May 16, 1915, III:15; SDN/AH, Obregón to Carranza, January 5, 1915, XI/481.5/221:120:48, January 16, 1915, XI/481.5/221:120:82; SDN/AH, Millán to Carranza, January 19, 1915, XI/481.5/221:120:87.

11. C/ADN, Aguirre Escobar to Coss, January 13, 1915, MP/7115/1, C/T, Carranza to Obregón et al., February 16, 1915, XXI-4; INEHRM, Narváez and Narváez to Carranza, January 10, 1915, 1:6/2:49; SDN/AH, Dávila et al. to Carranza, January 9, 1915, XI/481.5/221:120:58.

12. C/ADN, Coss to Carranza, December 9, 1914, MP/7115/2; JB, Coss to Carranza, February 5, 1915, I:18; PG, Martínez to González, September 8, 1915, 15; *Monitor* (Mexico City), May 2, 1915; del Castillo, *Puebla*, 246–8; Knight, *Mexican*, 2:255, 452–3.

13. C/T, Coss to Espinosa Mireles, [n.d.] 1915, XXI-4; C/T, Carranza to Medina, March 13, April 11, 1915, XXI-4; C/T, Medina to Carranza, [n.d.] 1915, XXI-4; C/T, Carranza to Lechuga, March 24, 1915, XXI-4; C/T, Carranza to Coss, April 11, 1915, XXI-4; JB, Lechuga to Carranza, March 23, 1915, II:13; VC, Medina to Carranza, May 5, 1915, 38:4148.

14. C/T, Tejada to Carranza, March 27, 29, 1915, XXI-4; C/T, Norzagaray to Carranza, April 4, 11, 28, 1915, XXI-4; C/T, Tejada to Carranza, April 25, 1915, XXI-4; JB, [Carranza] to Coss, April 7, 15, 22, 1915, I:18.

15. C/ADN, Carranza to Coss, April 23, 1915, MP/7115/1; C/T, Coss to Carranza, [n.d.] 1915, XXI-4; C/T, Carranza to Coss, April 19, 1915, XXI-4; RDS, Jenkins to Shanklin, May 14, 1915, 45:134; RGG, Ugalde to [González Garza], [n.d. 1915], 16:348; VC, Martínez to Carranza, April 10, 1915, 35:3728; *Monitor* (Mexico City), May 2, 1915; Knight, *Mexican*, 2:453.

16. SDN/AH, Narváez to Carranza, [n.d. 1915], XI/481.5/221:120:5; SDN/AH, Martínez to Carranza, May 3, 1915, XI/481.5/221:120:151; VC, Martínez to Carranza, April 10, 1915, 35:3728; *Mexican Herald*, May 14, 1915.

17. C/T, Carranza to Dávila, May 13, 1915, XXI-4; JB, Carranza to Obregón, May 14, 1915, III:15; JB, [Carranza] to Lechuga, May 14, 1915, II:13; JB, Lechuga to Carranza, May 15, 1915, II:13; RDS, Jenkins to Shanklin, May 14, 1915, 45:134; SDN/AH, Coss to Carranza, April 29, 1915, XI/481.5/221:120:133; SDN/AH,

Cervantes to Carranza, April 29, 1915, XI/481.5/221:120:130, May 13, 1915, XI/481.5/221:120:193; SDN/AH, Tejada to Espinosa Mireles, May 12, 1915, XI/481.5/221:120:201; Buve, *El movimiento*, 342.

18. C/T, Garza to Barragán, [n.d.] 1915, XXI-4; JB, González to Carranza, June 2, 1915, II:4; SDN/AC, Jefe Armas to Subsec. Guerra, August 3, 1915, X/III.2:24; SDN/AH, Olarte et al.—declaration, May 12, 1915, XI/481.5/221:120:167; SDN/AH, Báez to Méndez, May 16, 1915, XI/481.5/221:120:202; VC, Guaneros et al. to Carranza, May 14, 1915, 39:4280; Barragán, *Historia*, 2:333–5; *Pueblo*, May 18, 22, 23, 1915.

19. C/T, Cervantes to Carranza, [n.d.] 1915, XXI-4; C/T, González to Director, June 20, 1915, LXVIII-4; C/T, González to Carranza, March 20, 1916, XXI-4; PG, Coss to González, September 21, 22, 1915, 8; PG, González to Coss, September 21, 1915, 8, September 22, 1915, 7; RDS, Mitchell to Sec. State, March 30, 1929, 89:916; SDN/AC, Pesqueira to Carranza, March 12, 1916, X/III.2:24; SDN/AC, Jefe Estado Mayor to Pesqueira, March 28, 1916, X/III.2:62; SDN/AC, Acosta to Obregón, December 14, 1916, X/III.2:77; SDN/AC, Dieguez to Subsec. Guerra, December 25, 1917, X/III.2:100; SDN/AC, Neiva to Subsec. Guerra, April 2, 1918, X/III.2:152; Matute, *Historia—La carrera*, 105–6.

20. C/T, Carranza to Cervantes, April 18, 1915, XXI-4; JB, Cervantes to Barragán, May 4, 1915, V:21; MWG, Carranza to Cervantes, May 6, 1914, 15:2213; Peral, *Gobernantes*, 181–2.

21. C/T, Carranza to Martínez, May 5, 1915, XXI-4; PG, Cervantes to González, August 11, 1915, 7.

22. PG, Cervantes to González, August 11, 1915, 7.

23. *Demócrata*, March 16, 1916; Cervantes, *Decretos*, 1–132; del Castillo, *Puebla*, 254–6; Gamboa Ojeda, "El movimiento," 366–8.

24. PG, Cervantes to González, August 11, 1915, 7; PG, Narváez to González, September 10, 1915, 18; RDS, Jenkins to Shanklin, June 28, 1915, 47:708; RDS, Jenkins to Silliman, July 20, 1915, 47:119; VC, Soldados to Carranza, February 10, [1916], 148:16979; VC, Narváez to Carranza, May 15, 1916, 77:8548; Cordero y Torres, *Diccionario*, 3:4755; Ruíz, *Great*, 380.

25. JB, Cervantes to Carranza, August 6, 1915, I:17; PG, Cervantes to González, August 11, 1915, 7; PG, Téllez et al. to González, October 24, 1915, 16; PG, Hernández et al. to González, October 26, 1915, 16; PG, Miranda et al. to González, October 27, 1915, 16; PG, Tepox to González, November 29, 1915, 16; VC, Unda to Carranza, October 4, 1915, 54:5975.

26. PG, González to Medina, October 25, 1915, 22; PG, Pachcan et al. to González, November 30, 1915, 16; RG/PR, González to Sec. Gobernación, November 30, 1915, 154:95; VC, Medina to Carranza, May 5, 1915, 38:4148.

27. PG, Zepeda to González, [n.d. 1916], 26B.

28. C/T, Cervantes to Carranza, April 3, 1916, XXI-4; SDN/AC, Hoja servicios, [n.d.], XI/III.2:43–4; Peral, *Gobernantes*, 183–4; Womack, *Zapata*, 293.

29. VC, Rodríquez to Carranza, May 10, 1916, 77:8151; VC, Narváez to Carranza, May 15, 1916, 77:8548; VC, Frigueras to Carranza, September 25, 1916, 96:10931; Castro, *Informe*, 1–47; *Aguilas y Estrellas*, March 1917, 2; Cordero y Torres, *Crónicas* (1966), 263–4; Velasco, *Autobiografía*, 75.

30. *Periódico Oficial*, May–December 1916.

31. VC, Serrano to Carranza, November 10, 1916, 102:11705; *Prensa*, June 25, 1918.

32. RGG, Contreras to González Garza, April 21, 1915, 14:128; Cordero y Torres, *Poetas*, 40–1; LaFrance, *Mexican*, 204–9; Peral, *Los que*, 243; Sarmiento, *Puebla*, 330.

33. GM, Cartal [Paz]—report, September 27, 1916, 28:2:53; VC, Narváez to Carranza, May 15, 1916, 77:8548; VC, Aguirre to Carranza, October 4, 1916, 98:11123; VC, Serrano to Carranza, November 10, 1916, 102:11705; *Demócrata*, December 4, 1916.

34. MWG, "Memoria campaña," August 28, 1914, 19:2753; Contreras Cruz et al., *Puebla*, 5:273–5; Benjamin, *La Revolución*, 19–21.

35. C/ADN, Yáñez to Carranza, November 11, 1914, MP/7115/2; C/T, Coss to Carranza, March 6, 1915, XXI-4; CIM, Cardoso to Governor, November 18, 1918, 1:375; CIM, Gutiérrez Quijano and Cardoso to Oficina Propaganda, February 3, 1916, 2:183; INEHRM, Carrillo et al. to Narváez, November 11, 1914, 1:6/7.7; PG, Campaña constitucionalista, August 29, 1914, 48; SDN/AC, Ruíz—broadside, December 28, 1914, 876–7.XI/III/3-2623:22; *Demócrata*, September 17, 1914, October 21, 1915, April 3, 1916; *Pueblo*, May 7, 1915; *Revolución*, April 5, 1915; Peral, *Gobernantes*, 176–7.

36. Garner, *La revolución*, 134.

37. INEHRM, Narváez—manuscript, [n.d.], 1:6/1:11; INEHRM, Narváez and del Castillo—"La mujer poblana," [n.d.] 1950, 1:6/9:1; Jaime Espinosa, "Rosa," 83–5, 104, 111; Rocha, "Guadalupe," 1:332–3.

38. C/T, Cervantes to Carranza, [n.d.] 1915, XXI-4; C/T, Narváez to Carranza, [n.d.] 1915, XXI-4; INEHRM, Certificate, April 25, 1915, 1:6/4:1; INEHRM, Narvácz to Carranza, July 31, 1915, 1:6/4:4–6; SDN/AH, Narváez to Carranza, May 1, 1915, XI/481.5/221:120:144; VC, Narváez to Carranza, April 26, 1915, 37:3998, May 7, 1915, 39:4184; VC, Nuncio C.—certificate, May 11, 1915, 39:4240; VC, Badillo and García to Velázquez, May 12, 1915, 39:4256; VC, Vilchis to Carranza, June 27, 1916, 86:9616; VC, Rojas et al. to Carranza, June 25, 1916, 86:9589; VC, Pérez to Carranza, August 25, 1916, 92:10390; VC, Lucas et al. to Carranza, August 13, 1916, 92:10391; *Demócrata*, September 9, 1915; *Pueblo*, August 20, September 4, 1915; Cordero y Torres, *Crónicas* (1955), 11–2; Jaime Espinosa, "Rosa," 112–6; Rocha, "Guadalupe," 1:335–6.

39. C/T, Narváez to Carranza, January 27, June 19, 21, 22, 29, 1916, XXI-4; JB, Narváez to Carranza, July 26, 1915, II:17; RG/PR, Cervantes and García to Sec. Gobernación, July 1, 1915, 150:83; SDN/AH, Sotres y Olaco to Carranza,

May 25, 1915, XI/481.5/221:120:208; VC, Betanza de Galván to Carranza, July 16, 1916, 88:9846; VC, Narváez to Carranza, April 20, 1915, 36:3892; *Estudiante*, January 19, 1919; *Pueblo*, April 17, May 6, 9, 1915; Jaime Espinosa, "Rosa," 107, 109–10, 114, 119–24; Rocha, "Guadalupe," 1:337–40.

40. VC, Betanzo de Galván to Carranza, July 16, 1916, 88:9846.

41. VC, Soldados to Carranza, February 10, [1916], 148:16979; VC, Vilchis to Carranza, June 27, 1916, 86:9616; Jaime Espinosa, "Rosa," 122–3, 126.

42. Joseph, *Revolution*, 105.

43. C/T, Carranza to Narváez, February 12, 1916, XXI-4; C/T, Narváez to Carranza, February 13, 14, 1916, XXI-4; PG, Solís Bede to González, May 8, 1916, 24; RG/PR, Oficial Mayor to Sec. Gobernación, February 14, 1917, 198:82; VC, Betanzo de Galván to Carranza, July 16, 1916, 88:9846; VC, R. vda. de Narváez to Carranza, October 5, 1916, 98:11141; Jaime Espinosa, "Rosa," 122–3, 126.

44. Jaime Espinosa, "Rosa," 101.

45. C/T, Velázquez to Carranza, March 26, 1915, XXI-4; C/T, Hermoso and Serdán to Carranza, January 26, 1915, XXI-4; INEHRM, Narváez—minutes, February 24, 1915, 1:6/2:53; SDN/AH, Atl to Carranza, January 26, 1915, XI/481.5/221:120:95; *Pueblo*, October 22, 1914; Cordero y Torres, *Historia compendiada*, 2:520.

46. INEHRM, Narváez et al.—proclamation, July 26, 1915, 1:6/2:54; PG, Cervantes to González, August 11, 1915, 7; VC, Partido—minutes, July 8, 1915, 44:4842, July 14, 1915, 45:4910.

47. *Excélsior*, April 28, 30, 1917; *Demócrata*, September 19, October 4, 26, November 3, 7, December 18, 30, 1916, April 27, 1917; *Pueblo*, October 11, 26, 1916; del Castillo, *Puebla*, 243–4.

48. *Periódico Oficial*, June 8, December 7, 1915; Cervantes, *Decretos*, 6–16, 66–88.

49. PG, Moreno to González, June 3, 1915, 3; PG, Rueda to González, October 4, 1915, 26A; VC, Correligionario to Carranza, July 4, 1915, 44:4786; Castro, *Informe*, 26–31; Cervantes, *Decretos*, 6–16, 66–88; Cervantes, *Informe*, 4–6; *Pueblo*, August 5, 1915; *Universal*, February 9, 1917.

50. Falcón, *Revolución*, 71.

51. Fabela and Fabela, *Documentos*, 4:118–9; *Puebla a través*, 141.

52. C/T, Medina to Carranza, [n.d.] 1915, XXI-4; *Pueblo*, April 11, 13, 19, May 1, 1915; Garner, *La revolución*, 133, 138.

53. C/T, Carranza to Gavira, January 3, 1915, XXI-4; C/T, Carranza to Coss, April 27, 1915, XXI-4; PG, González to Medina, October 25, 1915, 22; RG/PR, González to Sec. Gobernación, November 30, 1915, 154:95; VC, Medina to Carranza, May 5, 1915, 38:4148; *Periódico Oficial*, April 27, 1915; *Pueblo*, August 4, 1915; Lear, *Workers*, 341.

54. Acuña, *Memoria*, 349–50.

55. PG, Alatriste to González, August 23, 1916, 3, September 1, 1916, 3; RG/PR, Pérez Méndez to Sec. Gobernación, October 10, 1916, 177:12; VC, Vilchis et

al. to Carranza, September 29, 1916, 97:11044; *Demócrata*, October 4, 8, 1916; *Pueblo*, September 7, 1916; LaFrance, *Mexican*, 43, 102, 227; Tecuanhuey, *Los conflictos*, 236.

56. INEHRM, Narváez to Galván, August 21, 1916, 1:6/6:62; PG, Alatriste to González, September 1, 1916, 3; VC, Vilchis et al. to Carranza, September 29, 1916, 97:11044; *Pueblo*, February 1, 1915, September 6, 8, 1916; Jaime Espinosa, "Rosa," 124.

57. C/T, Guazil et al. to Carranza, September 21, 1916, XXI-4; RG/PR, Díaz Z. to Sec. Gobernación, September 22, 1916, 177:13; VC, Mayorga et al. to Carranza, September 23, 1916, 96:10897; VC, Figueres to Carranza, September 25, 1916, 96:10931; VC, Ramírez et al. to Carranza, September 29, 1916, 97:11056; Ruíz, *Great*, 374.

58. *Demócrata*, October 8, December 13, 1916.

59. GM, Cartal [Paz]—report, September 27, 1916, 28:2:53; JFL, del Castillo and Cano to Lucas, October 10, 1916, 1916; JFL, Lucas to Partido Liberal, October 16, 1916, 1916; VC, Narváez to Carranza, October 20, 1916, 99:11331; *Demócrata*, October 7, 1916; *Pueblo*, October 11, 1916; Moreno, *Los hombres*, 265–6; Cumberland, *Constitutionalist*, 327 8; *Puebla a través*, 166.

60. Enríquez Perea, *Memorias*, 214–29; Niemeyer, *Revolution*, 39, 263–7; Tecuanhuey, *Los conflictos*, 238–42.

61. *Pueblo*, April 27, 1917. National vote totals: Carranza (797,305), González (11,615), Obregón (4008).

62. *Demócrata*, March 14, April 28, 30, 1917; *Excélsior*, May 24, 1917; Camp, *Mexican*, 267, 369; Tecuanhuey, *Los conflictos*, 246.

63. VC, Franco et al. to Carranza, December 13, 1915, 63:6947.

64. SDN/AH, Medina—speech, March 25, 1917, XI/481.5/223:120:38; *Demócrata*, November 13, 14, 19, December 4, 6, 1916; *Universal*, February 17, 1917, del Castillo, *Puebla*, 259–61; Tecuanhuey, *Los conflictos*, 252–4.

65. JB, del Castillo to Barragán, May 11, 1917, V:18; SDN/AH, Medina to Carranza, May 22, 1917, XI/481.5/223:120:67; *Pueblo*, June 12, 1917; *Universal*, June 11, 1917; del Castillo, *Puebla*, 259–61.

66. SDN/AH, Medina to Carranza, April 24, 1917, XI/481.5/223:120:59, June 10, 1917, XI/481.5/223:120:75; *Pueblo*, June 12, 1917; *Universal*, June 7, 11, 1917.

67. SDN/AC, Gracia to Sec. Guerra, January 30, 1917, XI/III/3-2791:28, April 14, 1917, XI/III/3-2791:48; *Pueblo*, May 18, 1917; *Universal*, June 11, 1917.

68. *Demócrata*, March 30, 31, April 17, 19, 22, 1917; *Excélsior*, April 17, 22, 1917; *Pueblo*, April 1, 7, 13, 18, 20, 1917; del Castillo, *Puebla*, 259–61; Camp, *Mexican*, 194–5; Cruz, *Pastor*, 394–9; Knight, *Mexican*, 2:123, 474–5; Martínez Guzmán and Chávez Ramírez, *Durango*, 204, 214–21; Tecuanhuey, *Los conflictos*, 255.

69. *Pueblo*, April 1, 1917; del Castillo, *Puebla*, 259–61; Camp, *Mexican*, 32–3; Peral, *Gobernantes*, 185–6.

70. *Universal,* June 8, 1917; Falcón and García, *La semilla,* 47, 86; O'Gorman, *Historia,* 150, 272.

71. Abud Flores, *Campeche,* 61; García Ugarte, *Génesis,* 99, 102; Oikión Solano, *El constitucionalismo,* 494–506, 528.

72. SDN/AH, Gracia to Carranza, June 18, 1917, XI/481.3/223:120:82; *Pueblo,* May 12, 14, 16–8, 24, 25, 31, June 2, 3, 5–7, 9, 18, 1917; *Universal,* June 4, 5, 7–11, 1917; del Castillo, *Puebla,* 259–61.

73. JB, Sec. Gobernación to Carranza, June 12, 1917, IX:21; SDN/AH, Medina to Carranza, June 5, 1917, XI/481.5/223:120:72; SDN/AH, Rodríguez et al. to Carranza, June 9, 1917, XI/481.5/223:120:73; *Excélsior,* June 29, 1917; *Pueblo,* June 10, 14, 18, 1917; *Universal,* June 10, 12, 13, 15, 1917.

74. ACE/E, Márquez Galindo et al. to Legislature, July 14, 1917, CCX-I:9.

75. ACE/E, Report, [July n.d.], 1917, CCIX-II:3; Bosques—interview; *Pueblo,* June 2, 1917.

76. CR, Espinosa to Convención, December 30, 1914, 3:4:7; EZ, [Anonymous] to Zapata, December 22, 1914, 17:9:78; JA, Mendoza et al.—decree, December 22, 1914, 2:173; JA, Sevada and Cordero to Convención Revolucionaria Local, December 23, 1914, 2:174; JFL, Méndez Galicia—manifesto, December 4, 1914, Scrapbook; RGG, Palacios Moreno to González Garza, February 2, 1915, 19:123; *Convención,* December 31, 1914; *Mexican Herald,* December 27, 30, 31, 1914, January 1, 1915; *Monitor* (Mexico City), December 24, 29, 31, 1914.

77. CR, Salgado to Asamblea Revolucionaria, May 28, 1915, 7:7:1; EZ, Espinosa to Palafox, January 1, 1915, 15:5:10; EZ, Palafox to Espinosa, January 2, 1915, 15:5:11; *Monitor* (Mexico City), January 8, 1915.

78. JFL, Ramírez to Lucas, December 11, 1914, Scrapbook; JFL, Márquez—decree, March 27, 1915, Scrapbook; RGG, González Garza to Convención, February 3, 1915, 19:122; *Monitor* (Mexico City), December 19, 1914, May 15, 16, 1915.

79. EZ, Guerrero et al. to Zapata, February 29, 1916, 11:6:45.

80. Garciadiego Dantán, "Higinio," 455–8; Kuri Camacho, *La realidad,* 2:76–8; Ramírez Rancaño, *La revolución,* 85–122.

81. CGS, Mendoza López Schwertfegert—decree, January 8, 1916, 1:2:47–8; CGS, Zapata—decree, August 15, 1917, 1:3:87–8; GM, Zapata—Ley Libertades Municipales, September 15, 1916, 30:12:231; JA, Zapata—decree, September 15, 1915, 3:267; Womack, *Zapata,* 264–5.

82. CGS, Zubiría y Campa et al.—decree, October 25, 1915, 1:2:6–7; GM, Zapata—circular, May 31, 1916, 30:12:230; GM, Zapata—law, March 5, 1917, 28:3:104; GM, Montaña—circular, March 12, 1917, 28:1:11; GM, Zúñiga—circular, March 28, 1917, 28:1:30, April 14, 1917, 28:1:30; JA, Mendoza López Schwertfegert et al.—decree, November 2, 1915, 3:205, December 1, 1915, 3:216; Womack, *Zapata,* 279–80.

83. GM, Díaz Soto y Gama et al.—decree, December 12, 1916, 28:2:87; GM, Cacique and Martínez to Pres. Asociación Defensora, January 8, 1917, 28:22:525;

GM, Palafox—regulation, May 23, 1917, 29:10:579; GM, Canova and Amilco–decree, September 13, 1917, 28:20:426; Womack, *Zapata*, 275–6.

84. EZ, López et al. to Zapata, January 20, 1915, 4:1:183; EZ, Miramón et al. to Zapata, June 7, 1915, 8:4:106; EZ, Tapia to Zapata, August 1, 1915, 9:4:2; EZ, Flores et al.—manifesto, October 5, 1916, 12:18:2; EZ, Bonifaz to Zapata, March 6, 1917, 13:7:6; EZ, Villalid to Ayaquica, May 18, 1917, 13:15:5; Henderson, *Worm*, 54.

85. Benjamin, *Rich*, 129, 138; Henderson, *In the Absence*, 235–6; Joseph, *Revolution*, 95–8, 103, 114.

6. Economic and Social Policy, 1914–1917

1. VC, Durán to Carranza, July 26, 1915, 46:5060; Castro, *Informe*, 33–4.

2. C/T, Castro to Carranza, March 8, 1916, XXI-4; SDN/AC, García to González, July 6, 1915, X/III.2:688; *Mexican Herald*, September 30, 1914; *Periódico Oficial*, September 29, October 2, 27, 1914; *Pueblo*, October 27, 1914; Benjamin, *Rich*, 122; Falcón, *Revolución*, 104, 112; Garner, *La revolución*, 133.

3. C/T, Cervantes to Carranza, January 17, February 2, 1916, XXI-4; C/T, Carranza to Cervantes, January 19, February 3, 1916, XXI-4; JB, Carranza to Acuña, June 28, 1915, I:12.

4. Cervantes, *Decretos*, 89–96.

5. C/T, Cervantes to Carranza, [n.d.] 1915, February 2, 1916, XXI-4; SDN/AH, Cervantes to Carranza, May 12, 1915, XI/481.5/221:120:7; SRE, Hohler to Dávalos, February 16, 1916, 16-18-193; VC, Rodiles to Governor, October 5, 1915, 55:6182; *Demócrata*, September 22, December 22, 1915; *Mexican Herald*, September 23, 1915; *Periódico Oficial*, May 11, June 22, September 28, 1915, January 25, 1916; *Pueblo*, May 13, September 23, 25, 1915; Cervantes, *Decretos*, 3–5, 105–6, 110, 128; Cervantes, *Informe*, 7–8.

6. *Pueblo*, June 20, 1917; *Universal*, February 27, 1917; Castro, *Informe*, 34–40.

7. ACE/E, Castro—informe, July 8, 1917, 18:33; *Pueblo*, May 16, 26, 1916.

8. C/T, Carranza to Rojas, April 27, 1915, XXI-4; TO, Comandante Militar—circular, August 28, 1914, 422; *Periódico Oficial*, September 15, 1914, April 6, 1915; Gamboa Ojeda, *Los empresarios*, 93, 95; McCaleb, *Present*, 226–9.

9. C/T, Tejada to Carranza, March 7, 1915, XXI-4; C/T, Carranza to Coss, April 6, 11, 1915, XXI-4; SDN/AH, Lucas to Carranza, December 23, 1914, XI/481.5/220:119:743; Falcón, *Revolución*, 136–7; *Historical Notes*, 20–1.

10. CIM, Gutiérrez Quijano and Cardoso to Castro, June 7, 1916, 2:326–7; PG, Ortíz to González, June 23, 1915, 17; PG, López to González, April 6, 1916, 19; VC, Ramírez to Carranza, April 25, 1915, 37:3972; *Pueblo*, August 9, 1915; *Demócrata*, November 29, 1915, January 26, November 13, 1916.

11. JB, García to Carranza, August 2, 1915, II:2; VC, Brito R. to Carranza, October 4, 1916, 98:11125.

12. *Periódico Oficial*, October 12, 1915.

13. CDHM, Nieto to Procurador, December 16, 1915, 50:335:8:—; CDHM, Banco Oriental—report, February 17, 1916, 50:335:8:—; González Loscertales, "Bases," 284–5; Manero, *La reforma*, 270–80. For a history of the Banco Oriental, see Salazar Ibargüen, "El Banco."

14. GM, Cartal [Paz]—report, September 27, 1916, 28:2:53; Knight, *Mexican*, 2:409; McCaleb, *Present*, 236–42.

15. CDHM, [Ministro] to Estrada, October 18, 1916, 50:335:8:—; CDHM, Ministro to Ministro de Estado, March 17, 1917, 50:331:1:30, May 22, 1917, 50:332:1:1; *Demócrata*, October 18, 1916; *Pueblo*, September 25, October 17, 19, 1916, June 29, 1917; *Universal*, December 31, 1916; Knight, *Mexican*, 2:409; McCaleb, *Present*, 243–6, 256–9.

16. CDHM, [Ministro] to [Ministro Estado], November 17, 1916, 49:315:1:10; CTB, Ferrocarriles Nacionales Mexicanos—report, August 31, 1920, 11:F-9/267:2283:119, 134–5; CTB, Gurza to Pérez, December 19, 1920, 11:F-9/267:2283:108–10; VC, Pani to Carranza, April 17, 1915, 36:3838, April 19, 1915, 36:3873; VC, Pani to Carranza, March 13, 1916, 70:7640; Knight, *Mexican*, 2:406–7; Ruíz, *Great*, 276–7.

17. CIM, Sánchez Gavito and Cardoso to Raygadas, October 31, 1915, 2:35–6; C/T, Carranza to Coss, February 27, 1915, XXI-4; PG, Aldama y Hno. to González, September 8, 1915, 5; RDS, Dismuckes to Navy Dept., February 10, 1916, 51:563; RDS, Canada to Lansing, February 21, 1916, 59:543–4; VC, [Anonymous] to Carranza, September 27, 1915, 53:5867; WFB, Wood—typescript, January 13, 1916, 148; *Demócrata*, November 1, 1916, April 6, 1917; Falcón, *Revolución*, 116.

18. PG, González to Pani, October 16, 1915, 8; RG/PR, Cervantes to Sec. Gobernación, March 2, 1916, 154:94; SDN/AC, Sec. Guerra to Sánchez, October 31, 1916, XI/III/1-405:401.

19. C/T, Pescador to Carranza, December 26, 1916, XXI-4; JB, Carranza to Oficiales, September 28, 1915, III:28; SDN/AC, López to Sec. Guerra, December 11, 1915, D/III/3-172:60; SDN/AC, Ejército Oriente to Sec. Guerra, May 16, 1916, XI/III/2-403:126; SDN/AC, Serrano to Sánchez, June 12, 1916, XI/III/1-405:396; SDN/AC, Godínez to Jefe Depto. Justicia, December 5, 1916, XI/III/1-405:404; SDN/AC, Villaseñor to Castro, June 5, 1917, XI/III/1-372:364; SDN/AC, Enríquez to Rochín, August 23, 1917, XI/III/1-372:371; VC, Preboste General—report, March 12, 1916, 70:7624.

20. CIM, Cardoso to Coss, November 17, 1914, 1:370, November 30, 1914, 1:383–5; DT, González Cosío Hnos. to DT, December 29, 1914, 80:19:1; GBFO, Sánchez y Cía. to Russell, November 11, 1914, 2034:19; GBFO, Hohler to Foreign Office, December 24, 1914, 2040:432; RDS, Jenkins to Shanklin, November 18, 1914, 43:93–4; RDS, Canada to Bryan, November 19, 1914, 42:1154–5; Gamboa Ojeda, *Los empresarios*, 89–90.

21. CIM, Sánchez Gavito and Cardoso to Governor, June 28, 1915, 1:433–42; CIM, Cardoso to Pani, October 27, 1915, 2:26; CIM, Gutiérrez Quijano and Cardoso to Castro, July 24, 1916, 2:357–8; Cervantes, *Informe*, 4; *Universal*, February 24, 1917.

22. CIM, Sánchez Gavito and Cardoso to Governor, August 12, 1915, 1:469–71; CIM, Sánchez Gavito and Cardoso to Tesorero, September 22, 1915, 1:492; CIM, Sánchez Gavito and Cardoso to Quien Corresponde, October 14, 1915, 1:9; CIM, Cardoso to Pani, November 19, 1915, 2:50; CIM, Gutiérrez Quijano and Cardoso to Carranza, March 3, 1916, 2:230; CIM, Gutiérrez Quijano and Cardoso to Ruíz, August 7, 1916, 2:368; CIM, Cardoso to Castro, August 12, 1916, 2:375; C/T, Cervantes to Carranza, [n.d.] 1915, XXI-4; C/T, Millán to Carranza, November 8, 1915, XXI-4; C/T, Certuche to Carranza, December 24, 1915, XXI-4; JB, Cervantes to Carranza, June 26, [1915], I:17; PG, Rosete et al. to González, January 4, 1916, 26B; SDN/AH, Cervantes to Carranza, [n.d., 1915], XI/481.5/221:120:1; *Demócrata*, December 20, 1915, January 25, 1916; *Periódico Oficial*, January 25, 1916; Ramírez Rancaño, *Burguesía*, 179–89.

23. CIM, Gutiérrez Quijano and Cardoso to Pontón, May 10, 1917, 3:113.

24. *Mexican Herald*, November 22, 1914; Knight, *Mexican*, 2:316, 319; Ruíz, *Labor*, 50.

25. Ramírez Rancaño, *Burguesía*, 142.

26. CIM, Cardoso to Sec. Hacienda, September 1, 1914, 1:261–4; CIM, Cardoso to González, September 4, 1914, 1:266–7; CIM, Cardoso to Carranza, September 29, 1914, 1:314–7; DT, Cardoso to DT, September 9, 1914, 88:15:10–1, October 15, 1914, 89:11:36–7; *Periódico Oficial*, September 15, 1914; Falcón and García, *La semilla*, 87 8; Joseph, *Revolution*, 109 10; Ramírez Rancaño, *Burguesía*, 152–4; Rivero Quijano, *La revolución*, 2:399–400. The 1912 accord, agreed to by government, labor, and owners, established a voluntary system that set a minimum wage, maximum work day, and other conditions; see LaFrance, "Labour," 59–74.

27. CIM, Cardoso to Sec. General Estado, September 17, 1914, 1:193–294, 298–9, November 11, 1914, 1:368–9; CIM, Sánchez Gavito and Cardoso to Depto. Trabajo, March 25, 1915, 1:398–9; DT, Director to Governor, September 17, 1914, 88:15:25; DT, Cardoso to Carranza, September 30, 1914, 88:16:2–4; DT, Muñoz to Sec. Fomento, November 14, 1914, 87:11:1, November 20, 1914, 87:11:4; VC, López Jiménez to Rouaix, December 19, 1914, 23:2228; *Mexican Herald*, October 8, 24, 1914; Gutiérrez Álvarez, "El conflicto," 405; Ramírez Rancaño, *Burguesía*, 154–63.

28. CIM, Sánchez Gavito and Cardoso to González, June 5, 1915, 1:414; DT, Carranza—decree, March 22, 1915, 50:29:2; PG, Martínez to González, May 26, 1915, 34, May 26, 1915, 8; VC, Martínez to Carranza, April 27, 1915, 37:4023; VC, González to Carranza, June 28, 1915, 43:4719; *Mexican Herald*, March 2, 1915; Acuña, *Memoria*, 337–8; Ramírez Rancaño, *Burguesía*, 175–9.

29. C/T, Cervantes to Carranza, January 31, 1916, XXI-4; DT, Rosete to DT, August 3, 1915, 104:3:4; DT, Tlacuilo et al. to DT, August 5, 1915, 103:14:2; DT, Cortés to López Jiménez, August 13, 1915, 104:3:1; DT, Director to Rosete, August 14, 1915, 104:3:5.

30. VC, Cervantes to Carranza, August 10, 1915, 48:5288; *Demócrata*, October 15, 1915; *Mexican Herald*, August 21, 23, 1915; *Pueblo*, August 7, 1915.

31. *Mexican Herald*, August 13, 1915; *Periódico Oficial*, July 6, 1915; *Pueblo*, March 2, 1915; Cervantes, *Decretos*, 41–2.

32. CIM, Gutiérrez Quijano and Cardoso to Governor, December 11, 1915, 2:92–4; DT, Furlong y Cía. to DT, May 26, 1916, 108:27:1–2, May 31, 1916, 108:27:7; *Pueblo*, September 4, 1915; *Periódico Oficial*, September 28, December 21, 1915; Joseph, *Revolution*, 109–10; Cervantes, *Decretos*, 107–9, 125–6.

33. CIM, Gutiérrez Quijano and Cardoso to Governor, January 29, 1916, 2:173; CIM, Gutiérrez Quijano and Cardoso to Castro, May 31, 1916, 2:313–5, June 10, 1916, 2:330–1; RG/PR, Gutiérrez Quijano and Cardoso to Carranza, December 24, 1915, 156:25; SRE, Cervantes to Riach, January 25, 31, 1916, 16-16-93; *Demócrata*, December 24, 25, 1915.

34. CIM, Gutiérrez Quijano and Cardoso to Castro, June 9, 1916, 2:328; CIM, Gutiérrez Quijano and Cardoso to González, September 24, 1916, 2:390; CIM, Gutiérrez Quijano and Cardoso to Gómez Haro, October 3, 1916, 2:401; C/T, Rosete to Carranza, February 26, 1916, XXI-4; C/T, Castro to Carranza, May [n.d.], June 3, 1916, XXI-4; DT, Gutiérrez Quijano and Cardoso to González, January 26, 1916, 108:35:2; VC, Rosete to Carranza, January 13, 1916, 65:7222; Lear, *Workers*, 332–9.

35. CIM, Gutiérrez Quijano and Cardoso to González, October 4, 1916, 2:402, October 28, 1916, 2:417, November 28, 1916, 2:470, December 4, 1916, 2:478, December 9, 1916, 2:480–1; RDS, Canada to Lansing, December 1, 1916, 58:339–40; VC, Rascón et al. to Zertuche, November 8, 1916, 102:11654; *Demócrata*, November 3, 11, 14, December 6, 20, 1916; Lear, *Workers*, 323–39.

36. CIM, Cardoso to Noriega y Cía., March 30, 1917, 3:71; *Demócrata*, March 24, 1917; Gómez Álvarez, *Puebla*, 57–8; Ramírez Rancaño, *Burguesía*, 189–92.

37. CDHM, Ministro to Ministro Estado, April 24, 1917, 50:331:1:38; CIM, Gutiérrez Quijano and Cardoso to Lavat, May 1, 1917, 3:106–7; RDS, Summerlin to Sec. State, May 17, 1917, 162:881; *Demócrata*, April 22, 1917; Gamboa Ojeda, "Acerca," 66–7; Ramírez Rancaño, *Burguesía*, 192–3, 198–9.

38. CIM, Gutiérrez Quijano and Cardoso to Castro, May 24, 1917, 3:144–5, May 30, 1917, 3:151–2; *Excélsior*, May 29, 1917; *Pueblo*, May 26, 30, 1917; *Universal*, June 4, 1917; Gómez Álvarez, *Puebla*, 58–9.

39. C/T, Carranza to González, August 26, 1914, XXI-4, August 28, 1914, XXI-4; MWG, Barrón to González, September 18, 1914, 19:2734; SDN/AC, Carrera Peña to Barbosa, October 9, 1914, D/III/3-172:40; *Pueblo*, October 20, November 12, 1914; Cordero y Torres, *Historia compendiada*, 2:427; Falcón, *Revolución*, 116–22; Knight, *Mexican*, 2:446.

40. VC, Rodríguez to Carranza, March 8, 1915, 30:3205; *Periódico Oficial,* October 6, 1914; *Pueblo,* October 3, 22, 1914.

41. C/T, Carranza to Coss, April 26, 1915, XXI-4.

42. C/T, Estrada to Carranza, February 15, 23, March 11, 1916, XXI-4; C/T, Carranza to Estrada, February 18, March 2, 1916, XXI-4; C/T, Nieto to Carranza, February 25, 1916, XXI-4; C/T, Acuña to Cervantes, March 6, 1916, XXI-4; C/T, Narváez to Carranza, March 15, 1916, XXI-4; C/T, Cervantes to Carranza, March 16, 23, 27, 30, 1916, XXI-4; C/T, Carranza to Cervantes, March 25, 1916, XXI-4; VC, Ortíz Rubio to Carranza, August 3, 1916, 90:10117.

43. Esparza, *Gillow,* 148–52; Gillow y Zavala, *Reminiscencias,* 404–5.

44. ABF, Cox to Fall, [December n.d., 1919], 40:1824; ABF, F.J.K. to Fall, December 13, 1919, 40:1822; DRF, Jones with Jenkins—interview, May 13, 1918, 118; RDS, Jenkins to Shanklin, June 28, 1915, 47:708–10; SDN/AH, Cervantes to Carranza, June 17, 1915, XI/481.5/221:120:223; SRE, Bonillas to Medina, November 1, 1919, 16-28-1(I); SRE, Cabrera to Sec. Relaciones Exteriores, May 20, 1918, 42-26-95; Cervantes, *Decretos,* 33–5; Espinosa Yglesias, *Fundación,* 12; Paxman, "William," 12–5.

45. C/ADN, Cabrera to Carranza, May 1, 1917, MP/7115/2; RG/PR, González to Sec. Gobernación, January 11, 1917, 221:71; RG/PR, León to Sec. Gobernación, January 24, 1917, 223:75; *Demócrata,* September 11, October 2, 16, 1915; *Pueblo,* September 12, 1915; Velasco, *Autobiografía,* 79.

46. TO, Ramírez to González, February 24, 1913, 411; *Mexican Herald,* September 5, 1914; *Pueblo,* October 1, 1914; Walker Sarmiento, "La reforma," 8–9.

47. TO, Coss and Muñoz to Ciudadanos, November 10, 1914, 421; *Periódico Oficial,* October 2, 9, 1914; *Pueblo,* October 20, 1914.

48. C/T, Sánchez Gavito to Carranza, March 3, 1915, XXI-4; C/T, Carranza to Coss, March 15, 1915, XXI-4; JB, Cruz to Carranza, [February n.d., 1915], I:18; JB, Lechuga to Carranza, March 14, 1915, III:3; VC, de Gante to Carranza, March 13, 1915, 31:3285.

49. VC, Cervantes to Carranza, August 25, 1915, 50:5473; *Demócrata,* September 23, 1915; *Periódico Oficial,* June 15, 1915; *Pueblo,* September 23, October 12, 1915; Cervantes, *Decretos,* 24–6.

50. ARM, Carranza to Rouaix, January 19, 1916, 60:99:272; C/T, Márquez to Carranza, June 30, 1916, XXI-4; JB, Duvallon—report, December 20, 1916, I:12; PG, González to Cervantes, December 4, 1915, 7; SDN/AC, Castro to Sec. Guerra, March 2, 1917, 876–7.XI/III/3-2623:192; SDN/AH, Medina to Carranza, May 9, 1916, XI/481.5/222:120:20; SDN/AH, Valencia et al. to Sec. Guerra, January 25, 1917, XI/481.5/223:120:8; VC, Tenorio and Gumersindo to Carranza, December 30, 1915, 64:7107; VC, Galves et al. to Carranza, January 9, 1916, 65:7187; VC, Marcario et al. to Carranza, January 10, 1916, 65:7197; VC, Castro to Carranza, June 22, 1916, 85:9524; *Demócrata,* March 2, 1917; *Periódico Oficial,* May 23, 1916; *Universal,* January 22, 1917; Cumberland, *Constitutionalist,* 242; Knight, *Mexican,* 2:468–9.

51. VC, Carreón et al. to Carranza, June 24, 1916, 86:9565; García Ugarte, *Génesis*, 121–2; Garner, *La revolución*, 165–6; Henderson, *Worm*, 60–2; Sánchez Flores, *Zacapoaxtla*, 247–8.

52. Castro, *Informe*, 15–7; Cervantes, *Informe*, 3; México, Sec. Agricultura, *Estadísticas*, 40.

53. Falcón, *Revolución*, 135–6; García Ugarte, *Génesis*, 65, 80, 89–95; Oikión Solano, *El constitucionalismo*, 406–13; Wasserman, *Persistent*, 19. See Ochoa, *Feeding*, for a study of government basic foods policy in subsequent decades.

54. CDHM, Memorandum, May 27, 1915, 48:311:29:1; DT, Juárez to Valero, October 10, 1914, 85:2:1.

55. CIM, Turnbull to Governor, February 23, 1915, 1:388–9; INEHRM, Oficina Información—handbill, April 24, 1915, 11:2:7–8; VC, Barradas to Carranza, March 17, 1915, 32:3337; *Mexican Herald*, September 12, 1914; *Monitor* (Mexico City), April 8, 1915; *Periódico Oficial*, September 15, 18, October 6, 13, 27, 1914, March 9, 23, 1915; *Pueblo*, October 16, 28, 31, 1914, March 10, 1915.

56. C/T, Carranza to Coss, February 23, 1915, XXI-4; PG, Vázquez and Martínez to González, June 9, 1915, 24; PG, González to Cervantes, June 11, 1915, 24; PG, Martínez to González, September 8, 1915, 15; RDS, [Anonymous] to Canada, January 21, 1915, 43:—; VC, Pani to Carranza, March 30, 1915, 33:3571; VC, Silva to Carranza, May 5, 1915, 38:4142.

57. C/T, Carranza to Coss, March 12–4, 1915, XXI-4; JB, Obregón to Carranza, August 22, 1915, III:24; PG, Cía. Comercial Puebla to González, August 11, 1915, 8; *New York Sun*, May 28, 29, 1915.

58. C/T, Carranza to Obregón, February 3, 1915, XXI-4; C/T, Carranza to Coss, February 3, 14, 22, March 9, 16, 17, 26, 28, 1915, XXI-4; C/T, Millán to Aguilar, March 25, 1915, XXI-4; JB, Obregón to Carranza, March 9, 1915, III:2; JB, Carranza to Coss, April 20, 1915, I:18; VC, Barradas to Carranza, March 17, 1915, 32:3337.

59. CDHM, Cervantes—decree, June 1, 1915, 48:311:29:1; CDHM, Agente Confidencial to Acuña, July 5, 1915, 48:311:29:1; CDHM, Aldama y Hno. to Zubarán Capmany, July 9, 1915, 48:311:29:1; PG, Colmenares Ríos to González, July 23, 1915, 12; SRE, de Villera to Subsec. Relaciones Exteriores, August 5, 1915, 16-15-97; VC, Largarda to Carranza, August 5, 1915, 47:5198; *El Demócrata*, August 16, 20, September 4, 1915; *Mexican Herald*, June 7, 1915; *Periódico Oficial*, June 15, 1915; *Pueblo*, August 7, 8, 20, 1915; Cervantes, *Decretos*, 17–9.

60. CDHM, Memorandum, May 27, 1915, 48:311:29:1; CDHM, Rivero Quijano to Casares y Gil, June 25, 1915, 48:311:29:1; JB, Cervantes to Carranza, July 1, 1915, I:17; JB, Carranza to Obregón, August 23, 1915, III:24.

61. C/T, Cervantes to Carranza, [n.d.] 1915, XXI-4; C/T, Carranza to Arredondo, July 1, 1915, XXI-4; PG, Cervantes to González, July 12, 1915, 19; PG, Valderrama to González, June 25, 1915, 14; RDS, Jenkins to Shanklin, May 14, 1915, 45:314–6; RG/PR, Cervantes to Sec. Gobernación, August 7, 1915, 154:92;

VC, Oficina Información—report, August 4, 1915, 47:5183; VC, Cervantes to Carranza, August 25, 1915, 50:5512; *Monitor* (Mexico City), May 24, 1915.

62. C/T, Bandera y Mata to Carranza, [n.d.] 1915, XXI-4; C/T, Suáres Ruisecos to Méndez, December 20, 1915, XXI-4; C/T, Millán to Carranza, December 29, 1915, XXI-4; PG, Somohano to González, September 14, 1915, 27; VC, Oficina Información—memorandum, July 14, 1915, 45:4917; *Demócrata*, August 20, 1915; *Mexican Herald*, August 23, 1915; *Pueblo*, April 19, May, 5, 18, August 3, 9, 16, 19, 1915.

63. C/T, Cervantes to Carranza, [n.d.] 1915, XXI-4; *Periódico Oficial*, September 21, 1915; *Mexican Herald*, September 16, 1915; *Pueblo*, September 16, 19, 1915; Cervantes, *Decretos*, 102–4.

64. VC, Soldados Constitucionalistas to Carranza, February 10, [1916], 148:16979; *Demócrata*, November 11, 15, 1915; *Pueblo*, January 7, May 27, June 11, 1916.

65. AAA, Asociación Internacional México to Rider, September 13, 1915, 20:367; *Demócrata*, December 24, 1915, January 7, April 14, 1916; *Mexican Herald*, October 5, 1915; *Pueblo*, August 11, 1916; Cervantes, *Informe*, 2–3.

66. C/T, Cervantes to Carranza, March 24, 1916, XXI-4; VC, Carranza to Cabrera, December 19, 1914, 23:2233; VC, Torres to Carranza, July 8, 1915, 44:4850; VC, Cervantes to Carranza, August 5, 1915, 47:5195; VC, Rosales to Zorrilla, March 10, 1916, 70:7609; VC, Narvácz to Zorrilla, March 23, 1916, 72:7821; *Convención*, December 23, 1914; *Periódico Oficial*, June 29, November 23, December 14, 1915; Castro, *Informe*, 31–2; Cervantes, *Decretos*, 27–8, 36–40, 111–7.

67. VC, Cabrera to Carranza, February 23, 1915, 28:3031; VC, Neri to Díaz vda. de Bendejo, February 11, 1916, 67.7399, *Boletín del Consejo Superior de Salubridad*, August 1915, 1–2, 12, October 1915, 4–5, December 1915, 6–7; *Demócrata*, October 15, 1915; *Periódico Oficial*, March 21, 1916; Paredes Colín, *El distrito*, 112.

68. CDHM, Ministro to Ministro Estado, September 13, 1916, 49:327:21: —; *Demócrata*, November 11, 19, December 6, 15, 1915; *Mexican Herald*, October 5, 1915; *Periódico Oficial*, December 28, 1915; *Pueblo*, February 17, 1916; Cervantes, *Decretos*, 118–21; Cordero y Torres, *Crónicas* (1966), 61; Cordero y Torres, *Diccionario*, 2:3899; Wood, *Revolution*, 31–7.

69. CIM, Gutiérrez Quijano and Cardoso to Castro, April 27, 1917, 3:96; C/T, Cervantes to Carranza, [n.d.] 1915, February 29, 1916, XXI-4; FM, Echeverría to Vda. de Serdán, October 19, 1914, 90; INEHRM, Narváez—minutes, February 18, 1915, 1:6/2:51; PG, Montaño to González, October 15, 1915, 20; *Demócrata*, December 11, 1915, March 5, 16, 1916; *Mexican Herald*, February 17, 1915; *Pueblo*, August 8, 13, 1915; Castro, *Informe*, 31–3; Cervantes, *Informe*, 7.

70. García Ugarte, *Génesis*, 62, 77.

71. C/T, Cervantes to Carranza, [n.d.] 1915, XXI-4; RG/PR, Narváez to Carranza, October 24, 1915, 155:75; SDN/AH, Cervantes to Carranza, [n.d.], XI/

481.5/221:120:7; TO, Mora to Pres. Consejo Administración Superior, October 21, 1914, 921; *Demócrata*, November 29, 1915, March 7, 1917; *Pueblo*, February 5, October 12, 1916; *Universal*, January 13, 24, February 17, 22, 27, 1917; Cervantes, *Decretos*, 122–3.

72. C/T, Cervantes to Carranza, February 29, 1916, XXI-4; VC, Lazcano et al. to Carranza, February 24, 1916, 68:—; Joseph, *Revolution*, 105–6.

73. C/T, Coss to Carranza, [n.d.] 1915, XXI-4; Castro, *Informe*, 20–2.

74. C/T, Carranza to Coss, January 22, 1915, XXI-4; C/T, Cervantes to Carranza, [n.d.] 1915, XXI-4; VC, Vázquez to Carranza, May 10, 1915, 39:4222; VC, Castro to Carranza, December 19, 1916, 107:12258; *Demócrata*, January 5, March 16, October 25, 1916; *Pueblo*, August 16, 1915, January 25, 1916, January 8, February 5, 1917; *Universal*, January 4, 1917; Castro, *Informe*, 20–6; Puebla (city), *Proyecto*, 13–4.

75. PG, Cervantes to González, January 24, 1916, 7; *Pueblo*, February 6, 1916; Cervantes, *Decretos . . . contra el analfabetismo*, 1–15; Gamboa Ojeda, "El movimiento," 368; Oikión Solano, *El constituionalismo*, 419–21; Joseph, *Revolution*, 107–8.

76. VC, Oficina Información—bulletin, February 17, 1916, 68:7442; VC, Bermúdez et al. to Carranza, March 26, 1916, 72:7836; *Estudiante*, March 9, August 3, 1919; *Pueblo*, October 17, 22, 1914, June 7, July 1, 15, 1916; Richmond, *Venustiano*, 174.

77. Knight, *Mexican*, 2:501; Ruíz, *Great*, 413–4.

78. WFB, Bryan-memorandum, November 15, 1919, 145[1]; Cordero y Torres, *Historia compendiada*, 2:429–31; Esparza, *Gillow*, 148–9; Gillow, *Reminiscencias*, 392–5; Gómez Haro, *D. Ramón*, 55–6; Márquez, *Monseñor*, 35–6; Ramírez Rancaño, "El destierro," 31, 38–9; Serafin Sodi, *Monografías*, 91–2.

79. EZ, Doret to Zapata, April 13, 1915, 7:5:19; SDN/AH, Coss to Carranza, January 21, 1915, XI/481.5/221:120:89; Cordero y Torres, *Historia del periodismo*, 98, 204; Medel M., *El convento*, 127; Palomera, *La obra*, 335; Peral, *Gobernantes*, 176–7.

80. CR, Coss to Pres. Convención, October 29, 1914, 4:2:18–21; VC, Hernández to Carranza, May 5, 1915, 38:4144; *Demócrata*, October 31, 1914, April 11, 1916; *Mexican Herald*, December 21, 1914; *Pueblo*, November 1, 1914; Cordero y Torres, *Historia compendiada*, 1:205; Ramírez Rancaño, *La revolución*, 74.

81. C/T, Carranza to Cervantes, March 2, 1916, XXI-4; PG, Cervantes to González, August 11, 1915, 7; RDS, Jenkins to Shanklin, June 28, 1915, 47:708–10; *Periódico Oficial*, July 13, 1915; Cervantes, *Decretos*, 43–53; Cordero y Torres, *Diccionario*, 2:2642; Cordero y Torres, *Historia compendiada*, 2:432; Palomera, *La obra*, 335–6.

82. Falcón, *Revolución*, 91; Falcón and García, *La semilla*, 88; García Ugarte, *Génesis*, 65–6; Garner, *La revolución*, 143–5.

83. *Demócrata*, November 4, 1914, April 8, 1916; *Pueblo*, January 20, April 12, 1916; Gamboa Ojeda, "El movimiento," 368; García Ugarte, *Génesis*, 66; Joseph, *Revolution*, 106; Palomera, *La obra*, 335–6.

84. RG/PR, Picazo to Sec. Gobernación, December 26, 1916, 219:25; RG/PR, Castro to Subsec. Gobernación, April 11, 1917, 219:25; *Demócrata*, April 8, 1916; Cordero y Torres, *Historia compendiada*, 2:431–2; Gamboa Ojeda, "El movimiento," 370.

85. RG/PR, Pérez to Aguirre Berlanga, February 28, 1917, 177:11; RG/PR, Castro to Subsec. Gobernación, March 15, 1917, 177:11, May 15, 1917, 193:29; SDN/AH, Santa Fe to Carranza, February 27, 1917, XI/481.5/223:120:17; SDN/AH, Castro to Carranza, March 30, 1917, XI/481.5/223:120:33; *Pueblo*, September 29, 1916, June 20, 1917.

86. GM, Ayaquica et al.—circular, December 21, 1916, 30:12:233; GM, Zapata—decree, March 5, 1917, 28:3:104; EZ, Mesa to Zapata, March 11, 1915, 18:3:95; EZ, Arellano to Zapata, December 8, 1915, 19.8.14; JA, Palafox et al. decree, November 17, 1915, 3:210; PG, Andrade to González, December 31, 1915, 4.

87. GM, Mentado to Zapata, February 16, 1917, 30:14:260.

88. EZ, Fuentes—financial statement, January 31, 1915, 25:2:31, 66; EZ, Gálvez et al.—financial statement, April 30, 1915, 25:2:70.

89. EZ, Osorio to Zapata, May 17, 1915, 8:2:131; EZ, Vargas to Zapata, January 3, 1917, 13:1:3.

90. EZ, Reyes Márquez to Zapata, January 22, 1915, 4:2:33; EZ, Muniver to Zapata, February 23, 1915, 6:1:42; RDS, Scott to Dismuckes, March 29, 1916, 52:937; *Historical Notes*, 20–1; Kuri Camacho, *La realidad*, 2:78–80.

91. CGS, Zapata—decree, October 10, 1914, 1:3:41; EZ, Aguilar and García to Zapata, March 16, 1915, 18:3:116; GM, Reyes Márquez to Zapata, March 13, 1915, 28:18:340; GM, Díaz Soto y Gama to Zapata, January 30, 1916, 30:11:229; GM, Díaz Soto y Gama—report, January 10, 1917, 30:13:244; JA, Mendoza López Schwertfegert et al.—decree, December 27, 1915, 3:225; RGG, González Garza to Ledesma, February 7, 1915, 7:283; RGG, Mejía to González Garza, March 28, 1915, 9:243; RGG, González Garza to Mejía, March 29, 1915, 9.244; RGG, Ayaquica to González Garza, June 2, 1915, 18:1; RR, Zapata—decree, February 11, 1915, 3:46:801, February 9, 1916, 3:46:815.

92. CDHM, Ministro—report, January 2, 1915, 48:310:2:14.

93. CGS, Palafox et al.—decree, January 19, 1916, 1:2:50–3; CGS, Zapata—decree, February 3, 1917, 1:3:68–70; RR, Zapata—decree, September 8, 1914, 3:46:743; RR, Palafox to Zapata, January 11, 1915, 3:46:795; Brunk, *Emiliano*, 148–53; Knight, *Mexican*, 2:189; Womack, *Zapata*, 230–1.

94. RR, Damián to Zapata, September 25, 28, 1914, 3:43:756; RR, Damián—decree, February 5, 1915, 3:43:763; RR, Ayaquica to Zapata, May 10, 1915, 3:50:859; Fabela and Fabela, *Documentos*, 21:131–3, 168–72, 174–5; Henderson, *Worm*, 60–2; Hoyos Hernández, "Vida," 118.

95. EZ, López et al. to Zapata, June 27, 1915, 8:6:57; SRE, Hohler to Palafox, May 26, 1915, 13-1-53; Knight, *Mexican*, 2:190–1.

96. Womack, *Zapata*, 229–36.

97. Gilly, *La revolución*, 253–308.

98. FM, Policia Reservada—memorandum, December 26, 1914, 75; RG/PR, Calzado to Sec. Gobernación, September 29, 1916, 225:99.

99. CR, Cariño to Jefe Armas, February 1, 1916, 10:1:4; EZ, Damián to Zapata, January 29, 1915, 4:2:193; EZ, Zapata to Mendoza, March 12, 1915, 7:1:65; EZ, Ramírez and Sánchez to Zapata, May 8, 1915, 19:1:45; EZ, Ayaquica to Zapata, May 10, 1915, 19:1:61; EZ, Silva to Espinosa, May 16, 1915, 8:2:103; EZ, Reyes Márquez to Zapata, June 7, 1915, 8:4:101; EZ, Romero et al. to Zapata, June 15, 1915, 8:5:64; EZ, Rosas et al. to Zapata, July 12, 1915, 9:2:8; EZ, Morán to Zapata, September 15, 1915, 10:2:19; EZ, Arellano et al. to Zapata, October 24, 1915, 10:6:22; EZ, López et al. to Zapata, January 30, 1916, 11:3:34; GM, Palafox to Zapata, February 7, 1916, 27:2:19; JA, Palafox to Mendoza, February 19, 1916, 3:243; JA, Paz to Zapata, August 16, 1916, 3:265; RR, Ayaquica to Zapata, May 10, 1915, 3:50:859, June 17, 1915, 3:43:760; VC, Marcario et al. to Carranza, January 10, 1916, 65:7197; *Demócrata*, April 7, 1917; Fabela and Fabela, *Documentos*, 21:207–8; Henderson, *Worm*, 50–2, 60–2; Hoyos Hernández, "Vida," 118–9; Ramírez Rancaño, *La revolución*, 92–4.

100. EZ, Damián to Zapata, April 7, 1915, 7:4:54; EZ, Reyes Márquez to Zapata, May 4, 1915, 8:1:86; EZ, Osorio to Zapata, May 17, 1915, 8:2:131; EZ, Lucero to Damián, July 9, 1915, 9:1:76; GM, Martínez to Asociación Defensora, March 11, 1917, 28:3:107; JA, Zapata to Jefes, Oficiales, etc., February 9, 1916, 3:240; PG, Andrade to González, December 31, 1915, 4; RGG, Ayaquica to González Garza, March 10, 1915, 13:20; Brunk, *Emiliano*, 181; Hoyos Hernández, "Vida," 135.

101. C/T, Medina to Carranza, March 12, 1915, XXI-4; EZ, Ayaquica to Zapata, March 10, 1915, 6:4:139; EZ, Herrera to Zapata, April 28, 1915, 7:6:43; EZ, Alcaide to Zapata, June 2, 1915, 8:4:27; EZ, Vázquez to Zapata, July 26, 1915, 19:3:75; EZ, Magaña to Zapata, May 30, 1917, 13:15:64; GM, Zapata—decree, April 10, 1917, 28:3:111; RGG, Zapata to González Garza, May 18, 1915, 47:478; RGG, González Garza to Zapata, May 19, 1915, 47:477; RGG, Méndez et al. to González Garza, May 22, 1915, 19:31; RGG, Nieto to González Garza, May 24, 1915, 19:30; RGG, Belaunzarán to González Garza, June 4, 1915, 19:14; *Mexican Herald*, December 29, 1914; Galindo, *A través*, 110–48; Henderson, *Worm*, 54–5; Knight, *Mexican*, 2:370–1, 416.

102. CGS, Montaña et al.—decree, November 27, 1915, 1:2:27–9; GM, Zúñiga—circulars, March 28, 1917, 28:10:245, 28:1:28, 28:1:29, April 13, 1917, 27:18:422, 28:1:41, 28:1:42, April 17, 1917, 27:18:424, May 13, 1917, 28:10:252, September 15, 1917, 28:10:253; GM, Zapata to Mendoza, August 22, 1917, 27:18:424; GM, Zapata–reform program, April 10, 1919, 30:36:579; JA, Montaña et al.—decree, November 20, 1915, 3:214; RR, Montaña to Pres. Municipales,

January 20, 1917, 3:46:835; RR, Depto. Instrucción Pública to Pres. Municipales, March 28, 1917, 3:46:841; Hoyos Hernández, "Vida," 55–6.

103. GM, Morales et al.—report, February 5, 1917, 28:3:94; GM, Torres—report, March 5, 1917, 28:3:103; GM, Zúñiga-circular, April 17, 1917, 27:18:424; GM, Report, May 31, 1917, 28:21:503; GM, Sánchez et al. to Ayaquica, February 14, 1918, 29:2:57; GM, Espíritu to Ayaquica, February 23, 1918, 29:2:86; GM, Bonilla to Ayaquica, March 15, 1918, 29:4:330.

104. Joseph, *Revolution*, 103–10.

7. Politics, 1917–1920

1. JB, Cabrera to Barragán, July 21, 1917, V:15; Meyer, *Luis*, 11–4; Niemeyer, *Revolution*, 45; Palavicini, *Los diputados*, 1:327; Peral, *Gobernantes*, 185–6; Porras y López, *Luis*, 17–8.

2. ACE/E, Cabrera to Legislature, October 16, 1919, CCXVIII:321.

3. *Estudiante*, March 23, 1919; *Prensa*, July 20, 1919, *Universal*, August 12, 1917; Navarro Rojas, *Conflictos*, 61.

4. *Demócrata*, December 26, 1919; *Estudiante*, March 16, 1918; *Excélsior*, September 22, 1917; *Monitor* (Puebla), December 25, 1918, April 2, May 3, 1919; *New York Times*, March 14, 1921; *Prensa*, August 1, 1918.

5. *Monitor* (Puebla), June 23, 1919; *Excélsior*, October 1, 2, 1919; del Castillo, *Puebla*, 261–2; Peral, *Gobernantes*, 185–6.

6. *Prensa*, August 28, 1918, July 23, August 21, 1919; Benjamin, *La Revolución*, 99–110.

7. *Prensa*, May 9, 10, July 19, 1918; Benjamin, *La Revolución*, 110.

8. ACE/A, 23:April 14, 1918; *Estudiante*, November 24, 1918, July 20, 1919; *Monitor* (Puebla), November 13, 1919; *Universal*, November 30, 1917, April 16, May 11, 1918.

9. *Estudiante*, June 16, 30, 1918, March 16, 1919; *Monitor* (Puebla), March 19, 1919; Cordero y Torres, *Crónicas* (1955), 119–20; Cordero y Torres, *Historia compendiada*, 425–6.

10. *Demócrata*, August 2, 1919; *Estudiante*, March 16, May 4, 1919; *Excélsior*, September 29, 1918, March 25, 27, 29, April 28, 1919; *Monitor* (Puebla), October 1, 3, 4, 22, 23, November 29, 1918, February 19, 23, April 13, 30, June 17, 19, 1919; *Universal*, September 30, 1918, January 28, April 5, 1919; Cordero y Torres, *Historia del periodismo*, 516–7, 473–4.

11. ACE/E, Cabrera—informe, January 15, 1920, CCXVI-11:201; VC, Junta Directiva to Carranza, July 25, 1919, 137:15741; *Estudiante*, March 30, 1919, January 4, 1920; *Excélsior*, July 26, 29, 1919; *Prensa*, July 25, 26, 1919; *Universal*, July 31, August 2, 1919; Cordero y Torres, *Historia del periodismo*, 206.

12. ACE/E, Cabrera to Legislature, September 3, 1919, CCXVIII:315; ACE/E, Legislature—decree, September 13, 1919, CCXVIII:315; RE, Estrada to Cabrera,

October 25, 1919, 2:21:779; *Demócrata*, September 14, 17, 20, 1919; *Estudiante*, September 28, 1919; *Excélsior*, September 14, 15, 20, 24, October 1, 1919; *Monitor* (Puebla), September 12, 1919; *Prensa*, September 20, 1919; *Universal*, September 20, 25, 1919; Cordero y Torres, *Diccionario*, 1:1289.

13. C/T, González to León de Garay, February 3, 1920, MIX-3; C/T, Ramírez to González, February 6, 1920, MIX-3; J1D/A, Valle Gagern to Juez, December 16, 1919, 283:356; J1D/A, León de Garay to Juez, January 28, 1920, 284:20; J1D/A, Director to Juez, February 14, 1920, 285:38; *Demócrata*, December 23, 1919; *Excélsior*, December 18, 1919, February 28, 1920; *Monitor* (Puebla), November 12, December 18, 1919; *Universal*, December 19, 1919; Cordero y Torres, *Historia del periodismo*, 101–13; Peral, *Diccionario*, 425–6.

14. SDN/AH, Cabrera to Carranza, October 31, 1917, XI/481.5/223:120:160; *Prensa*, February 22, March 2, 1918; *Universal*, November 3, 17, 1917, August 27, 1919; U.S. Senate, *Investigation*, 2:2078.

15. Cumberland, "Jenkins," 586–607; LaFrance, "Jenkins"; Paxman, "William," 15–6.

16. ACE/E, Cabrera—informe, September 30, 1917, January 15, July 15, 1918, CCX-I:4; ACE/E, Cabrera to Legislature, July 22, 1919, CCXXVIII:297; *Excélsior*, September 25, 1917, January 6, August 6, October 10, 1919, June 12, 1920; *Monitor* (Puebla), October 25, 1918; *Periódico Oficial*, September 25, 1917; *Pueblo*, September 12, 13, 25, 1917; *Universal*, January 4, 1918.

17. ACE/E, Cabrera—informe, September 30, 1917, January 15, July 15, 1918, CCX-I:4; RG/PR, Nomura and Zalce to Subsec. Estado, December 29, 1917, 175:10; SDN/AH, Cabrera to Carranza, October 3, 1917, XU/481.5/223:120:143; *Prensa*, August 6, February 12, 1918; *Excélsior*, December 31, 1917; *Universal*, August 20, 1917; Cabrera, *Informe*, 24–5; Jacobs, *Ranchero*, 105; Wasserman, *Persistent*, 17.

18. ACE/A, 23:July 21, 27, 1917; ACE/E, Cabrera to Legislature, July 21, 27, September 24, 1917, CCX-I:12; ACE/E, Legislature to Cabrera, July 23, 27, September 27, 1917, CCX-I:12; *Periódico Oficial*, August 7, October 2, 1917; *Universal*, August 11, 1917.

19. ACE/A, 23:January 18, March 4, 11, 1918; ACE/E, Hinojosa et al. to Legislature, January 18, 1918, CCX-I:12; ACE/E, Márquez Galindo et al. to Legislature, March 5, 1918, CCX-I:12; Bosques—interview; *Demócrata*, March 6, 1918; *Estudiante*, July 21, 1918; *Prensa*, January 19, March 12, 1918; *Universal*, January 21, 22, March 6, 1918; del Castillo, *Puebla*, 261. The principal independent deputies were Aurelio Aja (Acatlán), Gilberto Bosques (Puebla), Celerino Cano (Puebla), and Agustín Verdín (Matamoros).

20. ACE/E, Cabrera to Legislature, March 30, 1918, CCX-I:12; *Excélsior*, September 21, 1918; *Prensa*, April 2, 3, 1918; *Universal*, April 3, 1918.

21. ACE/A, 23:April 15, 1918; Bosques—interview; *Demócrata*, June 18, September 5, 1918; *Excélsior*, July 17, 25, September 6, 21, 1918; *Prensa*, February 20, March 5, April 7, 1918.

22. ACE/A, 24:May 27, 1919; ACE/E, Corfero et al. to Legislature, May 24,1919, CCX-I:12; *Excélsior*, January 30, 1919; *Monitor* (Puebla), January 29, April 20, 1919.

23. ACE/E, Sánchez to Legislature, July 2, 1921, CCX-I:12; ACE/E, Domínguez Martínez to Sánchez, July 13, 1921, CCX-I:12; Garner, *La revolución*, 141; Wasserman, *Persistent*, 15.

24. ACE/E, Palacios et al. to Legislature, April 10, 1918, CCXVI-11:204; *Excélsior*, November 12, December 8, 1917, September 1, 1918.

25. ACE/E, Cabrera—informe, July 15, 1918, CCX-1:4, January 15, 1920, CCXVI-11:201; ACE/E, Cabrera to Legislature, February 3, 1920, CCXX:379; *Demócrata*, August 2, 1918; *Estudiante*, June 22, October 5, 1919; *Excélsior*, July 22, 1919; *Monitor* (Puebla), March 7, May 10, July 20, 1919.

26. *Estudiante*, July 13, 1919; *Excélsior*, January 25, 1919, February 20, 1920; Cabrera, *Informe*, 5–8.

27. ACE/A, 24:October 8, 1919; ACE/E, Cabrera—informe, January 15, 1920, CCXVI-11:201; GO, Bretón—broadside, April 22, 1914, 19:11:12; *Excélsior*, December 8, 1918, February 9, September 20, 1919, June 6, 1920; *Monitor* (Puebla), October 17, 29, November 10, December 7, 1918, January 1, September 19, 1919; *Prensa*, September 28, 29, October 15, 1918, August 6, 1919; Peral, *Gobernantes*, 213–4.

28. ACE/E, Cabrera—informe, January 15, 1918, CCX-I:4; CTB, Sánchez to Obregón, July 26, 1919, 11:D-5/185:1254:72; *Prensa*, January 8, 12, 15, 1918; *Pueblo*, November 2, 1917; Puebla (state), *Constitución*, 16, 25, 29–32; Puebla (state), *Ley orgánica municipal*, 1–60.

29. ACE/A, 23:October 17, 18, 1918; *Prensa*, October 18, 1918; *Monitor* (Puebla), October 18, 1918; Cabrera, *Informe*, 10 2; Puebla (state), *Ley orgánica de los artículos*, 1–48.

30. ACE/A, 23:January 28, 1918, March 6, 1918; ACE/E, Cabrera—informe, July 15, 1918, CCX-I:4; *Excélsior*, December 11, 1917; *Monitor* (Puebla), October 8, 20, November 21, December 31, 1918, March 22, 1919; *Pueblo*, September 12, 13, 1917; *Universal*, January 8, 25, 1918.

31. CTB, Sánchez to Obregón, July 26, 1919, 11:D-5/185:1254:72; Velasco, *Autobiografía*, 82.

32. ACE/A, 24:April 3, 1919; INEHRM, Narváez to Carranza, April 27, 1919, 1:6/4:13–15; *Demócrata*, January 25, 1919; *Monitor* (Puebla), January 10, March 7, 1919; *Excélsior*, January 17, 1919; *Periódico Oficial*, January 21, February 4, 25, 1919; *Universal*, January 17, 1919.

33. ACE/E, Vilchis et al. to Legislature, February 26, 1919, CCXVII-11:270; ACE/E, Cabrera to Legislature, January 15, 1920, CCXVII-11:201; *Demócrata*, February 21, March 21, 1919; *Excélsior*, February 18, 1919; *Monitor* (Puebla), February 5, 25, 26, 1919; *Universal*, March 20, 1919.

34. ACE/E, Aparicio et al. to Legislature, March 24, 1919, CCXVII-11:270; *Demócrata*, March 25, 26, 1919; *Excélsior*, March 27, 31, 1919; *Universal*, March 26, 1919.

35. ACE/E, Cabrera to Legislature, April 12, 1919, CCXVII-11:270; *Demócrata*, March 29, 1919; *Excélsior*, March 27, 28, 1919; *Monitor* (Puebla), April 16, 1919; *Universal*, April 13, 15, 24, 1919.

36. ACE/E, Álvarez to Sec. General, March 20, 1919, CCXVII-11:270; ACE/E, Toxqui Vda. de Blanca to Legislature, July 25, 1919, CCXVIII:306; ACE/E, Cabrera to Legislature, January 15, 1920, CCXVI-11; AJE/I, Guzmán to Juez, September 6, 1919, 1919:3; INEHRM, Narváez to Carranza, April 27, 1919, 1:6/4:13–5; J1D/A, Casco to Garrido, February 22, 1919, 276:63; *Excélsior*, March 8, April 13, 21, 22, 1919; *Monitor* (Puebla), January 22, February 22, March 7, April 12, 15, 21, 24, June, 8, 10, September 6, 7, 1919; *Universal*, February 11, 25, April 20, September 7, 8, 1919.

37. ACE/A, 24:October 11, 1919; ACE/E, Garrido to Legislature, March 8, 1919, CCXVII-11:270; ACE/E, Cordero et al. to Carranza, March 27, 1919, CCXVII-11:270; ACE/E, Cabrera to Legislature, October 11, 1919, CCXVIII-11:322, January 15, 1920, CCXVI-11:201; INEHRM, Narváez to Carranza, April 27, 1919, 1:6/4:13-5; SDN/AC, Muñoz to Castro, March 28, 1919, XI/III.2:252; *Demócrata*, February 8, 16, 20, 1919; *Excélsior*, February 12, March 29, 30, April 3, 9, 10, 1919; *Monitor* (Puebla), February 10, March 29, April 3, 5, 8, August 9, 1919; *Prensa*, September 17, October 17, 1919; *Universal*, February 8, 19, 21, March 30, April 7, 1919.

38. ACE/A, 24:October 11, 1919; ACE/E, Aparicio et al. to Legislature, February 18, 1919, CCXVII-1:270; ACE/E, Cabrera to Legislature, October 11, 1919, CCXVIII-11:322, January 15, 1920, CCXVI-11:201; *Demócrata*, July 9, November 24, 1919; *Excélsior*, June 18, 19, 1919; *Monitor* (Puebla), March 6, 7, April 10, 11, 16, June 7, 17, August 6, 1919, January 23, 1920; *Prensa*, October 10, 28, 1919; *Universal*, March 5, April 9, July 9, 1919.

39. ACE/E, Cabrera to Legislature, September 11, 1919, CCXVI-11: 317; RE, Estrada to Cabrera, October 25, 1919, 2:21:779; *Demócrata*, November 10, December 8, 1919; *Estudiante*, September 28, November 2, 9, December 14, 1919; *Excélsior*, October 2, 13, 1919; *Monitor* (Puebla), October 1, 1919; *Prensa*, December 21, 1919.

40. ACE/E, Cano et al. to Legislature, February 2, 1918, CCXII-1:76; JB, de la Sierra to Gil Farías, March 4, 1918, X:23; JB, Narváez to Carranza, October 17, 1918, IX:29, January 28, 1919, IX:29; JB, García et al.–handbill, [December n.d., 1918], IX:29; *Prensa*, January 30, February 5, June 25, 1918, July 22, 1919.

41. ARM, Tirado et al.—report, October [n.d.], 1917, 67:107:284; FIC, Partido Liberal Constitucionalista—platform, June 26, 1918, 11:13:14; *Excélsior*, July 9, 1918; *Universal*, October 6, 1918; Abud Flores, *Campeche*, 63–4.

42. ACE/E, Vilchis to Legislature, April 14, 1918, CCXVII:301; *Monitor* (Puebla), October 12, 1918.

43. ACE/A, 24:April 23, 1919; CTB, Sánchez to Obregón, July 26, 1919, 11:D-5/185:1254:72; CTB, Partido Liberal to Obregón, August [n.d.], 1919, 11:N-

02/506:1576:7-8; *Estudiante*, July 14, 28, 1918; *Prensa*, June 11, 22, August 3, 1918; *Universal*, June 20, 1918.

44. *Monitor* (Puebla), October 2, 4–6, 25, November 12–5, 1918; *Palabra*, September 29, 1918.

45. ACE/A, 24:April 23, 1919; CTB, Partido Liberal to Obregón, August [n.d.], 1919, 11:N-02/506:1576:7–8; *Monitor* (Puebla), October 1, 5, 9, 15, 22, 23, November 2, 24–6, December 6, 1918, March 7, September 26, 1919.

46. *Prensa*, June 25, 1918.

47. Knight, *Mexican*, 2:452–3; Ruíz, *Great*, 218–9.

48. CTB, Hill to Obregón, February 27, 1919, 11:H-5/138:886:12–3, April 20, 1919, 11:H-1/355:1425:13–4, 17; CTB, Sánchez to Obregón, July 26, 1919, 11:D-5/185:1254:72; CTB, Partido Liberal to Obregón, August [n.d.], 1919, 11:N-02/506:1576:8; CTB, Narvácz to Obregón, [September n.d., 1919], 11:N-02/506:1576:9; Aguirre, *Mis memorias*, 305–9.

49. CTB, Partido Liberal Independiente—program, July [n.d.], 1919, 11:23:2005:1; CTB, Sánchez to Obregón, July 26, 1919, 11:D-5/185:1254:72; CTB, Sánchez Pontón to Obregón, October 12, 1919, 11:23:2005:11, October 13, 1919, 11:23:2005:9; CTB, Sánchez to Romero, October 19, 1919, 11:1324:4198:4.

50. AA, [Flores] to [Estrada], November 26, 1919, II:5:62, October 22, 1922, II:5:46; CTB, Contador Atone to Obregón, April 16, 1919, 11:A-03/6:754:1–2; CTB, Hill to Obregón, April 20, 1919, 11:H-1/355:1425:13–4, April 20, 1919, 11:H-1/355:1425:17, July 29, 1919, 11:H-1/355:1425:135–6, [June n.d., 1919], 11:H-1/355:1425:63; CTB, Ruíz to Obregón, June 5, 1919, 11:R-051/688:1758:1; CTB, Oropesa to Obregón, June 30, 1919, 11:1086:3960:1; CTB, Lara to Obregón, June 28, 1919, 11:L-05/391:1461:1, September 5, 1919, 11:L-05/391:1461:3, October 10, 1919, 11:L-05/391:1461:5; CTB, Novelo—report, [September n.d., 1919], 11:N-1/517:1587:82–5; CTB, Pérez to Obregón, November 17, 1919, 11:23:2005:19; J1D/P, García—report, May 27, 1919, 45:67; RE, Rivera to Estrada, September 19, 1919, 2:21:770; *Prensa*, July 1, 9, October 3, 14, 30, 1919; Taibo, *Los bolshevikis*, 40.

51. CTB, Hill to Obregón, May 1, 1919, 11:H-1/355:1425:31; *Estudiante*, November 2, 9, December 14, 1919; *Excélsior*, February 2, 1920; *Universal*, February 16, 19, March 11, 1920.

52. CTB, Narváez to Obregón, August 28, 1919, 11:N-02/506:1576:1; CTB, Sánchez to Obregón, September 13, 1919, 11:S-019/712:1782:1; CTB, Vilchis to Obregón, November 16, 1919, 11:23:2005:19; JB, Narváez to Gil Farías, March 28, 1920, IX:29; *Estudiante*, November 30, December 7, 1919; *Monitor* (Puebla), September 14, 1919.

53. AA, Flores to Estrada, August 26, 1919, II:5:30; CTB, Novelo to Obregón, August 8, 1919, 11:N-1/517:1587:22; CTB, Hill to Obregón, August 5, 1919, 11:H-1/355:1425:149; CTB, Limón to Obregón, August 12, 1920, 11:840:3715:1; CTB, Torreblanca to Sánchez, September 28, 1919, 11:S-019/712:1782:1; JFL,

Rouaix to Lucas, February 10, 1920, 1920s-1930s; RE, Rivera to Estrada, September 24, 1919, 2:21:771; *Universal*, November 12, 1919; Ruvalcaba, *Campaña*, 3:228. Rouaix's gubernatorial campaign was just under way in April 1920 when the Obregón rebellion erupted. He remained loyal to Carranza, was arrested, and later released, but his prospects to become Puebla's governor had again been frustrated; see *Demócrata*, April 15, 21, 25, 28, 30, 1920; *Excélsior*, April 17, 23–5, 1920; Peral, *El pelelismo*, 56–9.

54. *Universal*, April 9, 1920; Ruvalcaba, *Campaña*, 3:282.

8. Economic and Social Policy, 1917–1920

1. ACE/E, Cabrera to Legislature, January 15, 1920, CCXVI-11:201.

2. ACE/E, Cabrera to Legislature, January 15, 1918, CCX-1:4; *El Universal*, August 11, 14, 16, 1917.

3. ACE/A, 23:January 29, 1918; ACE/E, Cabrera to Legislature, September 30, 1917, CCX-1:4; *Excélsior*, December 15, 20, 1917; *Pueblo*, December 23, 1917; *Universal*, August 26, December 15, 1917. The estimated budget for the state in fiscal year 1918 was 1.65 million pesos in income and 2.32 million pesos in outlays for a deficit of approximately 670,000 pesos; see *Demócrata*, April 15, 1918. In his 1919 report to the legislature, Cabrera claimed the state ended 1918 with a 100,000-peso deficit, either reflecting more revenues collected than projected or innovative bookkeeping; see Cabrera, *Informe*, 63. He reported a 150,000-peso deficit for 1919; see ACE/E, Cabrera to Legislature, January 15, 1920, CCXVI-11:201. In early 1919 the state had an estimated total accumulated debt of 2,000,000 pesos; see *Prensa*, January 4, 1919.

4. *Universal*, August 19, 1917. The projected income to the state from all municipalities for 1919 was 993,000 pesos, 660,000 or 66 percent of which was predicted to come from Puebla City; see *Periódico Oficial*, December 31, 1918.

5. ACE/A, 23:February 4, 1918; *Demócrata*, May 11, 1918; *Estudiante*, September 1, 1918; *Monitor* (Puebla), October 12, 1918.

6. RG/PR, Jiménez et al. to Carranza, August 26, 1918, 226:34; RG/PR, Cabrera to Sec. Gobernación, October 16, 1918, 252:75; RG/PR, Sec. General to Sec. Gobernación, October 25, 1918, 226:34; *Excélsior*, November 2, 1917; *Pueblo*, October 27, 1917; *Universal*, November 1, December 20, 29, 1917, February 8, 1918.

7. ACE/E, Cabrera to Legislature, January 15, 1920, CCXVI-11:201; *Excélsior*, December 24, 1917; *Periódico Oficial*, December 25, 1917; *Universal*, January 19, 1918.

8. ACE/E, Cabrera to Legislature, January 15, 1920, CCXVI-11:201; *Demócrata*, August 25, 1919; *Excélsior*, August 9, 21, 1919; *Monitor* (Puebla), August 20, 1919; *Universal*, December 17, 1917.

9. *Demócrata*, July 25, September 24, 1919; *Excélsior*, January 6, August 28, October 24, 30, November 11, December 14, 27, 1919; *Monitor* (Puebla), July 4, 1919, August 27, October 18, 24, November 12, 1919; *Universal*, July 25, August 11, November 11, 1919.

10. ACE/E, Cabrera to Legislature, February 15, 1919, CCXVII-1:246, April 14, 1919, CCX-1:12; *Excélsior*, October 16, 1919; *Monitor* (Puebla), March 8, 1919.

11. VC, Correligionario to Carranza, July 4, 1915, 44:4786; VC, Cabrera to Carranza, January 30, 1919, 129:14801; Cabrera, *Informe*, 65–9; *Demócrata*, July 4, August 1, 19, 1918, May 8, 1919; *Excélsior*, December 15, 17, 1917, August 19, October 21, December 8, 1918, March 24, April 25, 1919; *Monitor* (Puebla), October 1, December 7, 16, 1918; *Prensa*, June 21, November 20, 1918, July 3, 1919; *Universal*, December 15, 18, 1917.

12. ACE/E, Cabrera to Legislature, January 15, 1920, CCXVI-11:201; CIM, Report, November 24, 1917, 3:460; CIM, González Cosío and Cardoso to Tesorero, December 6, 1917, 3:476; CIM, Gómez and Gómez Haro to Confederación Fabril, May 8, 1919, 7:38; *Excélsior*, August 25, 1919, February 14, 1920; *Monitor* (Puebla), August 24, 1919; *Prensa*, December 25, 1918; *Universal*, February 16, 1920.

13. ACE/A, 24:October 8, 1919, January 24, 30, 1920; GBFO, Conway to Brown, May 2, 1919, 3830:330; GBFO, Cummins to Foreign Office, May 2, 1919, 3829:24; RG/PR, Reydadas to Sec. Gobernación, December 14, 1915, 154:93; TLP, Board Directors—reports, December 31, 1916, 294, December 31, 1917, 313, December 31, 1918, 361, December 31, 1919, 354; VC, Cabrera to Carranza, January 30, 1919, 129:14801; *Excélsior*, May 1–4, 20, June 20, 1919, April 21, 1920; *Monitor* (Puebla), April 30, May 1, 3, 10, June 17, 18, 21, 1919, *Prensa*, April 2, 1918; *Universal*, January 28, 1918, July 12, 1919.

14. Aguilar Camín, *La frontera*, 427–8, 431, 435.

15. ACE/E, Cabrera to Legislature, January 15, 1918, CCX-1:4, April 14, 1919, CCX-I:12; *Demócrata* August 11, 1919; *Excélsior*, December 31, 1917, August 11, 1919; *Monitor* (Puebla), August 10, 1919.

16. *Demócrata*, March 10, 1920; *Excélsior*, March 8, 10, 1919; *Prensa*, June 5, 1918; *Universal*, May 25, June 7, 1918, March 10, 1920.

17. *Demócrata*, July 24, August 4, 1918; *Excélsior*, July 11, 16, September 5, 8, 1918; *Prensa*, April 19, 1918; *Pueblo*, August 12, October 14, 1917; *Universal*, August 31, 1917, June 20, 22, 1918. As of early 1920, currency from 24 different banks, including the Oriental, circulated in Puebla with values ranging from 9 to 74 centavos to the face value of one peso; see *Monitor* (Puebla), February 24, 1920.

18. CIM, Gómez to Carranza, November 28, 1918, 5:248; *Demócrata*, May 23, December 31, 1918, October 19, 1919; *Excélsior*, November 18, 21, 24, December 1, 20, 1918; *Monitor* (Puebla), September 24, November 7, 23, 1919; *Prensa*, November 23, 1918; *Universal*, January 30, June 25, September 13, 1919.

19. CIM, Gómez to Comisión Monetaria, December 14, 1918, 5:263; *Excélsior,* December 6, 1917; *Monitor* (Puebla), November 22, December 10, 19, 1918, April 9, 10, 15, 1919; *Prensa,* November 23, 1918; *Pueblo,* December 8, 1917.

20. CIM, Artasánchez and Gómez Haro to Sec. Hacienda, October 31, 1919, 7:418; *Excélsior,* January 17, February 2, March 22, 1920; *Universal,* January 17, February 13, 16, 26, March 11, 20, April 10, 1920.

21. CIM, Gómez and Cardoso to Sec. Comunicaciones, August 30, 1918, 5:22, September 24, 1918, 5:126–7; CIM, Gómez and Gómez Haro to Vilchis, January 23, 1919, 5:311; GBFO, Barclay to Curzon, March 10, 1919, 3828:62–3; RDS, Eberhardt to Dunn, September 5, 1919, 67:248–9; VC, Fontes to Carranza, June 1, 1919, 135:15365; VC, Durán et al. to Carranza, 136:15553; *Demócrata,* June 16, 1919; *Monitor* (Puebla), March 12, June 14, 20, 1919; *Universal,* June 17, 1919; Knight, *Mexican,* 2:407.

22. CIM, Santos Gavito and Cardoso to Sec. General, August 17, 1917, 3:274–5; CIM, González Cosío and Cardoso to Sec. General, December 29, 1917, 3:496; CIM, Gómez and Cardoso to Cabrera, August 7, 1918, 4:474–6; CIM, Gómez and Cardoso to Jefe Armas, August 15, 1918, 4:481; *Excélsior,* September 25, 1917, March 5, October 29, November 29, 1919; *Monitor* (Puebla), October 27, 28, 1919; *Universal,* August 2, 17, 1917, June 8, 1919; Gamboa Ojeda, *Los empresarios,* 91–2.

23. CDHM, Ministro to de la Torre, June 27, 1918, 51:353:7:–; CIM, Artasánchez et al. to Sec. Hacienda, July 21, 1917, 3:207–9; CIM, González Cosío and Cardoso to Cabrera, January 24, 1918, 4:23–4; CIM, González Cosío and Goytia to Governor, March 6, 1918, 4:81–2; CIM, Gómez and Cardoso to Mestre, July 13, 1918, 4:331–2; CIM, Gómez and Cardoso to Mexican Consuls Lima and Buenos Aires, July 16, 1918, 4:423, 427; CIM, Furlong and Gómez Haro to Confederación Fabril, August 23, 1919, 7:217; *Excélsior,* November 27, December 16, 1917; *Monitor* (Puebla), September 25, 1919; *Universal,* November 29, December 16, 1917; Ramírez Rancaño, *Burguesía,* 208–40, 257; Rivero Quijano, *La revolución,* 2:408–10.

24. *Excélsior,* May 23, 1917; *Pueblo,* May 23, 1917; Bortz, "Revolution," 683; Joseph, *Revolution,* 110.

25. CIM, Santos Gavito and Cardoso to Artasánchez, July 9, 1917, 3:195; CIM, Santos Gavito and Cardoso to House of Deputies, September 7, 1917, 3:292; *Excélsior,* September 26, December 6, 1917; Gamboa Ojeda, *La urdimbre,* 327; Ramírez Rancaño, *Burguesía,* 240–57.

26. ACE/E, Cabrera to Legislature, September 30, 1917, CCX-1:4, July 15, 1918, CCX-1:4; CIM, Gutiérrez Quijano and Cardoso to Isunza et al., June 9, 1917, 3:159–61; CIM, Gutiérrez Quijano and Cardoso to Sec. General, June 16, 1917, 3:169; CIM, [Cardoso] to Confederación Fabril, June 30, 1917, 3:179; CIM, Hijos de Díaz Rubín et al. to Governor, September 24, 1917, 3:318–21; CIM, Santos Gavito and Cardoso to Sec. General, September 27, 1917, 3:323–30; CIM, Santos Gavito to Goytia, October 18, 1917, 3:377–8; *Excélsior,* September 16,

October 2, December 31, 1917; *Periódico Oficial,* October 9, November 13, December 25, 1917, January 8, 1918; *Pueblo,* September 16, October 5, 20, 23, 1917; *Universal,* January 1, February 12, 1918.

27. ACE/A, 23:March 5–7, 1918; ACE/E, Cabrera to Legislature, July 15, 1918, CCX-1:4, March 7, 1918, CCXII-2:98; C/ADN, Cabrera to Carranza, March 5, 1918, MP/7115/3; CDHM, Quijano Rueda to Duque de Amalfi, March 14, 1918, 51:368:1:1; CIM, González Cosío and Cardoso to Mestre, February 12, 1918, 4:48; CIM, González Cosío and Cardoso to Governor, February 28, 1918, 4:70–1; CIM, González Cosío Hnos. et al. to Governor, March 8, 1918, 4:89–90; DT, CIM to Cabrera, February 25, 1918, 126:6:6; DT, Cabrera and Moto–broadside, March 7, 1918, 124:8:83; DT, DT to Sec. Industria, May 10, 1918, 126:5:3; Bosques—interview; *Demócrata,* November 19, 1917, March 1, 4, 6, 8, 1918; *Prensa,* February 24, 27, March 6–8, 1918; *Pueblo,* November 17, 1917; *Universal,* February 13, 28, March 4, 6–8, 1918; Ankerson, *Agrarian,* 87; Gamboa Ojeda, "Acerca," 63–80; Gamboa Ojeda, *La urdimbre,* 297; Lear, *Workers,* 343; Saragoza, *Monterrey,* 110–3.

28. ACE/A, 23:March 12, April 5, 20, 1918; CDHM, Ministro to Ministro Estado, March 25, 1918, 51:351:3:14; CDHM, Quijano Rueda to Duque de Amalfi, May 1, 1918, 51:368:1:1; *Demócrata,* April 25, 1918; *Prensa,* March 8, 16, 17, April 2, 17, 19, 24, May 3, 10, 21, 1918; *Universal,* March 12, 25, April 19, 1918.

29. DT, DT to Federación Sindicatos, April 23, 1918, 126:6:14; *Demócrata,* March 28, April 12, 15, 25, May 6, 1918; *Prensa,* March 14, 17, April 18, 23, 24, May 18, 1918; *Universal,* March 31, April 1, 14, 19, 21, 24, 1918.

30. ACE/E, Cabrera to Legislature, July 15, 1918, CCX-1:4; C/ADN, Galván to Carranza, April 17, 1918, MP/7115/3; CIM, González Cosío and Cardoso to Governor, May 31, 1918, 4:267–8, June 6, 1918, 4:294; CIM, González Cosío and Cardoso to Matienzo, June 6, 1918, 4:299; C/T, Castro to Carranza, June 10, 1918, XXI-4; DT, Llaguno to Carranza, May 4, 1918, 126:7:1; DT, Mestre to Pani, June 10, 1918, 126:6:20; *Demócrata,* May 6, 11, 30, June 4, 5, 8, 9, 11, 1918; *Prensa,* April 18, 19, 24, May 7, 29, 30, June 7, 11, 12, 25, 1918; *Universal,* June 13, 14, 1918.

31. CIM, González Cosío and Cardoso to Castro, June 3, 1918, 4:278–9; *Excélsior,* January 1, 1920; *Monitor* (Puebla), December 28, 1919; *Prensa,* June 6, 1918; *Universal,* January 2, 1920.

32. CIM, Gómez and Gómez Haro to Governor, May 9, 1919, 7:41–4; CROM, CROM to Maza, [n.d. 1920], 1; DT, Sánchez de Tagle to DT, May 31, 1919, 169:32:2; DT, Sánchez Gavito y Cía. to Sec. Industria, January 17, 1920, 164:31:4–5; RDS, Summerlin to Sec. State, June 18, 1919, 162:1226; *Excélsior,* August 20, 1919; *Monitor* (Puebla), June 21, August 21, 23, 1919; *Universal,* October 25, November 8, December 31, 1919; Barbosa Cano, *La CROM,* 139; Gamboa Ojeda, *La urdimbre,* 301, 314.

33. DT, Betz et al. to Poulat, October 6, 1919, 169:34:5; DT, Subsec. Industria to Betz et al., October 14, 1919, 169:34:2; DT, Subsec. Industria to Ortega

and Carranza, October 21, 1919, 169:34:4; DT, Artasánchez and Gómez Haro to Sec. Industria, February 27, 1920, 213:33:2–3; *Demócrata*, July 12, August 23, 1918; *Excélsior*, September 21, 1918, August 6, 1919; *Monitor* (Puebla), March 15, 27, August 6, 1919; *Prensa*, July 11, 1918, July 18, 1919; *Universal*, March 13, 14, May 5, September 27, December 7, 1919; Bortz, "Revolution," 671–5; Bortz, "Without," 287–8; Gamboa Ojeda, *La urdimbre*, 300–2, 306, 308–9; Saragoza, *Monterrey*, 110.

34. GBFO, Cummins to Curzon, January 20, 1919, 3826:446; MQG, León to Ministerio Público, January 18, 1919, ms.; RG/PR, Toscano to Carranza, February 20, 1918, 259:12; RG/PR, Cabrera to Sec. Gobernación, March 20, 1918, 259:12; *Demócrata*, September 14, 1919; *Excélsior*, July 11, September 7, 14, 1919; *Monitor* (Puebla), March 19, 20, July 10, August 7, 1919; *Prensa*, June 5, 1918, September 6, 1919; *Universal*, February 1, 1919.

35. Falcón, *Revolución*, 117; Falcón and García, *La semilla*, 92; Martínez Guzmán and Chávez Ramírez, *Durango*, 247; Oikión Solano, *El constitucionalismo*, 361, 525; Saragoza, *Monterrey*, 109; Tobler, *La revolución*, 386; Wasserman, *Persistent*, 22, 28, 75–6.

36. McBride reports 381 haciendas and 878 ranchos in the state as of 1910; see *Land*, 78, 98. *Universal* claims 460 haciendas, 1746 ranchos, and 65,965 fincas; see February 14, 1918.

37. ACE/E, Cabrera to Legislature, January 20, 1920, CCXVI-II:201; J1D/A, Couttolenc to Juez Distrito, December 3, 1919, 283:338; J1D/A, Escalante to Juez Distrito, December 30, 1919, 283:338; J1D/A, Sec. de Acuerdos Supreme Court–report, October 20, 1927, 283:338; VC, Parra to Juez Distrito, December 20, 1919, 143:16561; *Demócrata*, June 24, 1919; *Excélsior*, November 13, 20, 1917; *Monitor* (Puebla), August 4, 1919; *Prensa*, May 1, 9, 1918; García Ugarte, *Génesis*, 130; Garner, *La revolución*, 166; Walker Sarmiento, "La reforma," 17–8, 43–4.

38. J1D/A, Salmerón et al. to Juez Distrito, February 6, 1919, 276:56; RG/PR, Gómez and Durán to Carranza, March 12, 1918, 261:2; *Demócrata*, October 25, 1918; *Monitor* (Puebla), December 15, 1918; *Periódico Oficial*, April 9, 16, 1918, October 7, 1919, January 13, 1920; Walker Sarmiento, "La reforma," 17, 21.

39. ACE/E, Cabrera to Legislature, January 15, 1918, CCX-I:4, January 20, 1920, CCXVI-II:201; RG/PR, Cabrera to Sec. Gobernación, December 31, 1918, 240:67; SDN/AH, Presno et al. to Carranza, October 4, 1918, XI/481.5/224:121:202; SDN/AH, González Cosío Hnos. et al. to Carranza, October 16, 1918, XI/481.5/224:121:210; *Excélsior*, December 6, 1917, October 26, 29, 1918; *Monitor* (Puebla), October 26, 1918, February 23, 1919; *Periódico Oficial*, September 2, 1919; *Prensa*, September 22, 1918; Buve, *El movimiento*, 196–7, 346–7; Cabrera, *Informe*, 50–1; Ramírez Rancaño, *La revolución*, 197–200.

40. RG/PR, Cabrera to Sec. Gobernación, November 9, 1918, 240:67.

41. DRF, Jones with Jenkins—interview, May 13, 1918, 118; *Estudiante*, June 22, 1919; *Excélsior*, May 25, 1919; *Monitor* (Puebla), August 4, 1919; *Univer-*

sal, March 25, 1918, February 20, March 5, 22, May 24, 1919; Dussaud, "Agrarian," 18–23; Falcón and García, *La semilla*, 90–1; Walker Sarmiento, "La reforma," 39–41.

42. J2D/A, García et al. to Juez Distrito, April 16, 1920, 14:112; J2D/P, Procurador to Ministerio Público, March 5, 1920, 1:14; *Demócrata*, March 6, 1918; *Estudiante*, June 22, 1919; *Excélsior*, August 30, November 4, 1918, October 24, 1919; *Monitor* (Puebla), January 2, 3, March 27, 28, October 4, 1919; *Prensa*, April 27, May 31, July 7, 20, 1918, October 8, 1919; *Universal*, February 14, 1919, April 1, 1920; Dussaud, "Agrarian," 11–8.

43. RG/PR, Lavat to Sec. Gobernación, July 26, 1918, 231:33, July 26, 1918, 239:95; RG/PR, Pérez et al. to Carranza, October 15, 1918, 246:2; SDN/AC, Pres. Comisión Nacional Agraria to Subsec. Guerra, July 3, 1918, D/III/3-172:155; SDN/ AH, Castro to Carranza, March 22, 1918, XI/481.5/224:109–10; SDN/AH, Lozano Cardoso to Carranza, April 23, 1918, XI/481.5/224:123; VC, Anonymous– memorandum, October 4, 1917, 117:13316; VC, Anonymous–memorandum, [n.d.], 152:17375; *Monitor* (Puebla), October 30, November 1, 1918, March 7, October 4, 1919; *Prensa*, May 12, 26, June 7, December 8, 1918; *Universal*, June 16, 1918; Pettus, *Rosalie*, 41–8.

44. ACE/E, Montes et al. to Governor, December 30, 1917, CCXII-I:118; AJE/I, Álvarez to Juez Criminal, October 13, 1919, 1919:4; PHO, Interview— Flores, [n.d.] 1/140:/:40–1; *Monitor* (Puebla), November 1, 13, 1919.

45. ACE/E, Solís and Sánchez to Legislature, November [n.d.], 1917, CCXI-IV:62; CTB, Partido Liberal to Obregón, August [n.d.], 1919, 11:N-02/506:1576:8; RG/PR, Cabrera–circular, June 27, 1918, 240:67; RG/PR, Cabrera to Sec. Gobernación, October 16, 1918, 252:77, November 9, 1918, 240:67, December 31, 1918, 240:67; RG/PR, Sánchez to Sec. Gobernación, December 25, 1918, 254:61; *Demócrata*, June 21, 1918; *Excélsior*, November 18, 1917, July 18, 1918; *Prensa*, November 17, 1917, June 9, 1918; *Universal*, March 7, 1918.

46. DT, Sánchez de Tagle to DT, June 5, 1919, 170:12:1; J1D/A, Leyva et al. to Juez Distrito, March 5, 1919, 276:85; J1D/A, Arrellaga to Juez Distrito, March 15, 1919, 276:85; *Excélsior*, June 6, 1919; *Monitor* (Puebla), June 5, August 24, September 12, 1919; *Prensa*, May 24, 1918; *Universal*, February 13, March 14, June 29, August 9, 24, 1919; Tannenbaum, *Mexican*, 150; Vélez Pliego, "Marcelino," 159–77.

47. ACE/E, Cabrera to Legislature, January 15, 1918, CCX-I:4, January 20, 1920, CCXVI-II:201; CTB, Sánchez to Obregón, July 26, 1919, 11:D-5/ 185:1254:72; RG/PR, Pérez et al. to Carranza, October 15, 1918, 246:2; TLP, Board Directors—reports, December 31, 1918, 361, December 31, 1919, 354; *Demócrata*, April 12, 1920; *Excélsior*, March 8, April 23, 1919; *Monitor* (Puebla), February 16, 23, May 7, 18, October 14, 16, 17, 1919; *Universal*, January 17, 1918, February 11, 22, 23, 28, 1919; Cabrera, *Informe*, 55–6; Pettus, *Rosalie*, 56–8.

48. *Demócrata*, March 2, 1918; *Monitor* (Puebla), June 18, 1919; *Prensa*, February 11, 29, 1918; *Universal*, August 28, 1917; Pettus, *Rosalie*, 37–40.

49. CNA, *Resoluciones presidenciales*, 1917–20, 1–7; Cámara Agrícola, *Memorial*, n.p.; México, Sec. Agricultura, *Estadísticas*, 40; Matute, *Historia—Las dificultades*, 202; McBride, *Land*, 165. As of early 1918, 40 towns had petitioned for restitutions and another 243 for dotations; of these the state had approved 38 and the federal government 12; see ACE/E, Cabrera to Legislature, January 15, 1918, CCX-I:4; *Universal*, January 17, 1918. By mid-1918 some 500 villages had requested dotations of which the state (although not yet the federal government) had dealt with 50; see *Prensa*, August 2, 1918.

50. Ankerson, *Agrarian*, 87–8; Benjamin, *Rich*, 118–9, 130–1; Joseph, *Revolution*, 82–3, 114, 130–1, 306; Oikión Solano, *El constitucionalismo*, 453, 524; Wasserman, *Persistent*, 23.

51. Tannenbaum, *Mexican*, 403, 471.

52. ACE/E, Cabrera to Legislature, January 20, 1920, CCXVI-II:201; *Monitor* (Puebla), June 22, August 4, November 1, 1919; *Prensa*, July 18, 1918; *Universal*, June 20, 1918, February 16, 1919; Oikión Solano, *El constitucionalismo*, 454–9; Simonian, *Land*, 87–93.

53. ACE/E, Cabrera to Legislature, September 30, 1917, CCX-I:4, April 14, 1919, CCX-I:12; RDS, Row to Sec. State, October 10, 1917, 161:105, October 17, 1917, 161:136–7; RDS, Peabody to Polk, November 13, 1917, 62:131; RG/PR, Rocha to Aguirre Berlanga, August 10, 1917, 231:1; RG/PR, Cabrera to Sec. Gobernación, August 23, 1917, 231:1; *Excélsior*, June 19, October 6, 9, 1917; *Pueblo*, August 20, 1917; *Universal*, August 30, 1917.

54. ACE/E, Cabrera to Legislature, January 15, July 15, 1918, CCX–I:4; CIM, González Cosío and Cardoso to Sánchez Gavito, January 18, 1918, 4:14; RG/PR, González to Aguirre Berlanga, October 22, 1917, 179:47; *Demócrata*, May 26, June 22, 1918; *Excélsior*, November 29, December 5, 1917, January 25, 1919; *Monitor* (Puebla), January 17, 24, 1919; *Periódico Oficial*, October 23, 1917; *Prensa*, January 24, March 5, May 26, June 5, 8, 1918; *Universal*, November 15, 29, 1917, January 15, 17, March 6, June 7, 13, 1918.

55. RG/PR, Cañeda to Sec. Gobernación, November 16, 1917, 227:67; RG/PR, Rojas to Sec. Gobernación, February 2, 1918, 217:21; RG/PR, González to Aguirre Berlanga, February 4, 1918, 254:4; RG/PR, Fontes to Aguirre Berlanga, February 6, 1918, 254:3; RG/PR, Sec. Gobernación to Rojas, February 8, 1918, 217:21; RG/PR, Cabrera to Aguirre Berlanga, February 13, 1918, 217:21; SDN/AH, Ovallas to O. de Salarich, January 16, 1918, XI/481.5/224:25; *Prensa*, January 23, 1918; *Universal*, September 10, 1918.

56. RG/PR, Cabrera to Sec. Gobernación, February 15, 1918, 243:38; *Demócrata*, January 25, 29, 1919; *Excélsior*, December 19, 22, 28, 1917; *Prensa*, January 23, July 3, 1918; *Universal*, November 10, 14, December 17, 1917, September 19, 1918, January 26, 1919; Cordero y Torres, *Historia compendiada*, 2:37; U.S., Senate, *Investigation*, 2:2078–9.

57. ACE/A, 24:June 13, 1919; ACE/E, Cabrera to Legislature, January 15, 1918, CCX-I:4; AJE/I, *El Perico* (Puebla), July 6, 1919, 1919:5; *Demócrata*, July 6,

11, 25, 1919; *Excélsior*, July 19, 1918; *Prensa*, January 20, June 23, 1918, July 20, 1919; *Pueblo*, September 13, 1917; *Universal*, August 18, 20, December 3, 1917, January 23, May 30, 1918.

58. ABF, Sarah to Warren, December 4, 1919, 36:–; *Demócrata*, November 3, 6, 14, 20, 1917, July 10, 21, August 2, 1918, January 22, July 6, 11, 25, October 9, 1919; *Excélsior*, December 9, 20, 1917; *Prensa*, April 14, 24, August 29, September 4, 1918; *Pueblo*, October 13, December 21, 1917; *Universal*, August 21, 1917, January 5, February 16, 28, 1918; Torres Bautista, "La basura," 237–43.

59. *Excélsior*, October 27, 1918; *Monitor* (Puebla), October 14–7, 19, 22, 23, 27, 29, November 2, 1918; *Prensa*, October 16–20, 23, 24, 1918; Comisión Central Caridad, *Memoria*, 6; Gamboa Ojeda, "Epidemia," 94; García Ugarte, *Génesis* 116–7.

60. *Excélsior*, November 3, 5, 1918; *Monitor* (Puebla), November 2, 4, 1918; *Prensa*, November 3, 1918; Comisión Central Caridad, *Memoria*, 23, 24, 80.

61. *Excélsior* October 23, 25, 29, 31, November 3–5, 7, 8, 1918; *Estudiante*, November 3, 1918; *Monitor* (Puebla), October 22–8, 31, November 1, 2, 5, 6, 1918; *Prensa*, October 26, November 1, 1918; *Universal*, October 26, 1918; Gamboa Ojeda, "Epidemia," 96–7.

62. *Demócrata*, November 2, 1918; *Excélsior*, October 31, November 7, 13, 23, 1918; *Monitor* (Puebla), October 25, 30, November 1, 3, 6, 1918; *Prensa*, October 22, 27, November 1, 6–8, 12, 14, 17, 30, 1918; *Universal*, October 22, 1918; Candaredo, *Zacatlán*, 38; Comisión Central Caridad, *Memoria*, 27; Hoyos Hernández, "Vida," 143; Ramírez Rancaño, *La revolución*, 200–1.

63. *Universal*, January 2, 1919; Knight, *Mexican*, 2:421–2, 623; Matute, *Historia—Las dificultades*, 226; Patterson and Pyle, "Geography," 14, 15; Puebla (state), *Estudio*, 8; Velasco, *Autobiografía*, 82; Womack, "Mexican," 185. Cabrera reported that an estimated 26,000 men from Puebla had died fighting in the revolution; see ACE/E, Cabrera to Legislature, January 15, 1918, CCX-I:4. *Universal* also claimed that flu-related deaths totaled more than battle fatalities for the country as a whole, 436,000 and 300,000, respectively; see January 2, 1919.

64. CIM, Gómez and Polo de Olaguíbel to Furlong y Cía., October 30, 1918, 5:178; *Excélsior*, October 27, 31, November 1, 1918; *Monitor* (Puebla), October 24, 25, 27, 29, 30, 1918; *Prensa*, November 13, 1918; *Universal*, October 30, November 14, 1918; Comisión Central Caridad, *Memoria*, 6, 7–19; Gamboa Ojeda, "Epidemia," 97–100, 106–9; Velasco, *Autobiografía*, 81.

65. ACE/A, 23:October 31, 1918; *Demócrata*, November 4, 7, 1918; *Monitor* (Puebla), November 2–4, 1918; *Prensa*, November 5, 1918.

66. *Demócrata*, November 7, 1918; *Excélsior*, October 31, November 4, 7, 8, 1918; *Monitor* (Puebla), November 2, 4, 6, 8, 1918; *Prensa*, January 8, November 7, 8, 10, 13, 17, 1918; *Universal*, October 29, 1918; Comisión Central Caridad, *Memoria*, 20–1; Gamboa Ojeda, "Epidemia," 107–8.

67. *Estudiante*, November 3, 1918, August 10, 1919; *Excélsior*, October 31, 1918.

68. México, Dirección General Estadística, *Compendio*, 3–4; Puebla (state), Consejo Estatal, *Estudio*, 8.

69. ACE/E, Cabrera to Legislature, September 30, 1917, January 15, 1918, CCX-I:4, January 15, 1920, CCXVI:201; CIM, Gómez Haro to Moto, January 31, 1920, 7:483; *Excélsior*, December 15, 1917, December 17, 1918, February 7, 15, 1919; *Prensa*, July 6, 13,1918; *Pueblo*, October 16, 29, 1917; *Universal*, November 10, 1917, March 7, 1918, January 31, March 14, 21, 1919, January 19, February 3, 1920; Garner, *La revolución*, 146–9; México, Dirección General Estadística, *Compendio*, 50; Paredes Colín, *El distrito*, 14; Puebla (state), *Ley de educación*, 1–26.

70. ACE/E, Cabrera to Legislature, September 30, 1917, CCX-I:4; *Universal*, February 6, 13, 1918; Navarro Rojas, *Conflictos*, 63.

71. *Estudiante*, April 28, May 5, 12, June 16, 30, July 28, September 22, October 13, 1918, July 6, 1919; *Prensa*, April 9, May 7, September 24, 1918; Cordero y Torres, *Poetas*, 136–7; Navarro Rojas, *Conflictos*, 63–4.

72. ACE/E, Cabrera to Legislature, January 15, 1920, CCXVI:201; J2D/A, Díaz et al. to Juez Distrito, July 25, 1919, 10:134; J2D/A, Cabrera to Juez Distrito, July 29, August 5, 1919, 10:134, August 14, 1919, 10:152; J2D/A, Bonilla—ruling, July 30, 1919, 10:134; J2D/A, Álvarez to Juez Distrito, July 31, 1919, 10:134; J2D/A, Bonilla to Cabrera, August 7, 1919, 10:134; J2D/A, Supreme Court-ruling, September 9, 1919, 10:134; SDN/AH, Narváez to Carranza, July 12, 1918, XI/481.5/224:121; *Demócrata*, September 11, 1919; *Estudiante*, July 21, 1918, July 27, August 3, 10, 13, September 9, 1919; *Excélsior*, July 10, 18, 1918, August 2, 5, 23, September 12, 1919; *Monitor* (Puebla), July 25, August 4–6, 1919; *Prensa*, August 6, September 12, 1919; *Universal*, July 25, 28, August 6, 8, 1919.

73. J2D/A, Pérez Peña et al. to Juez Distrito, July 26, 1919, 10:135–9; J2D/A, Díaz to Juez Distrito, August 2, 1919, 10:134; J2D/A, Sec. General to Juez Distrito, August 4, 1919, 10:134; *Demócrata*, July 30, September 25, 1919; *Estudiante*, December 7, 1919; *Excélsior*, September 6, 12, 15, 26, 27, October 20, 1919; *Monitor* (Puebla), July 27, 28, September 5, 14, 20, 25, 1919; *Prensa*, September 5, 1919; *Universal*, July 28, 29, August 2, September 22, 25, 27, 1919; Puebla (state), *Reglamento*, 3–4.

74. *Demócrata*, November 5, 1919, March 18, 1920; *Estudiante*, November 2, 9, 1919; *Monitor* (Puebla), December 7, 1919; *Prensa*, September 6, 20, October 25, 1919; *Universal*, October 25, November 2, 1919; Garner, *La revolución*, 149.

75. ACE/E, Guerrero to Legislature, July 25,1919, CCXVIII:292; *Demócrata*, July 29, 30, August 2, 1919; *Excélsior*, August 23, 1919; *Monitor* (Puebla), July 27, 28, August 2, 1919; *Prensa*, July 27, September 12, 1919; *Universal*, July 28, 29, August 2, 1919.

76. RG/PR, Isla to Carranza, September 1, 1917, 193:26; RG/PR, Cabrera to Subsec. Gobernación, November 3, 10, 1917, 193:31, February 6, 1918, 235:6, April 8, 1918, 244:70, July 19, 1918, 233:19; *Demócrata*, June 29, 1918; *Prensa*, April 30, May 17, June 20, 1918; *Pueblo*, December 7, 1917; *Universal*, April 18, May 26, June 29, 1918.

77. JB, Montes de Oca to Gil Farias, August 17, 1918, IX:27; RG/PR, Pérez Aranda to Sec. Gobernación, June 8, 1917, 193:27; RG/PR, Cabrera to Subsec. Gobernación, September 17, 1917, 236:118; SDN/AH, Montes de Oca to Carranza, September 17, 1918, XI/481.5/224:197; Cordero y Torres, *Diccionario*, 1:1265; *Excélsior*, July 15, 1918, February 1, April 28, May 25, 1919, April 23, 24, 1920; *Monitor* (Puebla), June 8, 1919; *Prensa*, April 13, 21, May 22, 23, June 22, 23, July 17, 1918; *Universal*, April 23, 1920; Unión Popular Puebla, *Semana*, 1–20; U.S., Senate, *Investigation*, 2:2071–2; Velasco, *Autobiografía*, 81–2.

78. *Demócrata*, May 20, June 1, 9, 10, 1919; *Excélsior*, June 3, 9, October 12, 1919, January 8, April 16, 1920; *Monitor* (Puebla), May 29, June 4, 9, 20, October 12, 1919; *Prensa*, June 5, 1919; *Universal*, February 3, 1917, May 20, June 10, 1919, April 19, 1920; Palomera, *La obra*, 350.

79. Martínez Assad, *El laboratorio*, 22, 29, 38.

9. War, 1917–1920

1. ACE/E, Cabrera to Legislature, January 15, 1920, CCXVI-11:201.

2. EZ, Bonilla to Zapata, June 16, 1917, 13:17:9; EZ, Magaña to Zapata, July 8, 1917, 14:1:24, July 27, 1917, 14:3:10; GM, Alfaro to Ayaquica, March 17, 1918, 29:4:337; RDS, Canada to Lansing, August 15, 1917, 61:408, October 16, 1917, 61:987; SDN/AC, Gracia to Sec. Guerra, October 14, 1917, XI//III/3-2791:176; *Demócrata*, July 8, 1918; *Excélsior*, October 14, December 1, 28, 1917, August 22, 28, 1918; *Prensa*, August 4, 22, 1918; *Universal*, November 11, 14, December 1, 1917, February 21, March 29, 1918, Womack, *Zapata*, 281–2.

3. GM, Córdova to Magaña, February 21, 1918, 29:12:603; SDN/AH, Cabrera to Carranza, August 14, 1917, XI/481.5/223:102, October 18, 1917, XI/481.5/223:151; VC, Soldados to Carranza, February 10, [1918], 148:16979; *Demócrata*, April 5, May 12, 1918; *Excélsior*, November 29, 1917; *Prensa*, April 5, 6, 1918; *Universal*, November 29, 1917, January 12, April 4–6, 1918.

4. EZ, Mejía to Zapata, July 10, 1917, 14:1:27; EZ, Ayaquica et al. to Zapata, August 8, 1917, 14:4:25; GM, Zapata to Magaña, November 8, 1917, 29:1:4; GM, Rojas to Ayaquica, February 10, 1918, 29:2:48; GM, Caballero to Ayaquica, March 8, 1918, 29:4:293; GM, Mentuche to Ayaquica, March 22, 1918, 29:4:360; GM, Bonilla et al. to Ayaquica, March 29, 1918, 29:4:395; GM, Magaña to Zapata, May 2, 1918, 27:15:–; GM, Aguilar to Magaña, May 15, 1918, 27:15:317; GM, Zapata–circular, June 1, 1918, 30:17:283; JA, Palafox to Mendoza, August 20, 1917, 4:311; SDN/AH, Narváez to Carranza, September 25, 1917, XI/481.5/223:124; VC, Vélez et al. to Carranza, May 15, 1919, 133:15259; *Demócrata*, March 18, 1918; *Excélsior*, November 15, 1917, September 12, October 14, 16, 1918, April 23, 1919; *Monitor* (Puebla), October 8, 10, 11, 13, 15, 1918; *Prensa*, December 28, 1918; *Pueblo*, October 24, November 30, 1917; *Universal*, August 30, December 5, 18, 19, 1917; Chaffee, *Adoption*, 19.

5. *Demócrata*, July 4, 1918; *Excélsior*, December 11, 1917, November 2, December 13, 26, 1918, January 8, March 28, April 10, October 16, 1919; *Monitor* (Puebla), October 26, 29, 1918, January 1, 5, 1919; *Prensa*, August 3, November 29, December 28, 1918; *Universal*, December 10, 20, 1917, June 3, October 29, 1918, January 8, 9, 31, April 1, 1919; Knight, *Mexican*, 2:366.

6. GM, Zapata to Magaña, October 24, 1918, 30:25:451; *Monitor* (Puebla), November 21, 22, 1918.

7. *Excélsior*, April 17, 21, 30, December 23, 1919; *Monitor* (Puebla), April 15, 20, 29, December 5, 1919; *Prensa*, December 4, 1919; *Universal*, December 5, 1919.

8. EZ, Magaña to Zapata, July 27, 1917, 14:3:10; EZ, Zapata to Magaña, August 1, 1917, 14:4:3.

9. EZ, Magaña to Zapata, August 25, 1917, 14:6:8; JB, División Oriente "Arenas" to Carranza, September 3, 1917, I:2; Henderson, *Worm*, 62–3; Ramírez Rancaño, *La revolución*, 155–62.

10. EZ, Magaña to Zapata, July 30, 1917, 14:3:18, August 5, 1917, 14:4:12; EZ, Ayaquica et al. to [Zapata], August 8, 1917, 14:4:25; EZ, Ayaquica to Zapata, August 10, 1917, 14:4:36; *Excélsior*, September 2, 5, 1917.

11. EZ, Magaña to Zapata, September 13, 1917, 14:8:2, September 23, 1917, 14:9:3; SDN/AH, Zochicali et al. to Carranza, September 18, 1918, XI/481.5/224:189; *Universal*, November 6, 7, 1917; Ramírez Rancaño, *La revolución*, 160–2.

12. *Excélsior*, August 13, 1918; *Universal*, April 28, 1918; Ramírez Rancaño, *La revolución*, 162–8.

13. *Excélsior*, August 17, 1918; *Monitor* (Puebla), October 1, November 28, 1918, August 9, 1919; *Universal*, September 20, 23, 1918; Ramírez Rancaño, *La revolución*, 171–8.

14. AA, Zapata to División Arenas, April 27, 1918, IX:31:28; AA, Zapata to Pueblos Zona Arenas, April 27, 1918, IX:31:29; C/ADN, Méndez to Cosío Robelo, April 28, 1918, MP/7115/2; RDS, Bonillas to Lansing, July 31, 1919, 67:29–31; RG/PR, Osorio et al. to Sec.Gobernación, December 10, 1918, 246:13; WFB, Report, [n.d.] 1919, 113.44; *Demócrata*, April 30, May 3, 5, 1918; *Excélsior*, August 16, November 30, December 4, 1918, August 6, 1919; *Monitor* (Puebla), October 23, 24, 29, 1918; *Prensa*, May 11, 16, 1918; *Universal*, April 28, 30, May 3, 5, 1918, June 2, December 23, 1919; Henderson, *Worm*, 68–9, 88; Matute, *Historia—Las dificultades*, 126–7; Ramírez Rancaño, *La revolución*, 171–203.

15. GM, Caraveo to [illegible], August 9, 1918, 29:12:600; *Demócrata*, May 7, September 2, 1918; *Excélsior*, July 20, August 17, September 23, October 7, November 29, December 28, 1918; *Universal*, May 15, 1918.

16. C/ADN, [illegible] to Barguera, August 15, 1918, MP/7115/3; C/ADN, Jefe Operaciones to Sec. Guerra, September 14, 1918, MP/7115/3; RDS, Churchill to State Dept., August 12, 1918, 64:369; RDS, Military Intelligence to State Dept., September 14, 1918, 64:617; RDS, Summerlin to Lansing, June 11, 1919, 65:1252; *Demócrata*, July 26, August 14, 19, October 3, December 31, 1918, April 8, June 11, 15, 1919; *Excélsior*, July, 18, 19, 21, 26, August 1, 5, 8, 17, 25, 29, September 11, 13,

14, October 3, November 22, 1918, March 1, April 7, 9, June 11, 14, 16, August 9, September 1, 7, 12, November 5, 1919; *Monitor* (Puebla), October 2, 3, November 27, 1918, February 28, June 4, 5, 10, 11, 13, August 8, October 24, 1919; *Prensa*, June 5, 16, August 4, 14, 22, October 2, 1918, June 5, 8, 10–2, August 8, 1919; *Universal*, September 12, October 22, November 1, 1918, May 23, June 6, 11, 12, 15, August 9, 1919; *Puebla a través*, 166–7; Ramírez Rancaño, *La revolución*, 205–17.

17. *Demócrata*, June 15, July 22, 25, August 11, 22, November 13, 1919; *Excélsior*, August 2, November 30, 1918, June 10, July 18, 1919; *Monitor* (Puebla), May 10, October 28, 1919; *Prensa*, August 21, 1919; *Universal*, February 5, 1919.

18. *Prensa*, June 27, 1919.

19. J2D/A, Arenas to Juez Distrito, March 1, 1920, 12:54; J2D/A, Quintana et al. to Juez Distrito, March 3, 1920, 12:54; SDN/AC, Urquizo to Sánchez, March 2, 1920, XI/III/1-405:1252; SDN/AC, Sánchez to Subsec. Guerra, March 3, 1920, XI/III/1-405:1250; SDN/AH, Bonilla to Carranza, March 3, 1920, XI/481.5/226:2; *Demócrata*, March 1, 4, 5, 1920; *Excélsior*, January 15, March 1, 4, 1920; *Universal*, March 1, 3–5, 1920; Cordero y Torres (1955), *Crónicas*, 198–202; Henderson, *Worm*, 88; Ramírez Rancaño, *La revolución*, 231–50.

20. GBFO, Holloway to York, May 13, 1919, 3830:387–8; RG/PR, Conway to Sec. Gobernación, March 26, 1918, 242:62; *Excélsior*, August 8, September 16, 18, 1918; *Prensa*, March 23, May 29, 1918; *Universal*, August 16, 1917, June 23, September 29, 1918, April 2, 1919.

21. Thomson with LaFrance, *Patriotism*, 305–7. For full treatment of Barrios, see Brewster, *Militarism*.

22. SDN/AH, Morales to Carranza, August 12, 1917, XI/481.5/223:95; *Pueblo*, August 14, 16, 26, 1917; *Universal*, August 14, 16, 23, 26, 30, 1917; del Castillo, *Puebla*, 262; Kuri Camacho, *La realidad*, 2:85–7.

23. C/ADN, Castro to Subsec. Guerra, June 27, 1918, MP/7115/3; SDN/AH, Barrios to Subsec. Guerra, January 28, 1918, XI/481.5/224:39; SDN/AH, Cabrera to Carranza, March 2, 1918, XI/481.5/224:96; VC, Tejeda to Aguilar, December 21, 1918, 128:14528; *Demócrata*, March 3, 20, September 1, 1918, January 18, 1919; *Excélsior*, August 16, 1918, November 11, 1919; *Prensa*, March 2, 8, April 10, 11, 1918; *Pueblo*, September 7, 1917; *Universal*, August 31, 1917, March 3, April 9, December 14, 1918, January 23, February 20, November 1, December 22, 1919; Márquez, *El verdadero*, 55–8, 77.

24. ACE/E, Cabrera to Legislature, July 15, 1918, CCX-I:4; *Excélsior*, December 24, 1917, January 7, August 24, 1919; *Monitor* (Puebla), July 5, 1919; *Prensa*, July 19, 1918; *Universal*, December 24, 1917, October 24, 1918; Garciadiego Dantán, "Higinio," 463–71; Matute, *Historia—Las dificultades*, 135.

25. C/ADN, Castro to Subsec. Guerra, March 2, 1918, MP/7115/2; *Demócrata*, March 6, April 5, 1918; *Excélsior*, July 3, 1919; *Prensa*, July 20, 1918; *Universal*, August 22, 1917.

26. C/ADN, Villarreal to Ríos, August 15, 1919, MP/7115/3; RDS, Summerlin to Lansing, January 9, 1918, 62:784–5; SDN/AH, Cabrera to Carranza, March 2,

1918, XI/481.5/224:96; *Demócrata*, May 12, 23, August 21, 1919; *Excélsior*, July 22, December 16, 21, 1917, August 1, 8, October 29, December 4, 16, 1918, January 22, February 9, May 5, 13, July 10, 15, August 20, 1919; *Monitor* (Puebla), December 3, 1918, January 21, March 18, April 16, May 11, June 29, July 5, 13, 1919; *Prensa*, September 12, 1918, August 19, 20, 29, September 18, 1919; *Universal*, December 24, 1917, February 23, March 6, 9, April 9–11, 1918, May 23, June 2, July 31, August 15, 20, 21, 1919; Henderson, *Félix*, 138–40; Knight, *Mexican*, 2:390; Matute, *Historia—Las dificultades*, 131, 137–8.

27. ACE/E, Cabrera to Legislature, July 15, 1918, CCX-I:4; C/ADN, Carranza to Cabrera, February 19, 26, 1918, MP/7115/2; JB, Narváez to Carranza, [July 9, 1918], VIII:5; RG/PR, Cabrera to Sec. Gobernación, October 19, 1918, 247:6; VC, Anonymous—memorandum, January 7, 1919, 129:14721; VC, Anonymous to Carranza, July 25, 1919, 137:15744; *Demócrata*, November 19, 1917; *Excélsior*, October 12, November 19, 1917, January 13, December 28, 1919; *Monitor* (Puebla), July 15, 1919; *Universal*, August 12, 1919.

28. ACE/E, Cabrera to Legislature, January 15, 1920, CCXVI-II:201; C/T, de la Llave to González, February 10, 1920, MIX-3; RDS, Campbell to Military Intelligence, July 1,1918, 64:145; RDS, Foster to Lansing, May 12, 1919, 65:1039-40; RDS, Eberhardt to Dunn, September 5, 1919, 67:247; *Excélsior*, September 10, 1917, April 26, June 2, 24, 1919, January 9, 13, 1920; *Monitor* (Puebla), July 21, August 5, 17, 27, 1919; *Universal*, February 5, March 28, 1919, January 8, 9, May 26, 29, 1920; Henderson, *Félix*, 140-5; Matute, *Historia—Las dificultades*, 133.

29. C/ADN, Medina to Carranza, August 21, 1917, MP/7115/3; C/ADN, Sec. Gobierno to Carranza, October 25, 1917, MP/7115/3; C/T, Castro to Carranza, June 9, 1918, XXI-4; JFL, Santa Fé to Lucas, July 20, 1917, 1917; RDS, Summerlin to Lansing, February 19, 1918, 62:1120; RG/PR, Rodríquez and López Lima to Subsec. Estado, August 14, 1917, 172:37; RG/PR, Subsec. Gobernación to Subsec. Estado, October 25, 1917, 172:37; RG/PR, Rojas to Aguirre Berlanga, February 2, 1918, 243:39; SDN/AC, Real to Ramos Sánchez, May 30,1921, XI/III/1-405:1949; SDN/AH, Cabrera to Carranza, February 22, 1918, XI/481.5/224:79, February 26, 1918, XI/481.5/224:88; VC, Vera to Aguilar, December 18, 1917, 120:13587; VC, Carrera to Carranza, June 1, 1918, 123:13822; *Universal*, August 31, 1917, January 14, February 19-21, 25, March 1, 1918.

30. *Prensa*, July 20, 1919; Falcón, *Revolución*, 101-3; Mijangos Díaz, *La revolución*, 203-8.

31. SDN/AC, Cervantes to Castro, September 1, 1917, XI/III-2:152; *Estudiante*, May 4, 1919; *Excélsior*, September 2, 1917; *Prensa*, July 3, 1918; *Universal*, August 30, 1917.

32. *Excélsior*, December 3, 19, 1918; *Monitor* (Puebla), December 30, 1918, February 25, 1919; *Prensa*, February 26, 1918, September 24, 1919; Ruíz, *Great*, 260; Womack, *Zapata*, 293, 312.

33. *Prensa*, March 5, April 6, June 14, 22, 23, 27, July 3, 6, September 25, 1918, July 1, 8, 20, 1919.

34. *Excélsior*, December 20, 1917; *Prensa*, January 18, 1918; *Universal*, January 21, February 1, 1918.

35. ACE/E, Cabrera–report, January 15, 1920, CCXVI-II:201; C/T, Cervantes to Carranza, February 15, 1916, XXI-4; GO, Cuartel General Ejército Libertador–*Boletín*, May 25, 1918, 19:12:28; JB, Cervantes to Carranza, July 12, [1915], I:17, [September n.d., 1915], I:17; PG, Cervantes to González, July 19, 1915, 25, September 13, 1915, 11, February 14, 1916, 7; PG, Castro to González, April 24, 1916, 47; SDN/AH, Cabrera to Carranza, February 25, 1918, XI/481.5/224:84; *Excélsior*, February 18, 23, 1919; *Monitor* (Puebla), January 24, February 10, 19, April 10, June 12, 1919; Cervantes, *Informe*, 5.

36. J1D/A, Gracia Jr. to Juez Distrito, January 24, 1919, 275:20; J1D/A, Barrera to Juez Distrito, January 27, 1919, 275:20; SDN/AC, Gracia to Carranza, February 4, 1920, XI/III/3-2791:420; *Excélsior*, January 29, 1919; *Monitor* (Puebla), January 25, 28, 29, February 7, 1919.

37. SDN/AC, Juez Militar to Sánchez, September 26, 1919, D/III/3-172:675; SDN/AC, Cabrera to Juez Militar, October 13, 1919, D/III/3-172:688; SDN/AC, Sec. Guerra to Jefe Plaza, December 11, 1919, D/III/3-172.692, *Prensa*, June 25, 1918.

38. SDN/AC, Sec. Guerra–memorandum, March 14, 1918, XI/III/1-372:1520; *Excélsior*, August 31, 1918; *Monitor* (Puebla), October 25, 1918; *Prensa*, January 23, 24, 28, February 9, 12, September 8, 29, November 5, 1918; *Universal*, February 14, 1918.

39. *Excélsior*, December 19, 1918, April 3, May 4, June 6, 1919; *Monitor* (Puebla), October 12, 16, December 11, 13, 1918, January 18, April 24, 30, May 3, June 13, July 11, September 7, 1919, March 15, 1920; *Universal*, August 31, 1917, November 7, 1919.

40. JB, Narváez to Carranza, December 17, 1918, IX:29; *Estudiante*, August 10, 1919; *Monitor* (Puebla), December 24, 1918, May 17, 1919.

41. LaFrance, "Military."

42. RDS, Campbell to Military Intelligence, July 1, 1918, 64:145; SDN/AC, Cervantes to Castro, September 1, 1917, XI/III-2:152; SDN/AC, Yepez to Castro, September 18, 1917, XI/III-2:157; SDN/AC, Muñoz to Castro, January 7, 1919, XI/III-2:240; SDN/AC, Sánchez to Sec. Guerra, August 9, 1919, XI/III/1-405:303; SDN/AH, Castro–decree, May 21, 1918, XI/481.5/224:0; *Demócrata*, November 27, 1917, June 2, July 12, August 10, 1918, May 13, 18, 29, 1919; *Estudiante*, June 1, 1919; *Monitor* (Puebla), October 1, 2, November 27, 1918; *Excélsior*, July 7, 8, 11, August 21, September 10, 16, 20, 23-5, 28, 1918, May 14, 15, 1919, February 6, 1920; *Prensa*, May 8, 17, June 9, 25, 26, 28, 29, July 2, 17, September 5, 26, 1918; *Universal*, April 13, September 28, 1918, May 15, 29, 31, 1919.

43. ACE/E, Cabrera–Informe, January 15, 1920, CCXVI-II:201; MI, Weekly Report, October 20, 1919, 1:101; *Monitor* (Puebla), May 17, August 11, 17, 1919; *Universal*, August 11, 1919.

44. LaFrance, "Military."

10. Regime Ends, State Continues

1. CTB, Vega Bernal—decree, April 19, 1920, 11:1560:4432:1; CTB, Salas–memorandum, May 28, 1920, 11:836:3711:2; CTB, Sánchez to Obregón, June 1, 1920, 11:1398:4272:3; CTB, Barbosa to Obregón, May 30, 1920, 11:148:3024:1; *Demócrata*, April 25, May 3, 1920; *Excélsior*, April 27, 1920; *Monitor* (Puebla), May 3, 1920; *Universal*, May 5, 1920.

2. GBFO, Hardacker to King, May 20, 1920, 4494:50; *Demócrata*, May 3, 1920; *Excélsior*, May 4, 5, 1920; *Monitor* (Puebla), May 3, 1920; *Universal*, April 29, May 3, 5, 10, 11, 1920; del Castillo, *Puebla*, 263–4.

3. GBFO, Hardacker to King, May 20, 1920, 4494:50; RDS, Summerlin to Lansing, June 15, 1920, 72:266; *Crónica*, May 26, 1920; *Excélsior*, May 4, 18, 19, 1920; *Monitor* (Puebla), May 3, 1920, April 27, 1921; *Universal*, May 11, 1920; Cordero y Torres, *Diccionario*, 3:5062.

4. JA, Acuña Rosete to Amezcua, May 26, 1920, 5:424; PHO, Sánchez Pontón–interview, April [n.d.], 1961, 1/20:/:40; *Monitor* (Puebla), May 8, 11, 1920; *Universal*, May 10, 16, 1920; Almazán, "Memorias," December 26, 1957; Cabrera, *La herencia*, 114–6; del Castillo, *Puebla*, 278–80; Garciadiego Dantán, "La revuelta," 86–91; Márquez, *El verdadero*, 86–91, 111–3, 159; Matute, *Historia—La carrera*, 125–30; Richmond, *Venustiano*, 234–5; Urquizo, *México*, 103–4.

5. FM, Pérez Fernández to President, July 13, 1920, 91; FM, Balderas Márquez to de la Huerta, July 13, 1920, 91; RDS, Summerlin to Lansing, July 6, 1920, 72:982; *Crónica*, July 6, 8, 15, 16, 18, September 10, 11, 1920; *Demócrata*, October 19, 1920; *Excélsior*, July 6, 10, 12, 14, 15, 29, 1920; *Monitor* (Puebla), April 18, 19, 1921; *Universal*, July 4, 6, 7, 13, 15–7, September 11, 1920; Romero Flores, *Historia*, 155.

6. *Excélsior*, May 26, June 1, 1920; *Monitor* (Puebla), May 24, 1920; del Castillo, *Puebla*, 263–4.

7. *Monitor* (Puebla), May 8, 1920; *Periódico Oficial*, May 11, 1920.

8. FM, Suárez to President, June 27, 1920, 91; FM, Rojas to President, July 1, 1920, 91; *Crónica*, May 14, 19, June 6, 7, 9–11, 26, 1920; *Excélsior*, May 10, 12, 23, 29, June, 1, 6, 10, 12, 18, July 3, 1920; *Monitor* (Puebla), May 11, 20, 26, 1920; *Periódico Oficial*, June 8, 1920; *Universal*, June 3, 5, 10, 18, 19, July 1, 3, 8, 1920.

9. GBFO, Hardacker to King, May 20, 1920, 4494:50; RDS, Jenkins to Summerlin, May 10, 1920, 71:937–8. Jenkins, with criminal charges hanging over him related to his kidnapping of October 1919, also had a more personal reason to curry favor with Rojas.

10. CTB, Rivas et al. to de la Huerta et al., June [n.d.], 1920, 11:23:2005:24; FM, Rojas to President, June 11, 1920, 90; RDS, Summerlin to Lansing, May 18, 1920, 71:613–4; *Crónica*, June 21, 22, 1920; *Excélsior*, May 3, June 12, 1920; *Prensa*, July 3, 4, 1920; *Universal*, May 11, June 5, 1920.

11. *Excélsior*, June 14, 1920.

12. CTB, Aguilar to Obregón, July 10, 1920, 11:9:2025:2; RDS, Summerlin to Lansing, June 8, 1920, 72:182; SDN/AC, Calles to Morales, July 7, 1920, D/ III/3-172:280; *Crónica*, July 10, 1920; *Excélsior*, May 29, June 7, 16, 1920; *Universal*, July 11, 1920.

13. FM, Gaviola, Jr. to Sec. Gobernación, July 13, 1920, 91; PHO, Sánchez Pontón–interview, April [n.d.], 1961, 1/20:/:40; *Crónica*, July 8–10, 13, 1920; *Excélsior*, July 8, 13, 1920; *Universal*, June 23, July 8, 14, 1920.

14. AA, Rojas to Aguirre, June 21, 1920, II:6:100–1; FM, Rojas to President, June 21, 1920, 91; FM, Gutiérrez Ituarte to de la Huerta, July 9, 1920, 9; FM, del Razo to President, July 10, 1920, 91; FM, Domínguez Martínez to President, July 10, 1920, 91; FM, Gaviola, Jr. to Sec. Gobernación, July 13, 1920, 91; *Crónica*, June 21, July 14, 1920; *Universal*, July 8, 9, 12, 1920.

15. FM, Bosques et al. to de la Huerta, June 23, 1920, 91; *Crónica*, June 23, 24, 1920; *Excélsior*, June 23, 25, 1920; *Universal*, June 24, 1920.

16. CTB, Sánchez Pontón to Obregón, July 21, 1920, 11:1407:4281:1; FM, Rojas to President, July 16, 1920, 91; FM, Labastida to President, July 16, 19, 1920, 91; FM, Cruz to President, July 17, 1920, 91, FM, Frías to President, July 19, 1920, 91; FM, Sánchez Pontón to President, July 21, 1920, 91; JT, Rojas to Treviño, July 21, 1920, 25:110:13218–9; RDS, Summerlin to Lansing, July 20, 1920, 72:1142; *Crónica*, July 17, 1920; *Excélsior*, July 17, 21, 22, 1920; *Universal*, July 17, 19–24, 1920.

17. FM, Gaviola, Jr. to Sec. Gobernación, July 30, 1920, 91; FM, Hernández and Díaz to President, July 27, 1920, 91; FM, Sánchez Pontón to President, July 30, 31, 1920, 91; J2D/A, Robles Moscoso et al. to Juez Distrito, July 29, 1920, 11·160; PHO, Sánchez Pontón interview, April [n.d.], 1961, 1/20:/:41; *Cronica*, July 23, 25, 29–31, August 8, 1920; *Excélsior*, July 30, 31, 1920; *Universal*, July 29, 31, September 3, 1920.

18. CTB, Macuil to Obregón, August 8, 1920, 11:466:2482:1; CTB, Rosaín and Baldcras to Obregón, August 9, 1920, 11:1329:4203:1; FM, Ventura and Pérez to President, July 27, 1920, 91; FM, Saloma, Jr. to President, July 27, 1920, 91; FM, Blanco to President, July 28, 1920, 91; FM, Lucas to President, July 30, 1920, 91; FM, Mendoza to President, July 30, 1920, 91; FM, Talavera to President, July 30, 1920, 91; FM, Luque to President, August 3, 1920, 92; FM, Flores Martínez to President, August 5, 1920, 92; FM, Rojas to de la Huerta, September 7, 1920, 92; RDS, Hanna to Lansing, October 27, 1920, 73:1032; *Crónica*, August 2–4, 1920; *Universal*, August 3, 11, 1920; Aguirre, *Mis memorias*, 326–7; Ruvalcaba, *Campaña*, 5:371–2.

BIBLIOGRAPHY

Unpublished Documentary Sources

AA: Mexico City, UNAM, Amado Aguirre. Cited, box:file:document.

AAA: Whaddon Hall, England, Archiv des Auswärtigen Amtes (German Foreign Ministry Archives, 1867–1920, Latin America), microfilm. Cited, roll:document.

ABF: Albuquerque, University of New Mexico, Albert Bacon Fall, microfilm. Cited, roll:document.

ACE/A: Puebla, Archivo del Congreso del Estado, Actas de Sesiones Públicas. Cited, legislature:date.

ACE/E: Puebla, Archivo del Congreso del Estado, Libros de Expedientes. Cited, volume:file.

AJE/I: Puebla, INAH, Archivo Judicial del Estado. Cited, year:bundle.

ARD: Mexico City, Archivo General de la Nación, Alfredo Robles Domínguez. Cited, volume:file:document.

ARM: Mexico City, INAH Museum, Archivo de la Revolución Mexicana (Patronato Sonora), microfilm. Cited, roll:volume:page.

C/ADN: Mexico City, El Colegio de México, Archivo de la Secretaría de la Defensa Nacional, microfilm. Cited, roll.

CDHM: Mexico City, El Colegio de México, Correspondencia Diplomática Hispano Mexicano, microfilm. Cited, roll:box:file:number.

CGS: Mexico City, Archivo General de la Nación, Cuartel General del Sur. Cited, box:file:document.

CIM: Puebla, Cámara Textil de Puebla y Tlaxcala, Centro Industrial Mexicano, Fondo IV. Cited, book:page.

CNA: Mexico City, Archivo General de la Nación, Comisión Nacional Agraria. Cited, volume.

CR: Mexico City, Archivo General de la Nación, Convención Revolucionaria. Cited, box:file:document.

CROM: Puebla, Universidad Autónoma de Puebla, Confederación Regional d Obreras Mexicanas, microfilm. Cited, roll.

C/T: Mexico City, Condumex, Telegramas. Cited, fondo.

CTB: Mexico City, Fideicomiso Archivo Plutarco Elías Calles-Fernando Torreblanca. Cited, fund:file:inventory:document.

DRF: Los Angeles, Occidental College, Edward L. Doheny Research Foundation. Cited, interview number.

DT: Mexico City, Archivo General de la Nación, Departamento de Trabajo. Cited, box:file:document.

EZ: Mexico City, Archivo General de la Nación, Emiliano Zapata. Cited, box:file:document.

FD: Mexico City, Condumex, Félix Díaz. Cited, folder:document.

FIC: Mexico City, Archivo General de la Nación, Fernando Iglesias Calderón. Cited, box:file:document.

FM: Mexico City, Archivo General de la Nación, Francisco I. Madero. Cited, box.

GBFO: London, Public Record Office, Foreign Office Records, General Correspondence-Political-Mexico, Series 371, microfilm. Cited, file: document.

GM: Mexico City, UNAM, Gildardo Magaña. Cited, box:file:document.

GO: Mexico City, Archivo General de la Nación, Genovevo de la O. Cited, box:file:document.

INEHRM: Mexico City, Archivo General de la Nación, Instituto Nacional de Estudios Históricos de la Revolución Mexicana. Cited, box:file: document.

J1D/A: Puebla, Archivo General del Estado, Juzgado 1o de Distrito, Sección de Amparos. Cited, box:file.

J1D/P: Puebla, Archivo General del Estado, Juzgado 1o de Distrito, Sección de Procesos. Cited, box, file.

J2D/A: Puebla, Archivo General del Estado, Juzgado 2o de Distrito, Sección de Amparos. Cited, box:file.

J2D/P: Puebla: Archivo General del Estado, Juzgado 2o de Distrito, Sección de Procesos. Cited, box:file.

JA: Mexico City, Condumex, Jenaro Amezcua. Cited, folder:document.

JB: Mexico City, UNAM, Juan Barragán. Cited, box:file.

JFL: Puebla, In the possession of Ing. Eduardo Ayala Gaytán and Sra. Graciela García Lucas de Ayala, Juan Francisco Lucas. Cited, folder.

JT: Mexico City, UNAM, Jacinto Treviño. Cited, box:file:document.

MGR: Mexico City, Archivo General de la Nación, Manuel González Ramírez. Cited, volume:page.

MI: Washington, DC, National Archives, United States Military Intelligence Reports, microfilm. Cited, roll:document.

MQG: Cholula, Puebla, Universidad de las Américas, Miguel Quintana G. Cited, manuscripts (ms.).

MWG: Mexico City, Condumex, Manuel W. González. Cited, folder: document.

PG: Austin, University of Texas, Nettie Lee Benson Collection, Pablo González, microfilm. Cited, roll.

PHO: Mexico City, INAH Museum, Archivo de la Palabra, Programa de Historia Oral. Cited, series:volume:page.

RDS: Washington, DC, National Archives, Records of the Department of State Relating to the Internal Affairs of Mexico, 1910–1929, Record Group 59, microfilm. Cited, roll:document.

RE: Mexico City, UNAM, Roque Estrada. Cited, box:file:document.

RG/G: Mexico City, Archivo General de la Nación, Ramo de Gobernación, Gobernación. Cited, file.

RGG: Mexico City, Universidad Panamericana, Roque González Garza. Cited, folder:document.

RG/PR: Mexico City, Archivo General de la Nación, Ramo de Gobernación, Período Revolucionario. Cited, box:file.

RR: Mexico City, Archivo General de la Nación, Colección Revolución. Cited, box:file:document.

SDN/AC: Mexico City, Secretaría de la Defensa Nacional, Archivo de Cancelados. Cited, file:document.

SDN/AH: Mexico City, Secretaría de la Defensa Nacional, Archivo Histórico. Cited, file:document.

SRE: Mexico City, Secretaría de Relaciones Exteriores. Cited, file.

TLP: Cambridge, Massachusetts, Harvard University, Baker Library, Puebla Tramway, Light and Power Company Records. Cited, folder.

TO: Tetela de Ocampo, Puebla, Archivo Municipal. Cited, box.

VC: Mexico City, Condumex, Venustiano Carranza. Cited, folder: document.

WFB: Austin, University of Texas, Nettie Lee Benson Collection, William F. Buckley. Cited, folder.

Interviews

Barbosa, Miguel. Tehuacán, Puebla, August 22, 1998 (conducted by Rogelio Sánchez López).

Bosques, Gilberto. Mexico City, August 14, 1993.

Published Primary Works

Acuña, Jesús. *Memoria de la Secretaría de Gobernación correspondiente al período revolucionario entre el 19 de febrero de 1913 y el 30 de noviembre de 1916.* Mexico City: Talleres Linotipográficas de "Revista de Revistas," 1916.

Aguirre, Amado. *Mis memorias de campaña: Apuntes para la historia.* N.p.: n.p., 1953.

Almazán, Juan Andreu. *En legítima defensa.* Mexico City: n.p., [1952?].

_____. "Memorias del general Juan Andreu Almazán." *El Universal* (Mexico City), 1957–1958.

Barbosa Cano, Fabio. *La CROM de Luis N. Morones a Antonio J. Hernández.* Puebla: Universidad Autónoma de Puebla, 1980.

Bravo Izquierdo, Donato. *Un soldado del pueblo.* Puebla: Editorial Periodística e Impresora de Puebla, 1964.

Cabrera, Alfonso. *Informe que el c. gobernador, dr. Alfonso Cabrera, presenta a la h. XXIV Legislatura del Estado de Puebla el día primero de enero de 1919.* [Puebla: n.p., 1919].

Cabrera, Luis. *La herencia de Carranza.* Mexico City: Imprenta Nacional, 1920.

Cámara Agrícola Nacional de Puebla. *Memorial de la Cámara Agrícola Nacional de Puebla presentado al c. Presidente de la República.* Puebla: Imprenta "La Enseñanza Objetiva," 1922.

Casasola, Agustín Víctor, ed. *Historia gráfica de la revolución mexicana, 1900–1940.* 6 vols. Mexico City: Archivo Casasola, n.d.

Castro, Cesáreo. *Informe rendido por el ciudadano gobernador interino general de división Don Cesáreo Castro, ante la XXIII Legislatura del Estado.* Puebla: Escuela de Artes y Oficios del Estado, 1917.

Cervantes, Luis G. *Decretos expedidos por el gobernador del Estado, cnel. dr. Luis G. Cervantes.* Puebla: Imprenta del Hospicio y Escuela de Artes y Oficios del Estado, 1916.

_____. *Decretos expedidos por el gobernador del Estado de Puebla, cnel. dr. Luis G. Cervantes: Contra el analfabetismo.* Puebla: n.p., 1916.

_____. *Informe leído por el ciudadano gobernador del Estado, cor. dr. Luis G. Cervantes, en el 56o concierto cívico-popular.* Puebla: Oficina de Propaganda del Gobierno del Estado, 1916.

Comisión Central de Caridad. *Memoria documentada de la campaña contra "La Influenza Española."* Puebla: Escuela Linotipográfica Salesiana, 1919.

del Castillo, Porfirio. *Puebla y Tlaxcala en los días de la revolución.* Mexico City: n.p., 1953.

Fabela, Isidro, and Fabela, Josefina E. de, eds. *Documentos históricos de la revolución mexicana*. 27 vols. Mexico City: Editorial Jus and Fondo de Cultura Económica, 1960–1973.

Galindo, Miguel. *A través de la Sierra: Diario de un soldado*. Mexico City: Imprenta de "El Dragón," 1924.

Gillow y Zavala, Eulogio. *Reminiscencias del ilmo. y rmo. sr. dr. d. Eulogio Gillow y Zavala, Arzobispo de Antequera, Oaxaca*. Los Angeles, CA: Escuela Linotipográfica Salesiana, 1921.

González Ramírez, Manuel, ed. *Fuentes para la historia de la revolución mexicana*. 5 vols. Mexico City: Fondo de Cultura Económica, 1954–1957.

México, Dirección General de Estadística, Informática y Evaluación. *Compendio histórico: Estadísticas vitales, 1893–1993*. Mexico City: Secretaría de Salud, 1993.

———, Secretaría de Agricultura y Fomento, Comisión Nacional Agraria. *Estadísticas, 1915–1927*. Mexico City: Talleres Gráficos de la Nación, 1928.

Obregón, Alvaro. *Ocho mil kilómetros en campaña*. Mexico City: Fondo de Cultura Económica, 1959 (originally published 1917).

Palavicini, Félix F. *Los diputados: Lo que se ve y lo que no se ve de la cámara*. 2 vols. 2d ed. Mexico City: Imprenta Francesa, 1915.

Pettus, Daisy Caden, ed. *The Rosalie Evans Letters from Mexico*. Indianapolis: Bobbs-Merrill, 1926.

Puebla (city). *Proyecto de ley del municipio libre para el Estado de Puebla*. Puebla: Escuela Linotipográfica Salesiana, 1916.

Puebla (state). Consejo Estatal de Población. *Estudio demográfico de Puebla*. Puebla: Gobierno del Estado, 1985.

———. *Constitución política del Estado*. Puebla: Escuela de Artes y Oficios del Estado, 1917.

———. *Estudio demográfico de Puebla*. Puebla: Gobierno del Estado, 1985.

———. *Ley de educación primaria para las escuelas del Estado de Puebla*. Puebla: Talleres Gráficos de "La Prensa," 1919.

———. *Ley orgánica de los artículos 26, 27 y 103 de la Constitución del Edo. de Puebla*. Puebla: Imprenta "La Enseñanza Objetiva," 1918.

———. *Ley orgánica municipal del Estado de Puebla*. Puebla: Talleres Gráficos de "La Prensa," 1917.

———. *Reglamento general del Colegio del Estado*. Puebla: Escuela de Artes y Oficios del Estado, 1919.

Unión Popular de Puebla para la Acción Social. *Semana social en Puebla*. Puebla: Escuela Linotipográfica Salesiana, 1919.

United States. Senate. *Investigation of Mexican Affairs: Preliminary Report and Hearings of the Committee on Foreign Relations, United States Senate, 66th Congress, 2d Session.* 2 vols. Washington, DC: Government Printing Office, 1920.

Velasco, Francisco de. *Autobiografía.* Puebla: Grupo Editorial Bohemia Poblana, 1946.

Periodicals

Aguilas y Estrellas (Puebla City)
El Amigo de la Verdad (Puebla City)
Boletín del Consejo Superior de Salubridad del Estado de Puebla (Puebla City)
Boletín del Departamento de Trabajo (Mexico City)
La Convención (Mexico City)
La Crónica (Puebla City)
El Demócrata (Mexico City)
El Diario (Mexico City)
El Estudiante (Puebla City)
El Excélsior (Mexico City)
El Imparcial (Mexico City)
El Independiente (Mexico City)
El Liberal (Mexico City)
The Mexican Herald (Mexico City)
El Monitor (Mexico City)
El Monitor (Puebla City)
El Monitor Republicano (Mexico City)
New York Sun (New York City)
New York Times (New York City)
La Opinión (Puebla City)
El País (Mexico City)
La Palabra (Puebla City)
El Periódico Oficial del Estado de Puebla (Puebla City)
La Prensa (Puebla City)
El Pueblo (Mexico City)
El Renovador (Tetela de Ocampo)
Revista Moderna (Puebla City)
La Revolución (Puebla City)
El Universal (Mexico City)

Secondary Works

Abud Flores, José Alberto. *Campeche: Revolución y movimiento social, 1911–1923.* Mexico City: Instituto Nacional de Estudios Históricos de la Revolución Mexicana, and Campeche: Universidad Autónoma de Campeche, 1992.

Aguilar Camín, Héctor. *La frontera nómada: Sonora y la revolución mexicana.* Mexico City: Siglo XXI Editores, 1977.

_____. "The Relevant Tradition: Sonoran Leaders in the Revolution," 92–123. In D. A. Brading, ed. *Caudillo and Peasant in the Mexican Revolution.* Cambridge, England: Cambridge University Press, 1980.

Álvarez Aguilar, Luis Fernando; Olga Cárdenas Trueba; and Alfredo Hernández Murillo. *Carmen Serdán y la Junta Revolucionario de Puebla.* Mexico City: Instituto Nacional de Estudios Históricos de la Revolución Mexicana, 1993.

Ankerson, Dudley. *Agrarian Warlord: Saturnino Cedillo and the Mexican Revolution in San Luis Potosí.* DeKalb: Northern Illinois University Press, 1984.

Ávila Palafox, Ricardo. *¿Revolución en el Estado de México?* Mexico City: Instituto Nacional de Antropología e Historia, and Toluca: Gobierno del Estado de México, 1988.

Barragán Rodríguez, Juan. *Historia del ejército y de la revolución constitucionalista.* 3 vols. Mexico City: Instituto Nacional de Estudios Históricos de la Revolución Mexicana, 1985–1986.

Benjamin, Thomas. *La Revolución: Mexico's Great Revolution as Memory, Myth, and History.* Austin: University of Texas Press, 2000.

_____. *A Rich Land, a Poor People: Politics and Society in Modern Chiapas.* Albuquerque: University of New Mexico Press, 1989.

Bortz, Jeffrey. "The Revolution, the Labour Regime and Conditions of Work in the Cotton Textile Industry in Mexico, 1910–1927." *Journal of Latin American Studies* 32:3(October 2000): 671–703.

_____. "Without Any More Law Than Their Own Caprice: Cotton Textile Workers and the Challenge to Factory Authority during the Mexican Revolution." *International Review of Social History* 42:2(August 1997): 253–288.

Brewster, Keith. *Militarism, Ethnicity, and Politics in the Sierra Norte de Puebla, 1917–1930.* Tucson: University of Arizona Press, 2003.

Brunk, Samuel. *¡Emiliano Zapata!: Revolution and Betrayal; A Life of Emiliano Zapata.* Albuquerque: University of New Mexico Press, 1995.

Buve, Raymond. "La historia social del campo tlaxcalteca en la era liberal, 1854–1911: Logros y problemas," 201–220. In Shulamit Goldsmit and Guillermo Zermeño, eds. *La responsabilidad del historiador: Homenaje a Moisés Navarro*. Mexico City: Departamento de Historia, Universidad Iberoamericana, 1992.

_____. *El movimiento revolucionario en Tlaxcala*. Tlaxcala: Universidad Autónoma de Tlaxcala, and Mexico City: Universidad Iberoamericana, 1994.

Camp, Roderic A. *Mexican Political Biographies, 1884–1935*. Austin: University of Texas Press, 1991.

Candaredo, Baudelio. *Zacatlán: Ensayo histórico*. Puebla: Centro de Estudios Históricos de Puebla, 1979.

Carmagnani, Marcello. "El federalismo liberal mexicano," 135–179. In Marcello Carmagnani, ed. *Federalismos latinoamericanos: México, Brasil, Argentina*. Mexico City: El Colegio de México and Fondo de Cultura Económica, 1993.

Ceballos Ramírez, Manuel. *El catolicismo social: Un tercero en discordia; Rerum Novarum: La "cuestión social" y la movilización de los católicos mexicanos, 1891–1911*. Mexico City: El Colegio de México, 1991.

Chaffee, Arthur William. "The Adoption of Modern Agricultural Facilities by Subsistence Farmers in Central Mexico." Ph.D. dissertation, Ohio State University, 1968.

Contreras Cruz, Carlos, ed. *Puebla: Una historia compartida*. Puebla: Gobierno del Estado, and Instituto de Ciencias Sociales y Humanidades, Universidad Autónoma de Puebla, and Mexico City: Instituto de Investigaciones Dr. José María Luis Mora, 1993.

_____, Nydia E. Cruz Barrera, and Francisco Téllez Guerrero, eds. *Puebla: Textos de su historia*. 5 vols. Puebla: Gobierno del Estado, and Instituto de Ciencias Sociales y Humanidades, Universidad Autónoma de Puebla, and Mexico City: Instituto de Investigaciones Dr. José María Luis Mora, 1993.

Cordero y Torres, Enrique. *Crónicas de mi ciudad*. Puebla: Grupo Editorial Bohemia Poblana, 1955, 1966.

_____. *Diccionario general de Puebla*. 4 vols. Puebla: Centro de Estudios Históricos de Puebla, 1958.

_____. *Historia compendiada del Estado de Puebla, 1531–1963*. 3 vols. Puebla: Grupo Editorial Bohemia Poblana, 1965–1966.

_____. *Historia del periodismo en Puebla, 1820–1946*. Puebla: Grupo Editorial Bohemia Poblana, 1947.

_____. *Poetas y escritores poblanos: Por origen o adopción, 1900–1943*. Puebla: Casa Editora Nieto, n.d.

Cruz, Salvador. *Vida y obra de Pastor Rouaix*. Mexico City: Instituto Nacional de Antropología e Historia, 1980.

Cumberland, Charles C. "The Jenkins Case and Mexican-American Relations." *Hispanic American Historical Review* 31:4 (November 1951): 586–607.

_____. *Mexican Revolution: The Constitutionalist Years*. Austin: University of Texas Press, 1972.

Dussaud, Claude Philippe. "Agrarian Politics, Violence, and the Struggle for Social Control in Puebla from 1918 to 1927: The Case of Rosalie Evans." M.A. thesis, University of Virginia, 1990.

Enríquez Perea, Alberto, ed. *Memorias de un constituyente: José Álvarez y Álvarez de la Cadena*. Mexico City: *El Nacional* and Instituto de Investigaciones Dr. José María Luis Mora, 1992.

Esparza, Manuel. *Gillow durante el porfiriato y la revolución en Oaxaca, 1887–1922*. Oaxaca: Gobierno del Estado, 1985.

Espinosa Yglesias, Manuel. *Fundación Mary Street Jenkins: México, 1954–1988*. Mexico City: n.p., 1988.

Falcón, Romana. *Revolución y caciquismo: San Luis Potosí, 1910–1938*. Mexico City: El Colegio de México, 1984.

_____, and Soledad García. *La semilla en el surco: Adalberto Tejeda y el radicalismo en Veracruz, 1883–1960*. Mexico City: El Colegio de México, and Jalapa: Gobierno del Estado de Veracruz, 1986.

Gamboa Ojeda, Leticia. "Acerca de la huelga textil de 1918 en Puebla." *Boletín de Investigación del Movimiento Obrero* 4:7(May 1984): 63–80.

_____. *Camerino Z. Mendoza y la revolución maderista entre Orizaba y Tehuacán*. Puebla: Ayuntamiento del Municipio de Puebla, 1999.

_____. *Los empresarios de ayer: El grupo dominante en la industria textil de Puebla, 1906–1929*. Puebla: Universidad Autónoma de Puebla, 1985.

_____. "Epidemia de influenza de 1918: Sanidad y política en la Ciudad de Puebla." *Quipu* 8:1(January–April 1991): 91–109.

_____. "Los españoles en la Ciudad de Puebla hacia 1930," 190–217. In Clara E. Lida, ed. *Una inmigración privilegiada: Comerciantes, empresarios y profesionales españoles en México en los siglos XIX y XX*. Madrid: Alianza Editorial, 1994.

_____. "El movimiento revolucionario, 1906–1917," 342–372. In Carlos Cruz Contreras, ed. *Puebla: Una historia compartida*. Puebla: Gobierno del Estado and Instituto de Ciencias Sociales y Humanidades,

Universidad Autónoma de Puebla, and Mexico City: Instituto de Investigaciones Dr. José María Luis Mora, 1993.

_____. *La urdimbre y la trama: Historia social de los obreros textiles de Atlixco, 1899–1924*. Mexico City: Fondo de Cultura Económica, and Puebla: Benemérita Universidad Autónoma de Puebla, 2001.

Garciadiego Dantán, Javier. "Alemania y la revolución mexicana." *Foro Internacional* 32:4 (April–September 1992): 429–448.

_____. "Higinio Aguilar: Milicia, rebelión y corrupción como *modus vivendi*." *Historia Mexicana* 41:3(January–March 1992): 437–488.

_____. "Revolución constitucionalista y contrarrevolución: Movimientos reaccionarios en México, 1914–1920." Ph.D. dissertation, El Colegio de México, 1981.

_____. "La revuelta de Agua Prieta." Licenciatura thesis, Facultad de Ciencias Políticas y Sociales, Universidad Nacional Autónoma de México, 1974.

García Ugarte, Marta Eugenia. *Génesis del porvenir: Sociedad y política en Querétaro, 1913–1940*. Mexico City: Fondo de Cultura Económica and Instituto de Investigaciones Sociales, Universidad Nacional Autónoma de México, and Querétaro: Gobierno del Estado, 1997.

Garner, Paul H. "Constitutionalist Reconstruction in Oaxaca, 1915–1920," 79–90. In Wil Pansters and Arij Ouweneel, eds. *Region, State and Capitalism in Mexico: Nineteenth and Twentieth Centuries*. Amsterdam: CEDLA, 1989.

_____. *La revolución en la provincia: Sobernía estatal y caudillismo en las montañas de Oaxaca, 1910–1920*. Mexico City: Fondo de Cultura Económica, 1988.

Gilly, Adolfo. *La revolución interrumpida, México, 1910–1920: Una guerra campesina por la tierra y el poder*. Mexico City: Ediciones "El Caballito," 1971.

Gómez Álvarez, Cristina. *Puebla: Los obreros textiles en la revolución, 1911–1918*. Puebla: Cuadernos de la Casa Presno, Centro de Investigaciones Históricas y Sociales, Instituto de Ciencias, Universidad Autónoma de Puebla, 1989.

Gómez Haro, Enrique. *D. Ramón Ibarra y González: Primer arzobispo de Puebla*. Mexico City: Escuela Linotipográfica Salesiana, 1918.

González Loscertales, Vicente. "Bases para el análisis socio-económico de la colonia española de México en 1910." *Revista de Indias* 39(January–December 1979): 267–295.

Guardino, Peter F. *Peasants, Politics, and the Formation of Mexico's National State: Guerrero, 1800–1857*. Stanford: Stanford University Press, 1996.

Guerra, François-Xavier. *México: Del antiguo régimen a la revolución.* 2 vols. Mexico City: Fondo de Cultura Económica, 1988, trans. Sergio Fernández Bravo (originally published in French, 1985).

Gutiérrez Álvarez, Coralia. "El conflicto social en la industrial textil: Empresarios y obreros de Puebla-Tlaxcala, 1892–1914." Ph.D. dissertation, El Colegio de México, 1995.

———. *Experiencias contrastadas: Industrialización y conflictos en los textiles del centro-oriente de México, 1884–1917.* Mexico City: El Colegio de México, and Puebla: Instituto de Ciencias Sociales y Humanidades, Benemérita Universidad Autónoma de Puebla, 2000.

Hart, John Mason. *Revolutionary Mexico: The Coming and Process of the Mexican Revolution.* Berkeley: University of California Press, 1987.

Henderson, Peter V. N. *Félix Díaz, the Porfirians, and the Mexican Revolution.* Lincoln: University of Nebraska Press, 1981.

———. *In the Absence of Don Porfirio: Francisco León de la Barra and the Mexican Revolution.* Wilmington, DE: SR Books, 2000.

Henderson, Timothy J. *The Worm in the Wheat: Rosalie Evans and Agrarian Struggle in the Puebla-Tlaxcala Valley of Mexico, 1906–1927.* Durham, NC: Duke University Press, 1998.

Hernández Chávez, Alicia. "Federalismo y gobernabilidad en México," 263–299. In Marcello Carmagnani, ed. *Federalismos latinoamericanos: México, Brasil, Argentina.* Mexico City: El Colegio de México and Fondo de Cultura Económica, 1993.

———. "Militares y negocios en la revolución mexicana." *Historia Mexicana* 34:2 (October–December 1984): 181–212.

———. *La tradición republicana del buen gobierno.* Mexico City: El Colegio de México and Fondo de Cultura Económica, 1993.

Hernández Enríquez, Gustavo Abel. *Historia moderna de Puebla.* Vol. 1: *Gobierno del doctor Alfonso Cabrera Lobato, 1917–1920.* Vol. 2: *El período de la anarquía constitucional, 1920–1924.* [Puebla]: n.p., 1986–1988.

Historical Notes on Coins of the Mexican Revolution, 1913–1917. Mexico City: n.p., 1932.

Hoyos Hernández, Luis. "Vida rural y conflictos sociales en el municipio de Tehuitzingo, Estado de Puebla, 1895–1920." Licenciatura thesis, Colegio de Historia, Universidad Autónoma de Puebla, 1994.

Jacobs, Ian. *Ranchero Revolt: The Mexican Revolution in Guerrero.* Austin: University of Texas Press, 1982.

Jaime Espinosa, María Elizabeth. "Rosa y Guadalupe Narváez Bautista durante la revolución en Puebla de 1910 a 1917." Masters thesis, Instituto de Investigaciones Dr. José María Luis Mora, 1996.

Joseph, Gilbert M. *Revolution from Without: Yucatán, Mexico, and the United States, 1880–1924*. Cambridge, England: Cambridge University Press, 1982.

_____, and Daniel Nugent, eds. *Everyday Forms of State Formation: Revolution and the Negotiation of Rule in Modern Mexico*. Durham, NC: Duke University Press, 1994.

Juárez Lucas, Patricio. "Conflictos y movilidad política en el Estado de Puebla, 1916–1928." Licenciatura thesis, Colegio de Historia, Benemérita Universidad Autónoma de Puebla, 1999.

Katz, Friedrich. *The Life and Times of Pancho Villa*. Stanford, CA: Stanford University Press, 1998.

_____. *The Secret War in Mexico: Europe, the United States and the Mexican Revolution*. Chicago: University of Chicago Press, 1981.

Knight, Alan. *The Mexican Revolution*. 2 vols. Cambridge, England: Cambridge University Press, 1986.

_____. "Peasant and Caudillo in Revolutionary Mexico, 1910–1917," 17–58. In D.A. Brading, ed. *Caudillo and Peasant in the Mexican Revolution*. Cambridge, England: Cambridge University Press, 1980.

Kuri Camacho, Ramón. *Micro historia de Chignahuapan*. 3 vols. Chignahuapan, Pue.: Ayuntamiento del Municipio, 1985.

LaFrance, David G. "The Jenkins Kidnapping: Confronting the Myth." Unpublished manuscript, 2003.

_____. "Labour and the Mexican Revolution: President Francisco I. Madero and the Puebla Textile Workers." *Boletín de Estudios Latinoamericanos y del Caribe* (Amsterdam), no. 34(June 1983): 59–74.

_____. *The Mexican Revolution in Puebla, 1908–1913: The Maderista Movement and the Failure of Liberal Reform*. Wilmington, DE: Scholarly Resources, 1989.

_____. "The Military as Political and Socioeconomic Actor in the Mexican Revolution: The State of Puebla, 1910–1924." *International Studies* (Łódź) 4 (2003): forthcoming.

Lear, John. *Workers, Neighbors, and Citizens: The Revolution in Mexico City*. Lincoln: University of Nebraska Press, 2001.

Mallon, Florencia E. *Peasant and Nation: The Making of Post-Colonial Mexico and Peru*. Berkeley: University of California Press, 1995.

_____. "Reflections on the Ruins: Everyday Forms of State Formation in Nineteenth-Century Mexico," 69–106. In Gilbert M. Joseph and Daniel Nugent, eds. *Everyday Forms of State Formation: Revolution and the Negotiation of Rule in Modern Mexico*. Durham, NC: Duke University Press, 1994.

Manero, Antonio. *La reforma bancaria en la revolución constitucionalista.* Mexico City: Talleres Gráficos de la Nación, 1958.

Márquez, Miguel B. *El verdadero Tlaxcalantongo: ¿Quiénes son los responsables de esta tragedia?* Mexico City: A. P. Márquez, 1941.

Márquez, Octaviano. *Monseñor Ramón Ibarra y González.* Mexico City: Editorial Jus, 1973.

Martínez Assad, Carlos. *El laboratorio de la revolución: El Tabasco garridista.* Mexico City: Siglo XXI Editores, 1979.

Martínez Guzmán, Gabino, and Juan Ángel Chávez Ramírez. *Durango: Un volcán en erupción.* Mexico City: Fondo de Cultura Económica, and Durango: Secretaría de Educación, Cultura, y Deporte, Gobierno del Estado, 1998.

Matute, Álvaro. *Historia de la revolución mexicana, 1917–1924: La carrera del caudillo.* Mexico City: El Colegio de México, 1980.

————. *Historia de la revolución mexicana, 1917–1924: Las dificultades del nuevo estado.* Mexico City: El Colegio de México, 1995.

McBride, George McCutchen. *The Land Systems of Mexico.* New York: Octagon Books, 1971 (originally published 1923).

McCaleb, Walter Flavius. *Present and Past Banking in Mexico.* New York: Harper and Brothers Publishers, 1920.

Medel M., José V. *El convento de Sta. Mónica: Museo colonial.* 3d ed. Puebla: Editorial Puebla, 1943.

Mendieta Alatorre, Ángeles. *Carmen Serdán.* Puebla. Centro de Estudios Históricos de Puebla, 1971.

Meyer, Eugenia, ed. *Luis Cabrera: Teórico y crítico de la revolución.* Mexico City: Sepsetentas, 1972.

Meyer, Jean. "Los obreros en la revolución mexicana: Los 'Batallones Rojos.'" *Historia Mexicana* 21:1(July–September 1971): 1–37.

Meyer, Michael C. *Huerta: A Political Portrait.* Lincoln: University of Nebraska Press, 1972.

Mijangos Díaz, Eduardo Nomelí. *La revolución y el poder político en Michoacán, 1910–1920.* Morelia: Instituto de Investigaciones Históricas, Universidad Michoacana de San Nicolás de Hidalgo, 1997.

Moreno, Daniel. *Los hombres de la revolución: 40 estudios biográficos.* Mexico City: LibroMex Editores, 1960.

Navarro Rojas, Luis. *Conflictos estudiantiles y poder estatal en Puebla, 1900–1925.* Puebla: Gobierno del Estado and Benemérita Universidad Autónoma de Puebla, 1999.

Niemeyer, E. V., Jr. *Revolution at Querétaro: The Mexican Constitutional Convention of 1916–1917.* Austin: University of Texas Press, 1974.

Ochoa, Enrique C. *Feeding Mexico: The Political Uses of Food since 1910.* Wilmington, DE: Scholarly Resources, 2000.

O'Gorman, Edmundo. *Historia de las divisiones territoriales de México.* 3d ed. Mexico City: Editorial Manuel Porrúa, 1966.

Oikión Solano, Verónica. *El constitucionalismo en Michoacán: El período de los gobiernos militares, 1914–1917.* Mexico City: Consejo Nacional para la Cultura y las Artes, 1992.

Palacios, Enrique Juan. *Puebla: Su territorio y sus habitantes.* Mexico City: Secretaría de Fomento, 1917.

Palomera, Esteban J. *La obra educativa de los Jesuitas en Puebla, 1578–1945.* Mexico City: Universidad Iberoamericana, 1999.

Paredes Colín, Joaquín. *El distrito de Tehuacán.* Mexico City: Tipografía Comercial Don Bosco, 1960.

Patterson, K. David, and Gerald F. Pyle. "The Geography and Mortality of the 1918 Influenza Pandemic." *Bulletin of the History of Medicine* 65:1(Spring 1991): 4–21.

Paxman, Andrew William. "William Jenkins, the Private Sector and the Modern Mexican State." M.A. thesis, Latin American Studies, University of California, Berkeley, 2002.

Peral, Miguel Ángel. *Diccionario histórico, biográfico, y geográfico del Estado de Puebla.* Puebla: Editorial PAC, 1979.

____. *Gobernantes de Puebla.* Mexico City: Editorial PAC, 1975.

____. *Los que fueron a la revolución.* Mexico City: Editorial PAC, 1976.

____. *El pelelismo en México: Biografía de un político con anverso y reverso.* Mexico City: Editorial PAC, 1951.

Perry, Laurens Ballard. *Juárez and Díaz: Machine Politics in Mexico.* DeKalb: Northern Illinois University Press, 1978.

Pineda Gómez, Francisco Javier. "La revolución de fuera, segunda parte, 1912–1914: Historia de la guerra zapatista y análisis de discurso." Ph.D. dissertation, Escuela Nacional de Antropología e Historia, 2002.

Porras y López, Armando. *Luis Cabrera: Revolucionario e intelectual.* Mexico City: Editorial Manuel Porrúa, 1968.

Puebla a través de los siglos. Puebla: El Sol de Puebla, 1962.

Quirk, Robert E. *The Mexican Revolution, 1914–1915: The Convention of Aguascalientes.* New York: W.W. Norton, 1970.

Ramírez Granados, Agustín. *El 19o Batallón de los obreros de Puebla: Desde su fundación en el año de 1914 hasta 1918 que salió rumbo al norte de la República.* [Puebla]: n.p., n.d.

Ramírez Rancaño, Mario. *Burguesía textil y política en la revolución mexicana.* Mexico City: Instituto de Investigaciones Sociales, Universidad Nacional Autónoma de México, 1987.

———. "El destierro de la cúpula de la iglesia durante la revolución." *Perspectivas Históricas* 2(July–December 1998): 11–43.

———. *La revolución en los volcanes: Domingo y Cirilo Arenas.* Mexico City: Instituto de Investigaciones Sociales, Universidad Nacional Autónoma de México, 1995.

Rendón Garcini, Ricardo. "Díaz y Cahuantzi: Un caso de relaciones entre el gobierno estatal y el federal," 132–147. In Hans Joachim König and Marianne Wiesebron, eds. *Nation Building in Nineteenth-Century Latin America: Dilemmas and Conflicts.* Leiden, The Netherlands: School of Asian, African and Amerindian Studies, University of Leiden, 1998.

Richmond, Douglas. *Venustiano Carranza's Nationalist Struggle, 1893–1920.* Lincoln: University of Nebraska Press, 1983.

Rivera Moreno, Donna. *Xochiapulco: Una gloria olvidada.* Puebla: Gobierno del Estado, 1991.

Rivero Quijano, Jesús. *La revolución industrial y la industria textil en México.* 2 vols. Mexico City: Editorial Joaquín Porrúa, 1990.

Rocha, Martha Eva. "Guadalupe Narváez y la Oficina de Información y Propaganda Revolucionaria en Puebla, 1915–1916," 331–343. En Jaime Bailón, Carlos Martínez Assad, and Pablo Serrano Álvarez, eds., *El siglo de la revolución mexicana.* 2 vols. Mexico City: Instituto Nacional de Estudios Históricos de la Revolución Mexicana, 2000.

Romero Flores, Jesús. *Historia del Congreso Constituyente, 1916–1917.* Querétaro: Gobierno del Estado, and Mexico City: Instituto Nacional de Estudios Históricos de la Revolución Mexicana, 1986.

Ruíz, Ramón Eduardo. *The Great Rebellion: Mexico, 1905–1924.* New York: W. W. Norton, 1980.

———. *Labor and the Ambivalent Revolutionaries: Mexico, 1911–1923.* Baltimore: Johns Hopkins University Press, 1976.

Ruvalcaba, Luis N., ed. *Campaña política del c. Alvaro Obregón: Candidato a la presidencia de la República, 1920–1924.* 5 vols. Mexico City: n.p., 1923.

Salazar Ibargüen, Columba. "El Banco Oriental de México: Primer banco de emisión en Puebla, 1900–1910." Licenciatura thesis, Colegio de Historia, Universidad Autónoma de Puebla, 1985.

Salinas Sandoval, María del Carmen. *Política y sociedad en los municipios del Estado de México, 1825–1880.* Toluca, Edo. de México: El Colegio Mexiquense, 1996.

Salmorán Marín, Miguel. *Diario de un pueblo: Acatlán de Osorio, Puebla.* Mexico City: Editorial Combatiente, 1995.

Sánchez Flores, Ramón. *Zacapoaxtla: República de Indios y villa de Españoles; Relación histórica.* Zacapoaxtla, Puebla: XIV Distrito Local Electoral, 1984.

Sánchez Lamego, Miguel A. *Historia militar de la revolución constitucionalista.* 5 vols. Mexico City: Instituto Nacional de Estudios Históricos de la Revolución Mexicana, 1956–1960.

Saragoza, Alex M. *The Monterrey Elite and the Mexican State, 1880–1940.* Austin: University of Texas Press, 1988.

Sarmiento, Miguel E. *Puebla ante la historia: La tradición y la leyenda.* Puebla: n.p., 1947.

Simonian, Lane. *Defending the Land of the Jaguar: A History of Conservation in Mexico.* Austin: University of Texas Press, 1995.

Sodi, José Antonio Serafín. *Monografías de San Martín Texmelucan y Hacienda de Chautla: Anécdota de "Tu ya no soplas."* [Puebla]: Secretaría de Educación Pública, 1978.

Taibo, Paco Ignacio II. *Los bolshevikis: Historia narrativa de los orígenes del comunismo en México, 1919–1925.* Mexico City: Editorial Joaquín Mortiz, 1986.

Tannenbaum, Frank. *The Mexican Agrarian Revolution.* New York: Macmillan, 1929.

Tecuanhuey Sandoval, Alicia. *Los conflictos electorales de la élite política en una época revolucionaria: Puebla, 1910–1917.* Mexico City: Instituto Nacional de Estudios Históricos de la Revolución Mexicana, 2001.

Thomson, Guy P. C. "Federalismo y cantonalismo en México, 1824–1892: Soberanía y territorialiadad." *Anuario* (Instituto de Estudios Históricos-Sociales, Facultad de Ciencias Humanas, Universidad Nacional del Centro de la Provincia de Buenos Aires, Tandil, Argentina), 10 (1995): 73–99.

———. "*Montaña* and *llanura* in the Politics of Central Mexico: The Case of Puebla, 1820–1920," 59–78. In Wil Pansters and Arij Ouweneel, eds. *Region, State and Capitalism in Mexico: Nineteenth and Twentieth Centuries.* Amsterdam: CEDLA, 1989.

———, with David G. LaFrance, *Patriotism, Politics, and Popular Liberalism in Nineteenth-Century Mexico: Juan Francisco Lucas and the Puebla Sierra.* Wilmington, DE: SR Books, 1999.

Tobler, Hans Werner. "La burguesía revolucionaria en México: Su origen y su papel, 1915–1935." *Historia Mexicana* 34:2(October–December 1984): 213–237.

———. *La revolución mexicana: Transformación social y cambio político, 1876–1940.* Mexico City: Alianza Editorial, 1994, trans. Juan José Utrilla and Angelika Scherp (originally published in German, 1984).

Torres Bautista, Mariano E. "La basura y sus destinos: Puebla, 1878–1925," 221–248. In Rosalvo Loreto L. and Francisco J. Cervantes B., eds. *La basura, el agua y la muerte en la Puebla de los Angeles, 1650–1925.* Mexico City: Editorial Claves Latinoamericanas, 1994.

Tutino, John. *From Insurrection to Revolution in Mexico: Social Bases of Agrarian Violence, 1750–1940.* Princeton: Princeton University Press, 1986.

————. "Revolutionary Confrontation, 1913–1917: Regions, Classes, and the New National State," 41–70. In Thomas Benjamin and Mark Wasserman, eds. *Provinces of the Revolution: Essays on Regional Mexican History, 1910–1929.* Albuquerque: University of New Mexico Press, 1990.

Urquizo, Francisco L. *México: Tlaxcalantongo, mayo de 1920.* Mexico City: Editorial Cultura, 1943.

Vanderwood, Paul J. "Response to Revolt: The Counter-Guerrilla Strategy of Porfirio Díaz." *Hispanic American Historical Review* 56:4(November 1976): 551–579.

————. "Resurveying the Mexican Revolution: Three Provocative New Syntheses and Their Shortfalls." *Mexican Studies/Estudios Mexicanos* 5:1(Winter 1989): 145–163.

Vela González, Francisco. *Diario de la revolución: Año de 1913.* Monterrey: Universidad de Nuevo León, 1971.

Vélez Pliego, Roberto M. "Marcelino G. Presno y la propiedad agraria en Puebla," 155–177. In Agustín Grajales and Lilián Illades, eds., *Presencia española en Puebla, siglos XVI–XX.* Puebla: Instituto de Ciencias Sociales y Humanidades, Benemérita Universidad Autónoma de Puebla, and Mexico City: Embajada de España en México, 2002.

Walker Sarmiento, Oscar. "La reforma agraria en el Estado de Puebla, 1917–1922." Licenciatura thesis, Colegio de Historia, Universidad Autónoma de Puebla, 1987.

Wasserman, Mark. *Persistent Oligarchs: Elites and Politics in Chihuahua, Mexico, 1910–1940.* Durham, NC: Duke University Press, 1993.

Wells, Allen, and Gilbert M. Joseph. *Summer of Discontent, Seasons of Upheaval: Elite Politics and Rural Insurgency in Yucatán, 1876–1915.* Stanford: Stanford University Press, 1996.

Womack, John, Jr. "The Mexican Revolution, 1910–1920," 125–200. In Leslie Bethell, ed. *Mexico since Independence.* Cambridge, England: Cambridge University Press, 1991.

————. *Zapata and the Mexican Revolution.* New York: Vintage Books, 1968.

Wood, Andrew Grant. *Revolution in the Street: Women, Workers, and Urban Protest in Veracruz, 1870–1927.* Wilmington, DE: SR Books, 2001.

Zoraida Vázquez, Josefina. "El federalismo mexicano, 1823–1847," 15–50. In Marcello Carmagnani, ed. *Federalismos latinoamericanos: México, Brasil, Argentina*. Mexico City: El Colegio de México and Fondo de Cultura Económica, 1993.

INDEX